# THE EAGLE AND THE VIRGIN

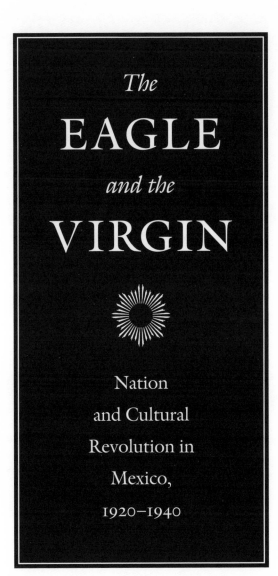

*The*

# EAGLE

## *and the*

# VIRGIN

Nation
and Cultural
Revolution in
Mexico,
1920–1940

EDITED BY MARY KAY VAUGHAN
AND STEPHEN E. LEWIS

Duke University Press
*Durham and London*
2006

© 2006 Duke University Press

All rights reserved

Printed in the United States of America on acid-free paper ∞

Designed by Erin Kirk New

Typeset in Galliard by Tseng Information Systems, Inc.

Library of Congress Cataloging-in-Publication Data appear on the last

printed page of this book.

# Contents

# List of Illustrations

Plates (between pages 118 and 119)

The Noche Mexicana and the Exhibition of Popular Arts

# Acknowledgments

The following institutions graciously granted permission to reproduce the images found in this book: the Amherst Special Collection at Amherst College, the collection of Andres Blaisten, the Archivo General del Estado de Nuevo León, the Archivo General de la Nación in Mexico City, the Biblioteca Lerdo de Tejada, the Art Archive, the Colección Museo Dolores Olmedo, the Davis Museum at Wellesley College, the Dirección General de Actividades Cinematográficas de la Universidad Nacional Autónoma de México, the Jacques and Natasha Gehman Collection of Mexican Art, and the Instituto Tlaxcalteca de Cultura.

We also wish to thank the following institutions and individuals for permission to reproduce the paintings of Diego Rivera, José Clemente Orozco, David Alfaro Siqueiros, Frida Kahlo, and María Izquierdo: the Instituto Nacional de Bellas Artes, the Banco de México, © Clemente Orozco V., Art © Estate of David Alfaro Siqueiros (SOMAPP/VAGA), Aurora Posadas Izquierdo, and Darlene Lutz. Thanks also to Sarah M. Lowe for permission to reproduce material from her book *Frida Kahlo*, Universe Series on Women (New York: Universe, 1991) and to Natalie Hanemann for preparing the maps.

Funds for the publication of this volume were provided by the Department of History and the General Research Board at the University of Maryland and by the Office of the Provost and the College of the Humanities and Fine Arts at California State University, Chico.

Finally, we thank our contributors for their work and patience, and Valerie Millholland, Miriam Angress, and the editorial staff and art production staff at Duke University Press for patiently guiding this volume to publication.

# Introduction

MARY KAY VAUGHAN AND STEPHEN E. LEWIS

In 1921, on the heels of the twentieth century's first social revolution, the Mexican government launched a nationalist movement celebrating the culture of Mexico's mestizo and indigenous peoples and recasting national history as a popular struggle against invasion, subjugation, and want. At the same time, it undertook an educational crusade to transform peoples whom reformers saw as downtrodden, oppressed, and divided into healthy patriots mobilized for modernity. Part of the government's vision is captured in Diego Rivera's mural of Mexican history painted on the walls of the National Palace. The Aztec eagle devouring a serpent is at the center and heart of this epic of conquest and betrayal, violence and exploitation, resistance and liberation (see plate 6).

The eagle was not the only symbol of national identity or Rivera's mural the only narrative of national memory and utopian vision constructed in the tumultuous years between 1920 and 1940. Artists associated with the government represented the nation in distinct ways. Radio and cinema contributed mightily to national identity formation but did not necessarily embrace the government's messages. Critically, thousands of Catholics opposed to official anti-Catholic campaigns identified with a figure absent from the state's symbolic repertoire: the Virgin of Guadalupe. The olive-skinned Virgin, worshiped at the site of Tonantzín, Nahuatl mother of the gods, earth, and corn, had become in the seventeenth and eighteenth centuries an icon of the creoles (the American-born European elite). She was proof of their autonomy from Spain and their linkage with the indigenous and mestizo majority. Made patron saint of New Spain in 1754, hers was the banner carried by the popular insurgents who struggled for Mexican independence in 1810 and the peasant armies of Emiliano Zapata who fought for justice and land in the revolution one century later. After 1920, the Virgin of Guadalupe became the symbol of the vilified and martyred Catholic Church.[1]

How did distinct symbols and practices, memories and utopian projections, coexist and intersect in these years of reform, protest, and state construction to forge one of the strongest cultural nations in the Western Hemisphere? These essays grapple with this question. They are organized in four parts. The first part addresses the aesthetics of nation building in popular arts, music, painting, and architecture. The second looks at utopian state projects of behavioral transformation in health, anticlericalism, and education and the ways Mexicans received these. The third examines the role of mass communications (roads, cinema, and radio) in nation formation. The fourth probes national identity formation as it took shape in distinct regions of the country among specific social groups—political Catholics, industrial workers, and middle-class women.

Overall, the essays illustrate five dimensions of the nation-building process emanating from the 1910 revolution. First, while the revolution marked deep ruptures with the past, national identity and memory construction were rooted in the nineteenth century. Second, nation building was a heterogeneous and contradictory process within the state and in relations between state and society. Third, the private sector, market development, and processes of secularization played an important role in national identity construction through technologies of transportation, communication, and representation. Governments tried to shape and regulate these, but they could not completely control them. Fourth, transnational processes empowered national identity formation in Mexico as much as they encouraged new forms of international domination and global interdependence. Fifth, these essays provide new insights into the gendered dimensions of nation formation. In the text that follows, we broadly define the terms "national identity," "memory," and "utopia" with reference to the essays in this volume.

## National Identity

National identity refers to the symbols, icons, discourses, and places created, disseminated, celebrated, and appropriated as national. In recent years, scholars have asked how nations are formed as imagined communities.[2] The flags, songs, monuments, medallions, and uniforms—the cultural artifacts marking the nation—may surge from wars, foreign invasions, revolutions, or migrations, but scholars generally concur that intellectuals, artists, and politicians (national, regional, and local) play a critical role in elaborating such symbols. Communications technologies disseminate them, as do civic, political, social, and cultural associations, as well as state laws and institutions. A central issue is the relationship between individual or institutional creators of national discourses and symbols and the popular cultures, or the beliefs and practices of the mass of citizens or subjects who make up the nation.

Historical research has tended to emphasize the imposition of national identity on popular culture.[3] In this volume, we want to pay particular attention to the reciprocal interaction between elites and popular culture in creating, disseminating, and appropriating symbols of national identity. Such interaction is salient to the Mexican case. Mexico experienced two great periods of civil war, revolution, and foreign invasion: the unstable initial years of independence from 1810 to 1867, and the Mexican Revolution of 1910 to 1917. In each case, dense, diverse popular mobilizations fueled politics, war, and state formation as feuding elites (foreign and national) sought to consolidate their power. These mobilizations created a reservoir for national imaginings that suggest a complex exchange between elites and popular forces in their construction.

Between 1829 and 1867, Mexico was four times invaded by foreign powers: Spain in 1829, France in 1838 and 1861, and the United States in 1846. Defense of the land against foreign armies and fraternizing among soldiers of "national" but diverse local origins fostered the growth of national identity, particularly when reinforced by new institutions and practices of loyalty, discipline, and sociability—armies, the national guard, military bands, patriotic juntas charged with organizing civic celebrations.[4] The experience generated a repertoire of anthems, marches, flags, songs, uniforms, heroes, slogans, stories —even consecrated body parts and bones.[5] Wars also create defining moments in nation construction as great victories and defeats in battle are etched into consciousness through monuments, statues, texts, and commemoration. Thus did the Niños Héroes, the five child cadets at the Colegio Militar, plunge to their death from the heights of Mexico City's Chapultepec Castle rather than surrender to the U.S. invaders. So also the Cinco de Mayo made its way early into the incipient national civic calendar as the day when Mexican Indian and mestizo soldiers bravely defeated French and Austrian armies at Puebla in 1862.

Shared heroes who had shed their blood that the *patria* might survive came to form a pantheon of icons resembling the Catholic saints. The two contending political factions of Liberals and Conservatives could agree on the inclusion of Father Hidalgo and Father Morelos, insurgents of independence. But in the second half of the nineteenth century, they were strongly divided about Benito Juárez, president from 1858 to 1872. For the Liberals, Juárez was a paragon of civic virtue and savior of the patria from foreign conquerors.[6] The Conservatives saw him as the devil incarnate for upholding the separation of church and state, divorcing Catholicism from official national identity, and sponsoring anticlerical legislation prohibiting church property, privileges, and worship (Meyer).[7] Communities of Liberal and Conservative affiliation developed distinct forms of patriotic celebration in the late nineteenth century (Vaughan).

The specter of masses of peasants and workers in the 1910 revolution was an even more powerful impetus to an interactive construction of national identity. Over a million people—one-tenth of the population—died in this conflagration. The revolution brought hunger, dislocation, disease, and death in its wake, but it also brought Mexicans together often under slogans that became national: "Tierra y libertad," "México para los mexicanos," and "Sufragio efectivo y no re-elección." As armies traversed the land, interacting in often brutal ways with each other and civilians, they also shared marches, waltzes, songs, myths, and stories (Velázquez and Vaughan). This demographic explosion contained powerful elements of cultural exchange and creativity that often achieved nationalist expression, particularly as Mexicans reacted to and mobilized around two U.S. invasions in 1914 and 1916. As Joanne Hershfield notes, filmmakers followed the armies, documenting battles and fiestas. These played to enthusiastic audiences who also welcomed movies on national themes.

As revolutionary armies descended on Mexico City, they generated a rage in popular theater and music reviews for the art and archetypes of regional, particularly rural, Mexico (Velázquez and Vaughan).[8] Academy- and European-trained artists joined the ferment, drawing inspiration from a popular culture that would provide the substance for a new nationalist art called forward by the charismatic visionary José Vasconcelos when he became minister of education in 1921. It is important to note that the repertoire of images, icons, and sounds deployed both by those who invaded the capital and by elite artists, intellectuals, performers, and entrepreneurs in the 1920s and 1930s was, to a large degree, the shared product in an ongoing transnational process of modern identity construction. In the nineteenth century, technological breakthroughs in transportation, communications, and representation had facilitated this deepening secularization. Its symbols and images were mediated by metropolitan expansion and an emerging order of nation-states.

Essays in this volume touch on three such prerevolutionary bodies of commodified images, types, objects, and sounds that informed postrevolutionary national identity formation. First, the iconography of *indigenismo*, a valorization of indigenous cultures, rested on knowledge and imagery accumulated from the late eighteenth century. European, North American, and Mexican intellectuals, scientists, explorers, lithographers, painters, and photographers had transformed Aztec, Mayan, and Zapotec ruins into archaeological sites and collected objects they displayed in museums and print. After their victory in 1867, the Mexican Liberals privileged Aztec civilization for its resistance to foreign conquest. In sculpture, painting, and opera, representations of pre-Columbian civilization in Greco-Roman neoclassical style flourished after 1870.[9]

Second, foreign travelers found in Mexico's green valleys, snowcapped volcanoes, cactus plants, and colorful market vendors the romantic, exotic "other." Mexican writers and artists contributed to this forging of popular archetypes: the *charro* horseman in tight black pants with silver buttons down the seams, his short, embroidered vest, and his leather boots; the *china poblana*, a mestiza beauty in sequined skirts, embroidered blouse, and satin slippers; the elegant women of the Tehuantepec Isthmus, majestic in full skirts, lace headdresses, and gold jewelry. Sanitized and stripped of context and squalor, these were pictured in postcards, books, advertisements, theater, concerts, and, by the turn of the century, the fledgling movie industry. Popular types, costumes, and dances had come to define regional identities and were performed and exhibited at the 1910 centennial celebrations.[10]

A third source of popular imagery surged with the contradictory results of modernization. For the proliferating press, engravers like José Guadalupe Posada depicted the faces of poverty and protest: prostitutes, criminals, the destitute, the diseased, the alcoholic, the violent and rebellious of the burgeoning cities and impoverished countryside.[11]

This repertoire was a key source for constructing a postrevolutionary nationalist aesthetics. What made the construction so powerful was its interaction with four related processes. The first was the sociopolitical upheaval of revolution. This coincided with a transnational movement of modernism in the arts that abandoned elite models of classical composition to discover authenticity, beauty, and energy in the primordial and primitive and gave rise in Mexico to a dazzling aestheticization of the popular in arts and crafts (López), painting (Rochfort, Oles, Lowe), and music (Velázquez and Vaughan).[12] Third, the emergence of mass society linked to urbanization and the meteoric rise of the mass media from the late 1920s privileged not only vintage popular types and genres but new ones in response to changing gendered subjectivities and social relations (Hershfield, Hayes, Velázquez and Vaughan). Products largely of the private sector, these were at the same time more conservative and more erotic than those created by artists directly associated with the state. Fourth, the fledgling national government showed an ability to mobilize this heterogeneous and contradictory array of cultural talent, genres, and symbolism as a means of consolidating control over a populace divided by needs and interests, regional and religious loyalties, and transnational and local political ideologies.

## National Memory

By "national memory" we refer to the narratives of a nation's past. States endorse a particular narrative of the nation that moves in tandem with the march of "civilization." Since the eighteenth century and until the Iranian Islamic revolution of 1978, this has been a linear history of scientific progress linked to the triumph of reason over dogma, magic, superstition, and violence.[13] Even when the foundational story of the nation celebrates a past golden age or a non-Western culture, these are usually endowed with virtues and vices defined by the standards of the modern West. Official narratives are what Pierre Nora calls "national pedagogies": they mobilize the past in order to move the individual into a particular future. As much as these histories affiliate a group of people, they generally order them into hierarchies reflecting differences in class, race, gender, and national space. As they create centers of power, knowledge, culture, progress, and authority, they fashion peripheries of backwardness and subordination. While they "include," they simultaneously "exclude" and "other" nonmembers.[14] Actors in the official national drama have been principally male elites.

Following the Liberals' defeat of the Catholic Conservatives and their French and Austrian allies in 1867, the Mexican Liberal Party gained control over official national memory. Ideologues elaborated their interpretation in school textbooks like Justo Sierra's *Historia patria*, or in master narratives such as his *La evolución política del pueblo mexicano* or the multiauthored *México a través de los siglos*.[15] These master narratives were written for foreign as well as national consumption. In an effort to attract foreign capital and immigration, these texts were published to overcome negative foreign accounts of bellicose and backward Mexico.[16] In this history, Mexico had its foundations in Indian civilization. The Spanish brought cultural, legal-administrative, and technological advances, but in their frenzied exploitation, they destroyed and buried Indian civilization. Liberal history promoted the Black Legend of a tyrannical, fanatical, backward Spain consonant with the late-nineteenth-century European hierarchy of nations, at the summit of which reigned Anglo-Saxon imperial power. Between 1810 and 1821, the "Mexican people," led by Miguel Hidalgo and José María Morelos, cast off the oppressive weight of Spanish colonialism and established a republic. Heroic men shed their blood in struggles against foreign invaders, who would dismember the patria, and Conservatives, who would restore the oppressive colony. Defeating their enemies, the Liberals secured the republic and proceeded under presidents Juárez and Díaz to foster national peace, stability, and progress through the development of communications, industries, markets, and schools.[17]

This history was disseminated through the arteries and institutions of a new civic space. The Bourbon kings began to secularize Mexico's profoundly religious public space in the late eighteenth century; Liberals after 1857 sought to demolish it.[18] They banned religious orders, property, processions, and garb and the ringing of church bells in an effort to confine religion to the church building—gestures more effective on paper than in practice. Renaming streets and schools for patriotic heroes, military victories, and political events, the Liberal government refurbished town plazas with gardens, statues of their heroes, and bandstands. New county office buildings called "municipal palaces" rivaled the church on the town square and generally included a huge clock to mark secular time. In larger population centers, the new space included opera houses, concert halls, libraries, academic societies, and museums. New technologies of communication and imaging fostered the circulation of official national memory through these venues, as did the growth of a reading public. However, in the still predominantly illiterate countryside, the spread of official national memory was not restricted to those who read or the adult males who voted. Imitating the socially inclusive colonial Catholic fiesta, civic ritual engaged distinct social classes, men, women, and children. Schoolchildren and brass bands were featured performers in the parades, choruses, and patriotic oratory that accompanied celebrations.[19] In Independence Day festivities, Liberals reenacted Father Hidalgo's cry for independence, but without his appeal to the Virgin of Guadalupe.

One should not exaggerate the spread of this national memory. Alan Knight has argued that in 1910, Mexico was "less a nation than a geographical expression, a mosaic of regions and communities, introverted and jealous, ethnically and physically fragmented, and lacking common national sentiments."[20] Large sectors of the population in particular regions of the country (rural Chiapas, small rural communities, many living on haciendas, foreign-owned plantations, lumber camps, and other enterprises) were only superficially exposed to official national memories. Others were overtly hostile. The latter included indigenous groups like the Yaquis of Sonora, against whom Mexican Liberal armies made war to access the Yaqui ancestral lands for modern capitalist development (Lewis). Hostile as well were militant Catholics who, under church leadership, began a campaign of reconquest, building new parishes, forming workers' circles and women's groups, developing a vigorous press and program of social reform (Bantjes, Meyer). In 1895 they convinced the pope to consecrate the Virgin of Guadalupe queen of the Americas. In 1910 they created the Mexican National Catholic Party (Meyer, Fernández). Their version of Mexican history was unequivocally antiliberal, Catholic, and Hispanist or pro-Spanish.

But official national memory appealed to many, including new sectors created by the rapid process of foreign-led modernization: an enlarged middle class and a more modern, incipient working class. Identifying with the nation and adopting the behaviors and artifacts of modernity were part of middle-class formation in this period. Many members of this sector, however, felt that their aspirations for representative government and social mobility were stifled by a partnership between foreign capital and a new Mexican oligarchy held together by the dictatorship of Porfirio Díaz. Certain sectors of workers, principally those in the lead industries of textiles, railroads, and mining, saw themselves discriminated against by foreign managers. In the first decade of the twentieth century, workers in these industries launched major strikes targeting foreign privilege and abuse. These groups, along with significant portions of the dislocated and dispossessed peasantry, mobilized in the 1910 revolution.[21]

The revolution revised but did not abandon Porfirian national memory. Explored in these essays, particularly in mural art and education, the revolutionary version of history constructed over time placed greater emphasis on Mexico's indigenous foundations and contemporary cultures and the role of the popular classes in the long, tragic march toward liberation. It condemned Porfirio Díaz as a dictator who undermined democratic liberties and facilitated the exploitation of his own people by foreign capitalists, landlords, and priests. The revolution became a rebellion of *el pueblo*—the peasants, workers, and middle classes—for national self-determination, freedom, and material well-being to be achieved through alliance with the postrevolutionary state. The new history created unity where it had never existed.[22] Out of the bloody conflict between revolutionary leaders and factions, a singular pantheon of new heroes emerged over time: Francisco I. Madero, Venustiano Carranza, Álvaro Obregón, Emiliano Zapata, and eventually Pancho Villa (Olsen). The constitution of 1917 became the new unifying document that promised land reform, workers' rights, a curbing of church power, and national control over natural resources and economic development. As mural depictions of the revolution attest, women entered this official drama in greater numbers than before, but as supports to male principals—witnesses, sex objects, fertility symbols, mothers, and teachers of male-generated knowledge.

To disseminate this revolutionary national memory, governments intensified and extended their use of existing channels. They expanded and centralized the system of public schools and multiplied the number of civic festivals, parades, street names, and sites (monuments, statues, museums, archaeological ruins). New genres emerged in painting and mural art, music, dance, and film. In the 1930s, the government made use of the radio. If this official version of national memory showed signs of achieving incipient hegemony by the end of the 1930s, it did so within a diverse and conflictive field of artistic, rhetorical, and intellectual expression—in film, the plastic arts, architecture, textbooks, and music. As essays in this volume show, distinct social sectors in different geographical regions forged national memories in opposition to, and interaction with, official messages. New groups emerging from the revolution such as unionized workers or land reform recipients (*agraristas*) made considerable use of government-generated symbols, icons, and memories to confirm their power and shape their identities while inevitably integrating these into specific local repertoires.

## Utopia and Cultural Revolution

Utopian visions surged in the heat and hope of revolution: Diego Rivera's vision of a Marxist workers' revolution (Rochfort); a Catholic utopia of order, hierarchy, and faith (Meyer); a secular utopia that had buried religion forever (Bantjes). To varying degrees, these relate to the utopia most central to these essays: the dream of behavioral transformation. In the first three quarters of the twentieth century, leaders of postcolonial nations felt the imperative to "catch up" with the modern West by sanitizing and transforming the behavior of their populations in order to compete productively and on a more equal basis with the very nation-states that had imperialized them.[23]

Standard revolutionary historiography has portrayed the Porfirians as being indifferent to the welfare and productive capacity of the Mexican population. In their dreams for the development of a mythical abundance of natural resources, Porfirians placed their faith in an influx of foreign capital, talent, and technology.[24] In this heyday of evolutionary theories of white racial superiority, their own predominantly nonwhite population was inferior in its biological destiny and thus an obstacle to national progress. They hoped they would whiten themselves through European immigration. When few came, the argument goes, they had to consider "improving" their own population. In fact, research increasingly shows the serious interest of Porfirian statesmen, scientists, and professionals in education, hygiene, sanitation, medicine, and rehabilitative criminology, or what Michel Foucault defines as biopolitics: a focus on the health, productivity, and discipline of a given population.[25]

Middle-class revolutionaries intensified this focus. Harboring their predecessors' dreams of harvesting Mexico's imagined riches, they were convinced that development depended on the Mexicans themselves and that Mexicans required a behavioral transformation. General Salvador Alvarado, governor of Yucatán in 1915, exhorted:

> If we, the lucky inhabitants of this privileged land, keep sleeping, if we are not strong, aggressive, and enterprising in the exploitation of our fabulous wealth, take heed—other races more enterprising, aggressive, and tenacious will come and whether we like it or not, they will take what is today ours, our lands, forest, livestock, homes. They will have shown more force in the struggle for survival and our children will shine their shoes.

He called for a campaign of regeneration. "If all sleeping minds enter into action," he exhorted, "the propelling work of evolution will be more intense and effective." "Everyone to the factory, shop and home! Let us create the religion of duty!"[26]

Postrevolutionary governments roundly rejected notions of biological destiny and inferiority to embrace principles of environmental determinism. They drew on the work of the anthropologist Franz Boas, professor at Columbia University and first director of the Escuela Internacional de Antropología, opened in Mexico in 1910. Boas's theory of cultural relativism challenged nineteenth-century theories of racial evolution. Mexican reformers called for a cultural revolution that would transform behavior through education, health and hygiene reform, property redistribution, defanaticization, and political access. The reformers were not a monolithic group: individuals supported some programs more than others and did so from distinct political positions. But whether they embraced the new ideologies of *indigenismo*, linking Mexico's essence to indigenous culture, or *mestizaje*, celebrating racial and cultural mixture, reformers did not abandon the language or the evolutionary approach of nineteenth-century racialist theory: they would transform a "backward, degenerate, diseased" people into healthy, scientific patriots mobilized for development.[27]

One dominant trope in the early years of reform came from Mexico's North, represented by the presidents Álvaro Obregón, Plutarco Elías Calles, and General Salvador Alvarado. Anglophiles hoping to pragmatize Mexican culture along the lines of that of the United States, they regarded central and southern Mexico as the sick and lethargic consequence of Spanish oppression and Catholic obscurantism. Over time, official rhetoric diluted the Anglophilic dimension in favor of a class analysis: Mexicans were diseased because landlords, priests, and foreign capitalists had exploited and oppressed them (Bliss, Vaughan).

Mexican reformers participated in a transnational milieu of scientific knowledge, technique, and expertise disseminated through publications, congresses, and educational exchanges.[28] Boas's cultural relativism was but one current operating in this milieu. Eugenics, the movement to "improve" racial stock through reproductive policy, was another (Bliss).[29] The Mexican program of population management and social engineering was to be carried out by teachers, social workers, medical and hygiene personnel, ethnographers, and statisticians. They operated through schools, home visits, clinics, fieldwork, jails, courts, and public radio and print campaigns. They aimed to eradicate tuberculosis, syphilis, and alcoholism, the three "social diseases," along with prostitution, gambling, and violence. They promoted sports, modern medicine, home economics, and puericulture, or the science of child raising. Their gendered policies imagined a nuclear patriarchal family headed by a sober, productive male breadwinner and a scientifically informed homemaker and mother of clean, patriotic children who regularly attended school. Entrepreneurs in the private sector and print and radio advertising supported this program, peddling dental and bodily hygiene, cleaning products for the home, and store-bought medicines and vitamins. However, advertising's reach remained largely urban between 1920 and 1940.

The program of behavioral modernization involved an extensive investigation of the "Indian" by ethnographers, anthropologists, demographers, and teachers. When the anthropologist Manuel Gamio began to study the population of Teotihuacán during the revolution, he moved from a biological to a cultural definition of race following his mentor Franz Boas. In his fieldwork, Gamio encountered fluidity and hybridity in both cultural and somatic traits.[30] As Stephen Lewis explains in his essay in this volume, an intense effort to specify the location and characteristics of indigenous societies and languages occurred simultaneously with the implementation of a uniform policy of behavioral modification and incorporation. Not until the mid-1930s did professionals show signs of recognizing the value of preserving cultural differences and indigenous languages.

Historians have disputed popular response to the government's behavioral reforms. Some, focused on religion, have tended to portray the postrevolutionary state as an aggressive bulldozer attempting to run over a uniform, homogeneous, resistant peasant community. There is good reason for this. In response to President Calles's attack on the church, Catholic mobilization triggered a dreadful, bloody civil war in western Mexico known as the Cristiada (1926–29) (Meyer). Anticlerical educational policy between 1932 and 1935 also drew widespread opposition (Bantjes, Vaughan, Lewis). The strong critiques of the state by Adrian Bantjes and Jean Meyer in this volume capture the fanaticism and violence of revolutionary Jacobinism as well as the religious fervor of Catholics.

Anticlericalism notwithstanding, most scholars stress the heterogeneity among state agents and rural communities, their capacities for negotiation, the state's willingness to subordinate cultural issues to politics, and the importance of the marketplace (Vaughan, Waters, Lewis). All agree that the short-term success of government programs was limited. Rightly or wrongly, they were often associated with campaigns against the church. The reformers' unconsidered faith in the cosmopolitan science of the moment and their attitudes of superiority limited their impact. Critically, the government lacked the technical capacity, economic resources, and unified will to implement its social programs fully and effectively. Within the state, agencies often came into conflict with one another while disputes raged over policy and jurisdiction at the national, regional, local, and institutional levels. The reformers' prescriptions, often incompatible with popular needs and economic capacities, frequently clashed with local cultural practices that reformers openly disdained. The greater a community's familiarity with, and access to, modern products, the more it was open to experimentation and appropriation. Where power relations were in flux and state reforms (particularly land and labor reforms) helped to empower new social groups, there was often greater openness to government behavioral initiatives. However, even in these communities, struggles ensued over the meanings of modernity, health, masculinity, femininity, childhood, work, and recreation. Everywhere it was difficult to undercut loyalty to the Virgin of Guadalupe and a multitude of local saints.

In the end, selective appropriation occurred. Many rural communities began to respond positively to social reform prescriptions only after 1940, when the religious controversy died down and demilitarization brought greater peace and stability. The government was able to provide more assistance in the form of water, agricultural inputs, minimal health protections, roads, and a subsidized fleet of buses that linked remote villages to urban markets. The expanded market made available canned foods, Coca-Cola, and the wonder drug penicillin, which reduced infant mortality and ended the obsession with bacterial diseases. These benefits were few and not evenly distributed. As Wendy Waters shows in her story of Tepoztlán's road, they were negotiated and selected by communities proud of their traditions.

Although pride in local traditions had grown in the cultural struggles over meaning and practice that raged between 1920 and 1940, such pride was not simply the result of local resistance. It was endorsed by another dimension of the postrevolutionary cultural revolution. It is not unusual in nation-building processes to combine a campaign for behavioral modernization with attempts to mobilize and unify populations around a mystical, folkloric past.[31] Postrevolutionary cultural nationalism flourished in a modernist recovery and aestheticization not only of the pre-Hispanic and colonial past but also of contemporary popular culture. As Rick López shows, Dr. Atl elevated to the category of pure art a *rebozo* (shawl) or lacquered bowl likely crafted in the very conditions of misery and religious devotion that social reformers sought to abolish. Within the transnational and national contexts in which these two parallel mobilizations—the aesthetic and the behavioral—unfolded, their apparent contradiction emerges more as a capacious, flexible ambivalence.

The Mexican Revolution occurred within a significant geopolitical shift that had profound cultural implications. After 1898, the United States emerged as a major imperial power in Latin America following the U.S. intervention in the Cuban struggle for liberation from Spain. The United States turned Puerto Rico into a colony and Cuba into a semicolony. In the years immediately following, U.S. troops invaded Nicaragua, Haiti, and the Dominican Republic. These aggressions unleashed a strong response from Latin American intellectuals, who began to contrast the aggressive, mechanistic, industrial culture of the northern colossus with the spiritual, soulful, and telluric culture of Latin America.[32] If the violence and devastation of World War I contributed to this movement by discrediting notions of European cultural superiority, it left Latin America, particularly Mexico, face to face with the aggressive northern power—Caliban to Latin America's Ariel, as the Uruguayan writer José Enrique Rodó imagined it. Mexican intellectuals were keenly aware that the U.S. had twice invaded Mexico during the revolution. The United States emerged from the war as the world's only creditor nation and, in 1920, had reduced Mexico to pariah status by refusing to recognize or extend credit to a revolutionary nation whose constitution threatened the sanctity of private property.

Part of the euphoria of cultural nationalist movements is often their assertion that their societies contain in their past and culture the seeds for improving on and surpassing European/Anglo civilization. José Vasconcelos proudly challenged the United States. His theory of the Cosmic Race declared Latin America superior to Europe and North America because of its historical fostering of racial and cultural intermixing, its tolerance, and its spiritual creativity. When he called on Mexican artists and intellectuals to paint, compose, dance, write, and display their national culture, they came forward, well trained by virtue of the Porfirian state's educational policies, fully conversant with transnational modernist discourses and techniques, and committed to immersing themselves in the plethora of popular art that surrounded them. The result was perhaps the most successful achievement of the transnational modernist movement: abjuring "bourgeois elitism" and transcending the limitations of positivist science and academic formalism, they effectively celebrated the popular in revolutionary forms and techniques.[33]

If we consider that Mexican revolutionary state builders faced a triple challenge of establishing governance over a disparate, mobilized, and needy population, preparing it for economic competition and membership in the world of "civilized nations," and negotiating a more equal relationship with metropolitan nations (particularly the United States), we can understand how and why they eagerly enlisted artists and intellectuals. Artistic production provided the polish for the muddied boots of the "backwoods" military generals who ruled postrevolutionary Mexico. They sorely needed this cultural capital to negotiate with the outside world. As the essays in this volume by Rick López, Desmond Rochfort, James Oles, and Marco Velázquez and Mary Kay Vaughan suggest, Mexican murals, crafts, and music played a critical role in crafting a rapprochement with the United States. U.S. artists, intellectuals, collectors, and powerful patrons—including U.S. ambassador to Mexico Dwight Morrow and the oil magnate and financier Nelson Rockefeller—became immediately engaged. They organized exhibits for Mexican crafts in New York and other U.S. cities; debuted the music of Carlos Chávez; invited Rivera, Orozco, and Siqueiros to paint walls in Detroit, San Francisco, Los Angeles, and New York; and contributed mightily to the investigation, preservation, and revitalization of "folkloric" culture and arts in Mexico.[34] Artistic achievement marked Mexico's entry into the cosmopolitan club of nations, overcoming or at least counter-acting prevailing images of Mexican bellicosity, savagery, and backwardness. At the same time, art became a potent medium through which Mexico was subordinated to U.S. hegemony. In addition to their role in diplomacy, Mexican artists and their foreign interpreters contributed to the folklorization and exoticization of Mexico (Rochfort, Lowe, Oles, Zavala).

Domestically, cultural nationalism contributed to uniting a divided nation. Mexico came of age as a nation in March 1938 when president Lázaro Cárdenas expropriated the oil wells from Anglo-American corporations. The act provoked a groundswell of support from the Mexican people, mobilized by schoolteachers, unions, the radio, businessmen's associations, and even the Catholic Church. For weeks, thick crowds packed the Avenida Juárez and the Alameda, waiting to donate their animals, rings, pesos, sewing machines, and jewels to contingents of Mexican women who received them with first lady Amalia Solórzano at the Palacio de Bellas Artes (Olsen). Artists gave their paintings, photographs, and sculptures. Writers penned poems. Musicians composed *corridos*. In cities all over the country, Mexicans marched carrying placards that read "For the foreign chickens, Mexican roosters!" and "Hidalgo 1810: Cárdenas 1938."[35]

In 1938 President Cárdenas reorganized the state political party as the Partido Revolucionario Mexicano (renamed the PRI in 1946) incorporating the military, organized workers (Confederación de Trabajadores de Mexico or CTM), peasants (Confederación Nacional Campesina or CNC), and the middle classes (Confederación Nacional de Organizaciones Populares or CNOP). There is little doubt that cultural nationalism served the authoritarian, single-party state in its governance. But what Claudio Lomnitz, in his conclusion to this volume, calls the pragmatism and eclecticism of this state—its recognition of the need to leave its dreams of radical transformation incomplete—makes it distinct from contemporary fascist and communist regimes. Pragmatic negotiation became a source of its strength and consensus building.

When in a pivotal gesture of conciliation in 1940 president Manuel Ávila Camacho declared himself a Catholic, he confirmed the defeat of postrevolutionary antireligiosity. On the other hand, he invited the participation of the church and Catholics according to the rules of a secular state. The desacralization of religious culture and its resacralization as the art and culture of a national patrimony became an enormous resource for state and society alike as they experienced ever-deepening and uneven processes of modernization. Such a secular, ecumenical framework permitted the continued valorization and revalorization of indigenous cultures in their religious devotion and their prescientific communal practices. It condoned the proliferation of the image of the Virgin of Guadalupe in increasingly modern incarnations—tattooed on the chests and arms of young men, dangled from the rearview mirrors of taxicabs, buses, and trucks, leading bicycling pilgrims over superhighways to her shrine in Mexico City. The multiple, polyphonic symbols of popular culture now fully identified as national could be manipulated to represent the ultramodern, sexualized persona of Frida Kahlo, the struggles of workers for dignity and social justice, the communal traditions of Zapotec weavers, and Catholic Hispanist desires for the preservation of patriarchy and class boundaries. As the essays in this volume suggest, this symbolic cultural repertoire was a powerful force in the making of modern Mexico, a process of dynamic hybridity that transcended categories of assimilation and acculturation.

## Notes

1. The Virgin's history is told in David Brading, *Mexican Phoenix: Our Lady of Guadalupe; Image and Tradition across Five Centuries* (New York: Cambridge University Press, 2001); Stafford Poole, *Our Lady of Guadalupe: The Origins and Sources of a Mexican National Symbol, 1531–1707* (Tucson: University of Arizona Press, 1995); Jacques Lafaye, *Quetzalcóatl and Guadalupe: The Formation of Mexican National Consciousness, 1531–1813* (Chicago: University of Chicago Press, 1976); and Karla Zarebska and Alejandro Gómez de Tuddo, *Guadalupe* (Oaxaca, 2002). On creole nationalism, see David Brading, *The First America: The Spanish Monarchy, Creole Patriots, and the Liberal State, 1492–1867* (Cambridge: Cambridge University Press, 1991), 358–72, 639–40; and Claudio Lomnitz, *Deep Mexico, Silent Mexico* (Minneapolis: University of Minnesota Press, 2001), 16–24.

2. The seminal and most cited work is Benedict Anderson, *Imagined Communities: Reflections on the Origin and Spread of Nationalism* (London: Verso, 1983). See also Homi K. Bhabha, *The Nation and Narration* (New York: Routledge, 1990); Eric Hobsbawm and Terrence Ranger, *The Invention of Tradition* (New York: Cambridge University Press, 1983); and Partha Chaterjee, *Nationalist Thought and the Colonial World* (Minneapolis: University of Minnesota Press, 1993). For a brief historiographic account of this literature, see Geoff Eley and Ronald Grigor Suny, *Becoming National: A Reader* (New York: Oxford University Press, 1996), 8–26.

3. For example, Anderson, *Imagined Communities*; Hobsbawm and Ranger, *The Invention of Tradition*; Elie Kedourie, *Nationalism in Asia and Africa* (London: Weidenfeld and Nicolson, 1971), 73–77, 92–93, 106; and Ernest Gellner, *Nations and Nationalism* (Oxford: Blackwell, 1983), 48–49, 55–62.

4. See, among others, Guy P. C. Thomson, "Bulwarks of Patriotic Liberalism: The

National Guard, Philharmonic Corps, and Patriotic Juntas in Mexico (1847–1888)," *Journal of Latin American Studies* 22 (1989): 31–68; "The Ceremonial and Political Roles of Village Bands, 1846–1974," in *Rituals of Rule, Rituals of Resistance: Public Celebrations and Popular Culture in Mexico*, ed. William H. Beezley, Cheryl Martin, and William French (Wilmington: Scholarly Resources, 1994), 300–336; Florencia Mallon, *Peasant and Nation: The Making of Postcolonial Mexico and Peru* (Berkeley: University of California Press, 1995); William H. Beezley and David Lorey, *Viva México! Viva la Independencia! Celebrations of September 16th* (Wilmington: Scholarly Resources, 2001); and Annick Lemperiere, "La ciudad de Mexico, 1780–1869: Del espacio barroco al espacio republicana," in *Hacia otra historia del arte en México: De la estructuración colonial a la exigencia nacional, 1780-1860*, vol. 1, ed. Esther Acevedo (Mexico City: Conaculta, 2001), 149–64.

5. On blood, bones, and body parts in Mexican national identity, see Lomnitz, *Deep Mexico*, 88–90; and Mallon, *Peasant and Nation*, 276–309.

6. Lomnitz, *Deep Mexico*, 95; Charles Hale, *The Transformation of Mexican Liberalism in Late Nineteenth Century Mexico* (Princeton: Princeton University Press, 1989); and Brian Hamnett, *Juárez* (London: Longman, 1994).

7. Names in parentheses refer to a contributor's essay in this volume.

8. Ricardo Pérez Montfort, *Estampas del nacionalismo popular mexicana: Ensayos sobre cultura popular y nación* (Mexico City: CIESAS, 1994), 142–46, 199–221; Roberto Blancarte, "Indigenismo, hispanismo, y panamericanismo en la cultura popular mexicana de 1920 a 1940," in *Historia de la iglesia católica en México (1929–1982)* (Mexico City: Colegio Mexiquense and Fondo de Cultura Económica, 1992), 344–46.

9. The literature on prerevolutionary indigenismo is now vast. See, among others, David Brading, *The First America*, 364–67, 450–65, 523–30, 638–39; Enrique Florescano, *Etnia, estado y nación* (Mexico City: Taurus, 1996), 392–93; Enrique Florescano, "Imágenes de la patria en la época de la Reforma y el Porfiriato" (unpublished manuscript, 2003), 9–17; Stacie Widdifield, *The Embodiment of the National in Late Nineteenth Century Mexican Painting* (Tucson: University of Arizona Press, 1996), 42–45; Benjamin Keen, *The Aztec Image in Western Thought* (New Brunswick: Rutgers University Press, 1974); Barbara Tenenbaum, "Streetwise History: The Paseo de la Reforma and the Porfirian State, 1876–1910," in Beezley, Martin, and French, *Rituals of Rule*, 127–50; and Mauricio Tenorio, *Mexico at the World's Fairs: Crafting a Modern Nation* (Berkeley: University of California Press, 1998), 72–73, 184.

10. On travel literature and the exotic, see Mary Louise Pratt, *Imperial Eyes: Travel Writing and Transculturation* (New York: Rutgers University Press, 1992); on the genesis of Mexican images and popular types, see, among others, Florescano, "Imágenes," 6–9, 21; Rosa Casanova, "Un nuevo modo de representar: Fotografía en México, 1839–1864," in Acevedo, *Hacia otra historia*, vol. 1, 191–217; Deborah Poole, "An Image of 'Our Indian': Type Photographs and Racial Sentiments in Oaxaca, 1920–1940," *Hispanic American Historical Review* 84, no. 1 (2004); and various articles in *La Tehuana*,

*Artes de México*, no. 49 (2000), and *La China Poblana, Artes de México*, no. 66 (2003) (bilingual publications).

11. Rita Eder, *El arte en México: Autores, temas, problemas* (Mexico City: Conaculta Lotería Nacional, Fondo de Cultura Económica, 2001), 341–72; Fausto Ramírez, "Las ilustraciones de José Guadalupe Posada en *La Patria Ilustrada*," in *Signos de moderniza-ción y resistencias* (Mexico City: Museo Nacional del Arte, 1996).

12. On primitivism and modernist aesthetics, see Colin Rhodes, *Primitivism and Modern Art* (London: Thames and Hudson, 1994); for a similar movement in neigh-boring Cuba, see Robin D. Moore, *Nationalizing Blackness: Afrocubanismo and Artis-tic Revolution in Havana, 1920–1940* (Pittsburgh: University of Pittsburgh Press, 1997), 191–214.

13. Pierre Nora, "Between Memory and History: Les Lieux de Memoire," *Represen-tations* 20 (spring 1989): 7, 16; Elie Kedouri, *Nationalism in Asia and Africa* (Weidenfeld and Nicolson, 1971), 73–77, 92–93; and Mary Matossian, "Ideologies of Delayed In-dustrialization: Some Tensions and Ambiguities," in *Political Change in Underdeveloped Countries*, ed. John H. Kautsky (New York: Wiley, 1962), 254–64.

14. Partha Chatterjee, *The Nation and Its Fragments* (Princeton: Princeton University Press, 1993), 110–15; see also Edward Said, *The World, the Text, and the Critic* (Cam-bridge: Harvard University Press, 1983), 171.

15. Justo Sierra, *The Political Evolution of the Mexican People*, trans. Charles Cumber-land (Austin: University of Texas Press, 1969), originally published in 1900–1902; Sierra, *Historia patria* (Mexico City: SEP, 1922); *México a través de los siglos: Historia general y completa del desenvolvimiento social, político, religioso, militar, artístico, científico y literario de México desde la antigüedad más remota hasta la época actual*, 5 vols., ed. Vicente Riva Palacio (Barcelona: Espasa y Cía., 1887–89).

16. Tenorio, *Mexico at the World's Fairs*, 237–46.

17. From Sierra's *Historia patria*, in Vaughan, *The State, Education, and Social Class in Mexico, 1880–1928* (DeKalb: Northern Illinois University Press, 1982), 218–26.

18. See Annick Lemperiere's superb essay, "La ciudad de Mexico."

19. Guy P. C. Thomson, "Bulwarks," 31–68; and Vaughan, "The Construction of Patriotic Festival in Tecamachalco, Puebla, 1900–1946," in Beezley, Martin, and French, *Rituals of Rule*, 213–46.

20. Alan Knight, *The Mexican Revolution*, 2 vols. (1986; Lincoln: University of Ne-braska Press 1990), 1:2.

21. The historiography of the Mexican Revolution is understandably enormous. Par-ticularly informative is Alan Knight's discussion of this historiography in "The Mexi-can Revolution: Bourgeois? Nationalist? Or Just a 'Great Rebellion'?" *Bulletin of Latin American Research* 4, no. 2 (1985): 1–37. On nationalist sentiment in the revolution, see John Hart, *Revolutionary Mexico* (Berkeley: University of California Press, 1987).

22. Thomas Benjamin, *La Revolución: Mexico's Great Revolution as Memory, Myth, and History* (Austin: University of Texas Press, 2000).

23. See, among others, Matossian, "Ideologies of Delayed Industrialization"; and Tom Nairn, *The Breakup of Britain: Crisis in Neo-nationalism*, 2nd ed. (London: New Left Books, 1977), 332–41.

24. See Raymond Craib, "A Nationalist Metaphysics: State Fixations, National Maps, and the Geo-historical Imagination in Nineteenth Century Mexico," *Hispanic American Historical Review* 82, no. 1 (2002): 33–68.

25. On education, see Vaughan, *The State, Education, and Social Class*, 1–77; and Vaughan, "The Construction of Patriotic Festival"; on hygiene, see Claudia Agostini, *Monuments of Progress: Modernization and Public Health in Mexico (1876–1910)* (Boulder: University of Colorado Press, 2003); and Mauricio Tenorio Trillo, "1910 Mexico City: Space and Nation in the City of the Centenario," *Journal of Latin American Studies* 28 (February 1996): 75–104; on mental health, see Cristina Rivera Garza, " 'She neither Respected nor Obeyed Anyone': Inmates and Psychiatrists Debate Gender and Class at the General Insane Asylum La Castañeda Mexico, 1910–1930," *Hispanic American Historical Review* 81, nos. 3–4 (2001): 653–88; on criminology, see Pablo Piccato, *City of Suspects: Crime in Mexico City, 1900–31* (Durham: Duke University Press, 2002); and Robert Buffington, *Criminal and Citizen in Modern Mexico* (Lincoln: University of Nebraska Press, 2000). On biopolitics, see Michel Foucault, *The History of Sexuality, Volume I: An Introduction* (New York: Vintage, 1990), 140–44.

26. Salvador Alvarado, "Carta al Pueblo de Yucatán publicada en *La Voz de la Revolución*, 5 de mayo de 1916, aniversario de gloria para la patria mexicana," in *La cuestión de la tierra, 1915–1917: Colección de folletos para la historia de la revolución mexicana, dirigida por Jesús Silva Herzog* (Mexico City: Instituto Mexicano de Investigaciones Económicas, 1960); *Boletín de Educación* 1, no. 2 (1915): 252; and Antonio Mediz Bolio, *Salvador Alvarado* (Mexico City: SEP, 1968), 67.

27. See Alan Knight, "Racism, Revolution, and *Indigenismo*: México, 1910–1940," in *The Idea of Race in Latin America, 1870–1940*, ed. Richard Graham (Austin: University of Texas Press, 1990); and Vaughan, *Cultural Politics in Revolution: Teachers, Peasants and Schools in Mexico, 1930–1940* (Tucson: University of Arizona Press, 1997), 10–12, 25–46.

28. Victoria de Grazia, *How Fascism Ruled Women: Italy, 1922–1945* (Berkeley: University of California Press, 1992), 1–40.

29. See also Alexandra Minna Stern, "Mestizophilia, Biotypology and Eugenics in Post-revolutionary Mexico: Toward a History of Science and the State, 1920–1960," in *Race and Nation in Modern Latin America*, ed. Nancy P. Appelbaum, Anne S. Macpherson, and Karin Alejandra Rosemblatt (Chapel Hill: University of North Carolina Press, 2003), 187–210.

30. On Gamio at Teotihuacán, see, among others, David Brading, "Manuel Gamio and Official Indigenismo in Mexico," *Bulletin of Latin American Research* 7, no. 1 (1988): 75–89; and Alexander Dawson, *Indian and Nation in Revolutionary Mexico* (Tucson: University of Arizona Press, 2004), 9–17.

31. Claudio Lomnitz points out that a modern future and a traditional past go to-

gether in nation building. See *Deep Mexico*, 132–33; see also Chatterjee, *Nationalist Thought*, 49–53. Literature on cultural nationalism is extensive, but see in particular Anthony D. Smith, *The Dynamics of Cultural Nationalism* (London: Allen and Unwin, 1987); and Gellner, *Nations and Nationalism*, 53–62.

32. Lomnitz, *Deep Mexico*, 103–4; Frederick Pike, *The United States and Latin America: Myths and Stereotypes of Civilization and Nature* (Austin: University of Texas Press, 1992), 193–94; José Enrique Rodó, *Ariel* (Austin: University of Texas Press, 1988); Martin Stabb, *In Quest of Identity: Patterns in the Spanish American Essay of Ideas, 1890–1960* (Chapel Hill: University of North Carolina Press, 1967); and Vaughan, *The State, Education, and Social Class*, 239–66.

33. See Andreas Huyssen, *After the Great Divide: Modernism, Mass Culture, Postmodernism* (Bloomington: Indiana University Press, 1986). This otherwise excellent study does not mention Mexico.

34. See, among others, Susan Danly et al., *Casa Mañana: The Morrow Collection of Mexican Popular Arts* (Albuquerque: University of New Mexico Press, 2002); Helen Delpar, *The Enormous Vogue of Things Mexican: Cultural Relations between the U.S. and Mexico, 1920–1935* (Tuscaloosa: University of Alabama Press, 1992); Susannah Joel Glusker, *Anita Brenner: A Mind of Her Own* (Austin: University of Texas Press, 1998); Taylor Littleton, *The Color of Silver: William Spratling, His Life and Art* (Baton Rouge: Louisiana State University Press, 2000); Alejandra López Torres, "El renacimiento cultural bajo la mirada de Frances Toor," *Tzintzun* 34 (July–December 2001); Joan Mark, *The Silver Gringo: William Spratling and Taxco* (Albuquerque: University of New Mexico Press, 2000); and James Oles, *South of the Border: Mexico in the American Imagination, 1914–1947* (Washington: Smithsonian Institution, 1993).

35. Montfort, *Estampas*, 180–95.

# I

The
Aesthetics of
Nation
Building

# The Noche Mexicana
## and the Exhibition of Popular Arts:
## Two Ways of Exalting Indianness

RICK A. LÓPEZ

After watching the Mexican revolution from Europe, Dr. Atl (Gerardo Murillo), Roberto Montenegro, Jorge Enciso, and Adolfo Best Maugard, among other artists and intellectuals, answered the patriotic call to come home and help to rebuild the nation. Imbued with modernist sensibilities, they looked on Mexico and its people with new eyes, fascinated above all with the nation's distinctive nativist qualities. Living indigenous cultures, despite centuries of disparagement, seemed to offer a source for a new national culture that might unite the nation while propelling Mexico into the highest ranks of cultural modernity. In 1921 a number of these artists and intellectuals organized public displays for the massive state-sponsored celebration of the centennial of Mexico's independence. Among the most innovative of these events were the Exhibition of Popular Arts by Enciso, Montenegro, and Atl, and the Noche Mexicana by Best Maugard. Together they expressed the search for an indigenous-based national identity—an identity that event organizers hoped might help unite the historically fragmented, war-torn population.

Both events recast native craft industries from symbols of peasant backwardness into integral components of Mexican identity. Yet they represented contrasting visions of the role that indigenous cultures should play in the formation of the national self. They clashed in their assumptions about the relationship between Indianness and Mexicanness. Both reveal the extent to which the turn toward an "ethnicized" or "Indianized" definition of Mexico's national culture did not flow inevitably out of Mexico's historical experience, as is generally assumed, but instead resulted from a distinct movement led by cosmopolitan nationalists inside and outside the government. And far from occurring uniquely within Mexico, this generation's turn toward things native, and away from "Europeanized artificiality," occurred in a profoundly trans-national context in artistic and intellectual circles across Europe, Russia, the Americas, India, and Japan.

## The Centennial Celebrations

By mid-May 1921, when events sponsored by the newspaper *El Universal* and other private organizations had generated public excitement for the upcoming centennial, the new minister of foreign relations, Alberto Pani (recently re-turned from living in Paris), became convinced that the fledgling state should take the organizational and financial reins of the commemoration. Pani had previously stressed the need to study and publicize the diverse languages, cus-toms, aesthetics, and composition of the peoples of Mexico so as to unite them culturally. He conceded that rural cultures were crude and splintered, and that it might take years to forge a common culture. The government, he insisted, should play a leading role in this transformation. State sponsorship of a popu-larly oriented centennial celebration was a first step in this state-led transfor-mation.

President Álvaro Obregón, who saw the centennial celebrations as a means of crafting a populist image for his regime and a unifying identity for the frag-mented nation, backed Pani's plan. With a mere four months to coordinate one of the largest, most public displays in Mexican history, Obregón ordered his cabinet to appoint prominent intellectuals to a planning committee and immediately issued invitations to foreign envoys. After intense public debate, he won passage of a controversial one-time tax on middle- and upper-income earners to help fund the events.[1]

To contrast with what they defined as the elitist quality of Porfirio Díaz's 1910 centennial celebrations, the month-long commemoration was to be of "essentially popular character." But it was far from clear what the committee meant by "popular." Some of the events, such as street parades, offered public access. Others like bullfights, circuses, and sporting events had a proven appeal to nonelite audiences. As September drew near, promoters and journalists as-serted that this was not enough. The centennial needed events rooted in rural popular culture ("folk culture" and "indigenous culture" were other frequently invoked terms). Even the newspaper *Excélsior*, skeptical of the new cultural ori-entation, affirmed that the events should celebrate folk culture and not *cursi* (pretentious and tacky) European styles.[2]

But who were these rural popular classes of which everyone spoke, and how would their culture make the events more Mexican? This question posed a problem not only for the celebrations but also for the postrevolutionary regime, whose very mandate was based on its supposed advocacy of the popular classes that had fought in the revolution. Some people emphasized the country's Spanish colonial heritage as the basis for a shared cultural nation, while others emphasized a romanticized pre-Hispanic past. A brief glance at the statuary along Paseo de la Reforma sufficed to confirm that there was nothing particularly revolutionary about the celebration of Mexico's Spanish, Aztec, and Maya roots. What was new was that after the revolution these were joined by a novel populist discourse that cast rural Mexicans as Indian and placed their culture at the center of postrevolutionary national identity. The Noche Mexicana and the Exhibition of Popular Arts were among the centennial events that focused most self-consciously on this emerging interpretation of popular cultures.

### "The Germ for Artistic Expression"

In August 1921 the Centennial Committee contracted Adolfo Best Maugard to plan a garden party to celebrate the new paved roads and electric lighting in Chapultepec Park—an homage to modern improvements typical of the Porfiriato. Best transformed the staid gathering into an exuberant outpouring of postrevolutionary nationalism modeled after regional *ferias* (regional fairs) and christened it "Noche Mexicana."[3]

He drew inspiration from the indigenous aesthetics of his homeland. In New York at Columbia University, Best had worked for Franz Boas, pioneer in theories of cultural relativism. Best had illustrated pre-Hispanic pottery shards that would later inspire his own theory of a common seven-motif origin for world (and Mexican) art. In modernist avant-garde circles in Europe, he had become familiar with German and Russian neoromantic nationalism within a revalorization of intuition, emotion, and the primitive and veneration for popular traditions as carriers of the collective spirit.[4]

Best transformed the old-fashioned garden party into a grand experiment uniting cosmopolitan modernism, popular revolution, and postrevolutionary nationalism, so as to forge a new aesthetic vocabulary of Mexicanidad. A leading commentator declared the event unprecedented, magical, and "genuinely Mexican." Another announced that the "soul of the Republic, dispersed and almost forgotten by our foreign-oriented intellectuals," had been rediscovered and made palpable by the Noche Mexicana and the Exhibition of Popular Arts.

The Noche Mexicana, free to the general public, was reportedly packed with thousands of people from all walks of life, including special guests—President Obregón, foreign envoys, government officials, artists and literati, and members of prominent families. It won two repeat performances in September and October and was later restaged at the Teatro Arbeu.

As the park opened, visitors wandered along its newly paved roads, lit by the freshly installed electric streetlights and hundreds of small illuminated stars dangling from tree branches. Originally planned as the focus for a celebration of modernity, these became mere background for Best's gala tribute to a folkloric Mexicanidad. Guests wandered through the festival, stopping at the many booths from which elite white women served lower-class Mexican food and drinks. Best Maugard supervised the women's choice of regional costumes and saw to it that all the booths were "authentically" decorated "with blankets, woven mats, shawls, flags, and . . . art objects . . . typical of the Mexican nation." The "damas" sold "refreshments of the kind classically prepared in *tapatío* clay jugs [from Tonalá, outside Guadalajara] then served in gourds beautifully decorated by the Indians of Pátzcuaro." They also sold popular food and beverages—*pollo asado*, *enchiladas*, *tamales*, *buñuelos*, *atole*, and hot chocolate—served on ceramics from Guadalajara and Texcoco.[5]

At each street corner, guests encountered small stages on which Yucatecan troubadours, dancing *charros* and *chinas poblanas*, and Yaqui performers mesmerized the audience with "exotic" performances. A spectacular fireworks display inaugurated the evening's entertainment. Special guests were led to viewing stands constructed on the Avenida de Lago bridge, and everyone else pressed around the edges of the lake. From a brightly lit island stage in the middle of the lake, Miguel Lerdo de Tejada's 350-member Orquesta Típica del Centenario accompanied regional dancers attired in the beautiful costume of the Tehuana of the Oaxaca Isthmus. Then, from the side, a replica of the volcano Popocatépetl erupted from the waters with lights and pyrotechnics, topped off by an overflight of planes trailed by multicolored flames. Clapping hands, bold strings, and stomping feet drew attention back to the stage where over a hundred colorfully adorned chinas poblanas and charros burst into a modernized rendition of the *jarabe tapatío* entitled "Fantasía Mexicana."

"Fantasía Mexicana" had originally been staged by Best and choreographed by Anna Pavlova of the Ballets Russes in 1919 as an avant-garde performance in New York City, then repeated in Mexico the same year. The jarabe tapatío dated back to the colonial-era Jalisco but remained a regional dance and Mexico City vaudeville act until Pavlova's and Best's transformation (see fig-

FIG. 1. Anna Pavlova as a *china poblana*, *El Universal*, September 16, 1921. Photograph by Rick López. Courtesy of the Biblioteca Lerdo de Tejada, Mexico City.

ures 1 and 2). For the centennial, Maria Cristina Pereda, her brother, and Castro Padilla modified Pavlova's act, expanding it into a massive folkloric outpouring danced by several hundred couples. Their rendition would be reworked in 1929 by Gloria and Nelli Campobello, who would emerge as major choreographers of a revolutionary, folkloric, and nationalist aesthetic.[6]

In September 1921, the Noche Mexicana was novel in scale and bold in its celebration of previously devalued aesthetic forms. During the Porfiriato, artists had celebrated preconquest civilizations while disparaging contemporary indigenous people. Their handicrafts had been treated as embarrassing evidence of Mexican backwardness. Occasional attempts to bring them into national art did not transcend the conventions of European academicism. In his Noche Mexicana, Best did not suggest incorporating new subjects into old

FIG. 2. Performance of the *jarabe tapatío* with stage set by Adolfo Best Maugard.
Photograph by Rick López. Courtesy of Archives and Special Collections, Amherst
College. Reproduced from Frances Toor, *Mexican Folkways* 6, no. 1 (1930): 32.

artistic forms. He proposed a distinctive aesthetic language inspired by the
popular art of Mexico's "Indian classes."[7] He strove to demonstrate how popular traditions, when filtered and refined by the modern, cosmopolitan artist,
could provide the aesthetic expression of the Mexican nation.

The experiment was jolting. Some public response was decidedly negative.
But one of the most respected critics, Francisco Zamora (who went by the nom
de plume Jerónimo Coignard), raised his pen in Best's defense. Writing of the
Noche Mexicana (and its restaging in the Teatro Arbeu), Coignard conceded
that the dances were not great. Neither were they "una lata" (a tedious bore),
as "certain snobbish theater critics" had charged. The problem, he explained,
was that because Best called them "ballet," the audience expected more than
folk dances could deliver. Coignard agreed that classical ballet would have been
more refined, but he countered that such a performance would have offered
nothing new. Based on the "manner of Mexico," "Fantasía Mexicana" was
novel and praiseworthy.[8]

Coignard found himself pressed into the role of apologist for vernacular art. He lamented his countrymen's low regard for things "truly" Mexican. Rather than appreciate their own, most middle- and upper-class Mexicans lived "in the reflected images of other peoples, whom we have imitated as if we had no aesthetic traditions of our own from which to make our own art." This represented an unfortunate loss for the nation, because apart from European-ized art, "each country has its own vigorous manifestations, its own peculiar art born from the spontaneity and primitiveness of the humble classes." He con-ceded that popular aesthetic expression was crude, but it provided "the germ for artistic expression, ready to be developed and refined by men of talent" who could use it as the inspiration for a nationalist art that remained "faithful to the sentiments and thought of the popular soul of Mexico."

He complained that everyone loved Russian ballet, inspired by popular dances, but when Best created a performance based on "what is ours, we see it as disconcerting." To break away from foreign influences, Coignard recom-mended that Mexico's professional artists appropriate popular expression just as Europeans had done. By this formulation, popular aesthetics remained de-void of form or meaning until interpreted by elite artists with Western sensi-bilities. "Fantasía Mexicana," Coignard argued, needed to be understood as a revolutionary first step toward Mexico's nationalist modernity and aesthetic liberation.

Neither Coignard nor Best Maugard argued that popular arts had any di-rect value except as raw material for elite artists. José Vasconcelos, who left an unrivaled cultural stamp on 1920s Mexico, shared this perspective. Like that of Best and Coignard, Vasconcelos's populism was tempered by an unbending cultural elitism. As minister of public education, he supported efforts to pro-mote popular crafts, but he did not consider the vernacular industries to be "art." True art could not "arise spontaneously from the people." It had to be nurtured and required "intervention by the cultured artists." It also demanded state patronage, "since artists cannot produce anything when abandoned to their own resources, and only the government" was able to direct and system-atize artistic production. Vasconcelos advocated a nationalist regeneration that was sympathetic to the rural masses, but one that avoided sinking into what he saw as the morass of provincial and lower-class ignorance.

Despite commonalties, the vision that Best promoted through his Noche Mexicana drew on antirationalist modernism, not on Vasconcelos's classical liberal humanism. Vasconcelos saw all the lower classes as uniformly uncul-tured yet redeemable by Western humanism. Not surprisingly, he insisted that the highlight of the centennial events was a performance by a European opera company. Only the opera provided an edifying model for the masses—a model apart from bullfights, Indian beauty contests, popular music and dances, and exhibits of indigenous handicrafts. Best, by contrast, focused on a nativist search for the essence of the Mexican "race." He cast the rural poor as Indian and saw their culture as the germ of true Mexicanness. While Vasconcelos felt that Western art and Greek classics should be used to elevate the depraved masses, Best advocated the adoption of popular aesthetics "as a base from which to move forward [and] evolve" so as to produce "our own expression" that is "genuinely Mexican."[9]

Despite differences, Vasconcelos, Best Maugard, Coignard, and fellow travelers were united in their call for an elite-led transformation by "men of talent" such as themselves. Within this project, the main alternative came from an expanding group of artists and intellectuals that included Dr. Atl, Jorge Enciso, Roberto Montenegro, and Manuel Gamio. In their view, far from a mere "germ" for the creation of Mexicanidad, popular arts embodied the ultimate expression of a primordial Mexicanidad. Their Exhibition of Popular Arts emerged as one of the earliest public testaments to this perspective.

### "Making Known the Indian Civilization"

Today the Exhibition of Popular Arts lives on among art historians, collectors, *indigenistas*, and nationalists as one of the most important events in the history of popular arts, and as the most remembered event of the centennial. Yet it was not even on the original centennial agenda. The exhibition was dreamed up by Enciso and Montenegro, who offered to fill a slot left by the cancellation of the industrial fair, which was to have been the centennial's centerpiece.

The exhibition had three objectives. First, it would bring together popular art from every part of the republic on the assumption that these diverse arts shared a common aesthetic basis that, once recognized, might reveal an inherent national cohesiveness. Second, it would offer examples of what the organizers considered high-quality popular arts. The structure of the exhibition, the tours, the docents, and the catalog were to teach the audience why these objects should be considered art, rather than mere curiosities, and why they should be considered authentic national art, rather than evidence of national fragmentation or indigenous backwardness. Third, the organizers hoped to teach the urban middle and upper classes to admire and seek to acquire these newly valorized markers of Mexicanidad. Demand by a public willing to pay fair prices would, it was hoped, bring economic uplift to the countryside and encourage continued production of "authentic" popular art.

Only three months before the centennial, Enciso and Montenegro, together with their mentor Dr. Atl, won official confirmation as the Comisión de la Exposición de Arte Popular (hereafter the Comisión). In addition to time constraints, their aspiration to create an aesthetic encyclopedia of Mexico faced other obstacles. In all of Mexico there was not a single collection that was even vaguely comprehensive. Second, there was not a single person, group, or agency with the knowledge needed to assemble such a collection. Very little was known about the languages or cultures of rural Mexico, much less about their popular arts. To get the ball rolling, Enciso, Montenegro, and Atl contributed their own recently assembled collections and solicited contributions from close associates. They undertook a few minor collecting expeditions to areas they knew, such as Tonalá and Pátzcuaro. They also enlisted the collaboration and collections of the North American art dealer Frederick Davis and ethnologists Miguel Othón de Mendizábal and Renato Molina Enríquez at the recently created Department for the Promotion of Indigenous Industries (Departamento del Fomento de las Industrias Aborígenes) of the Museo Nacional.[10] Still, lacking local knowledge and objects, they turned to regional authorities.

Enciso sent a circular to state governors urging collaboration in this nationalist venture. Enciso explained that the Comisión sought objects of popular manufacture, whether for decoration (including paintings and toys) or for domestic use, "like furniture, weavings, blankets, belts and runners, shawls, indigenous outfits, silk embroidery, woolens, . . . [and] ceramics of all types of manufacture." He urged them to send "samples of the popular art" from their states.

To the Comisión's consternation, governors and their regional subordinates reported that the Indians in their states produced no art. Enciso sent a second missive in which he insisted that there was no region in the "vast territory" of Mexico where "the Indians do not offer manifestations of primitive art and talent, putting their hands to the products found in their native region." He explained that "these objects that they create, following the traditions of their ancestors and guided by their own artistic sensibility, . . . are works of art esteemed by the national and international public."

The circular promised long-term benefits in exchange for cooperation. He emphasized that the exhibition was "conceived as part of a political plan to rehabilitate our Indian classes" by promoting their crafts. He asked the governors to publicize the search and to teach the artisans about its potential benefits. The federal government, in turn, would cover all transportation costs and, on request, would sell the objects on the artisans' behalf.[11]

Locals familiar with their region's craft production were confused: Did the Comisión want the cheap objects produced by local impoverished artisans, or did it want works of art? This confusion frustrated Enciso, but he had no other choice than to rely on these contacts for collecting objects and information about producers.

Enciso was learning that didacticism and specificity were vital to the construction of popular art as a subject. If his request was to make sense on the local level, he had to teach local mediators which crafts the Comisión considered valuable and why they should be thought of as art. His efforts to create an encyclopedic exhibition were stymied by the gaps that emerged between his own modernist validation of authenticity, the collective subconscious, and the modern cultural nation, and local prejudice against "backward" Indians and their "curiosities."

Ironically, Enciso had to rely on local knowledge at the very moment he was attempting to transform local assumptions and power relations. He depended on local government authorities for information, the delivery of which might affect local structures of power. The more local his contacts, the more imbricated they were in structures of artisanal production and marketing, and thus the less willing they were to facilitate new direct contacts between artisans and urban connoisseurs and markets. The act of collecting Mexican arts was not neutral; it was a process that had to navigate among global intellectual trends, central authority, and local politics and economic relations.[12]

When the exhibition opened on September 19, 1921, at 85 Avenida Juárez, Montenegro, Atl, and Enciso were rewarded with rounds of praise from the public, state officials, and the press. At the opening, flags, banners, and a military band announced the arrival of President Obregón and his retinue of government ministers, the diplomatic corps, members of the Centennial Committee, regional representatives, and foreign envoys. The exhibition treated visitors to folk singers, Yucatecan dancers, Lerdo de Tejada's Orquesta Típica del Centenario, and a *merienda* (afternoon snack) of fresh tamales, *atole*, and chocolate served from decorated booths similar to those that would be used at the Noche Mexicana in the following week. The inauguration was by invitation only. Afterward the exhibition was free and open to the public. Contemporary accounts suggest heavy attendance by Mexicans of various classes and foreign visitors.

FIG. 3. A gallery in the Exhibition of Popular Arts. Photograph by Rick López. Reproduced from Frances Toor, *Mexican Popular Arts* (Mexico City: Studios of Frances Toor, 1939).

After witnessing a series of musical performances and dioramas, visitors followed tour guides through two floors of galleries crowded with popular objects arranged by category: lacquerware, ceramics, toys, weavings, wooden tools, paintings, and leatherwork. In place of the sparse walls typical of museum exhibitions, guests encountered rooms filled to capacity with objects arrayed on crowded shelves, stands, and tables, with textiles covering the walls. Designed to evoke the packed shelves of a curio shop or a stall in a regional outdoor market, the exhibition provided some of the flavor of the milieu where buyers might actually encounter such objects for sale (see figure 3). The exhibition taught visitors to recognize authentic popular arts and to identify them as "indigenous" and "*muy nuestro*." It also made clear that not just the objects but the entire way of life they represented was on display, and that value lay not in the visuality of the individual works but in the cultural wholeness of which they were a part.

The Exhibition of Popular Arts awoke public interest. On the one hand, the exhibition amazed audiences with displays they found "very exotic and original." On the other hand, it created a new appreciation for *artesanías* as artistic, nationalist, and commercially important. The exhibition also created a fashion in which "people of good taste" began to decorate their homes "in the style of the Exhibition." Families with money transformed entire rooms into miniature exhibitions, while those with lesser means confined artesanías to a special corner—practices that endured even as memory of the exhibition faded. The show also inspired elite painters in the aesthetic possibilities suggested by popular styles.

Like Best's ballet, the exhibition had its detractors. The critic S. Suárez Longoria argued that even though a group of misguided artists might call these crafts "popular arts" and put them in a museum, they remained mere trinkets and "curiosities." But even he conceded that the exhibition was an impressive nationalist achievement.[13] In the end, most of the public, including the harshest critics, received the exhibition as a positive sign of the ongoing cultural revolution and a vibrant expression of nationalism. Most importantly, critics, the general public, private enterprise, and the state all seemed to embrace the exhibition as an eye-opening revelation of the "real" Mexico.

### "La manera de ser del pueblo mexicano"

Roberto Montenegro and Jorge Enciso collected, curated, and promoted the exhibition. But their mentor Dr. Atl wrote the accompanying catalog. More than merely compiling an inventory, Atl provided readers with a groundbreaking treatise on how to judge the value of art, the nature of the Mexican peasantry, and the essence of the nation.

After a decade and a half of study and political activism in Rome, Paris, and Spain, Atl threw himself into the Mexican Revolution, first as a propagandist in Europe and then as a syndicalist and intellectual in Mexico, winning broad support for Carranza and, later, Obregón.[14] When the violence of the revolution subsided, Atl dedicated himself to national reconstruction. He assumed government posts, spearheading the mural movement and emerging as a dominant figure in the search for a Mexican aesthetic. Atl claimed disenchantment with the "-isms" of the European avant-garde art world. He charged that most European modernists were charlatans and opportunists working in cahoots with gallery owners and art critics to manipulate public opinion and to hijack the category of "modern." They conspired "against the feeling and aesthetics of the collective" and were antithetical to the revolutionary project of cultural regeneration.

He did not abandon European modernism altogether. In his search for Mexican authenticity, he found inspiration in Continental theories of intuition and the collective subconscious. He had read Kant, Fouillee, Schopenhauer, and particularly the French philosopher Henri Bergson. He concluded that popular arts represented the most intuitive, most genuine expression of the Mexican people and nation.

When Alberto Pani asked him to write the catalog, Atl jumped at the opportunity. Instead of a simple description of the objects, he wrote a thesis on race, authenticity, and postrevolutionary populist nationalism. The first edition of the catalog found a ready audience among Mexican and foreign intellectuals and artists and sold out almost immediately. Several months later, Pani, by then minister of industry and commerce, invited Atl to write a second, expanded edition. Pani's ministry initially hoped that the catalog's second edition might accompany the exhibition as it traveled to Brazil and Argentina, but Atl and Pani decided that it would be better to extend the time for the book so as to produce a better publication. Since Atl knew that the catalog would not travel with the show, he aimed it at a Mexican, rather than a South American, audience. Whereas the first edition was a slim catalog with short essays and few illustrations, the second edition ran into several hundred pages of argumentation and analysis.

Atl stated that "until now there has been no book to present, classify, or evaluate that which after revolutionary passion, is *lo más mexicano de México: las artes populares*" (the most Mexican of Mexico: the popular arts). The idea that popular arts were "the most Mexican" aspect of Mexico and the "most characteristic manifestations of the way of being of the Mexican people" (*la manera de ser del pueblo mexicano*) became central to their valorization. And the compelling manner in which Atl set out his assertion has made his book the single most influential, enduring work on Mexican popular art.

In 448 pages of text and lavish illustrations, *Las artes populares en México* constructed these as a transhistorical subject naturally delimited by, and cohesive within, Mexico's political borders. It was unique in its attention to *contemporary* arts rather than preconquest and colonial objects. Crucially, Atl excluded objects that he judged to be exclusively shaped by modern or foreign styles, materials, or uses. He reasoned that because items like the *talavera* (majolica) pottery of Puebla were not Indian in character, they were not reflective of the Mexican popular spirit and therefore had no place in a catalog concerned with "essentially Indian production" and the "great artistic sensibility" and "manual skill of the Mexican people [that] up to now have not been well understood" or appreciated. Though some of the included crafts, such as metal or leatherwork, had originated abroad, Atl assured his readers that unlike talavera, these arts had been interpreted and transformed by indigenous hands, such that they now carried "the stamp and vigor of the Indian races," which made them authentically Mexican. Unless they carried clear signs of Indianness, then, popular arts could not be considered truly Mexican.

Race and Indianness were central to Atl's promotion of artesanías. Indigenous cultural influences provided the shared traits and collective distinctiveness that constituted a "true national culture," something shared by populations throughout Mexico. *Mestizaje* (racial and cultural mixing) was emerging as the symbol of Mexican nationality, but mestizaje presented a distinct problem. The worthiness of the European side of this equation seemed self-evident. But the indigenous side still needed definition and validation. According to the emerging nationalist rhetoric first clearly articulated by Manuel Gamio in 1916, to be truly Mexican, one had to be part indigenous or at least to embrace the idea that indigenousness was vital to the national consciousness. Rejection of Mexico's contemporary indigenous peoples and cultures, de rigueur before the revolution, was now criticized as a mark of unpatriotic xenophilia. Even so, this did not resolve the problem that even the staunchest advocates of *indigenismo* remained uncertain what, if anything, was worth admiring in things Indian. Nor did Atl have much of a grasp of the specificities of Mexico's subcultures. Rather, he cast a modernist optic of the "primitive" onto a broad array of objects crafted by artists representing a diversity of subcultures, some urban as well as rural, and called them "Indian."

For Atl, Indians represented an unadulterated bastion of Mexican authenticity. They created their art intuitively from their, and the nation's, collective subconscious rather than from artificial learning or imitation of Europe. Atl stated that it "has not seemed appropriate to me to weigh down this monograph with technical definitions, chemical analysis of the primary materials employed in Indian ceramics, or erudite depositions." Such details were irrelevant when "dealing with things that are completely spontaneous and that must be shown simply, since they are that way [simple], so as not to present them out of character." The catalog and the Exhibition of Popular Arts constructed artesanías as Indian, spontaneous, and wholly Mexican in spirit. Crafts became art insofar as they were understood as embodiments of the natural, agentless expressions of the deep Mexican spiritual subconscious. While Atl validated both indigenous and mestizo arts, indigenousness remained central to their value. He insisted that Mexican crafts became more perfect and "more complete the more Indian their producers."

Atl's emphasis on Indianness, spontaneity, authenticity, the collective sub-conscious, manual industries, and premodernity did not make him *anti*modern. On the contrary, he saw such traits as providing Mexico with a distinct path *toward* modernization. He foretold that the "day is not far when most of the *manufacturas indígenas* will be substituted by products of mechaniza-tion." When that day comes, "this book . . . will have considerable importance" as a "testament to the intelligence and deep artistic sensibility of the Mexican people." Atl welcomed Mexico's belated "industrial evolution" and expressed his faith that traditional artisans would play a key role in constructing the coun-try's future modernity. Yet he also hoped that the "authentic" aesthetic tradi-tions of rural Mexican arts might be preserved by the creation of markets for "authentic" popular arts.

Atl distinguished between creating markets for popular arts, which he fa-vored, and creating popular arts for markets, which he condemned. Authentic crafts were the result "of a particular way of being, intimately tied to the idio-syncrasy of the producers," such that "to touch them," to affect their appearance or methods of production, was "to destroy them." He saw popular arts not as unchanging but rather as a fragile ecological system in which one had to take care not to disrupt the naturally evolving expression of indigenous artisans. He mocked Luis Murillo's efforts in Tonalá to "improve" pottery designs by try-ing to return them to a pre-Hispanic state through the introduction of ancient Aztec and Mayan designs. Equally misguided, according to Atl, were efforts to make the popular arts "evolve" into elite modern forms. He condemned the composer Manuel Ponce's creation of classical music based on popular Mexi-can tunes. One would presume that Atl similarly frowned on the ideas of Best Maugard, Jerónimo Coignard, and José Vasconcelos. "Popular music," Atl as-serted, "does not need to be dressed up, and the blanket of Oaxaca [and] the jug of Guadalajara do not need modifications." We should learn to appreciate "the works of the people just as they are," and "we should not try to transform them claiming a spirit of progress."[15] The only way to save the popular arts was by helping producers acquire primary materials, excusing artisans from taxation (so as to limit their need for cash), and creating urban markets where they could sell directly and liberate themselves from reliance on profiteering middlemen. Other kinds of assistance could "only result in prostitution of the Popular Arts."

According to Atl, the ideal artisan should demonstrate an intuitive passion for artistic creation, unencumbered with concerns about the market. Atl saw no better example of authentically Mexican artisans than those of Tonalá. Atl claimed to recall a conversation with the Tonaltecan artisan Jicarías Jimón, who supposedly stated: "I paint because something inside me drives me to work with melancholy—and I paint to cover the surface of a jug. I want only one thing: to be able to decorate my jugs so as to give them as gifts, not to sell them." That the artisan might have said this is questionable, but the fact that Atl claimed that Jimón did reveals Atl's idealization of indigenous artisans as primitive producers isolated from modern commercialization.

For particularly "authentic" places like Oaxaca or Tonalá, Atl's catalog juxtaposed photographs of artisans with images of their homes and artesanías. Like the objects they made, the artisans, their homes, and their entire way of life became embodiments of the vital spirit of Mexican authenticity and collective racial subconscious (see figure 4). Atl contrasted the idealized artisans of Tonalá to those of Metepec (near Toluca), whom he criticized for an apparent lack of dedication to the joys of creation. Their concern with the market, which had "nothing to do with the spirit of these arts," had supposedly corrupted their crafts. Unlike the Tonaltecos or Oaxaqueños, the artisans of Metepec symbolized the decadence and the wayward path that threatened all handicrafts and endangered the nation's pristine cultural patrimony.

Previously, art in Mexico had been valued primarily for its classical references, rationality, and highly refined skill. Atl veered from this trajectory even more profoundly than did Best Maugard. He insisted on the need to esteem popular art for its independence from Western visual traditions, for its rawness and immediacy, and for its spiritual authenticity derived from intuitive and subconscious impulses. He understood peasant and non-Western art as expressions of a creativity that did not originate from the individual artist. Such art was the expression of something larger than the artisans themselves, reflective of something deeper than their consciousness, and created by something more profound than mere technical process. Mexico's handicrafts were expressions of an entire collective history, of a race, and of a nation. Popular arts production could not be rationalized, and their aesthetics could not be improved on.

This issue separated the exhibition from the Noche Mexicana and, by extension, separated Atl, Montenegro, and Enciso from Best Maugard, Vasconcelos, Ponce, and Coignard. Whereas Best and Vasconcelos valued the popular as raw material for the creation of art or viewed its valorization as the first step toward attracting the popular classes into an appreciation of "high art," Atl,

FIG. 4. *Left*, jar by Adamo Galván of Tonalá; *right*, Tonalá artisan Ladislao Ortega, photographed as if he were the jar being valorized as passive and authentic. Reproduced from Dr. Atl, *Las artes populares en Mexico*, 2nd ed. (Mexico City, 1922).

Enciso, and Montenegro promoted popular arts as artistic creations in their own right.[16]

However, the exhibition catalog denied artisans any agency in the process of creation or even in their own lives, nor did it recognize their real practices. Dr. Atl's artisans did not learn, study, practice, refine their art, or make difficult economic and political decisions. Instead, they possessed innate skills as a result of being racially indigenous and culturally pristine. Any clear signs of agency or of modern Western influences invariably detracted from their work's value. The perspective embodied in the Exhibition of Popular Arts contrasted with that of the Noche Mexicana. But the exhibition's discourse was not inherently any more liberating for the artisan.

## Conclusion

The eventual embrace of a popularly based Mexicanidad was not an inevitable outcome of Mexican mestizaje, as is generally assumed. Neither was it born solely out of the revolution or from European modernism. Instead, postrevolutionary Mexican national identity was born out of a particular historical moment. Through the Noche Mexicana and the Exhibition of Popular Arts, we can begin to understand the uneven process by which popular arts were validated and embraced as part of the ideal of an inclusive primordialist national identity rooted in popular culture.

It was a time when Mexican intellectuals were returning from Europe, bringing with them ongoing conversations and philosophical problems that they had engaged in Rome, Paris, and Barcelona. They were drawn home in part by financial reasons, but above all by a desire to take part in rebuilding the nation after the first revolution of the century. Returnees looked at their homeland through a novel intellectual prism that reveled in its "exotic," non-European, indigenous qualities. Allied with the new state, they forged nationalist aesthetics and cultural criteria for reassessing the nature and value of art, the meaning of the nation, and the significance of indigenousness.

What emerged was a new way of thinking about the indigenous populations, national art, and what it meant to be Mexican. The Noche Mexicana embodied the argument that the culture of the masses was raw material for the production of an elevated national art by men of talent and training. The Exhibition of Popular Arts, by contrast, called for a more radical redefinition of aesthetic value. It singled out indigenousness as the most Mexican aspect of Mexico, and popular art as the most unmediated, most authentic expression of this Mexicanidad. It was from its immediacy and its independence from European training that such art derived its nationalist and aesthetic value. The Exhibition of Popular Arts and the Noche Mexicana together signaled a transition in Mexican thought, when the outlines of what was to be esteemed as vital to the postrevolutionary nation were far from clear. The view represented by Best's Noche Mexicana dominated the first part of the 1920s. But by the middle of the decade, the view embodied in the Exhibition of Popular Arts gained ground and left its own mark on Mexico's national identity, on state policies, and on the conservation of the nation's cultural patrimony.

In the coming decades, Mexican intellectuals would devote their attention to studying the Mexican rural classes so as to make them known in new ways and to valorize rural aesthetics and material production as an essentialization of

*Mexicanidad auténtica*. They would advance rural exploration and cultural discovery based on metropolitan concerns for accumulating, systematizing, promulgating, and hierarchically ordering knowledge about the "real" Mexican nation in all its parts. In the hands of nationalist artists and literati and resident foreign sympathizers, the popular arts would become integral to the process of Mexican nation building. Even today, for Mexicans and foreigners alike, to hold in one's hands a piece of Mexican popular art is to hold something larger than a mere object; it is to hold Mexico in all its diversity, its rich past, its complex present, and its uncertain future. But oftentimes it is also to hold on to a "deep" Mexico in which the masses can contribute only passively to the nation, through their instincts and intuition, not through their self-determined cultural or political genius. In this way, the possibilities, but also the baggage, of the legacy of the Noche Mexicana and the Exhibition of Popular Arts remain with us today.

## Notes

1. Alberto Pani, *Una encuesta sobre educación popular* (Mexico, 1918); and Pani, "The Sanitary and Educational Problems of Mexico," *Annals of the American Academy of Political and Social Science* (1917), suppl., 22–26; L-E-955 to 966, 1921, Sría de Relaciones Ext., Archivo Histórico (hereafter AHSRE); 104-C5, 1921, Archivo General de la Nación, Presidencial Archives (hereafter AGN); José Vasconcelos, *El desastre*, 4th ed. (Mexico: Botas, 1938), 54–58; Dr. Atl, *Las artes populares en México* (1922; Mexico: INI, 1980), 7; *El Universal* (hereafter EU), July 8, 1921; May 14, 1921; July 19, 1921; July 17, 1921; August 24, 1921.

2. EU, May 15, 1921; May 21, 1921; editorial, *Excélsior* (hereafter EX), August 21, 1921.

3. L-E-1652, Libro de Actas, Acta no. 19, June 16, 1921, AHSRE; EU, June 25, 1921; September 6, 1921.

4. F. Boas to A. Best Maugard, December 8, 1926, American Philosophical Society, Professional Correspondence of Franz Boas, Philadelphia, Pa., Microfilm; A. Best Maugard, interview, 1964, BMP/59, Biblioteca del INBA, Archivo General (hereafter INBA); and Karen Cordero, "Para devolver su inocéncia a la nación," in *Abraham Angel y su tiempo* (Toluca: MBA, n.d.), 12–13.

5. EU, September 29, 1921; *El Universal Ilustrado* (hereafter EUI) 230 (September 29, 1921): 26–27; EU, September 1, 1921; September 6, 1921; September 28, 1921; EX, September 1, 1921.

6. EU, September 28–29, 1921; EX, September 1, 1921; Frances Toor, "El jarabe antiguo y moderno," *Mexican Folkways* (hereafter MF) 6, no. 1 (1930): 32–33.

7. A. Best Maugard, "Conferencia sobre México" (from a speech, October 2, 1922, San Francisco), BMP/59, INBA; José Juan Tablada, "La función social del arte," and

Pedro Henríquez Ureña, "Arte Mexicano," in Adolfo Best Maugard, *Método de dibujo: Tradición, resurgimiento y evolución del arte mexicano* (Mexico City: SEP, 1923); and Cordero, "Para devolver," 18.

8. Jerónimo Coignard (Francisco Zamora), "El valor efectivo de ballet mexicano," *EUI* 4, no. 232 (October 13, 1921): 32.

9. Vasconcelos, *El desastre*, 23, 56–57; Best, *Manuales*, 9, 17–18.

10. *EU*, June 2, 1921; June 5, 1921; June 25, 1921; September 25, 1921. Atl, "Artes Populares de Mexico," typescript, unpublished 3rd ed. of *Artes Populares en México*, caja 4a, exp. 2, Fondo Reservado de la Biblioteca Nacional de México, Archivo Doctor Atl (hereafter BNA); Atl, *Artes* (1980), 21–27; Gov. of Yuc., circ. 5075, July 6, 1921, leg. 680, Archivo General del Edo. de Yucatán, Ejecutivo/Gobernación, Mérida, Yucatán (hereafter AGY); L-E-1652, Libro de Actas, Acta 8, June 3, 1921, AHSRE.

11. Gov. of Yuc., circular 5075, July 6, 1921; Jorge Enciso to Gov. of Yucatán, July 13, 1921; and Gov. of Yucatán to the Comisión Organizadora de la Fiestas del Centenario, July 27, 1921, legajo 680, AGY; "La Exposición de Arte Popular," *EU*, July 8, 1921.

12. For a discussion of these local tensions, see Rick López, "*Lo más mexicano de México*: Popular Arts, Indians, and Urban Intellectuals in the Ethnicization of Postrevolutionary National Culture, 1920–1972" (Ph.D. diss., Yale University, 2001).

13. *EU*, September 19–20, 1921; *EX*, September 20, 1921; Frances Toor, "Mexican Folkways," *MF* 7, no. 4 (October–December 1932): 205–11; Atl, *Artes* (1980), 21–22; Frances Toor, *Mexican Popular Arts* (Mexico City: Frances Toor Studios, 1939), 11; S. Suárez Longoria, "La exposición de arte popular," *Azulejos*, October 1921, 29–30.

14. Dr. Atl, typescript, "El mundo será Comunista," n.d., caja 2, exp. 41; Atl, typescript, "La revolución mexicana y los mexicanos en París," n.d., caja 2a, exp. 94; Atl, typescript, "Primer Guión para la autobiografía," 1959, caja 6, exp. 5; typescript, "Notas de un serie de entrevistas," caja 6, exp. 9, BNA; and José Clemente Orozco, *Autobiografía* (1945; Mexico City: Era, 1996), 40–45.

15. Dr. Atl, typescript, "Sobre las modas pictóricos," n.d., caja 2a, exp. 106; Atl, typescript with marginalia, n.d., caja 4a, exp. 10, BNA. Also see Juan del Sena, "El Doctor Atl conferencista," *EUI* 5, no. 194 (January 2, 1921): 8–9; Atl, *Las artes populares en México*, 2nd ed., 2 vols. (Mexico City: Librería "Cultural," 1922); Atl, *Artes* (1980), 7–49, 437–44; Atl, "Artes Populares de Mexico," unpublished 3rd ed., caja 4a, exp. 2, BNA; M. Teresa Pomar A., "Presentación," in Atl, *Artes* (1980), ix; and Manuel Gamio, *Forjando patria* (1916; Mexico City: Editorial Porrúa, 1992). For a discussion of the international, national, and local impacts of projects to create a market for popular arts, see López, "*Lo más mexicano de México*."

16. Atl, *Artes* (1980), n.p., 28, 46–47, 86, 110, 125, 135, 150–53, 443–44.

# The Sickle, the Serpent, and the Soil:
## History, Revolution, Nationhood, and Modernity
## in the Murals of Diego Rivera, José Clemente Orozco,
## and David Alfaro Siqueiros

DESMOND ROCHFORT

If by the end of the 1920s the radical impulses emanating from the Mexican Revolution were beginning to be molded into a centralized politics, for most of that decade the postrevolutionary state was a fragile proposition, contested and coveted by forces of the Left and Right. In those heady, unpredictable years, artists were as prominent players as political and military actors. Among the artists, none played a greater role in defining the nation to itself and the rest of the world as the muralists. They provided the visual vocabulary and narratives of nation in monumental and publicly accessible images that encoded the history, experiences, traditions, and culture of peasants, workers, Indians, and artisans that came to be defined as the Mexican *pueblo*. Although the movement of mural painting was the creation of several artists over many decades, Diego Rivera (1887–1957), José Clemente Orozco (1883–1949), and David Alfaro Siqueiros (1897–1974) stand above the rest. They started the movement. Their murals have traditionally been interpreted as providing its singularly radical artistic purpose. This essay focuses on their evolving production between 1922 and 1940.

Commissioned in 1922 by José Vasconcelos to paint the walls of the Escuela Nacional Preparatoria in the center of Mexico City, the artists first worked within the religious and compositional traditions of the Italian Renaissance. Rivera's *Creation* reflected some of his immersion in modernism acquired during his long stay in Europe but was more directly influenced by his familiarity with Italian and Byzantine painting. Siqueiros's cherubic angel and Orozco's blonde Madonna and child were far removed from their experiences in the

Mexican Revolution. Both had followed Dr. Atl to Orizaba, where they edited
and illustrated *La Vanguardia*, the newspaper aimed at recruiting worker soldiers for the Red Battalions.[1]

In late 1923, the Obregón government faced a major rebellion from conservatives in the military and political nationalists under the leadership of Adolfo
de la Huerta. In January 1924, de la Huerta's supporters assassinated Felipe
Carrillo Puerto, the socialist governor of Yucatán and self-styled champion of
the peasantry. In the wake of the rebellion and following the deepening radicalism of industrial workers and peasants, Mexico found itself caught, as the
art historian Antonio Rodríguez has written,

> between two fires: on one side the Left as we will call it, with the workers' move-
> ment and most radical adherents of the Revolution, who wanted to continue the
> 1910–1917 struggle to its final conclusion, and on the other the reactionary forces,
> with the spiritual and well-organized support of the clergy. . . . Obregón had the
> sense to lean on the more progressive forces—the workmen, the advanced intellec-
> tuals, the painters, who . . . rushed into the fray to defend [him]. . . . This explains
> to a great extent how painters and other intellectuals became radicals. . . . There
> were other factors. Among these . . . the ever-increasing influence of the October
> revolution in Russia.[2]

Rodríguez refers to the Syndicate of Technical Workers, Painters, and Sculptors formed in late 1922 by those working on Vasconcelos's commissions.
Siqueiros drew up its manifesto in response to the de la Huerta rebellion.
In March 1924, he published the manifesto in *El Machete*, the union's agit-
prop newspaper, which Siqueiros called "our calling card to the mass organizations . . . [our] access to the workers . . . [our] bonds to the Communist Party."[3]
The manifesto declared:

> The Syndicate of Technical Workers, Painters, and Sculptors directs itself to the
> native races humiliated for centuries; to the soldiers made into hangmen by their
> officers; to the workers and peasants scourged by the rich; and to the intellectuals
> who do not flatter the bourgeoisie. . . . Our fundamental aesthetic goal must be to
> socialize artistic expression. . . . The creators of beauty must use their best efforts
> to produce ideological works of art for the people; art must no longer be the ex-
> pression of individual satisfaction, which it is today, but should aim to become a
> fighting, educative art for all.[4]

The political and social events surrounding the formation of the syndicate
neither caused nor explained the dramatic change that occurred in the frescoes

of Orozco and Siqueiros or the less sudden but no less fundamental change in Rivera's work. However, they form a context in which it is possible to see how Vasconcelos's philosophical idealism and the aesthetic metaphysics of the first mural commissions collided with, were taken over, and, in the case of the muralists, were transformed by a momentarily radicalizing politics.

The change in Orozco's images was particularly striking as he moved from an essentially apolitical and metaphysical European imagery to create along the walls and inner stairwell of the Preparatoria a series of monumental, powerful, often tragic images of the revolution. Along the corridor walls of the ground-floor patio, he created *The Trench* (plate 1), *The Destruction of the Old Order*, and *The Strike*, three huge panels that have entered the iconography of his pene-trating vision of human tragedy and pathos. In *The Trench*, wrote Antonio Rodríguez, "There are no stirring hymns to drive heroes toward enemy bayo-nets, no waving standards to enthuse the timid. Here everything is dignified like death or like fire which, consumed and purified, resolves in ashes.... There is no lyric passion, no lamentation.... There is not enthusiasm. Neither is there despair."[5] A confirmation of what an extraordinary and powerful painter Orozco would turn out to be, *The Trench*, like his two adjacent panels, reveals Orozco as the creator of an eerie stillness, in which monumentalism freezes in time the violence of movement.

Along the same wall, Orozco, who began his career as a cartoonist in the opposition press, mocked both the revolutionaries and their opponents with a tragic pessimism that would come to distinguish his work. *The Trinity* was a telling indictment of revolutionary idealism betrayed by its own zeal. The central figure depicts a revolutionary brandishing a rifle but blinded by his red Jacobin cap. The right-hand figure, its hands severed from the wrists, watches helplessly as the figure on its left prays for salvation. In *The Rich Banquet While the Workers Fight*, oversize caricatures of the fat, hideous, and debauched rich feast and drink while workers fight among themselves, their disputes sustaining the banquet of the bourgeoisie.

Orozco's murals became the targets of intense criticism and fury from con-servative groups. During the de la Huerta uprising, the Damas Católicas and conservative students defaced the murals. In response to protests, Vasconce-los ordered Orozco and Siqueiros to cease painting. Salvador Novo, an art critic and member of the Contemporáneos group of poets, described Orozco's murals as "repulsive pictures, aiming to awaken in the spectator, instead of aes-thetic emotions, an anarchistic fury if he is penniless, or if he is wealthy, to make his knees buckle with fright."[6]

In his first murals in the Preparatoria, Siqueiros lacked the maturity to syn-
thesize his largely European artistic preparation with his direct experience in
the Mexican Revolution. The beginnings of this synthesis began with his panel
*Burial of the Sacrificed Worker*, dedicated to the memory of Felipe Carrillo
Puerto. *Burial* marks the point at which Siqueiros consciously decided to abandon "symbolic, cosmogenic, sentimental, abstract folkloric terms," as he put it,
in order to create works of political and social content. While embellishments
like the hammer and sickle on top of the coffin suggest his enthusiasm for revolutionary Marxism, *Burial* expresses a religious sentiment shared by all three
muralists at this time.

Diego Rivera's murals painted in the Ministry of Education (SEP) and the
National Agricultural School at Chapingo between 1923 and 1928 represent
the most significant stage in the development of the movement as a radical
national public art. By the end of 1922, the French muralist Jean Charlot observed that Rivera's Italian memories began to fade as he began to look "his
own country in the face and find her beautiful."[7] Vasconcelos sent Rivera to
visit the Tehuantepec Isthmus, images of which crop up in a corner of his Creation mural in an abundance of lush tropical foliage and figures with Indian
faces. But it was in the murals he painted in the SEP and at Chapingo that his
aesthetic embraces the idea that the nation's culture was both the product and
possession of the people. In 235 individual fresco panels covering fifteen thousand square feet in the SEP, Rivera aimed "to reflect the social life of Mexico
as I saw it, and through my vision of the truth to show the masses the outline
of the future."[8] The frescoes were thematically divided according to the architectural subdivision of the colonial building with two adjacent courtyards and
two upper floors.

On the ground floor of the Labor Courtyard, he began his cycle depicting
the industries and agriculture of Mexico's regions. The influence of his visit to
Tehuantepec came through in a series of frescoes on the theme of the Tehuanas,
showing the industries of this largely indigenous and mythically matriarchal
southern society. In contrast to these somewhat folkloric, exotic panels, Rivera
followed with a series of more monumental panels on the south wall depicting the toil and hardship of iron and mining workers from northern Mexico.
In images depicting western Mexico's agricultural, mining, and pottery industries, he synthesized his national subject matter with his knowledge of Italian
Renaissance religious painting to create an evocative fusion of the Christian,
Euro-Indian imagery typical of colonial churches and intimately familiar to
millions of Mexicans. In *Entry into the Mine* (plate 2), the miners, carrying

pickaxes, shovels, and pit props over their shoulders, echo the biblical story of the road to Calvary. In the adjacent panel, *Exit from the Mine*, the outstretched stance of the miner being searched by a manager evokes the Crucifixion sacrifice. Farther along the wall, in the panel *The Embrace*, the unity expressed between peasant and industrial worker, with the peasant's sombrero resembling a halo and his serape a religious cloak, conveys all the religious passion of a secular annunciation of revolutionary brotherhood and constitutes one of the most striking and poetic elements in Rivera's artistic vocabulary.

Rivera continued to use such images in *Liberation of the Peon*. Here the allusion is to the descent from the cross and the lamentation, which Rivera employed to express the tragic freedom of death when the peasant is finally released from his life of drudgery and exploitation. By contrast, an adjacent panel entitled *The New School* expresses the notion of a different kind of freedom, gained through revolution as a dark-skinned woman teaches a circle of children and adults. A revolutionary soldier guards them while in the background campesinos plow their newly retrieved land.

As Rivera moved on to his Courtyard of the Fiestas, his mood changed. He described the atmosphere expressed in which "the people turned from their exhausting labors to their creative life, their joyful weddings, and their lively fiestas: the Burning of the Judases, the Yaqui Deer Dance, the Sandunga dance of the Tehuanas, the Dance of the Ribbons, the Corn Harvest Dance, the fiesta, offering, and dinner of the Day of the Dead." On every available wall space, Rivera painted hundreds of figures, creating a vast portrait of the Mexican people and capturing their extraordinary collective sociability. In this series, including the markedly political *Partition of the Land* (plate 3) and *Festival of the First of May*, Rivera celebrates. The murals exude an air of optimism and idealism, creating visual eulogies to the gains of the revolution and its hope for liberation. The compositions are made up of compacted groups of predominantly Indian figures. Their lack of background space, together with a tiered arrangement of figures, echoes the pictorial method of the Aztecs and Mayans. Unlike Orozco and Siqueiros, Rivera now embraced the postrevolutionary *indigenismo* promoted by artists and intellectuals such as Dr. Atl and Manuel Gamio. His insistent and repetitive image of the Indian as peasant rooted in the land becomes at this time his "authentic" representation of the essential Mexican, whose ancestry reaches back to Quetzalcóatl, the plumed serpent, and to ancient cities like Teotihuacán, recently excavated by Gamio.[9]

Rivera continued his decorations with murals painted in the adjacent stair-

well. From the ground up to the second floor, he represented what he described as

> an interpretative painting of the Mexican landscape rising from the sea to the hills
> and plateaus and mountain peaks. Alongside this representation of the ascending
> landscape was an accompanying view of the progress of man. Allegorical figures
> personified the ascending stages of the social evolution of the country from primi-
> tive society through the people's revolution to the liberated and fulfilled social
> order of the future.[10]

In contrast to the exotic, idealized, feminine representation of southern
Mexico on the lower levels of the stairs, Rivera painted scenes of Mexico's agricultural center and north on the top floor of the stairwell. This is the Mexico
of the hacienda, landlord, and peasant: of exploitation and revolution. In a
panel entitled *Mechanization of the Countryside* (plate 4), a goddesslike figure
swathed in red strikes down the landlord and his cohorts with a triple-headed
lightning bolt. Next to them sits an Indian woman, her hands and lap filled
with corn; she symbolizes the earth's fertility turned into abundance by the
campesino driving a tractor and by the dams, electric towers, factories, and
airplanes that symbolize the male conquest of nature through reason, science,
and technology.

The final frescoes along the second floor of the Courtyard of the Fiestas include twenty-six panels illustrating the stanzas from three revolutionary *corridos*, or popular songs: "The Ballad of Zapata," "The 1910 Mexican Agrarian
Revolution," and "Así será la revolución proletaria." Here Rivera acknowledges
his great debt to the engraver José Guadalupe Posada, whose popular images
of satire and social criticism, of impoverishment and protest, had appeared in
the broadsheets of the Porfirian penny press. Although the two agrarian frescoes were painted nearly two years before the proletarian corrido, which Rivera
completed following his first trip to the Soviet Union in 1928, all are characterized by a recurring motif: the contrast between an idealized revolution and the
wicked opponents and detractors of revolution—the capitalists of Wall Street,
John D. Rockefeller, J. P. Morgan, and Henry Ford, decadent rich Mexican
men with scantily dressed prostitutes, and the intellectuals who served them.
To defend and ensure this embattled revolution, Frida Kahlo distributes arms
from the center of *The Arsenal* (plate 5), David Alfaro Siqueiros appears at the
left in army uniform, and to the right stand the photographer Tina Modotti
and her lover, the Cuban Communist Julio Antonio Mello, who would be assassinated in 1929.

By the time Rivera completed the SEP murals in 1928, he had created an epic portrait of the Mexican people. Notwithstanding accusations that he had indulged in the falsification of reality in his depictions of the revolution's history and trajectory, Rivera had synthesized his attachment to revolutionary socialism with an acute visual understanding of Mexican popular culture. He had recuperated many of its images that had been marginalized to broadsheets, ex-votos (vernacular religious pictures asking for or acknowledging a miracle), and workingmen's *pulquerías* and taverns. He crafted a popular vocabulary that enabled him to appeal to a public beyond the confines of the country's bourgeoisie and their intellectual supporters with their narrow literary culture. He created a foundation on which to convey to this much wider audience a sense of continuity with history and agency in an ongoing process.

Similarly, in his murals at the National Agricultural School in Chapingo, Rivera fused into a visual poem the consciousness of his country's peasant revolution with its long, deeply rooted history of spiritual-religious attachment to the land and its endless struggle against the forces of nature and voracious elites to keep it fertile, productive, and theirs. As a poetic narrative of revolutionary impulse and national texture, the Chapingo murals have few equals. The writer Louis Gillette described them as "the first of the great works born of socialist and agrarian materialism."[11] Rivera inscribed their central panel with a dedication: "To all those who fell, and to the thousands who will yet fall, in the fight for the land and to all those who make it fruitful by the labor of their hands. Earth manured with blood, bones and flesh!"

At the end of the 1920s, Rivera had achieved hegemonic status in the Mexican mural movement at home and abroad, but not without contradiction. Individualistic and opportunistic, he had shown little collective solidarity with the Syndicate. He held commissions from an increasingly conservative "revolutionary" government when his colleagues lost theirs. In 1929 the Communist Party expelled him when the Mexican president appointed Rivera director of the national art academy and he refused to take part in an antigovernment demonstration. Former comrades and fellow artists hurled virulent criticism against him as a "false revolutionary" and "millionaire artist for the establishment." In fact, he played an important role in the reconciliation between Mexico and the United States between 1926 and 1929. U.S. ambassador Dwight Morrow sponsored Rivera's decoration of the Cortés Palace in Cuernavaca and secured him commissions and exhibits in New York, California, and Detroit.

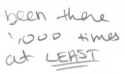

## Painting America

At the end of the 1920s and into the early 1930s, all three muralists established their reputations in the United States. Their painting here probed a common American identity and confronted the intersection between politics and
technology as the onset of the economic depression sent millions spiraling
into poverty and, for many, meant the collapse of capitalism. Rivera's California murals capture the utopian mirage of the "roaring twenties" and the
decade's claim to a society abundant with opportunity, prosperity, and well-
being. So too does the celebratory vision of modern industrial production in
his depiction of Henry Ford's River Rouge plant at the Detroit Institute of
Art. The work revealed nothing of its sociopolitical context of massive un-
employment, hunger, gangsterism, and Ford's own harsh response to organized labor. By contrast, in *Man at the Crossroads* at Rockefeller Center, Rivera
painted the revolutionary outcome that would spring from capitalism's conflicts and contradictions. When he refused to remove his portrait of Lenin,
Nelson Rockefeller fired Rivera and ordered the mural destroyed.[12]

In contrast to Rivera's optimistic vision of the modern world, Orozco's U.S.
murals rendered it with an encyclopedic display of entrapment, unfulfilled
promise, menace, and betrayal. At Dartmouth, he painted his *America, the New
World*. The American experience of European peoples conquering and sub-
jugating indigenous societies became the symbolic representation of a cyclical
history of idealism subverted by fallibility. He depicted "Anglo-America" not
as a world of exemplary democracy but as one of rigid conformity in which
polite orderliness eschewed all questioning and dissent. In *Modern Human
Sacrifice*, Orozco painted the mirror image of Aztec ritual. Young men are sacrificed on the altar of nationalism. The act is denounced in the tragic image of the
dead torso of an unknown soldier, whose body lies over a burning candle and
whose head is draped with a flag bearing the composite of many national emblems. This gratuitous sacrifice is sacralized in the modern, nationalist monumentalism of a wreath and funeral sermon.[13]

In Los Angeles, Siqueiros's murals included *Tropical America*, painted on the
side of the Plaza Art Center on Olvera Street in "Sonora Town," the city's poor,
largely Mexican barrio. He described the mural as depicting "our America,
of undernourished natives, of enslaved Indians and Negroes, that . . . inhabit
this most fertile land in which the richest and most ferocious people on earth
also live. And as a symbol of U.S. imperialism, the principal capitalist oppres-
sor, I used an Indian crucified on a double cross on top of which stood the

Yankee eagle of American finance."[14] The mural provoked a hostile response. The building's owner ordered it covered over with whitewash. Despite this setback, Siqueiros continued to experiment with new techniques and materials in public art. The experimental workshop he opened in New York in 1936 attracted a number of emerging American artists, including Jackson Pollock.[15]

## Probing Mexico's Memory and Future

In Mexico, the muralists' focus had shifted by the 1930s to an interpretation of the national past and future. In 1935, Rivera completed his epic mural *The History of Mexico* on the walls of the nation's most sacred and powerful precinct, the National Palace. The mural marked the visual institutionalization of a rhetoric of revolutionary emancipation and populist national identity grafted onto the nineteenth-century liberal national memory. The history Rivera configured on the central wall is a two-dimensional one, shorn of qualifications and complexities. He painted a heroic history of good and evil—a memory of betrayal and oppression, resistance and emancipation. The good and heroic defended Mexico from external violation. The bad was unmistakably associated with invasion, subjugation, and exploitation.

On the right wall, Rivera painted pre-Hispanic Mexico as a mixture of artistic achievement, agricultural abundance, and productive human energy interspersed with conflict, slavery, and human sacrifice. He makes no judgment about these contradictions. On the contrary, in the central panel, Mexican history arises out of the Spanish conquest as an ongoing struggle against colonial subjugation and dictatorship. At the center perches the Aztec eagle with a serpent in its mouth (plate 6). This is the symbolic national heart. Below the eagle, the last Aztec prince, Cuauhtémoc, battles the conquistador Hernán Cortés. Above the eagle are the heroes of independence, Fathers Hidalgo and Morelos. At the apex stand Obregón and Calles, presidents of postrevolutionary Mexico. Near them, Felipe Carrillo Puerto and Emiliano Zapata stand behind a banner unfurling the revolutionary slogan "Tierra y Libertad."

Under the arch to the right, Rivera painted the nineteenth-century liberal struggle against the Catholic conservatives. The Zapotec Indian president Juárez holds up the constitution of 1857. Under the left arch, the 1910 revolutionaries battle the forces of reaction—Díaz, foreign oil companies, hacienda owners, and priests. Venustiano Carranza displays the sacred text of revolution, the constitution of 1917, with its clauses affirming peasant and worker rights. Zapata stands next to a peasant soldier with the Plan de Ayala, his declaration for land reform, pegged to his chest. The outer arches display popular resistance to foreign invasions: against the United States in 1846, and against France between 1861 and 1867.

As with much history painting, Rivera's mural renders into the realm of myth every event and personage. If Mexican history texts and monuments had created the idea of the hero, Rivera painted him, a noble and untarnished being, in whose name politics are created and causes are followed, and around whom history is configured into meaningful constructions. In the final left-hand panel, Rivera portrayed the absorption of the Mexican working classes into history by including the image of Karl Marx and the Communist workers' movement. As with all heroic constructions, however, reality conspired to disrupt Rivera's expression of heroism, stripping it of its luster. His vision was negated by the realities of the revolution and its aftermath, for the influence of Plutarco Elías Calles, president from 1924 to 1928, and Jefe Máximo until 1934, had transformed the radical, heady days of the early 1920s into a regime of power-seeking corruption. Rivera's configuration of a heroic national ancestry provided a contemporary mythology the government could claim as its inheritance.

By the end of 1935, upon completing the National Palace mural, Rivera found himself at a crossroads: he had little more to say about twentieth-century society that would not be a retreat from his own proclaimed political beliefs or a stale repetition of assertions arising from those ideas. Meanwhile, José Clemente Orozco was rapidly emerging as the foremost muralist. In 1934, he returned from the United States to Guadalajara in the state of Jalisco to carry out a series of mural commissions for governor Everardo Topete. Over a period of four years, Orozco painted three great mural cycles: his searing indictment of the revolution's demagogues, *Political and Ideological Exploitation* (1936), at the University of Guadalajara (plate 7); his monumental *Hidalgo* (1937), in the Governor's Palace; and the cycle of the Spanish conquest, his most ambitious work, executed in 1938 in the Hospicio Cabañas, a former Catholic church and orphanage.[16]

Orozco opposed Rivera's utopian political mythologizing of revolutionary struggle and his folkloric indigenismo. For Orozco, the struggle for ideals and their betrayal by the fallibility of human beings that leads to greed, power, exploitation, and superstition dichotomized the human character, dooming it to tragic repetitions of failure, a theme powerfully reflected in *Political and Ideological Exploitation*. In this mural, Orozco depicts a group of wretched, emaciated beings set against a flaming background; they angrily gesticulate at a

group of figures opposite, barely disguised as the political heads of modern social revolutions, whose false rhetoric, leadership, and revolutionary ideology
Orozco sees as the cause of the abject failure of their project. The result, the
people's continued starvation, poverty, and death, is depicted in the right-hand
panel, with despotism, dictatorship, and corruption represented by a group of
ugly *caudillos* (political strongmen) in the left-hand panel.

But Orozco does not see the failure to achieve freedom and justice as something reducible to specific geographic areas, historical times, race, or cultures.
At the Hospicio, he did not embrace the cause of pre-Hispanic Mexico, nor did
he view the Spanish conquest in a totally negative light. In his vision of national
memory, he synthesized his preoccupation with the positive and negative aspects of history. In the east and west transepts, he painted images evoking the
cruel, barbaric world of ancient Indian Mexico, with its bloody sacrifices and
macabre dance rituals appeasing Huitzilopochtli, the Aztec god of war. Huge
metaphorical images in the ceiling panels introduce a crucial historical moment of an Indian world about to be transformed by dual military and spiritual
means. Along the length of the nave, Orozco painted the Spanish conquest
at its harshest. White European Renaissance man at his most aggressive, ac-
quisitive, and violent plunders and crushes the Indian world. The subjugation
appears total and final. A huge portrait of Philip II of Spain, dominated by a
dark cross with the monarch's crown, evokes the monarchical Catholicism at
the spiritual heart of the colonial enterprise.

Ensuing panels focus on the technological force of conquest. In his depiction of Hernán Cortés (*Dimensions*) and the mechanical horse (*The Violence
of Conquest*), Orozco's imagery conveys modern war in both man and animal
(plates 8 and 9). The armored Cortés, with a body of nuts, bolts, and pistons,
takes on the appearance of a machine. As Salvador Echavarria has observed,
these human and animal images transformed into demonic machines portray
the "engine age in its prime, the first product of the rising science of the Renaissance, which made the conquest possible."[17] In the image of the mechanical horse, the conquering animal becomes a modern battle tank. On its gro-
tesquely mechanical body, the image of the heraldic lion and tower of Castile,
closely resembling the tank's turret, appears on a banner.

Evocations of subjugated Indian Mexico are complemented in the nave by
images of cultural and spiritual transformation. Over the head of a kneeling
Indian, an imposing Franciscan priest holds a crucifix, its edges sharpened like
a sword. At the priest's side is a banner with the first letters of the European
alphabet. The conquest is simultaneously ruthless and harsh, charitable and

consoling. On the side walls of the nave and transepts, Orozco depicted what he saw as the positive effects and benefits of European colonialism. Portraits of El Greco and Cervantes symbolize the introduction of European art and culture. The portrait of the bishop Ruiz de Cabañas, founder of the orphanage, evokes the charity and help for the poor. Another fresco panel explores the transformation of Indian culture into colonial-mestizo culture.

In iconoclastic fashion, Orozco counterposed these positive images of the colonial legacy with panels depicting twentieth-century despotism and the rise of fascism. In deathly gray colors, modern demagogues gesticulate menacingly, and people march in a faceless, spiritless mass behind a foreground of barbed wire, presided over by a torso carrying a whip. Here the pessimistic Orozco comments on a legacy of despotism that seems to extend back through the power-seeking aggrandizement of the conquest to Aztec human sacrifice.

Orozco's mural was painted during a particularly significant period in the development of postrevolutionary Mexico. The latter half of the 1930s under the presidency of Lázaro Cárdenas could be characterized as a spirited revisiting of the egalitarian and nationalist thrust of the revolution. Cárdenas's nationalization of the oil industry in 1938, for example, marked, in the words of the politician Porfirio Muñoz Ledo, "the highest point of our revolution. Mexico came of age before the world by making sure that its sovereign rights would be respected, securing the basic principles of the constitution from outside attack."[18] In its political context, Orozco's cycle in the Hospicio Cabañas, with its ambivalent and somber vision of the contemporary world, suggests a deliberately powerful rebuttal of leftist nationalist rhetoric. Likewise, the complex duality of the national heritage, so vividly expressed in his images, cuts through Rivera's one-dimensional construction of officially sanctioned national memory.

Though Siqueiros had undoubtedly made innovative contributions to mural art, until his completion of *Portrait of the Bourgeoisie* in 1940 at the Electricians Union Building in Mexico City, his reputation and his murals had not yet entered the public domain to the extent of Rivera's or Orozco's. Siqueiros had painted fewer murals, and those he had done were not the result of major institutional commissions. They were either private projects far from the public gaze or were "radical" open-air street projects. In part, his obscurity is explained by his politics. Unlike Rivera, Siqueiros was an unflinching Communist and a strong supporter of Stalin on political, although not always artistic, issues.[19] Consistent with his politics, Siqueiros executed *Portrait of the Bour-*

*geoisie* on the walls of the Mexico City headquarters of the militant Electricians Union, where hundreds of workers could see it.

In *Portrait*, Siqueiros consolidated the development of a radical, innovative approach. His fully developed use of polyangular perspectives in the overall composition, of the industrial airbrush, and of nitrocellulose-based pyroxalin paint reflected a radical departure from the traditions within which Mexican muralism had largely been confined. This aesthetic would mark his identity as an artist of growing international reputation in the postwar years.[20]

The mural is a powerful and frightening critique of the age of the modern machine. Siqueiros highlighted his passionate denunciation of fascism by clothing it in the garb of a mechanical and industrial modernity. Political figures, their faces obscured by the hideous anonymity of their gas masks, stare out toward the viewer. Next to them, topped by a nightmarish mechanical eagle, is an "infernal machine," spewing money from its midsection, while, at its base, appear enmeshed, oppressed faces. Across the surface of the work, collages of photo-documentary imagery showing machinery and episodes of modern warfare intersect with each other.

Opposite, on the right-hand wall, more images derived from photo-documentary material of the Spanish Civil War depict the suffering and death of carpet-bombing. Siqueiros had fought in the war on the side of the Republicans against Franco, and his friend José Renau had provided him with the photomontage. On the left-hand wall, a ridiculous parrot figure representing fascist demagoguery winds up out of a machine, wildly gesticulating above a regimented, marching crowd (plate 10). The combined visual effect makes *Portrait of the Bourgeoisie* agonizing to view. Yet it is not without hope. On the opposite wall, an angry revolutionary worker aims his oversize rifle at the Fascists.

Although the global struggle against fascism in the 1930s would extend well into the next decade, this mural heralded the point of closure of much of what the prewar epoch had represented. In Mexico, the Cárdenas presidency was drawing to a close, and with it ended the most radical period in Mexican politics. Like Mexico at the outset of World War II, *Portrait of the Bourgeoisie* stands at the intersection of two distinct periods. With its theme rooted in the political culture of the 1930s, its aesthetic pointed decidedly in the direction of Siqueiros's well-established desire to create a unity between revolutionary content and form. Such a view had been present in much of his thinking throughout the thirties, in which he had tirelessly attempted to overhaul the approach to the mural with his constant experiments using innovative techniques and materials supported by new technological applications. However, the thinking that underpinned this aesthetic notion was in reality a utopian projection into the future, which would find its rationale in technologically based postwar economic growth.

## Conclusion

For the Mexican mural, the 1920s were a period of birth and formation. By the end of that decade, muralism had defined itself as a movement of revolutionary and popular culture. Its artists were part of a process of national definition, for which they provided the visual vocabularies and narratives. For the world at large, Mexican mural painting became a unique catalog of monumental and publicly accessible images that appeared to reflect the experiences, traditions, and culture of the popular masses, the peasants, workers, and Indians.

During the thirties, the twin themes of the national past and the realities of industrial modernity became principal preoccupations for the artists. The one reflected inward, constructing an identity by drawing on the experiences of a national history born from the encounter between European and indigenous peoples. The other looked outward and forward, interrogating and expressing the dilemmas and hopes of a complex, conflictive modernity toward which a new postrevolutionary Mexico was irrevocably propelled.

## Notes

1. On the Red Battalions, see Barry Carr, "The Casa del Obrero Mundial, Constitutionalism, and the Fact of February 1915," in *Work and Workers in the History of Mexico*, ed. Michael C. Meyer and Josefina Vázquez (Tucson: University of Arizona Press, 1979), 603–31.

2. Antonio Rodríguez, *A History of Mexican Mural Painting* (London: Thames and Hudson, 1969), 198.

3. Ibid. On the history of the Mexican Communist Party in Mexico and its relationship to the mural movement, see Barry Carr, "The Fate of the Vanguard under a Revolutionary State: Marxism's Contribution to the Construction of the Great Arch; Three Moments in the History of the Left, Communism and the Mural Movement," in *Everyday Forms of State Formation*, ed. Gilbert Joseph and Daniel Nugent (Durham: Duke University Press, 1994), 326–52, esp. 342–45.

4. The text of the manifesto is published in English in David Alfaro Siqueiros, *Art and Revolution* (London: Lawrence and Wishart, 1975), 24–25.

5. Rodríguez, *History*, 189.

6. Jean Charlot, *The Mexican Mural Renaissance* (New York: Hacker Books, 1979), 235.

7. Ibid., 143.

8. Diego Rivera, *My Art, My Life*, with Gladys March (New York: Citadel Press, 1960), 134. To supplement the selection of images reproduced in this volume, readers may consult the website www.diegorivera.com to see additional murals Rivero painted in the SEP, the agricultural school at Chapingo, and the National Palace.

9. On Rivera's indigenismo, see Barry Carr, "Fate of the Vanguard," 343–44.

10. Rivera, *My Art, My Life*, 136.

11. As quoted in Bertram D. Wolfe, *Diego Rivera, His Life and Times* (New York: Alfred A. Knopf, 1939), 234.

12. The mural remained covered for nearly seventy years. With financial and technical assistance from the Getty Research and Conservation Institutes, it is now being restored and the whitewash removed. Diego Rivera's U.S. murals can be found at www.diegorivera.com and www.diamondial.org/rivera.

13. Orozco's Dartmouth murals can be viewed at http://hoodmuseum.dartmouth .edu.

14. David Alfaro Siqueiros, *Mi respuesta, edición mexicana de arte público* (Mexico, 1960), 31–32.

15. Jackson Pollock, *The Hollow and the Bump* (New York: Carlton Miscellany, 1966), 85–86.

16. For Guadalajara murals not reproduced here, consult the websites www.peter langer.com and http://mexico.udg.mx.

17. Salvador Echavarria, *Orozco, Hospicio Cabañas* (Guadalajara: Planeación y Promo-ción, 1959), 28.

18. Porfirio Muñoz Ledo, *Mexico Today* (Philadelphia: Institute for the Study of Human Issues, 1973), 28.

19. For more information, see Siqueiros's "Open Letter to Soviet Painters, Sculptors and Engravers: A Reception Speech at the Soviet Academy of Art, October 17th, 1955," in Siqueiros, *Art and Revolution*, 176.

20. From a technical perspective, Mexican muralism was in many senses, particularly with Rivera, conventional and conservative. Siqueiros was the exception. For more on his experimentation, see Desmond Rochfort, *Mexican Muralists: Orozco, Rivera, Siqueiros* (New York: Chronicle Books, 1998), 185–217.

# Painting in the Shadow of the Big Three

Frida Kahlo
SARAH M. LOWE

Although in the last quarter of the twentieth century, Frida Kahlo (1907–54) and her painting became symbols of Mexico and modern womanhood, in her lifetime she had only one solo exhibit in Mexico, organized in 1953 by photographer Lola Álvarez Bravo. Today Kahlo's story is widely known. The daughter of a Hungarian Jewish photographer and Oaxacan mother, she was stricken with polio at the age of six. She was one of the pioneer women to study at the Escuela Nacional Preparatoria, and there in 1922 she watched Diego Rivera paint *The Creation*. In 1926, a gruesome traffic accident left her crippled, in pain, and unable to bear children. In 1929, she married Rivera. Sexually unfaithful, often separated, once divorced, and twice married, they were passionately devoted to each other. Yet their artistic styles and content were vastly different. Rivera painted a flamboyant, evolutionary panorama of Mexican history. Frida Kahlo concentrated Mexican history and the Mexican present in representations of herself.[1]

Women artists who paint self-portraits have had to overcome an already given meaning—the equation of female self-reflection with vanity. They have also had to invent images of the self that are, nevertheless, inscribed within a patriarchal order, one that defines women first in sexual terms. Women have been traditionally denied access to venues for presenting their own sense of self, and in light of these proscriptions, Frida Kahlo's production is especially remarkable. Her construction of self is at once complex and astonishingly straightforward: without a hint of self-pity or sentimentality, Kahlo depicts her dreams, fears, passions, and pain with a forthrightness that defies social and artistic restrictions.

In 1927 Kahlo painted *Pancho Villa and Adelita*. "Adelita" is one of many songs about the *soldaderas*, primarily working-class and poor women who left their homes to provide food and care for revolutionary soldiers and often fought alongside them.[2] "Adelita" is sung from the point of view of a sergeant who sings of his passion for his beloved, of his suffering heart, and of her fear of his dying in battle. He entreats Adelita to bury his remains in the sierra and weep for him should he perish.[3] It is a song as much about their mutual devotion as it is about devotion to the revolutionary future. Kahlo situates herself in the center of *Pancho Villa and Adelita* (plate 11), the eye of a storm, wearing a shimmering, off-the-shoulder evening dress, while around her, pictures seem to fall off the wall. Two male figures are sketchily painted in: one sits facing her; the other is faceless. Directly above Kahlo is a portrait of Pancho Villa; to his left is a painted vignette of the revolution, and to his right, a painting of a stage set or bar. In the image of the revolution, soldiers with several soldaderas are placed in and on top of a freight car, which is set in front of a summary rendering of one of the two great volcanic peaks that tower above the Valley of Mexico.

Although the painting's meaning remains enigmatic, Kahlo clearly identifies with Adelita. This painting is the earliest self-portrait in which she aspires to depict a specific aspect of her identity not simply as a Mexican, but as a Mexican woman. As Adelita's descendant, Kahlo places herself in solidarity with the soldaderas, some of whom became military officers. The soldadera, an inherently Mexican phenomenon, was mythologized in literature, graphically depicted by printmaker José Guadalupe Posada, and ennobled by Orozco.

Throughout her life Kahlo sympathized with leftist issues and participated in left-wing activism. This painting clearly indicates politicized consciousness, for she not only places herself in a historical relationship with Mexico's revolutionary past but also adopts an appropriate foremother. Kahlo's feeling of kinship with the soldadera at this point in her life is a logical extension of her other activities: in the same year that she painted *Pancho Villa and Adelita*, she joined the Communist Youth League, at a time when the Communists still hoped to effect the promised reforms of the revolution.[4] The fact that Mexico's preeminent artists were in leadership roles in the Communist Party may have attracted Kahlo to their ranks. As an artist, however, she resisted Communist mandates that circumscribed formal innovation in favor of social realism.

Kahlo's small, almost miniature, painting *Self-Portrait on the Border between Mexico and the United States*, painted during her visit to Detroit in 1932, is a strong example of her political acumen and insight. Kahlo's perspicacious allegory of the political arrangements between these two countries places at its center a full-length self-portrait, indicating Kahlo's sense of a personal position in a larger political arena, an early-twentieth-century avowal of the politics of the personal.[5] Kahlo's figure stands at the divide of two landscapes, the past on the left and the present on the right. On the Mexican land, a pyramid in ruins stands in an arid landscape, while on the right, undifferentiated American skyscrapers become the modern equivalent of this ancient temple. Where the cosmic forces of the sun and moon clash to create Mexican culture on the left, the Ford factory, whose smokestacks billow exhaust, gives forth the American flag, with the cynical suggestion that Ford not only makes cars but also creates national identity, literally out of thin air. In the Mexican foreground, desert plants thrive, and their roots (one of Kahlo's favored themes, which indicates life) extend deep into the earth. The only thing that flourishes in the sea of concrete on the right are sinister self-replicating machines and a trio of modern electrical appliances: a loudspeaker, a searchlight, and a generator that is plugged into the pedestal on which Kahlo places herself.

This image concretizes Kahlo's feelings of apprehension toward American imperialist policies. She wrote to a friend: "Mexico is as always disorganized and gone to the devil, the only thing that it retains is the immense beauty of the land and of the Indians. Each day the United States' ugliness steals away a piece of it, it is a sad thing, but people must eat and it can't be helped that the big fish eats the little one."[6]

*Self-Portrait on the Border* also reveals much about Kahlo's perceptions of her relationship with her husband, especially when read in contrast to Rivera's epic *Portrait of Detroit*, which he painted in the courtyard of the Detroit Institute of Arts, a project funded by Henry Ford. Rivera was dazzled by Detroit, which represented to him the center of American industry and the American worker. He aspired, he said, to place "the collective hero, the man-and-machine, higher than the old traditional heroes of art and legend."[7]

Not only with words but also in her painting, Kahlo seems to be poking fun at Rivera's grandiose stance. In their art, Kahlo and Rivera proceed with diametrically opposed models. He advances a grand symbolism, a macrocosm that takes as its starting point an anonymous worker and ultimately creates an idealized vision removed from the reality of concrete experience. Kahlo, on the other hand, paints in microcosm, with herself and her personal experience standing in the field of cosmic phenomena. To ground her image in the personal, Kahlo invokes a formal model drawn from popular art, a young girl's confirmation picture. Although she cloaks herself in distinctly Mexican dress and appears to be standing demurely on a pedestal, Kahlo mocks her submission by choosing to hold a cigarette in place of a fan, the required accoutrement of a lady. Thus in a parody of the confirmation picture, wherein girls offered their devotion to Christ, Kahlo seems to offer herself as a Mexican version of the New Woman.

The very small size of Kahlo's work, its private symbolic realm, in such marked contrast to Rivera's monumental, public fresco, might militate against comparing the two. But this is precisely where Kahlo's motive lies: she reinvents history painting as she parodies Rivera's mural. She reduces Rivera's grand symbolism into distilled opposites, thus intensifying the message. Kahlo takes a step beyond self-definition to self-creation in a strange, even fantastic, image, *My Birth*, painted in 1932 (plate 12). Kahlo does not simply depict her artistic genesis but reinvents the unknowable moment of her actual birth. It is a disturbing image on many levels: the austere setting, the utter isolation of the draped birthing woman depicted without a head, and the unusual viewpoint that results in a contorted and misshapen figure. In purely iconographic terms, *My Birth* is a radical adaptation of the depiction of the goddess Tlazolteotl, traditionally shown in the act of childbirth.

Kahlo sets *My Birth* within the ex-voto format, an especially appropriate choice, since the ex-voto customarily represents a supernatural event, which this surely is. The ex-voto mixes fact and fantasy, depicting an image of divine intervention to commemorate the miraculous recovery from a sickness or an accident. It pictures two registers of reality: the earthly—an incident recorded with journalistic verity—and the divine, in the form of a patron saint shown floating above the victim. This fusion of the real and the imaginary was enormously appealing to Kahlo, and it was this aspect of the ex-voto that she appropriated for her work.

Yet while using the form of the ex-voto, Kahlo forgoes any specific Catholic sense, and in lieu of a mystical guardian, she places on the wall in this sparse room a *retablo* of the Mater Dolorosa (Mother of Sorrows), another popular idiom for the expression of piety. Kahlo said that the Madonna was included not for religious reasons but as a "memory image," because a similar retablo was present when she was born.[8] The Virgin is depicted not wearing her usual crown of thorns but pierced with daggers, a peculiarly Mexican artistic innovation, presiding over the bloody birth of the full-grown Frida.[9] Significantly, though, this is an important traditional depiction. The Mater Dolorosa was invoked by believers to guard against sorrow or pain, or at the hour of death, which presents a paradox in this case.

It is likely that Kahlo identified with the Mater Dolorosa, who is often depicted shedding tears of sorrow for her lost son. In at least eight formal self-portraits—and in several letters where she drew caricatures of herself—Kahlo painted symbolic tears on her face. Perhaps biography may be used to corroborate the suggested affinity, for in Kahlo's mind, the three miscarriages/abortions she endured were literally lost children.[10] A figure from popular legend, La Llorona, the Weeping Woman, further establishes the association of tears and loss of a child, for like the Mother of Sorrows, La Llorona mourns her dead child.

It was Kahlo's custom to dress in indigenous Mexican clothes. She favored the long dresses from the Tehuantepec region of Oaxaca, embellishing herself with pre-Columbian earrings, necklaces, and bracelets. In part, Kahlo was motivated by a conscious disregard of appropriate bourgeois behavior, but it was equally a stance of solidarity with the people who wore and produced these beautiful objects. Accordingly, in many self-portraits Kahlo wears native blouses and skirts, with special care given to her hair, which was often rolled with brightly colored wool cords or fabrics into a headdress known as *tlacoyal*. So careful was Kahlo's attention to detail that the origin of each outfit can be determined, thus tangibly communicating important information about her culture, as well as about herself as a Mexican woman. It should be noted that Kahlo's Mexican dress and her use of Mexican sources was not simply a matter of conforming with the current impulse of Mexicanidad and the *indigenista* movement; Kahlo embraced her Mexican heritage because it gave her strength. She drew on a multiplicity of sources, constructing a polysemous self, one grounded in a native, but also female, existence.

Kahlo was attuned to the significance of specific costumes of a region, and that she used this knowledge to convey precise information is evident in her *Self-Portrait as a Tehuana* (or *Diego on My Mind*) from 1943 (plate 13). Other artists had painted the Tehuana in the recent past: it is likely Kahlo knew Roberto Montenegro's portrait of Rosa Rolando as a Tehuana and Matías Santoyo's Tehuana. These modernists were attracted to the abstract qualities of the extraordinary white lace *huipil*. This rectangular-shaped dress with openings for the head and arms was worn to cover the head, in the manner that other Mexican women wore a rebozo (shawl). For Montenegro and Santoyo, the potential political content inherent in the subject matter played a secondary role. Rather, the huipil allowed them a degree of formal experimentation. Neither is a likely visual source for Kahlo's image, which more closely resembles a colonial prototype of the *monjas coronadas*, or "crowned nuns," a distinct aspect within the larger genre of viceregal portraiture.[11] These portraits, whose origins are found in Catholic Europe, commemorated one of two events in a nun's life: her initiation into monastic life or her death. Before a novitiate entered the convent, her family commissioned a portrait, which they kept as a memento. As the bride of Christ, she was lavishly crowned with flowers, a custom unknown abroad but developed in Mexico as a continuation of the floral headdresses of Aztec ritual. The nun's flowers were preserved and reused for her deathbed portrait, paid for by the convent to perpetuate her memory within the religious community.

Kahlo's *Self-Portrait as a Tehuana* shares both explicit formal and implicit conceptual elements with the monjas coronadas. In each, the face is surrounded by an exuberance of detail, imparting a mystical quality to the disembodied heads. The Tehuantepec wedding dress that Kahlo wears further substantiates the implied correspondence between Kahlo and the novitiate. Another point of similarity is the inclusion of a second party portrayed in a small medallion. In the monjas coronadas, the nuns usually hold an image that depicts either the Virgin or Christ, indicating to whom the painting is dedicated. Instead of a medallion, Kahlo paints a portrait of Rivera as a "third eye," thus dedicating the image to him. Kahlo's attachment to Rivera, as expressed most profoundly in her diary, bears comparison to the nun's mystical marriage to Christ: "Diego is the beginning, the constructor, my baby, boyfriend, painter, my lover, 'my husband,' my friend, my mother, myself, and the universe."[12]

Just as Kahlo adapts the spatial and temporal organization of the ex-voto without any specific religiosity, so she transforms the overtly Catholic image of the bride of Christ into an emblem of personal symbolism. She accomplishes this by successfully combining the Catholic prototype with a readily recognizable native costume and its attendant connotations. She thus achieves an individual mystical expression without conventional sacred significance. In short, Kahlo created a desacralized syntax by mixing elements of Indian and Catholic art, myth and symbolism, a syncretic art form that in many ways reflects the basic dualistic approach to religion manifest in Mexico. For Kahlo, as for many Mexicans, ancient rites that survived in Indian rituals were celebrated at the same time as Catholic rites, without apparent contradiction. Kahlo simply reappropriated symbols and reorganized them into multivalent images, ultimately bereft of any theological content.

Kahlo is often held to be a surrealist despite the many aspects of her work that make such a definition questionable.[13] Some have argued against such a designation, insisting that Kahlo drew too heavily on her own experience.[14] One important difference between Kahlo and the French surrealists is that many of her formal innovations sprang not from intellectual constructs but from traditions in Mexican art: the odd spatial quality of the ex-votos, the mixing of human and animal forms often seen in Aztec images, and themes that to European eyes might have seemed morbid but were common in colonial art. If we are to believe André Breton, who saw Kahlo's painting as "pure surreality," and in fact sought to bring her into the club, then Kahlo may indeed be counted among its ranks. On the other hand, to place her neatly within this category is to ignore the complexity of her sources and motives. Thus perhaps we should ask: What are the surreal elements in Kahlo's work? What are her sources? To what extent is Kahlo indebted to European surrealism?

The definition of surrealism is complicated by its ever-changing cast of characters. Breton's tyrannical desire to dominate this circle, the factional fighting, vacillating alliances, and recurrent expulsions among the surrealists make it difficult to assign any single meaning. The initial group was dominated by the painters Max Ernst, Andre Masson, and Joan Miró, and thus the 1924 Manifesto of Surrealism reflects their reliance on automatism, accident, and biomorphism as means of expression—all elements that are, by and large, absent from Kahlo's idiom.[15] On the other hand, the impetus for using these methods to "express the functioning of the mind" is in fact close to the way Kahlo's paintings work.[16] The Second Manifesto of Surrealism (1929) reveals the influence of imagists such as Salvador Dalí and René Magritte, with whose realist style Kahlo had more in common. The spatial qualities evident in much of Kahlo's work are similar to the "landscapes of the mind" devised by the surrealists Yves Tanguy and Dalí.

Kahlo marshaled a variety of formal strategies to convey her personal symbology, and these coincide with surrealist means of expression. She had a high regard for the work of Henri Rousseau and Giorgio de Chirico, whom the surrealists cited among their progenitors. Thus it is not surprising that when Breton arrived in Mexico in the spring of 1938, he felt that Kahlo's work embodied the tenets of surrealism. But Kahlo's work was equally informed by stylistic conventions of her Mexican past. However, her recognition that these forms were viable for a modern artist may indeed have been informed by surrealist notions.

Kahlo herself was ambivalent about being called a surrealist and never fully identified herself with the movement. When interviewed in 1938, she claimed, with a degree of insincere indifference, "I didn't know I was a Surrealist until André Breton came to Mexico and told me I was."[17] Breton's trip to Mexico had a twofold purpose: under the auspices of the French Ministry of Foreign Affairs, he was obliged to present lectures on French culture. His private agenda, however, involved drawing artists into the surrealist fold. At the time, his international movement was stagnating and was no longer considered the cutting edge of the avant-garde, and so Breton was seeking supporters in other countries and arenas.

Breton's interest in pre-Columbian art fueled his desire to visit Mexico. But the interest of the European surrealists in non-Western art, which they imprecisely called "primitive," was at odds with Kahlo's own understanding.[18] The Europeans' "ethnographic" interest in Africa, Oceania, and to some extent Mesoamerica provided "other" religions and forms that enabled them to revitalize their work. Kahlo's incorporation of the formal and symbolic aspects of Aztec art may be seen within the context of Mexicanidad and understood as a search for her own indigenous history.

The place Mexico occupied in the surrealist imagination was stimulated not only by Breton's familiarity with pre-Columbian art but also no doubt by the account Antonin Artaud made after he had visited Mexico two years earlier. Breton had expelled Artaud from the surrealist group in 1926. As if not to be outdone by Artaud, who "discovered" the work of María Izquierdo, Breton made Kahlo his Mexican trophy. It is perhaps no coincidence that each returned to France with a female souvenir. Since they were predisposed to see Mexico as an exotic, distant, and mythic "other" place, only a woman artist could fully embody the otherness that Mexico signified. That both Kahlo and Izquierdo incorporated pre-Columbian sources in their work made them even more ideal representations of Mexican surrealism.

Breton's eulogistic, if somewhat self-serving, preface to Kahlo's 1938 exhibition at the Julien Levy Gallery in New York—in which he collapsed the idea of woman and Mexico—makes clear his sexualized construction of both Kahlo and her country. After declaring that her paintings had blossomed into "pure surreality," Breton then asserted, with a patronizing and provincial arrogance, that Kahlo had "no prior knowledge of the ideas motivating the activities of my friends and myself."[19] His presumption that Kahlo arrived at her formal resolutions intuitively has the effect of dismissing her conscious artistic decisions while perpetuating his self-proclaimed power to confer value on art that was otherwise inconsequential. Breton concluded: "I would like to add now that there is no art more exclusively feminine, in the sense that, in order to be as seductive as possible, it is only too willing to play alternately at being absolutely pure and absolutely pernicious."[20] In this striking display of reductive essentialism, Breton sexualized both Kahlo and her work, so that her art becomes merely a reflection of a masculine idea of the feminine.

Kahlo's work is incontrovertibly grounded in her identity as a Mexican, and the surrealist elements in her painting stem from her own cultural background.

In a short piece published the year Kahlo died, the artist and curator Susana
Gamboa accounted for Kahlo's imagery by specifically citing the long history
of Mexican art. She wrote that in treatment, Kahlo's painting "is imaginative
and fantastic, but the mood is poetic, full of age-old Mexican symbolism which
has less to do with Frida as an individual than with Mexico as an aesthetic
heritage."[21]

*A Few Small Nips* (plate 14), painted in 1935, offers an instance of Kahlo's application of popular art. It is among her most disturbing images and derives its
subject matter, in part, from imagery popularized by José Guadalupe Posada.
Posada's lurid prints of gruesome murders and ghastly accidents were in fact
visual recaps of recent events. Several postrevolutionary artists "discovered"
Posada. In their minds, his illustrations for broadsides and *corridos* formed a
crucial link between a folk tradition and Mexican modernist practice by providing the muralists with an art form that was inherently Mexican. Posada based
his work on popular art but cast off European aesthetics and thus represented
the earliest recent instance of an alternative artistic tradition.

Kahlo's attraction to Posada also lay in his macabre humor and shocking explicitness, similar in timbre to *A Few Small Nips*, which in turn was inspired by a
newspaper story of a brutal murder of a woman knifed to death by her drunken
husband. In keeping with Kahlo's sardonic sense of humor, the title derives
from the killer's answer upon being charged with murder: "But I only gave
her a few small nips."[22] This understatement contrasts with the exaggerated
depiction of blood, which splashes out onto the frame of the painting, literally into the viewer's space. While Posada is one source, such excess derives in
part from the graphic realism and directness of polychromatic sculpted images
of Christ's Passion found in Mexico's churches. Based on baroque models, the
Mexican versions' realistic colors and explicitness render the wounds of Christ
vividly and literally. For Kahlo, the mark of blood is woman's mark: she depicts
women riddled with puncture wounds, bleeding after an abortion or childbirth, spilling blood from a vein connected to her heart, or pierced with arrows.
However, the excessive use of blood removes this image from the traditional
symbolism associated with women. Usually blood is identified as the "curse"
of menses, a taboo, signifying filth and pollution, defilement and degradation.
On the other hand, the blood shed on the wedding night certifies virginity,
signals purity, and thus confers value on the bride.[23] For Kahlo, blood is not
symbolic; it is real—it is present in the everyday life of Mexico.

*A Few Small Nips* is not simply an indictment against violence inflicted on
women. Kahlo painted this image shortly after arriving back from her stay in

the United States. One wonders if, in part, the painting is a reaction to the shock of being back in Mexico after having to endure the "disgusting puritanism" and "endless pretension" of the dull, bland gringos. Kahlo preferred, in her words, the Mexican "thieves," "hijos de la chingada" (sons of bitches), and the *cabrones* (bastards) to the infuriating colorlessness of the North Americans.[24] Violence as part of life in Mexico was something Kahlo had experienced her entire life. "In Mexico killing is quite satisfactory and natural," she said of this image.[25] It was an inextricable part of her culture on which she reports rather than editorializes. Kahlo paints not the action of violence but its aftermath, its consequences.

*A Few Small Nips* is remarkable for the way Kahlo deftly overturns the established expectations of the female nude. The gritty reality of the scene, utterly lacking in any erotic overtones, undermines the conventional presentation of woman's body in art. Additionally, Kahlo's presentation of the convergence of sex and violence contrasts sharply with the manner in which surrealism treats the subject. Women's sexuality, as constructed by that male coterie, was decisively influenced by their reading of the Marquis de Sade, whose pornographic writing both affirmed and perpetuated the association of violence with female sexuality. Their idea of woman was structured on male fantasies. Indeed, although women played a central role in the conception of French surrealist ideology, they were relegated to the role of muse, the passive mediator between nature and creative man.[26] The elaborate surrealist constructions of the feminine are wholly inventive, whereas for Kahlo, being a woman was not imaginary. Unlike surrealist art, which glamorizes misogyny and in whose visual images women are portrayed with a stylized, sanitized elegance, Kahlo's painting serves as an explicit reminder of the concrete reality of daily violence in women's lives. Where the surrealists fantasized about the hidden mysteries of "la femme," Kahlo often exposes the internal, literally. The surrealists endeavored to evoke, visually or verbally, extraordinary realities drawn from the erotic, the exotic, and the unconscious: for Kahlo extraordinary realities were her present.

## María Izquierdo
### ADRIANA ZAVALA

Over the course of the 1930s and 1940s, the art world in Mexico City became the center of contentious debates over how Mexican identity should be defined and expressed in artistic terms. These debates emerged between artists who advocated the socially committed art emerging from the revolution, and artists who advocated more autonomous, formally experimental forms of art, which they termed "pure" or "new" art. Within the realm of pictorial expression, revolutionary nationalists embraced the concept that Mexicanness was defined in anticolonial and politicized terms and was in essence rooted in "Indian" tradition. By the late 1920s, artists like Rufino Tamayo, Agustín Lazo, Carlos Mérida, Manuel and Lola Álvarez Bravo, and María Izquierdo dissented.[27] They allied with a group of writers who founded and contributed to the avant-garde journals *Contemporáneos* (1928–31), *Examen* (1932), and *Taller* (1938–41).

Known as the Contemporáneos, this group of writers, among them Jaime Torres Bodet, Salvador Novo, José Gorostiza, Carlos Pellicer, Gilberto Owen, Jorge Cuesta, and Xavier Villaurrutia, asserted that the essence of being Mexican was best explored and expressed in dialogue with the latest international cultural currents. In their own writing, and in the pages of their journals, they sought actively to situate Mexican culture within a modern, urban, international context, defining it in terms as much informed by universal ideals as by local roots. In other words, they sought an alternative to "social art," especially the idea that twentieth-century Mexican art equated with an overt celebration of the "race" and with the politically homogenizing historical narratives offered up by the muralists, particularly Diego Rivera. Among the group, Salvador Novo most notoriously parodied revolutionary virility, of which Rivera was one of Mexico's most notorious poseurs.

In contrast to official postrevolutionary populism, the Contemporáneos advocated for a sophisticated aesthetic that was principally urban and middle class. While on one level they privileged the individual, sensual, and sometimes the melancholic, individual experience was firmly rooted simultaneously in a sense of the "difference" (vis-à-vis Europe or the United States) inherent in being Mexican. For the Contemporáneos, "social art," such as the novel of the revolution and Rivera's murals, represented an official image of Mexico, defined principally in rural terms. The Contemporáneos recognized the importance of Mexico's rural and Indian cultures but were committed to looking to the future of a modernized, optimally middle-class Mexico. Thus in 1932, the poet Xavier Villaurrutia affirmed that Mexican culture "could be firmly rooted and yet its branches remain free."[28] Given the official "Indianization" of the cultural nation, the challenges of the Contemporáneos and supporting artists were daring. Ultimately the Contemporáneos' hopes for an enlightened and more varied Mexican culture were fulfilled after 1940 rather than in the 1930s.[29]

The Contemporáneos staked their claim to an alternative definition of art and national identity in the first issue of *Contemporáneos*, in June 1928. There, in the midst of their sonnets, poems, and introspective essays on music and literature, they published a negative assessment of Rivera's art. Gabriel García Maroto wrote that Rivera's murals reduced art to a "mechanized and unrefined political-social instrument," bereft of the "fundamental values of *new* art."[30] By "new" García Maroto meant art that was more universal rather than nationalistic, and more self-referential, exploring creative expression rather than social concerns. Rivera retaliated against the Contemporáneos in a public conference in which he defended his murals, purportedly calling the Contemporáneos numerous epithets, including *maricas*, a derogatory reference to the homosexuality of some members of the group.[31]

This incident helps establish the climate in Mexico City's artistic community at the end of the 1920s. The artists who rallied around *Contemporáneos* were committed to making space for modes of expression based on difference, insofar as social art represented the normative. Indeed, Salvador Novo, Xavier Villaurrutia, and Agustín Lazo were openly gay, and their literary and pictorial works are infused with a homoerotic sensibility and desire, albeit carefully disguised. They also depicted the active, modern, and at least implicitly sexually emancipated woman. In 1930s Mexico, homosexual artists and female ones, such as Izquierdo and Lola Álvarez Bravo, who were divorced, found themselves at the margins of the "true" (nationalist, patriarchal) Mexican nation. It was precisely for her depictions of women, usually nude and often anguished, in primordial landscapes, rendered in small, opaque, almost overworked, watercolor paintings, that Izquierdo attracted the interest of the Contemporáneos.

María Izquierdo was born in 1902 in San Juan de los Lagos, Jalisco. By 1923 she had married Cándido Posadas and had three children. The couple moved to Mexico City, where in January 1928, despite apparently limited previous artistic training, Izquierdo enrolled at the National School of Fine Arts (NSFA). There she studied with the older academic generation, but also with newly appointed, younger faculty, among them Rufino Tamayo. Izquierdo remained at the school only until mid-1929.[32]

In August 1929, while a student at the NSFA, Izquierdo was singled out for praise by the school's new director, Diego Rivera. In an essay of September 1929, Rivera praised Izquierdo's work for its "fundamentally Mexican" qualities.[33] This assessment had major implications in the cultural context of late-1920s Mexico, since Rivera aggressively asserted his hegemony in defining Mexican identity. Given Rivera's allegiance to "social art" and the fact that he had just transformed the curriculum at the art school so as to train "worker-artists" who created "collective" works of art, one might assume that Izquierdo was producing socially oriented art.[34] Instead, she was producing images in a naive manner of painting, among them still lifes, landscapes, and portraits.

Her *Flower Vendors* (ca. 1927) features two indigenous women selling flowers in a market, a work that in its subject matter resembles Rivera's *Flower Day* (ca. 1925). However, unlike Rivera's lovingly rendered Indians, with gently downcast eyes, Izquierdo's flower vendors meet the viewer's gaze directly. Whether Izquierdo painted in a naive style out of choice or for lack of training remains an open debate. In the 1920s, a naive style of painting came into vogue. It was promulgated at the government-run "Open-Air Painting Schools" because it was deemed to express "innate" Mexicanness by emulating the flattened perspective, lack of modeling, and unblended and somewhat strident use of color characteristic of nineteenth-century provincial painters who lacked formal academic training. Artists as diverse as Abraham Angel, Manuel Rodríguez Lozano, and Frida Kahlo employed elements of this style to signal, variously, their allegiance to a modernist, less strictly naturalistic manner of rendering the human figure, or, as in Kahlo's case, an allegiance to "the people."

It was no doubt her painting style and simple subjects that led Rivera to single Izquierdo out, praising her "rich yet simple compositions" and her "warm and unusual color harmonies." While he concluded that her talent was "fundamentally Mexican," her gender and physical appearance were factors as well, because Rivera described her as "one of the most attractive artists recently discovered in Mexico." He predicted Izquierdo would become one of Mexico's most valued artists if she could avoid the "bastardizing influence of foreign painting."[35] With that statement, Rivera was signaling modernist tendencies among some Mexican artists, namely, Rufino Tamayo, recently appointed instructor at the NSFA and then involved with María Izquierdo.

She continued to receive Rivera's support through November 1929. In an unprecedented act, she was given a solo exhibition at the newly founded Galería de Arte Moderno, run by Carlos Mérida and Carlos Orozco Romero. Like Tamayo, Mérida and Orozco Romero's intellectual orientation and advocacy of "new" or "pure" painting affiliated them with the Contemporáneos. However, in Mexico City's cultural climate, they had to be cautious—the more so because the Galería was funded by the Mexico City Department of Civic Action. When Mérida described the gallery's mission, he stated its commitment to showing internationally recognized, established artists (e.g., Rivera), but also "emerging" Mexican art that exemplified "new values" and "original tendencies."[36] Mérida's conciliatory statement explains why Rivera wrote the catalog essay for Izquierdo's exhibition. Furthermore, it was a key to ensuring her success. In his essay, Rivera asserted that Izquierdo was *herself*, like her painting, "classically Mexican," so much so that he claimed that in her physical appearance she resembled an ancient carved stone deity.[37]

In Rivera's descriptions of Izquierdo's work, he was "claiming" her for his side in the debate over Mexican art. In 1928, Rufino Tamayo had asserted, "Mexicanism has been interpreted only folklorically and archaeologically, having more to do with anecdote than essence." Just returned from New York, Tamayo declared himself a supporter of French painting, "particularly the work of Picasso, Matisse, Braque and de Chirico."[38] In condemning "foreign painting," Rivera was no doubt aware of the interest it was generating anew among some Mexican artists. Furthermore, his description of Izquierdo as physically attractive in her "classically Mexican" (i.e., *mestiza*) appearance, coupled with the homophobic rancor he had unleashed against the Contemporáneos, points to the fact that "Mexicanness" for him was not just rooted in traditional culture but sustained by the normative patriarchal gender roles evident in his painting. However, after November 1929, Rivera fell silent about Izquierdo's work. Instead he shifted his interests to championing the cause of Frida Kahlo.[39]

It was in the midst of these contested definitions of cultural identity and appropriate "revolutionary" gender roles that key members of the group, among them Xavier Villaurrutia and José Gorostiza, began to pay critical attention to Izquierdo's work. Not only was she associated with Tamayo, but her painting, and her lifestyle as a newly divorced woman, responded in key ways to their interest in a complex, multifaceted definition of Mexicanidad. Their definition was based not on a single, essential identity but rather on a free play of the dichotomies between local and cosmopolitan, rural and urban, masculine and feminine, and social versus pure art.

Izquierdo's membership in the Contemporáneos group was confirmed when in September 1929, four of her paintings were reproduced in *Contemporáneos*. The illustrated paintings, all lost, included a female nude, a still life, and two portraits of male sitters, one of which depicted her ex-husband Cándido Posadas seated next to a book, a pipe, and a small sculpted female nude (figure 1). Of the four works, the nude is remarkably advanced in terms of Izquierdo's modeling of the figure, the overall mood conveyed, and the fact that, early in her career, she rendered a female nude so candidly. The work is replete with emotional ambiguity. In fact, it shows a woman who is rendered naked, rather than nude. She sits on an unmade bed, with one leg pulled up awkwardly to shield her body. The angularity of the figural composition and graphic modeling of the body suggest that Izquierdo had little interest in representing her sitter in a flattering or seductive way. Instead the woman's pensive expression, along with several compositional elements, including a framed photographic portrait of a man in a matador's costume, an extinguished candle, an open bottle of wine on the nightstand, and the disarray of clothing under the bed, evokes a sense of postcoital abandonment. The tired and pensive expression on the woman's face forces the viewer into a denaturalized, if still potentially titillating, voyeuristic position. The work thus subverts the accepted, ostensibly unthreatening relationship normally established in classically rendered images of the female body. Rather than inhabiting a world apart, this particular woman clearly inhabits a world emotionally and physically conditioned by the male presence. Rather than rendering a chaste, untouched nude, Izquierdo makes clear that the woman is anything but untouched.

Izquierdo's fashioning of the female body as modern rather than rural or traditionally Mexican is most evident when compared with Julio Castellanos's *Two Nudes* (1929).[40] Castellanos codes his subjects as rural and idyllic. They have dark hair and skin; their bodies are rounded and fecund. Their expressions are passive. Their bodies are left open by virtue of their seated position on painted wooden chairs, which along with the red tile floor and the simple geometric architecture locate them in rural Mexico. Here Castellanos engages with the Western pictorial tradition of equating the feminine with nature rather than with knowledge and Western culture. Here the viewer's desire for the women's bodies is hidden behind their positioning as timeless symbols of a premodern existence. Thus Castellanos has classicized Mexican womanhood.

Castellanos's painting contrasts powerfully with the mood evoked in Izquierdo's. Izquierdo's nude is located temporally and spatially within urban modernity and rendered sexually experienced. Her description of the female subject as naked, awkward, and sexual marks the body with what T. J. Clark has termed "particular and excessive fact," whereas Castellanos's rendition articulates the female body as a sign signifying the idealization of rural Mexico as well as generalized, purified desire.[41]

What is remarkable about Izquierdo's early nudes is her engagement with modern womanhood as a means to challenge canonical representations of the idealized or "naturalized" female nude. For an easel painter, and indeed for Izquierdo as a woman establishing herself in a male-dominated genre, the most

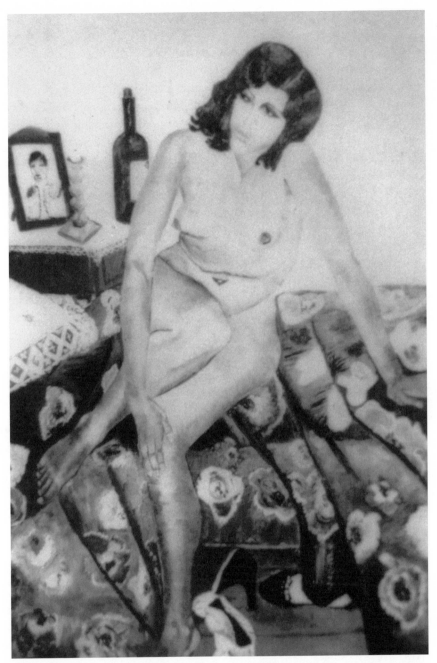

FIG. I. María Izquierdo, *Nude*, 1929. Original painting destroyed; reproduction in *Contemporáneos*, no. 16 (September 1929): 105. Photograph by Adriana Zavala from *Contemporáneos*.

audacious way to claim her space was to paint the female nude body, one of the most canonical and male-dominated of all subjects; however, her engagement is rebellious. Her works abuse the canon, even if ironically, by creating a temporally specific context that becomes highly confrontational. Having herself been described as "classically Mexican," she renders a resolutely modern, naked, sexual woman. In so doing, she does not reject the canon, for she could not afford to; instead, she overtly signals her dependence on it by *using* it and simultaneously rebelling in her "ironic *abuse* of it."[42]

Between 1932 and 1938, Izquierdo painted a series of over forty watercolors and gouache paintings that feature nude and naked women within primordial landscapes and represent one of the earliest focused engagements with the female nude in Mexican art.[43] In addition to nude women, the works are littered with classical architectural elements, mountains, horses, lions, and celestial orbs. A subseries includes circus and equestrian subjects that hint at the seedy, carnivalesque atmosphere of the *carpas*, itinerant sideshows that traveled throughout provincial and urban Mexico in the first half of the twentieth century.[44] What unites these works is Izquierdo's use of color, composition, and strange, uncanny narratives that pose interpretive challenges. While some works, such as *Allegory of Work* (1936), suggest both potentially sociopolitical concerns and surrealistic interests, others, such as *Woman with Horse* (1938), suggest melancholic rural Mexican subjects.

Between 1932 and 1934, three prominent Contemporáneos, Xavier Villaurrutia, Jorge Cuesta, and José Gorostiza, along with Gorostiza's younger brother Celestino, wrote essays inspired by Izquierdo's paintings. In 1932, Villaurrutia emphasized that she was a very different painter from the one singled out by Rivera in 1929. She had assimilated certain qualities of Tamayo's painting, but hers possessed a "lively and feminine sensuality," above all in their "delicious" coloration. He pronounced her one of the "most daring and yet harmonious colorists" within "new Mexican painting."[45] Izquierdo's works would have appealed to the poet, whose own "nocturnes" conjure very similar imagery.[46] With his praise, Villaurrutia accomplished multiple tasks. By promoting Izquierdo, he elevated Tamayo artistically above the stature of Rivera. By employing terms such as "delicious" and "feminine sensuality," he also subordinated her, positioning her as Tamayo's protégée in a manner that upheld Tamayo's masculine superiority.[47]

In 1933, when Izquierdo exhibited seventeen of her watercolor paintings at Frances Toor's Mexico City gallery, Jorge Cuesta wrote the catalog essay. He praised them precisely because he saw in them a critique of "painterly explorations of the Mexican spirit and character." Her painting did not succumb to extraneous elements such as sentimentalism, but was "*modern*."[48] While Cuesta acknowledged that her paintings invited a desire to search for meaning, he concluded that to search for meaning in art had grave consequences, and that her art should instead be accepted for what it was: "pure painting." A different strategy was employed at the opening of the exhibition, when José Gorostiza reverted to a patriarchal characterization of her works as "confessions of anguish, fear, solitude and bitterness."[49] Gorostiza linked that quality to Izquierdo's unique understanding of the modern Mexican psyche, a subject that would be crucial to the younger generation of Contemporáneos, principally Octavio Paz.

In November 1933, Celestino Gorostiza addressed both the "Mexican" and the emotive qualities of Izquierdo's work. He remarked that her *Mexicanness* was to be found not in the themes she treated but rather in her very spirit and the way in which her taste and temperament were manifest in her art.[50] He, like other critics before him, established an interdependence between her painting and her physicality, describing the power of her works as residing in the "viscera, between her heart and her mind." In other words, he described Izquierdo's painting as instinctive.

Despite identifying her creative impulses as instinctive, Celestino Gorostiza distanced Izquierdo from the notion that her work was excessively personal. He saw her painting as expressive yet serene, as conveying "moral strength and fortitude, rather than typically feminine sentimentality." Her "fortitude" was a "rare quality in a woman painter," because "the feminine artistic inclination is toward a sensibility of the flesh . . . that translates as excessive sentimentalism and tasteless pathological expressions of purely sexual states of mind." Although Gorostiza did not, with that criticism, identify any particular woman artist, it is likely that he was referring to Frida Kahlo, who had, in 1932, completed works such as *Henry Ford Hospital* (known at the time as *The Lost Desire*) and *My Birth*. The possibility seems strengthened by his denunciation of artists who expressed their Mexicanness through the forms and styles of folk art. He denigrated them as being "caught in a web of nationalism," and their work as being little more than "ornament suitable to adorn the fireplace mantel of the American tourist."[51]

From 1936 to 1938, Izquierdo painted a disturbing group of works among which are *Allegory of Work* (1936), *Allegory of Freedom* (1937), and *Woman with Horse* (1938) (plates 15, 16, 17). In each, Izquierdo appears to establish a corollary between sexual engagement and sexual labor. *Allegory of Work* represents a woman, who sits on the ground, covering her face with her hands. Before her are two columns, one erect at the top of the hill and the other lying on its side, pointing directly to the woman. Above her a huge pair of disembodied male legs straddle one of the volcanic hills, their torso disappearing into the clouds above. In front of the legs' genital area hovers a golden orb decorated with a moon and five stars. Whereas in many of Izquierdo's images the phallic symbolism is implicit, signified by columns and tree trunks, here the symbolism is overt and overwhelms the female figure. *Allegory of Freedom* depicts a winged, torch-bearing angel, flying away from a smokestack that spews a black cloud and toward the heavens, bearing a cluster of five severed female heads.

The visceral, seemingly Mexican yet simultaneously universal quality that Celestino Gorostiza identified in Izquierdo's paintings is displayed as well in *Woman with Horse* (1938). Here Izquierdo depicts a nude woman, seen from behind, who attempts to drape a bright red blanket over a horse as if preparing to mount it. A strange sense of instability occurs as a result of an ambiguous horizon line. The background plane blends directly into the ground plane, and a slightly darker diagonal wall recedes from the left. The woman's brown skin and black hair stand out against the predominant red hue of the flattened picture space. Her attempt to cover the horse can also be read as protective, as one of concealment and modesty, rendering her own nudity all the more strikingly noticeable. Her brown hips and buttocks are compositionally balanced against the round hindquarters of the horse. While the woman, the horse, and the architecture might evoke rural Mexico, ultimately there is nothing explicitly Mexican in this painting. Instead it invites an enjoyment of color, of compositional dynamism, and of a contemplation of the female form, which by virtue of the narrative elements in the painting can be read as naked and exposed just as readily as it can be read as nude, or in a "state of nature."

Some scholars have argued that Izquierdo's watercolors are located within rural Mexico by virtue of their color palette and certain recurring motifs, such as horses, classical architectural elements, tree stumps, and conical landforms reminiscent of volcanoes. Some have interpreted Izquierdo's ocher, brown, and red bodies as "Indian." On the contrary, she did little to explicitly Mexicanize her landscape settings. Further, by differentiating the skin tones of women in many of her watercolors, she seems to subvert the effort to collapse Mexico's racial diversity behind either *mestizaje*, the notion of racial fusion, or the concept of *indigenismo*. Rather, she creates a private and allegorical fantasy world by relying on a circumscribed pool of iconographic elements comprised of unclothed female bodies, classical architecture, horses, astrological bodies, and,

elsewhere, mermaids and lions. Although her critical supporters described Izquierdo's landscape settings as primordial and her women as Amazons, in the
images of *Allegory of Work* and *Allegory of Freedom*, her pictorial focus is on the
generalized oppression of women.

Izquierdo's interpretation of the female body within a culturally unspeci-
fied yet primordial world suggests that she was acutely aware of, and in dis-
agreement with, the image of woman advanced elsewhere. The numerous references in her works to female sexual agency function as a form of pictorial
resistance to the normalized system of exchange that typically surrounded the
female nude, demonstrated in works such as Castellanos's and Tamayo's; and
she also resisted the overtly self-referential use of the body typical of Kahlo.
Izquierdo's subversion of these representational conventions constitutes a kind
of self-effacement that can be understood as her pictorial response to the insistent linkage established by her supporters between her own physical characteristics and her painting. She, more than any of her peers, positioned the
female body as the site most conducive to examining, indeed subverting, the
full range of those conventions, eroticized, cultural, and otherwise. She did so
by anticipating her peers, male and female, and by locating the female nude
squarely and consistently at the center of a nocturnal, erotic, bizarre, and violent visual world. By constructing an allegorical and timeless world of nocturnal fantasy, she set her work in dialogue with advanced international painting
and particularly with the issues at the heart of surrealist practice as Mexican
artists understood it.

In 1938, the poet Rafael Solana wrote an essay in the journal *Taller*, a literary descendant of *Contemporáneos*.[52] He wrote: "This thing of María Izquierdo
is not painting as a conscious action ruled by the will and the intellect; this is
to secrete painting, in a natural, incontinent way, like crying or bleeding. . . .
María's is not painting born of the mind but of the flesh. . . . Two primordial elements characterize her painting: femininity and Mexicanidad."[53] His
description of her praxis as an uncontrolled incontinence akin to crying or
bleeding is an unremitting expression of his and other male artists' perception of art making as a gendered process. Further, in describing her artistic
process as unconscious, surreal, dreamlike, and visceral rather than intellectual, Solana summarized the way that Izquierdo's supporters had described her
work throughout the 1930s, linking her femininity to their definition of Mexicanidad. On the other hand, he noted her crucial subversive role as an artist
among her peers when he wrote: "Man never appears in María's painting except represented by a column . . . or a horse. He has no will of his own, but

acts only for the painter, for woman. María sees [the world] exclusively from the perspective of her femininity." Finally, Solana described her as a precursor to, and sage of, surrealism while simultaneously taking a swipe at French surrealism: "What the surrealists do not obtain by spying on and imitating the dream, María obtains by letting it speak and believing in it [rather than] torturing it with critical analysis. . . . María Izquierdo who allows to emerge from her depths . . . an acute expression of her art, should be considered a sage and a precursor. What others search for and express with artifice, in her has the value of being spontaneous and ingenuous."[54]

Perhaps Solana wrote to counter the claim of the French dissident surrealist Antonin Artaud, who "discovered" Izquierdo during a visit to Mexico in 1936 and called the women in her images a "caravan of nude Indians." Solana may also have been countering André Breton's 1938 "discovery" of Frida Kahlo as a "surrealist" and his eulogizing of Rivera as *the* revolutionary artist "incarnate [in] the eyes of an entire continent." Indeed, Breton singled out Kahlo's art as "casting the deciding vote between various pictorial tendencies [in Mexico]," a likely reference to debates between "social" and "new" art. Breton described Kahlo's work as "free from foreign influence," and as "prior to knowledge," by which he meant not just surrealism but western European artistic knowledge.[55] Solana's praise of Izquierdo as having a more natural understanding of surrealism was likely provoked by Breton's inaccurate claim that before his arrival in Mexico, Mexican artists had been unaware of surrealism. Thus, in praising Izquierdo, Solana sought to reclaim for Mexican artists and intellectuals an active rather than a passive engagement with the issues at the heart of both advanced painting and surrealist practice. He sought to reaffirm a more open definition of Mexicanidad, and he asserted that Izquierdo's sensually feminine work had value beyond excessively personal invocations of the national, the historical, and the folkloric. In the final analysis, the discourse apparently at play between Artaud, Breton, and Solana suggests that even as late as 1938, debates about the terms of Mexicanidad, and with it the terms of art, continued in complex ways among diverse groups of intellectuals.

Izquierdo's contribution to this process was multifold. She created works that subverted—through direct engagement and abuse—the canonical exemplar of the female nude. In so doing, her works suggest an exploration of an active female sexual subject and female erotic imagination that reterritorializes the female body in terms that suit women's, rather than men's, needs and desires. Yet as late as 1950, she felt compelled to dissemble that process publicly by distancing herself from "classical feminism." Finally, in the context of the gendered social order of postrevolutionary Mexico, Izquierdo was used by diverse male actors in their own competition for cultural hegemony and the right to utter the "final" word on the definition of essential Mexicanness. Ultimately, however, what is particularly provocative about Izquierdo's painting is the way in which her artistic engagement allied her with dissident groups, among them cultural cosmopolitans, homosexuals, and even dissident surrealists, who actively used their "difference" from the established order to create new spaces not just in the margins but increasingly at the center of the cultural order.

## The Mexican Experience of Marion and Grace Greenwood
### JAMES OLES

From the beginning, the so-called Mexican cultural renaissance of the post-revolutionary decades was a phenomenon constructed in part by outsiders, including promoters, curators, critics, and artists from the United States.[56] Many were particularly interested in the ambitious fresco cycles of Diego Rivera and José Clemente Orozco, the most visible and complex artistic statements of the 1920s and 1930s: in both scale and message, they were unlike anything to be found in the United States. Not surprisingly, these murals prompted several American artists to tackle the technical and compositional complexities of the medium.[57] Some sought to establish a mural renaissance back home, a goal finally realized during the New Deal. Others achieved mural commissions of their own in Mexico, in part because of their talent and enthusiasm, in part because they were living in the country during a resurgence of mural commissions in the early 1930s, when Rivera, Orozco, and David Alfaro Siqueiros were working in the United States.

The Mexican frescoes painted between 1933 and 1936 by two Brooklyn-born sisters, Marion (1909–70) and Grace Greenwood (1902–79), are among the most important works of public art created by Americans in the period.[58] Complex in terms of composition and rich in meaning, the Greenwoods' murals also complicate standard views of Mexican art that have privileged the prolific careers of Mexico's "Tres Grandes," a term that obscures the fact that Rivera, Orozco, and Siqueiros were not the only important muralists. Indeed, the Greenwoods' experience in Mexico confirms that Mexican muralism itself was more than a monolithic "movement" sponsored by the Ministry of Public Education. Rather, by the 1930s it was a heterogeneous force marked by competing and overlapping strategies played out by a wide range of participants.

In late December 1932, Marion Greenwood crossed the border by car, en

route to Mexico City. She had accepted an invitation to accompany the radical writer and journalist Josephine Herbst and her husband, John Hermann,
on their escape from the pressures of life in New York. As Greenwood later
wrote: "Like a good many of the younger American artists, I was attracted to
Mexico because it seemed to offer an inspiration and an opportunity that was
vital and American. American, that is, in the big sense of the New World, as
against the European influence that pervaded most painting at that time."[59]

Once in Mexico City, Greenwood met a fellow American artist named Pablo
O'Higgins, a member of Mexico's Communist Party since 1927 and a former
assistant to Rivera. Although both Marion and Grace Greenwood would also
become rather close to Rivera, neither sister ever studied with him or worked as
his assistant. Instead, O'Higgins taught Marion the rudiments of mural composition and technique (talents she later passed on to her sister) and helped
them both obtain commissions. He was also an insider who served as an important model for the success that a committed American could find in the
Mexico City art world.

Refugees from modern urban life, Herbst, Hermann, and Marion Greenwood soon fled the noisy capital for Taxco, a colonial town in the state of Guerrero that was then emerging as an important tourist destination. In January
1933, Greenwood received her first commission from the American owners of
the Hotel Taxqueño, a restored colonial mansion with modern conveniences.
This was not only a case of Americans helping a fellow citizen but an early example of private-sector appropriation of muralism for commercial purposes.
*Taxco Market* covers a small and irregular space on one wall of the hotel stair-
way, a constricted site that Greenwood used to her advantage. The fresco features local residents in the shaded plaza in front of Taxco's church of Santa
Prisca. Seated women sell pottery, fruits, and vegetables, while other peasants
carry bundles or merely watch and wait in the distance. As sites rich in local
culture, market scenes had been featured in the murals and easel paintings of
Rivera and other artists. For audiences in the United States, these scenes also
signaled a dramatic difference from increasingly sanitized and depersonalized
systems of retailing. Greenwood's emphasis on traditional costumes and her
elimination of any signs of modernization helped create an image of Taxco as
timeless, devoid of evidence of political or social progress, perfect for a relaxing
tourist.

Despite the relative conservatism of this first mural, which was not much
different from typical commercial postcard views, Greenwood began to move
politically to the left. She was inspired not only by the politics of Herbst,

Hermann, and O'Higgins but by a view, especially prevalent during the Depression, that Mexican community life was superior to American individualism. As she explained to her mother: "The world is in a terrible mess, and when people begin to have a group feeling instead of worrying about their own little lives . . . things will begin to straighten themselves out."[60] She connected this new political awareness to her practice as an artist: "In making frescos I have to study history and the Indians here, for the subject and themes have to be significant, not playing around with easel pictures—Herbst is teaching me all about Communism which gives one a wonderfully hopeful slant on life and it's something you can grasp, it's tangible and useful."[61]

Marion Greenwood's second fresco, *Landscape and Economy of Michoacán*, painted in 1933–34 for the Universidad Michoacana de San Nicolás de Hidalgo in Morelia, the Michoacán state capital, reveals a subtle but important transition in her understanding of the purpose of public art. Although the mural emphasizes local customs in a premodern setting, it takes labor rather than commerce as its basic theme. Greenwood was invited to paint the mural by the university's rector, Gustavo Corona, who certainly saw himself following in the footsteps of José Vasconcelos. Though her prior experience and radiant looks may have persuaded Corona to give Greenwood this important commission, the fact remains that any artist willing to make the trip would probably have been welcomed with open arms. Indeed, in the mid-1930s four other Americans, including Marion's sister Grace, obtained commissions from cultural and political leaders in Morelia eager to elevate their provincial city.

*Landscape and Economy of Michoacán* covers a broad horizontal space along a patio corridor in the university's main building (plate 18). This larger, more public site caused Greenwood some anxiety at the start of the project, prompting a self-justifying letter to Herbst (who had returned home in May 1933): "I'm afraid I have nothing to say, which has not been said before in the way of social significance and political attitudes . . . by Orozco and Rivera and many others. I am simply going to paint these people as I feel them in all their sadness, their apathy, and beauty. Hammers and sickles, and historical periods and personalities have been done to death. I have only become class-conscious in the last year, it would be an affectation for me to paint the usual propaganda at this period when I have nothing original to offer, whereas if I paint something I feel it might have much more significance."[62] Ultimately, however, Greenwood followed an example set by Rivera in the Ministry of Public Education. She addressed the region's geographic and cultural characteristics, focusing on three aspects of the rural economy she observed around Lake Pátzcuaro: fish-ing and repairing nets, harvesting wheat and corn, and manufacturing utilitarian folk crafts, specifically reed mats and pottery. As in Taxco, Greenwood emphasized Mexico's timeless folkways, but now she made their daily struggles a major theme of the mural. Above the central doorway, Greenwood painted a monumental Indian struggling to support the weight of a stone he carries on his back, a symbol of social burdens, but also a graphic refutation of persisting racist condemnations of Indian "laziness." She placed her signature over the skirt of a female potter grinding pigments on the right of the fresco. Notwithstanding her different nationality and the fact that she came from a middle-class background, Greenwood made a public (and even feminist) statement, identifying herself directly with an indigenous woman painter working for the community for little remuneration.

Nevertheless, the local population is again stoic, suffering the pains of its labors silently, far removed from political upheavals. This resistance to overt left-wing rhetoric reflects not only her anxieties that everything had "been said before," as well as her own tentative political consciousness, but also political complexities in Michoacán. For much of 1933, the state was marked by conflicts between those loyal to the revolutionary policies of former governor Lázaro Cárdenas and those allied with current governor Benigno Serrato, a devout Catholic. These tensions, which caused strike at the university while Greenwood was working, certainly did not encourage risk taking, and her reticence paid off: when Cárdenas visited Morelia in January 1934, during his campaign for the presidency, he viewed the fresco and thanked Greenwood for devoting a year of her life to his native state.[63]

In an article about the mural, Herbst focused on the work's deeper symbolic meanings: "The Mexican Indian has never gone down [but] his ways of life are doomed also to disappear before the onslaught of the machinery age which is slower in Mexico than in the States. Roads will come, gasoline stations sprout along the way, burros disappear. . . . But now, while there is still time, when ways of life are almost as ancient as the Indian himself, Marion Greenwood [has captured] the burden and beauty of this Indian life which is a cultural heritage not to be lost."[64] For Herbst, rural Mexico provided a reminder of what Americans had given up in the race for progress. A similar angst about the annihilation of tradition by the onslaught of modernity deeply informed contemporary discourse in both Mexico and the United States. But despite their sensitivity to cultural loss and their dedication to the proletariat, Herbst's and Greenwood's preservationist impulse was practically counterrevolutionary. In the defense of tradition, they consigned rural populations to a preindustrial age, isolated from the technological and social advances of the modern world. Like many artists, anthropologists, and writers of the time, Greenwood allowed the local population no agency to accept or reject change. It was only through an outsider's representation that the Tarascans' heritage could be saved.

Greenwood's greatest complaints about the months spent in Morelia related less to the tricky medium of fresco or the political rivalries that surrounded her commission than to the difficulty of living in an exceedingly provincial city, in a nation where women were still largely consigned to home and family. Working in public, she found her gender a hindrance primarily because she attracted several suitors and feared their advances would compromise her reputation, sexual as well as artistic. She also felt that her body restricted her as a muralist: "I wish my breasts and hips would disappear, they're in the way, and I look awful in pants."[65] In a comment that alludes to both these social and physical ordeals, she angrily confessed to Herbst: "If I was a man everything would be easier."[66]

Marion Greenwood's mural soon became a tourist attraction, and her success prompted commissions for other visiting American artists, including her sister, who was given a narrow vertical panel on the second story of the nearby Museo Michoacano. Grace Greenwood's allegorical fresco, entitled *Men and Machines* (1934), hailed the very modernity that threatened the rural folkways Marion Greenwood had memorialized. Five male workers, surrounded by enormous metal gears, seem to push and pull against unseen forces. The machine forms here play an ambiguous role, as a force with which and against which the proletariat must struggle. Grace's mural is particularly notable for its clichéd emphasis on the exclusively male realm of industry, unlike her sister's fresco, which acknowledged the importance of both genders in the rural workforce.

The Greenwoods' murals in Taxco and Morelia avoided explicit references to current politics. They reflect not only hesitant personal politics and the relative conservatism of their patrons and intended audiences, but also the fact that they were done in provincial isolation. These constraints were significantly lifted as the Greenwoods embarked on their final Mexican murals, designed for a Mexico City market initially known as Mercado del Carmen and later renamed in honor of president Abelardo Rodríguez (1932–34).

The sisters learned of the market project through Pablo O'Higgins in early 1934. While waiting for it to coalesce, they returned to New York, where they joined the Public Works of Art Project (PWAP), hoping to paint murals for Ellis

Island. When the PWAP was abruptly terminated, they returned to Mexico in October and found themselves embroiled in an even more complex situation. New lines were being drawn among the Mexican muralists. Siqueiros and several younger artists vehemently attacked the previous decade's murals as insufficiently revolutionary. In their view, these works had praised the peasant and worker but ignored ongoing class conflicts and social inequities. Such murals had tended to consolidate the rule of the current conservative regime. Though critics chiefly had in mind Rivera's frescoes in the Ministry of Public Education and National Palace, not to mention his work for American capitalists, their analysis applied equally to the Greenwoods' recent work.

Siqueiros's position emerged partly in reaction to Rivera's hegemony, partly to discredit Rivera's sympathies with Trotskyism, and partly to revitalize the discourse of muralism. In a 1934 article for the left-wing publication *New Masses*, Siqueiros attacked Rivera as a "snob" and "mental tourist." This article helped launch a quarrel that would culminate in the famous Siqueiros/Rivera debate in the Mexico City Palace of Fine Arts in August 1935. Though the debate was couched in terms of a struggle between Stalinists (headed by Siqueiros) and Trotskyites (led by Rivera), both sides were marked by inconsistencies that reveal personal as well as political motives. The debate, as well as the shift in Communist Party politics toward a popular front with "bourgeois" governments against war and fascism, would leave artists, including the Greenwoods, searching for new solutions in muddied waters.[67]

This controversy coincided with the end of the Maximato (1928–34), the period when former president Plutarco Elías Calles exerted control over three relatively weak successors. The political conservatism of the Maximato had sent Rivera, Orozco, and Siqueiros to seek opportunities in the United States, but ironically, mural commissions in Mexico increased during the Rodríguez administration. Facing the effects of the depression and searching for ways to deflect growing social protest, the administration promoted murals as one strategy for releasing tensions. Artists too young or inexperienced to have participated in the 1920s found official mural commissions through two progressive campaigns to improve Mexico City's infrastructure: the Ministry of Public Education's new primary schools and the Abelardo L. Rodríguez Market, sponsored by the Department of the Federal District (or DDF).

The Rodríguez Market, a bulky neocolonial edifice covering two square blocks, was a linchpin in the revitalization of a downtown working-class district. Murals were considered integral to the building, which included a theater, day care center, and offices of the Department of Civic Action, the cultural wing of the Federal District government and direct patron of the murals. The bureaucrats in charge were less interested in the art than in the propaganda value of the market as a symbol of the hygiene and modernization bestowed by a benevolent "revolutionary" regime.[68]

While the patrons encouraged themes related to nutrition and food distribution, most of the ten selected muralists soon shifted their attention to labor disputes, antifascist rallies, and Depression-era "readjustments" in the workforce. In part, this reveals the influence of the League of Revolutionary Writers and Artists (or LEAR), an organization founded by O'Higgins and others in 1933 and closely associated with the Communist Party.[69] Given the Rodríguez administration's anticommunism, however, LEAR kept its involvement out of the press. To calm official anxieties, the poet Antonio Mediz Bolio, head of the Department of Civic Action, supervised the political content of the preliminary sketches, while Diego Rivera was charged with approving their visual content. Rivera, however, seems to have been relatively lax in his role. For the most part, the muralists were allowed to do as they pleased, provided all work was completed within their contract's time frame. This was less a sign of government sympathies with their radical content than tolerance of the muralists' rhetoric as a smoke screen for the regime's conservative policies.

The Greenwoods were assigned a complex arrangement of walls covering almost three hundred square meters in the northeast corner of the building. The murals begin with small panels that face each other in a ground-floor foyer. From there, the walls expand into twin stairwells that lead to the second floor, where they meet in a single shared wall. The richly colored compositions lure visitors up the stairs, despite competition from the sights and smells of nearby stalls. The Greenwoods used Rivera's stairwell mural in the Ministry of Public Education as a model. Each began with images related to the raw materials (canals, mines), and then, just as Rivera moved upward through the Mexican landscape, the Greenwoods created a vertical progression emphasizing increasing industrialization and class consciousness. Like Rivera, they did research, including on-site visits, to ensure the "authenticity" of their subjects, thus building their political thesis in part on documentary facts. They both sought to draw viewers' attention to struggles affecting Mexico's rural and urban workforce, and to the threatening connections between fascism and capitalism made in the Communist press. O'Higgins had insisted that they "get immediate demands up on the walls with as little allegory as possible." In a letter to Herbst, Marion Greenwood clarified the issue: "Propaganda in art is most difficult these days because if you paint revolution, the people think it has already taken place. . . . All the government buildings have the most radical posters on them—'Down with Imperialism, Fascism,' 'Workers of the world, unite!' . . . The result is the most hopeless confusion in the minds of people— The only way to solve it in painting is to state the present miserable conditions but you don't dare paint the way out—if you don't want to fool the people."[70] Such comments reflect the ongoing debates over public art in a nation where revolutionary promises had yet to be fulfilled. Although both did eventually include "radical posters" in their murals, they are justified by their placement within a much more complex leftist framework.

Marion Greenwood's entire project is known today by the title *The Industrialization of the Countryside* (plate 19). In the ground-floor foyer, she painted the Jamaica terminal, where produce arrived by canal from agricultural zones in the city's south. By making loose reference to the DDF's ongoing restoration of the Jamaica Market and nearby canals, she presented the city government as an active force in improving urban life. On the east wall of the stairwell itself, peasants at work are juxtaposed with capitalist authorities (foreman, monopolist, and bookkeeper) to reveal the social problems lurking behind an otherwise blissful market scene. Greenwood reinforced the modernity of the setting through details like trucks and workers' overalls. The central or landing wall includes both generalized political commentaries and tragic vignettes of individual suffering. Here Greenwood moved far beyond the naturalistic spaces of her earlier work. Different scales are dramatically juxtaposed, and disparate activities and locales are piled up in a relatively shallow field. This sophisticated play between interrelated forms and actions, which conceal the underlying compositional structure, was one of the most important visual strategies she learned from Rivera's frescoes. She framed this wall with expanded treatments of the farmer (harvesting and processing sugar) and the worker (in a steel mill), the twin foundations of socialist society. Between them, two oversize fists hold a ticker tape: this sinuous emblem of capital floats above a banker, defended by a line of soldiers. In a call to arms, however, a group of workers threatens this display of authority.

The most chaotic scenes appear on the west wall. A collapsing bank facade and a tilted, cramped perspective create an unstable composition that leads to scenes of social strife. A line of marching soldiers, a Nazi flag, gun barrels, and a tank underscore Greenwood's belief that fascism, emerging from economic and social trauma, supported by the church and technology, means war. To the right, stevedores strike against a shipment of petroleum in an industrial port, perhaps Tampico. Here Greenwood made an explicit reference to her historical moment: an explosion of strikes gripped Mexico in 1935 as inflation rapidly eroded wages. Through inscribed red banners, she encouraged working-class resistance to war and fascism through the boycott of war materials, including oil. By tracing a progression from the ancient tranquillity of the canals to contemporary protests by industrial workers, Marion Greenwood summarized the complexities of Mexico's political and economic situation in the mid-1930s.

Grace Greenwood's mural cycle, known as *Mining*, follows a similar trajectory (plate 20). The ground-floor panel depicts a mining tragedy set deep within the earth. More explicitly proletarian than her sister's, the panel rallies visitors to commiserate with distant comrades. Other workers in this inventory of mining tasks push upward into a cutaway view of a mountain, situated in the mining town of Real del Monte, Hidalgo. On the remainder of the west wall, ore is transformed into molten silver while a foreman counts ingots. Like the seated accountant counting bundles of sugar cane in her sister's mural, this figure symbolizes the watchful presence of capitalism and is one of many iconographic parallels uniting the stairwells. Grace Greenwood divided her landing wall into two horizontal sectors. Above, money is coined at a mint. Two men representing local and foreign bankers dip their hands into a bin of gold coins (equivalent of the ticker tape in a corresponding location in Marion's mural) while a worker below looks on in anger. Like her sister, Grace too contrasted workers' starvation wages with gleaming wealth. Surprisingly, the most prominent figure, a worker in overalls in the foreground, remains passive, although others gesture aggressively toward the bankers.

On the south wall, Grace also moved from latent class conflict to actual revolt, here at a munitions factory. Outside, clusters of strikebreakers subdue strikers with poison gas. Inside, the tedium of factory labor is revealed by two lines of workers, whose bent backs resemble the tiers of shell cases before them. At the far left, a hint of triumph is indicated by a group of armed workers who have entered the factory. This focus on the munitions factory completes her survey of the life cycle of metals, moving from the extraction of precious metals to the destructive power of iron and steel.

Both sisters concluded their cycles with equally strong condemnations of war and fascism, the twin evils to be defeated by the Popular Front. The small panel at the top of the stair completes and joins the visual narratives in the stairwells. An urban worker and a campesino cooperate in the hanging and decoration of a red banner bearing the Communist Party slogan: "Workers of the World, Unite!" The wall serves as a concluding metaphor not only for the murals themselves but for the Greenwoods' own practice. The two workers

might even be read as symbols for the two young Americans, artists who had
adopted the overalls and wages of the working class to bring their message directly to the people. But whether because of the requisites of social realism, a
modest rejection of self-portraiture, or their reluctance to fully identify themselves with their proletarian subjects, the Greenwoods made their proxies men:
perhaps an overtly feminist statement, here at the conclusion of their greatest endeavor, would have questioned the very spirit of equality that had given
them this opportunity. In fact, men are the leading actors in both stairwells,
further evidence that the tropes of proletarian art were hard to avoid. And despite the internationalism of the Communist slogan, both sisters emphasized
easily identifiable Mexican types and events, surely to make the works personally relevant to their local proletarian audience.

Marion and Grace Greenwood successfully completed their murals in early
1936, just a few days after their contractual deadline of December 31, 1935. Yet
some of their colleagues, including Pablo O'Higgins, were dismissed before
their own murals were finished. The political transformations that emerged
as Cárdenas broke with Calles's conservative control in mid-1935 had left the
young muralists with new bureaucratic patrons who were hardly committed to
the glory of a past regime. The explicit political content of some of the murals
may also have contributed to the withdrawal of official support, though the
DDF was careful to emphasize that the contractual deadline, rather than cen-
sorship, was at issue. But a broader change in government propaganda policy
was also under way. One journalist noted that it had become essential "to use
every possible means to fight off a counterrevolutionary coup which the Cardenistas thought was imminent as a result of renewed Callista agitation in
1936. The press, the radio, the poster became the favored media. Funds were
withdrawn from mural work and shunted to more direct publicity."[71] Radio
programs, magazines, conferences, films, and "revolutionary posters" orches-
trated by the regime's Department of Press and Propaganda (or DAPP) took
precedence over more fixed, if less ephemeral, fresco paintings. Indeed, despite its radical reputation, the Cárdenas administration sponsored few murals:
Rivera, Orozco, and O'Higgins received just one federal commission each between 1934 and 1940.

In April 1936, soon after Marion and Grace Greenwood returned to the
United States following their extended residence in Mexico, the *Washington
Post* reported that Rivera had named them "the greatest living women mural
painters."[72] Rivera's personal ranking of the Greenwoods may not be that surprising, given that both were influenced by his work and that he had supervised

their murals in the Rodríguez Market. But in 1936 there were hardly any female muralists in Mexico, and none of greater importance than these two sisters. Indeed, although they benefited from the fact that other women had worked as assistants on earlier projects, the Greenwoods were the first women of any nationality to create important murals in Mexico.[73] In part, this is because even in postrevolutionary Mexico women were discouraged from assuming overly public roles. Though one could become an artist or even an art dealer, it was less easy to leave home to work on the scaffolds, wearing overalls like a common worker. Women muralists, by violating expected standards of dress and adopting a public role, had a difficult struggle. But the Greenwoods were also in the right place at the right time: eager to work in provincial locales where hotel owners or cultural officials hoped to bring muralism to new audiences; close allies of the well-connected Pablo O'Higgins; living in Mexico at the crest of a second wave of mural commissions following the renaissance of the early 1920s.

The Mexican experience of the Greenwoods reminds us of the crucial interrelationship between mural painting in the United States and Mexico, perhaps the only time in history when the art of the former was significantly dependent on the achievements of the latter. Like all the Americans who worked as muralists in Mexico in the 1930s, Marion and Grace Greenwood returned home to undertake new commissions under the federal arts projects of the Roosevelt administration, bringing direct experience with the Mexican model to audiences in the United States. And yet their American murals of the late 1930s and early 1940s kept to the restrictions of their New Deal patrons. They are not only smaller in scale, but entirely (and not surprisingly) devoid of revolutionary rhetoric, serving instead to confirm that the "American way of life" endured.

The Greenwoods' status as Americans working in Mexico ratified the international importance of Mexican muralism, just as Rivera, Orozco, and Siqueiros had when they brought their techniques and messages to the United States earlier in the 1930s. And if the Greenwoods' first murals were limited by the relative conservatism of their patrons, their Mexican context ultimately allowed and even encouraged them to create monumental and radical images that would never have been permitted in the United States. Their embrace of Marxist rhetoric may have been tentative, but even as fellow travelers, in the Rodríguez Market the sisters conquered the technical and compositional difficulties of fresco to create among the most powerful antifascist and proletarian works of their day.

# Notes

### FRIDA KAHLO

This section on Frida Kahlo is an excerpt from Sarah A. Lowe, *Frida Kahlo*, Universe Series on Women (New York: Universe, 1991), and has been reprinted with the permission of the author.

1. Studies of Frida abound. Among those in English, see Gannit Ankori, *Her Selves: Frida Kahlo's Poetics of Identity and Fragmentation* (Westport: Greenwood Press, 2002); Malka Drucker, *Frida Kahlo* (Albuquerque: University of New Mexico Press, 1995); Hayden Herrera, *Frida: A Biography of Frida Kahlo* (New York: Harper and Row, 1983); Margaret Lindauer, *Devouring Frida: The Art History and Popular Celebrity of Frida Kahlo* (Hanover: University Press of New England, 1999); and Martha Zamora, *Frida Kahlo: The Brush of Anguish* (San Francisco: Chronicle Books, 1990). For Frida Kahlo's paintings, see "Orazio Centaro's Art Images on the Web," www.ocaiw.com/catalog.

2. Anna Macías, *Against All Odds: The Feminist Movement in Mexico to 1940* (Westport, Conn.: Greenwood Press, 1982), 40; Elizabeth Salas, *Soldaderas in the Mexican Military: Myth and History* (Austin: University of Texas Press, 1990).

3. Frances Toor, *A Treasury of Mexican Folkways* (1947; New York: Bonanza Books, 1985), 310, 411–12.

4. Rupert Garcia, *Frida Kahlo: A Bibliography and Biographic Introduction* (Berkeley: University of California, Chicano Studies Library Publications Unit 3, 1983), 14.

5. See Terry Smith, "From the Margins: Modernity and the Case of Frida Kahlo," *Block* 8 (Hertfordshire, England) (August 1983): 11–23; and "Further Thoughts on Frida Kahlo," *Block* 9 (September 1983): 34–37. The painting can be found at www.ocaiw.com.

6. Frida Kahlo to Dr. Leo Eloesser, June 14, 1931. Cited in Herrera, *Frida*, 127.

7. Frida Kahlo, interview with Parker Lesley, Mexico City, May 27, 1939. Transcription courtesy of Hayden Herrera.

8. Ibid.

9. Gloria Giffords, *Mexican Folk Retablos: Masterpieces on Tin* (Tucson: University of Arizona Press, 1974), 47.

10. Raquel Tibol, *Frida Kahlo: Crónica, testimonios y aproximaciones* (Mexico City: Ediciones de Cultura Popular, 1977), 50.

11. See Emmanuel Pernoud's insightful essay, "Une autobiographie mystique: La peinture de Frida Kahlo," *Gazette de Beaux Arts* 101 (January 1983): 43–47.

12. Cited in Herrera, *Frida*, 379.

13. See, for example, Whitney Chadwick, *Women Artists and the Surrealist Movement* (Boston: Little Brown, 1985); and Erika Billeter and José Pierre, eds., *La femme et le surréalisme*, exhibition catalog, Lausanne, Musée Cantonal des Beaux Arts, 1987–88.

14. See Grace E. Porter, "The Fertile Torment of Frida Kahlo" (M.A. thesis, University of Maryland, 1981), which surveys the many opinions on Kahlo's relationship to surrealism.

15. Automatism is a means of moving beyond conscious thought to get at the unconscious. Surrealists also believed that accidents were intended to unlock the unconscious. With biomorphism they referred to abstract shapes resembling actual organic forms.

16. André Breton, *Manifeste du surrealisme* (Paris, 1924), 24, cited in William J. Rubin, *Dada, Surrealism and Their Heritage* (New York: Little, Brown, 1977), 64.

17. Bertram Wolf, "Rise of Another Rivera," *Vogue* 92 (October–November 1938): 64.

18. The problematic relation of "primitive" art to modern art has been addressed in reviews of the controversial exhibition Primitivism in Twentieth Century Art. See articles by Hal Foster, especially "The 'Primitive' Unconscious of Modern Art, or White Skin Black Masks," in *Recordings: Art, Spectacle, Cultural Politics*, ed. Hal Foster (Port Townsend, Wash.: Bay Press, 1985), 181–208; and James Clifford, *The Predicament of Culture: Twentieth Century Ethnography, Literature and Art* (Cambridge: Harvard University Press, 1988), 189–214, 117–51.

19. André Breton, "Frida Kahlo de Rivera," preface to *Frida Kahlo (Frida Rivera)* (New York: Julien Levy Gallery, 1938), reproduced and translated in *Frida Kahlo and Tina Modotti*, exhibition catalog, organized by Laura Mulvey and Peter Wollen (London: Whitechapel Art Gallery, 1982).

20. Ibid.

21. Susana Gamboa, "Portrait of the Artist," *Art News and Review* (London) 4 (March 21, 1953): 1.

22. Herrera, *Frida*, 180.

23. See Susan Gubar, "'The Blank Page' and Female Creativity," in *Writing and Sexual Difference*, ed. Elizabeth Abel (Chicago: University of Chicago Press, 1982), 73–94.

24. Frida Kahlo to Dr. Eloesser, undated. Cited in Herrera, *Frida*, 171–72.

25. Frida Kahlo, interview by Parker Lesley, Mexico City, May 27, 1939. Transcription courtesy of Hayden Herrera.

26. For a discussion on the problematic position of women in surrealism, see Rudolf E. Kuenzli, "Surrealism and Misogyny," in "Surrealism and Women," special issue, *Dada/Surrealism*, no. 18 (1990): 17–26.

### MARIA IZQUIERDO

27. For an early groundbreaking analysis of the Mexico City avant-garde and Izquierdo's place within it, see Olivier Debroise, *Figuras en el trópico, plástica mexicana, 1920–1940* (Mexico City: Ediciones Oceana, 1984).

28. Villaurrutia, in an interview with Febronio Ortega; see "Conversación con un escritor," *Revista de Revistas*, April 10, 1932, 24–25.

29. Salvador Oropesa, *The Contemporáneos Group: Rewriting Mexico in the Thirties and Forties* (Austin: University of Texas Press, 2003). Oropesa describes the Contemporáneos' cultural interests as "polyphonic" (xiii).

30. Gabriel Garcia Maroto, "La obra de Diego Rivera," *Contemporáneos* 1, no. 1 (June 1928): 43–75.

31. Recalled by Ermilo Abreu Gómez, "Contemporáneos," in *Las revistas literarias de México* (Mexico City: INBA, 1963), 166. Rivera parodied several members of the group in a panel on the third floor at the Ministry of Public Education, by depicting them as decadent aesthetes.

32. Biographical information is drawn from an unsigned typescript located in the María Izquierdo Archive, Fondo Especiales, Biblioteca del Centro Nacional de las Artes, Mexico City; Sylvia Navarrete, "María Izquierdo," in *María Izquierdo* (Mexico City: Centro Cultural/Arte Contemporáneo, 1988), 59–109; Elizabeth Ferrer, curator, *The True Poetry: The Art of María Izquierdo* (New York: Americas Society Art Gallery, 1997); Luis-Martín Lozano and Teresa del Conde, *María Izquierdo, 1902–1955* (Chicago: Mexican Fine Arts Center Museum, 1996).

33. Diego Rivera, "María Izquierdo," *El Universal*, September 25, 1929.

34. Diego Rivera, "Exposición de motivos para la formación del plan de estudios de la Escuela Central de Artes Plásticas de México" (1929), in *Diego Rivera: Arte y política*, ed. Raquel Tibol (Mexico City: Grijalbo, 1979), 87–94.

35. Rivera, "María Izquierdo," *El Universal*, September 25, 1929.

36. Mérida, "La Nueva Galería del Arte Moderno: The New Modern Art Gallery," *Mexican Folkways* 5, no. 4 (October–December 1929): 184–91.

37. Rivera, "María Izquierdo," exhibition catalog, Galería de Arte Moderno, November 6–17, 1929.

38. "Rufino Tamayo, pintor mexicano, nos habla de su arte," unidentified newspaper clipping, dated December 7, 1928, in Rufino Tamayo Archive, Centro de Investigación, Museo Rufino Tamayo, Mexico City; also cited in Raquel Tibol, "Cronología," in *Rufino Tamayo: del reflejo al sueño, 1920–1950* (Mexico City: Centro Cultural/Arte Contemporáneo, 1955), 50.

39. In 1947 he dismissed Izquierdo's abilities as a muralist. Arturo Adame Rodríguez, "Existe monopolio en la pintura, dice María Izquierdo," *Excelsior*, February 13, 1947, 1; and "María Izquierdo vs. Los Tres Grandes," *El Nacional*, October 2, 1947, sec. 2, p. 4. In her essay on Izquierdo's nationalism in the 1940s, Robin Greeley explores this incident. Robin Adele Greeley, "Painting Mexican Identities: Nationalism and Gender in the Work of María Izquierdo," *Oxford Art Journal* 23, no. 1 (2000): 51–72.

40. Castellanos's *Two Nudes* is in the collection of the Museo de Arte Moderno, Mexico City.

41. Clark, *The Painting of Modern Life: Paris in the Art of Manet and His Followers* (London: Thames and Hudson, 1985), 123–26.

42. The strategy of challenging canonical systems by abusing them ironically is discussed in Oropesa, *The Contemporáneos Group*, 19.

43. A great many of these works are illustrated in Navarrete, "María Izquierdo"; and Ferrer, *The True Poetry*.

44. See my discussion of *Circus Bareback Rider* (1932), Jack S. Blanton Museum, in Gabriel Pérez-Barreiro and Courtney Gilbert, eds., *Latin American Art in the Collection of the Jack S. Blanton Museum* (Austin: University of Texas Press, 2005).

45. Xavier Villaurrutia, "María Izquierdo," *Mexican Folkways* 7, no. 2 (August–September 1932): 138–42.

46. See, for example, Villaurrutia's "Nocturne: The Statue," published in *Contemporáneos*, no. 6 (November 1928): 324–25. In later editions, this poem appears with a dedication to the painter Agustín Lazo; see *Xavier Villaurrutia: Obras*, vol. 6, ed. Miguel Capistrán, Ali Chumacero, and Luís Mario Schneider (Mexico City: Fondo de Cultura Económica, 1966), 45.

47. My thinking to this point is informed by Marcia Brennan's observations on Georgia O'Keeffe; see her *Painting Gender, Constructing Theory: The Alfred Stieglitz Circle and American Formalist Aesthetics* (Cambridge: MIT Press, 2000).

48. Jorge Cuesta, "La pintura de María Izquierdo," exhibition catalog, "17 acuarelas de María Izquierdo," February 1933, Frances Toor Gallery, Mexico City.

49. José Gorostiza, "La pintura de María Izquierdo," typescript original dated February 1, 1933, in the María Izquierdo Archive, Galería de Arte Mexicano, Mexico City; probably presented at the opening of Izquierdo's exhibition; also published in *El Universal Ilustrado*, February 20, 1933, and included in the catalog "Exposición María Izquierdo: Oleos y acuarelas," Avenida Juárez 71, November 24–December 2, 1933.

50. Celestino Gorostiza's comments appear to have been presented at the closing of Izquierdo's exhibition at Frances Toor's gallery in February 1933; they were later published as "María Izquierdo, pintora mexicana," in *El Universal Gráfico*, November 1933, thus coinciding with her exhibition of oils and watercolors, held at a gallery on Avenida Juárez from November 24 to December 2, 1933.

51. Ibid.

52. Although the members of the Taller group were careful to distinguish themselves from what they termed the "intellectualism" of the Contemporáneos, they too assumed a universal perspective, which they placed, however, in the service of "destroying the bourgeoisie." See Octavio Paz, "Poesía mexicana moderna" (1954), in *Las peras del olmo* (Mexico City: Imprenta Universitaria, 1957), 72–75; reprinted in *Taller 1938–41*, facsimile ed. (Mexico City: Fondo de Cultura Económica, 1982), 10–12.

53. Rafael Solana, "María Izquierdo," *Taller* 1 (December 1938): 65.

54. Ibid., 65–80.

55. André Breton, "Frida Kahlo de Rivera," in *Surrealism and Painting* (Boston: ArtWorks/MFA Publications, 2002), 141–44. Breton's essay was originally written for Kahlo's exhibition at the Julien Levy Gallery, New York City, November 1938.

## MARION AND GRACE GREENWOOD

56. See James Oles, *South of the Border: Mexico in the American Imagination, 1914–1947* (Washington: Smithsonian, 1993).

57. In part because "American art" is the specific name of a field of study, and because "North American" can be problematic, the adjective "American" will at times be used in this essay to refer to the United States only.

58. For details and additional images, see Oles, "The Mexican Murals of Marion and Grace Greenwood," in *Out of Context: American Artists Abroad*, ed. Laura Fattal and Carol Salus (Westport: Greenwood Press, 2003); and *Las hermanas Greenwood en México* (Mexico City: Conaculta, 2000). See also Elinor Langer, *Josephine Herbst* (New York: Warner Books, 1985), esp. 140–45.

59. "My Murals in Mexico and the United States" (ca. 1941), 4. Marion Greenwood Archive, courtesy Robert Plate (MGA).

60. Marion Greenwood (MG) to her mother, April 30, 1933 (MGA). For a similar vision, see Stuart Chase, *Mexico: A Study of Two Americas* (New York: Macmillan, 1931).

61. MG to her mother, May 8, 1933 (MGA).

62. MG to Josephine Herbst, June 22, 1933. Josephine Herbst Papers, Yale Collection of American Literature, Beinecke Rare Book and Manuscript Library, Yale University (JHP).

63. S. L. A. Marshall, "Two Pretty American Sisters Find Adventure Painting Pictures on Mexican Walls," *Detroit News*, March 29, 1936.

64. Josephine Herbst, "The Artist's Progress," *Mexican Life* 11, no. 3 (March 1935): 24.

65. MG to JH, December 3, 1933 (JHP).

66. MG to JH, September 13, 1933 (JHP).

67. See Maricela González Cruz Manjarrez, *La polémica Siqueiros-Rivera: Planteamientos estético-políticos, 1934–1935* (Mexico City: Museo Dolores Olmedo Patiño, 1996).

68. Ramón Alva Guadarrama, Angel Bracho, Raúl Gamboa, Antonio Pujol, Pedro Rendón, Miguel Tzab, and O'Higgins also painted murals in the market. Isamu Noguchi, the last to join, created a cement relief adjacent to the Greenwoods' murals: see Oles, "International Themes for a Working Class Market: Noguchi in Mexico," *American Art* 15 (summer 2001): 10–33.

69. See Verna Carleton Millan, *Mexico Reborn* (Boston: Houghton Mifflin, 1939), 174. See also Francisco Reyes Palma, "La LEAR y su revista de frente cultural," *Memoria* 71 (October 1994): 25–31, 35–38.

70. O'Higgins to Grace Greenwood (GG) and MG, June 12, 1934 (MGA); MG to JH, December 15, 1934 (JHP).

71. J. H. Plenn, *Mexico Marches* (Indianapolis: Bobbs-Merrill, 1939), 339.

72. "Marion Greenwood Applauded for Steady Rise to Mural Fame," *Washington Post*, April 12, 1936.

73. The only other women who completed murals in Mexico in the 1930s were the American Ryah Ludins and the Mexican Aurora Reyes.

# *Mestizaje* and Musical Nationalism in Mexico

MARCO VELÁZQUEZ AND MARY KAY VAUGHAN

Contrary to official myth, Mexican musical nationalism was not born of the 1910 revolution. It was under way in the nineteenth century, when with optimistic cosmopolitanism it expressed a desire to join the circle of modern nations. Revolutionary musical nationalism had similar aspirations but delved more self-consciously inward to celebrate Mexican traditions and creativity in both classical and commercial popular music. The shift stemmed from initiatives of cultural actors within and outside governments in response to Porfirian and cosmopolitan musical trends; the democratizing, nationalizing dimensions of the revolution; and the emergence of the mass media. Within a broad process of secularization, musical nationalism was a movement of *mestizaje* or mixture—the intermingling of musics and musicians, rural and urban, regional, national, and transnational, classical and popular.

### Creating the Musical Nation: Nineteenth-Century Antecedents

The foreign invasions and wars that ravaged Mexico from 1810 to 1867 catalyzed musical nationalism. They introduced genres, instruments, musical formations, and repertoires and provoked a patriotic musical response. *Corridos*, popular news broadcasts in song, celebrated national defense and demonized the interloper.[1] The brass band, introduced in the French Revolution, became a major arm of war and nation-state formation. The conservative leader Antonio López de Santa Anna brought the Catalan bandmaster Jaime Nunó from Cuba to create a national network of military bands that numbered 230 by 1854. In a competition that Santa Anna convoked in 1853, Nunó wrote Mexico's national anthem. When crowds flocked to the concerts of the large bands accompanying the French and Austrian invaders in 1861, their Liberal opponent, Benito Juárez, ordered his military chiefs to create *cuerpos filarmónicos* and National Guard bands everywhere.[2]

From these emerged the municipal, town, military, and police bands that became the most popular musical form in the more peaceful decades after 1870. Bands opened new sound possibilities, musical and social sensibilities, associations, disciplines, and demand. They mixed regional with national and cosmopolitan repertoires, adding opera overtures, polkas, mazurkas, waltzes, and marches that had become newly accessible through sheet music. Bands became central to patriotic ritual. As fountains in town squares gave way in the Porfiriato to bandstands, musicians drew crowds to Independence Day and Cinco de Mayo celebrations.[3]

In indigenous communities, bands catalyzed musical mestizaje. They may have been expressive of factionalism and social differentiation, but they also helped to integrate communities suffering from the ruptures of war, the privatization of communal lands, and market growth. In concerts for visiting dignitaries, they presented a unified image to the outside world. In ceremonies in which village leaders passed their canes of command to new officers, they sanctified an internal order. In varying equations, the new bands coexisted with the *chirimía*, the sacred reed and drum ensemble that accompanied religious, life cycle, community, and curing rituals.[4] While preserving old forms of sociability, bands forged linkages to new imagined communities. In Oaxaca, Macedonio Alcalá's waltz "Dios nunca muere," with its plaintive, sentimental chords and graceful rhythms, became the state hymn. In an era of official anticlericalism, it linked patriotism with God. Still today, when they hear the waltz, Oaxaqueños stand and place their right hands on their hearts.

At a level removed from the bands was the Orquesta Típica. In 1884, the first Orquesta formed in Mexico City with the support of the National Conservatory. Its musicians performed in *charro* costume under the direction of Miguel Lerdo de Tejada. With chords, psaltery, wind instruments, harps, and marimbas, they played popular waltzes and romantic songs. "Aires nacionales mexicanos," their obligatory piece — particularly at international performances such as the Pan-American Exposition in Buffalo in 1901 — was a potpourri of traditional songs that included "Cielito lindo." They delighted Mexican elites and the aspiring middle classes — women with their parasols and men in their top hats who strolled in their finery in city parks and central plazas. With time, those of more modest means frequented these public spaces to enjoy the music. Their songbook, published in 1894, rapidly sold out.[5]

Improved transportation, communication, and urbanization in the late nineteenth century furthered the proliferation of regional popular musics and their transnational and national articulation. Of Moorish Andalusian origin, the *son* is a secular dance of courtship performed with skilled footwork (*zapa-*

*teado*) as the male circles the modest, alluring virgin until he conquers her. Its poetic or ironic verse is as important as its seductive rhythms and melodies. In Mexico, it acquired regional forms shaped by local criollo, mestizo, African, and indigenous traditions. The *jarabe tapatío* in Jalisco, the *huapango* in the Huasteca region of eastern Mexico, and the *sandunga* from the Tehuantepec Isthmus flourished in the late Porfiriato and would be iconized as national culture in music, dance, and mural painting in the 1920s.[6]

In the Porfiriato, composers responded to multiple transnational currents. Chilean and Peruvian genres, principally the *cueca*, penetrated the west coast of Guerrero and Oaxaca, giving rise to the *chilena*, a dance enjoyed far and wide in the Porfiriato.[7] Afro-Caribbean music arrived through a vigorous shipping triangle linking Havana, Veracruz, and Yucatán. In the 1880s, to the brothels, cabarets, and neighborhoods of the Gulf Coast cities, the Cubans introduced *danzón*, a genre based on a variation of the French counterdance brought to Cuba by Afro-Haitian slaves. By 1906, Mexicans listened to Cuban and Mexican orchestras play danzón on records cut by Victor and Columbia.[8]

At the turn of the century, sensual Cuban *boleros*, *habaneras*, and *claves* flooded Yucatán. At first, elites shunned the erotic African sounds and rhythms. That did not keep musicians from producing compositions, nor elite men from enjoying them in brothels. The songs quickly circulated in marketplaces and popular fiestas. The Yucatecan romantic song drew from these genres and from the Colombian *bambuco*, an African dance shaped by indigenous and Spanish traditions.[9]

A final force promoting musical nationalism came from educational institutions, particularly the National Conservatory. Until the beginning of the twentieth century, Italian influence held sway here. In 1887, a group of Conservatory musicians, including Ricardo Castro (1864–1907) and Gustavo Campo (1863–1934), broke away to found the Instituto Musical, favoring French music. Castro, who had studied in Europe, composed romantic piano pieces similar in style to Chopin and Liszt. He also wrote compositions based on Mexican melodies. His opera *Atzimba* told the story of the Spanish conquest of the Tarascan kingdom of Michoacán. Campa's opera *El rey poeta*, originally *Le roi poete* in French, celebrated Nezahualcóyotl, Aztec ruler of Texcoco.

Classical and popular music were closely linked. Conservatory graduates had limited employment opportunities and could find them in popular bands, the circus, churches, bullrings, music halls, puppet shows, elite clubs and salons, and, after 1900, movie theaters. In response to demand, they composed dozens of dances and military marches.[10]

In the first decade of the new century, classical composition flourished in dance songs. As Carlos Monsiváis notes, collaboration with poets marked this music with a profuse lyricism, bringing to an exquisite level of refinement a deeply rooted vernacular tradition. As the modernist poet Amado Nervo wrote: "To be a poet is predestination; it is to realize God in one's soul, to become the temple of the Holy Spirit."[11] A poetic waltz written for violins, psaltery, and piano became the ultimate expression of delicate, modern senti-ment. Many were composed for the perfumed salons of the aristocracy with their velvet-covered furnishings and their potted palms. Here Victorian vir-gins, their bodies imprisoned in tight corsets and ensconced in white, lightly touched the hands of eligible gentlemen, keeping a proper distance as they glided gracefully across the room. In 1899, Miguel Lerdo de Tejada composed the dance *La perjura*, with lyrics by Fernando Luna Drusina. In what Mon-siváis calls their "unabashed declaration of intimate, sexual infatuation," the poet's words scandalized Porfirian society:

> On the way to church I saw you, niña,
> Your beautiful face in flickering candlelight
> So pure and good, I loved you instantly
> Tender words I spoke to you,
> Gentle caresses I gave you
> And to see your breast filled with love
> I vowed to you to be forever true.

*La perjura* is said to mark the birth of the modern Mexican romantic song.[12]

In the first decade of the century, French influence replaced Italian at the Conservatory. In 1900 the government commissioned Gustavo Campa to visit European institutions. The purpose was to foment a Frenchification of Mexi-can culture, for to be modern was to "live in French: savoir vivre."[13] When Campa returned, the Conservatory revised its curriculum in a reorganization that enhanced the technical capacity of Mexican musicians. In the avalanche of revolution, European influence would not so much dominate as contribute to the crafting of a Mexican nationalist art music.

We emphasize European rather than specifically French influence because the two composers initially identified with revolutionary musical national-ism had studied in Germany. There, Julian Carrillo became wedded to a Ger-manic notion of compositional organicity. In the 1920s, as head of the Con-servatory, he would introduce to Mexico a modernist revolution that, like Arnold Schoenberg in Vienna, privileged new sounds (microtonality) outside the standard scale, but within a compositional unity.[14] Manuel M. Ponce, who studied in Bologna and Berlin, followed the Germanic path of incorporating popular songs into classical compositions. In 1907 he arranged the lullaby "La rancherita." In 1911 he wrote his *Rapsodia mexicana no. 1* based on the jarabe tapatío. In 1912 he composed the pathbreaking romantic song "Estrellita." In 1913 he gave his first public lecture on the subject of "music and the Mexican son."[15]

If the Frenchification of Porfirian "high" musical culture has been exaggerated, the emergence of a nationalist popular music based on Mexican traditions has been ignored. In September 1910, the Porfirian regime dedicated its energies to projecting the country's new modern image in the centennial fiestas. In this culminating moment of his long reign, Porfirio Díaz decided to visit Mexico City theaters. For this occasion, the great soprano María Conesa ("La Gatita Blanca") reappeared at the Teatro Principal. For her performance of Mexican and Spanish songs, La Gatita decided to embroider on her skirt the eagle, the emblem of the *patria* emblazoned on the national flag. This daring act of desacralization had the theater directors on pins and needles as they anticipated the response of Mexico's venerable president. After the curtain fell, they breathed sighs of relief as Porfirio Díaz and his wife, Doña Carmelita, approached the beautiful María and warmly congratulated her.[16] From then on, the Mexican eagle was often embroidered on the skirt of the twirling *china poblana*, who would emerge in the course of the revolution as a national icon and inseparable partner of the charro.

## Music and the Revolution of 1910

A few weeks later, revolutionary forces deposed Porfirio Díaz. In the revolution, they assaulted Porfirian social hierarchies, exclusions, and rules of sexual repression. It was a cultural, aesthetic, and erotic mobilization of enormous proportions and consequences.[17] As armies, fellow travelers, and refugees moved south from the northern states, they came into contact with one another. As they occupied the capital and central and southern states, they mingled with people from Mexico City, Puebla, Jalisco, Yucatán, Campeche, and Oaxaca. Campesinos from the South invaded pueblos and cities in central Mexico. The brass bands accompanying the armies exchanged repertoires in a vigorous musical effervescence and nationalization that combined cosmopolitan with more popular, regional, and rural traditions. This music was militarized in its marches, genteel and nostalgic in its waltzes. The emerging repertoire embraced the traditional (the jarabe) and the new (the fox-trot) as dancing became part and parcel of the military experience. Its corridos were at once gay, sad, lewd, and patriotic. Soldiers sang them at night around the campfire to guitars and on top of trains as they pulled out of cities, shooting off their guns. Band music was as essential to celebrating victory as to mourning defeat. Bands even played through battles. For combat, Pancho Villa preferred the march "Jesusita de Chihuahua."[18]

This revolution invaded the capital. The theater district, south and west of the Zócalo, was jammed with people as musical reviews, comedies, and vaudeville performances took up regional themes, icons, genres, and melodies: the charro, the china, the jarabe, the sandunga, the tehuana.[19] The Orquestas Típicas multiplied and incorporated more vernacular pieces and instruments. As Rick López has noted, in 1919 the world's premier ballerina, Anna Pavlova, danced the jarabe tapatío in a modern ballet staged by Adolfo Best Maugard.[20] The jarabe was quickly incorporated into official events, school programs, and civic festivals.

In his crusade for the expression and dissemination of national culture, education minister José Vasconcelos drew on this ferment—making the jarabe (known in the United States as the Mexican Hat Dance) the centerpiece of his monumental open-air festivals replete with workers' and children's choirs, gymnastic displays, bands, and Orquestas Típicas. But Vasconcelos preferred Beethoven to Mexican art composers, and the sentimental criollo songs of popular arrangers like Mario Talavera and "Tata Nacho" (Ignacio Fernández Esperón) to those of the maestro Manuel M. Ponce. In the aftermath of revolutionary violence, Vasconcelos favored the "refined beauty" of Hispanic tradition above the blood and barbarism he associated with the indigenous legacy.[21] While he created the mandate, institutions, forms, and channels for the emergence of a nationalist aesthetics, others more daring, modern, and inclusive than he would define those aesthetics.

## The Creation of a Nationalist Art Music

As early as 1915, Constitutionalist chief Venustiano Carranza asked the Conservatory to abandon foreign models and "recover the national."[22] But what was "national" music? Trained musicians launched a prolonged, intense dispute in the press, numerous ephemeral journals, two national congresses, several contests, and the classrooms and corridors of the Conservatory and the SEP.[23] Animating the debate were a younger generation of composers (Carlos Chávez, Silvestre Revueltas, Luis Sandi, Jerónimo Baqueiro Foster, Daniel

Castañeda, Francisco Domínguez), regional band musicians such as Candelario Huizar and Estanislao Mejía, and musical historians and ethnomusicologists (Jesús Romero, Rubén Campos, Vicente T. Mendoza). Some argued that Mexican music was no more than sixty years old, limited to its participation in the nineteenth-century European canon. Others wanted to include colonial music. Although all agreed that the current rage in romantic songs was not art music, most were interested in vernacular music. But what vernacular music — criollo, mestizo, Afro-Mexican, or indigenous? How was it to be incorporated into art music: in its "pure" forms or transposed into classical harmonies? Would it be transcribed, interpreted, or represented by modernist devices that challenged classical sound—the microtonality pushed by Julián Carrillo and his students, pentatonicism, a five-note scale used by Western composers to interpret the "primitive," non-Western Other, or another experimental form? Through what genres would a Mexican music be heard? The opera, march, waltz, salon piano poem, or military march of the Porfiriato or the modernist, folkloric ballet, symphony pieces, mass choral works, and film scores preferred by the younger composers?

We tell the story of the emergence of a Mexican art music through the career of Carlos Chávez (1900–1978). At first glance, such a focus would appear to undermine recent attempts to break with an official historiography that privileges the heroics of great men. But the new scholarship is also interested in cultural politics, and Chávez was an entrepreneur who knew how to mobilize a rich transnational pool of ideas, talent, energy, and support into a new hegemonic configuration that empowered at the same time that it selected, hierarchized, and excluded. Growing up in the revolution, Chávez instrumentalized revolutionary corridos and composed a ballet with an Aztec theme.[24] He befriended the irreverent Estridentista poets who burst on the scene declaring "Death to Father Hidalgo!" and "Chopin to the electric chair!" But at his 1921 concert, he played the late romantic pieces of Debussy and Ravel, the preferences of Chávez's mentor Ponce. At the age of twenty-two, Chávez left for Europe, found it insipid, and headed for New York, where the skyscrapers, avant-garde music circles, orchestras, and jazz clubs electrified him. He arrived at a key moment in early 1924 when Gershwin debuted "Rhapsody in Blue" and French expatriates Edgard Varèse, Dane Rudhyar, and Ernest Bloch introduced modernist music. They hailed the young New Yorker Leo Ornstein's "The Wild Men's Dance" as pure Bergsonian vital energy, the primitivism they expected from this land of nature and the machine, symbol of masculine conquest, production, and the demolition of tradition. The New World whirled with sounds and rhythms that challenged the stultifying formalism of decadent Europe: city noises, sirens, honking taxicabs, buzzing railroad stations, steamship whistles, airplane propellers. Dissonance captured the New World's multiethnicity and raciality. "Dissonance is democracy," declared Dane Rudhyar. From the city's concrete as from the mountains and prairies, the artist drew creative energy.[25]

Carlos Chávez thrived in New York and returned home with a mission. He weighed in on the debate raging in the press against Julián Carrillo's essay "Sonido 13" on microtonality. In a daring assault, Chávez dismissed the older and more powerful Carrillo from the nationalist movement. "Either we become Europeanized or we forge the basis of our nationality not in forms we see derivative of these sad cases of (tardy) importation."[26] He proceeded to debut a series of bold, dissonant, polyrhythmic pieces: "Energía," "Foxtrot," "Blues," and "HP" (Horsepower).

New York critics had heard his music as essentially Mexican, which meant an imagined Indianness. Olin Downs heard Chávez "tomahawking" and "scalping" the keyboard. Paul Rosenfeld described his "primitive singsong" as "Amerindian in its rigidity and peculiar earthy coarseness. . . . Undeluded, bony and dry as [Mexico's] own high deserts and peppery as chiles . . . savage . . . dusty, abrupt and squat as Toltec divinities." In Chávez's "Sonatina for Piano" and "Energía," Rosenfeld heard the "penetrating terror" of the barbarous Other.[27] As Leonora Saavedra notes, Mexican audiences did not recognize their country in Chávez's music. One critic wrote that "HP" sounded like "the unleashed energy of a fast train. The rhythm bounces around like a racing car on an obstacle course." But Chávez understood that modernist techniques might solve technical crises in Western music while serving as a means for integrating the distinct sounds of the Mexican vernacular into a national art music with a unique place in the cosmopolitan canon.[28]

In 1926, he returned to New York, composing, premiering his music with the International Composers' Guild and the Pan American Association of Composers. In 1932, Leopold Stokowski conducted the Philadelphia Orchestra in a performance of the ballet "HP," staged shortly after Diego Rivera's exhibit at the Museum of Modern Art. While "HP" celebrated the optimistic New World vision of youthful man unlimited in his creative capacities, it took up another trope popularized in Latin America after the U.S. seizure of Cuba and Puerto Rico in 1898. Chávez juxtaposed the cold industrialism of the United States to the natural Latin America of tropical luxuriance and primitive mystery. To the sensual strains of the tango, huapango, and sandunga, great papier-mâché pineapples, coconuts, and bananas designed by Diego Rivera danced across the stage.²⁹ It is not likely that either Chávez or Rivera saw this binary as one of inevitable dominance and subordination. Both harbored skepticism about the machine and, in the midst of the Depression, probably imagined a synthesis between North and South that might banish exploitation. In retrospect, however, both contributed to the folklorization and exoticization of Latin America.³⁰

Back home in 1928, Chávez made a proposal to the Mexico City Sindicato de Filarmónicos, whose members faced a terrible crisis as the shift to sound films eliminated their movie theater jobs. He suggested the formation of the Orquesta Sinfónica de México, for which he mobilized private, public, and trade union backing. In the OSM, Chávez united two rival groups — the popular musicians known as *jazzistas* and the classical ones. He intended the orchestra to serve as a platform for new Mexican composers. His strategy was didactic: to create a musical public that was modern, sophisticated, and broad. In concert programs, he mixed familiar classical with experimental music. The orchestra's performance of John Alden Carpenter's "Iris Skyscrapers" caused such a heated critique in the press that a repeat performance completely sold out.³¹ Moving into the Palacio de Bellas Artes in 1934, the OSM played for paying audiences and, with assistance from the government, gave free concerts in parks and at the Palacio for workers and schoolchildren.

In 1928, Chávez became director of the National Conservatory. Propelling renovation already under way there, he provoked a split. More conservative musicians formed the Escuela Nacional de Música at the National University, while Chávez affiliated the Conservatory with the SEP. Ponce returned from Paris and with Jesús Romero taught musical history that integrated a broad range and chronology of Mexican music. Silvestre Revueltas came back from the United States to teach violin, conduct the Conservatory orchestra, and compose a series of pathbreaking compositions, including penetrating scores for new Mexican films. Luis Sandi headed the program in choral music, a critical element in making a nationalist art music accessible to mass publics in civic events, schools, and union halls.³²

Research focused on transcribing, recording, and filming Mexican vernacular music and dance (indigenous, mestizo, and criollo), probing its history, collecting its instruments, and creating a calendar of popular fiestas and musical events. In 1933, the Orquesta Mexicana was formed, consisting of "typical" instruments ranging from the marimba and a panoply of guitars to the more indigenous chirimía, conch shells, drums, rattles, and gourds. Teaching musical creativity and composition, Chávez, Candelario Huizar, Jerónimo Baqueiro Foster, and others trained a new generation of outstanding symphonic composers—Daniel Ayala, Juan Pablo Moncayo, Blas Galindo, and Salvador Contreras. For his "Sones de mariachi," Blas Galindo traveled to Jalisco, Michoacán, and Nayarit. Moncayo went to Veracruz to record the *sones* for his vigorous "Huapango."

When Chávez headed the SEP Departamento de Bellas Artes in 1933–34, the audience for the new production widened. The number of public concerts multiplied. Luis Sandi introduced Yaqui and Maya dances and a broad repertoire of Mexican songs to the public schools.[33] As Joy Hayes writes in this volume, the SEP radio station broadcast an array of programs featuring art and vernacular music.

Chávez was a major actor in the hegemonization of a Mexican national art music. He was a polyphonic opportunist, adopting styles to play to the moment. An experimentalist in the 1920s, he became *indigenista* ("Sinfonía india," "Cantos de México") and proletarian ("Sinfonía proletaria") in the 1930s. In the triumphalist "Obertura republicana," he became synthetically postrevolutionary Mexican. The writer Jorge Cuesta denounced Chávez as a demagogic composer of state music. Chávez contributed to a hierarchization of Mexican music—one that privileged an art music that folklorized the vernacular, selected particular genres for classicization, and categorized vernacular musics as popular, traditional, mestizo, or indigenous (see the Hayes essay in this volume). As invigorating as the new musical configurations were, they limited creative and technical possibilities. A man who sidelined rivals and awarded loyalists, Chávez marginalized Manuel M. Ponce, whose musical capacity and technical training with Nadia Boulanger and Paul Dukas in Paris allowed him to resolve compositional questions the extraordinary but less trained Silvestre Revueltas could only ask.

Chávez's power to shape a repertoire was limited, among other factors, by audience taste. Mexican publics rejected modernist experimentation. As Saveedra notes, Revueltas's dramatic dissonance captured the rupture, conflict, and fault lines in Mexican society, but concertgoing audiences preferred the melodic folkloric lyricism of his "Colorines" and "Janitzio."[34] They preferred Chávez's "Obertura republicana" with its inclusion of Porfirian marches, waltzes, and revolutionary corridos to his atonal "indigenista" music. Together with Moncayo's majestic "Huapango," these expressed the vigor, grandeur, and forward thrust of the postrevolutionary society—particularly in its decade of bourgeois triumph and consolidation in the 1940s, when Chávez directed the orchestra of the Instituto Nacional de Bellas Artes, which he founded in 1946.

## Popular Musical Nationalism

In the 1920s, Mexico City's popular, public culture eroticized in an ambience of democratization, massification, and commodification. Amid the excitement, disorder, and influx of foreign and regional styles emerged the *chica moderna* — the modern girl who took off her corset, raised her skirt, bobbed her hair, and moved her body in new, more supple, ever so suggestive ways.[35] Elites, Damas Católicas, and government reformers may have confused them with prostitutes, but the young working-class women of the time did not as a rule see themselves this way. As much as they signed up for classes at the SEP's vocational schools, they flocked to the new dance halls, where they could fox-trot, tango, and Charleston. But it was danzón that dazzled them. The new Salón México, dubbed the Cathedral of Danzón, boasted three dance floors for different social groups—one for the *clases acomodadas*, another for the aspiring middle and working classes, and a third for the truly poor. A sign in this salon read: "We ask the gentlemen not to throw their lit cigar butts on the floor so as not to burn the women's feet."[36]

In the 1920s, ambitious regional politicians used music to create and deepen their political base. In 1921, for the centennial celebrations, Felipe Carrillo Puerto, socialist governor of Yucatán, sent La Trova Yucateca to Mexico City. They composed and sang a romantic song cultivated in the peninsula's Caribbean milieu and performed over XEY radio in Mérida, "La voz del Gran Partido Socialista." Much in the Mexican tradition, the poet's lyrics were as important as the rhythm and melody. The song that won over Mexico City was "Peregrina," composed and sung by Ricardo Palermín, with lyrics by Luis Rosaldo Vega. Commissioned by Felipe Carrillo Puerto, the poem declared his love for the North American journalist, art critic, and Mexican enthusiast Alma Reed:

> Peregrina, with your divine blue eyes
> And cheeks of rose, your ruby lips
> And hair radiant as the sun,
> You left the fir trees and the virgin snow
> To seek refuge in my palm trees under the sky of
> My tropical home.[37]

In August 1927, the facade of Mexico City's Teatro Lírico glittered with multicolored lights, banners, and streamers to mark the historic moment when composers and musicians came together to compete for even greater stardom in the "Concurso de Canciones Mexicanas."[38] Tata Nacho won first prize, but Guty Cárdenas stole the show. Just twenty-one years old, the Yucatecan troubadour sang his exquisite "Nunca," with lyrics by the peninsular poet Ricardo López Méndez:

> I know I will never kiss your lips of blushing red,
> I know I can never be the passion of your life.

Overnight, Guty Cárdenas conquered Mexico City, recording his songs with fledgling Mexican companies. In 1929 he left for the United States, where he recorded with Camden Records and then with Columbia in New York at the behest of Mexican Alfonso Esparza Oteo, musical director for Latin America. Guty Cárdenas wrote and recorded over two hundred songs animated by the company of Cuban, Colombian, and Puerto Rican musicians. All cut records and mingled with Harlem jazz musicians. In 1929 and 1930, Guty Cárdenas toured the United States, singing for President Hoover and concluding with a gala performance at the Teatro Mexico in Los Angeles. At the same time, he made two of the first Hollywood sound movies: *The Daring Lady* and *The Jazz King*.[39]

Returning to Mexico, Guty Cárdenas took to the airwaves of Mexico's new premier station, XEW, created by RCA Victor associates the Azcárraga brothers and located on the edge of the capital's theater district. Guty had his own show every evening sponsored by Picot, distributors of U.S.-made anti-indigestion tablets, an enormously popular product in a city now given to an exhausting nightlife. Doubtless Guty Cárdenas took them. Like the rest of the Trova, he was excessively fond of alcohol—it was part of his bohemian persona. The medicine must have helped him sustain the discipline of his extraordinary work pace. He helped compile XEW's *Cancionero Picot*, still today Mexico's most popular songbook. A meticulous composer, he framed his songs with the verse of well-known poets, Caribbean and Mexican. The Mayanist Antonio Mediz Bolio wrote the lyrics set by Guty to a sensual melody and haunting, tropical beat in "Caminante del Mayab," a piece later learned by Mexican schoolchildren.

On April 5, 1932, Guty Cárdenas worked on proofs of "Caminante del Mayab." In the afternoon, he walked to the XEW studios to prepare his evening program. As usual, program announcer Leopoldo de Samaniego held Guty's pistol, a necessary accessory of artists, politicians, soldiers, and gangsters in those rambunctious years. That night, Guty sang "Para olvidarte a ti" with a passion that surprised even his colleagues at the studio. It would be his last performance. After the show he walked with friends along Avenida Madero to the restaurant and cantina Salón Bach, a favorite bohemian meeting place. Over drinks, they quarreled with a group of Spaniards accompanying the Flamenco singer Jaime Carbonell "El Marroquín." In the shoot-out that ensued, Guty Cárdenas was killed. Just twenty-six years old, he immediately became a national symbol and legend of romantic tragedy.

Radio contributed mightily to an ascendant musical nationalism and its mestizaje of regional and foreign rhythms, sounds, and genres. Scholars have stressed the importance of government requirements that commercial radio give preference to Mexican music, but technology, profit margins, and publics were critical factors as well. Emilio Azcárraga, the entrepreneurial wizard of XEW, knew well that radio had to cater to popular tastes. As a technology, radio created a new relationship with its publics—that of the ear. It was not a question of hearing alone, for reading aloud was a centuries-old practice. It was a matter of distance between the broadcasting voice and the listener (an absence of real bodies with the inhibiting power their presence implied) that opened space for the imagination, liberty, and intimacy, linked to new sensations of sensuality, awareness of the body, and individualization. Radio's technology also required new sounds—no longer the robust voices of operas and reviews, but the soft, insinuating voice of the male crooner and the female torch singer.[40] By contrast, in instrumental music, the sound of chords proved too thin. Radio needed brass, big bands, and orchestras.

The driving actor was the public. Radio required and privileged forms of cultural capital forged outside elite institutions—in the streets, vaudeville tents and theaters, bars, brothels, town plazas, urban slums, and well-appointed parlors where young ladies practiced the piano.[41] Both commercial radio and its listeners were caught up in a frenzied moment of change. Radio had to switch performers and repertoires constantly because publics tired quickly and demanded novelty. Hundreds of would-be stars crowded outside the doors of XEW studios. If a particular performer did not show up, the producer went into the street and picked the lucky person who had been waiting for weeks. One afternoon, remembered Angelina Brushcetta, one of Agustín Lara's wives, "a little mulatto girl appeared at our door. She had a baby in her arms. Poorly but cleanly dressed, she asked the servant if her 'paisano' Agustín Lara was in."[42] Lara received her, listened to her sing, and immediately changed her name from

María Antonia del Carmen Peregrino de Cazarote to Toña la Negra. She became his lead interpreter on XEW. Soon she toured Mexico, the United States, and Latin America. Stories like Toña's sparked the imagination and dreams of thousands of young people, dreams of success that intertwined with and engraved in them notions of Mexicanidad. In the stars, they saw themselves and their desires. It helped that the 1930s and 1940s were a period of audience participation. Performers were attentive to their fans.[43] XEW programs were open to the public. Its studios held up to eight hundred people each. Thousands auditioned to perform on *La hora del aficionado*, modeled after the U.S. Amateur Hour, or *La hora del calcetín eterno*, for which mothers, youngsters in hand, waited for hours outside the studios to launch their children's careers.[44]

We choose here the Mexican bolero, the *mariachi*, and the *canción ranchera bravía* to illustrate the intersecting processes shaping Mexican musical nationalism. Both the bolero and the canción ranchera (with its interpreters, the mariachi) spoke to the anonymity of modernity, and particularly of the modern city—of its emancipatory possibilities as well as the solitude, nostalgia, and melancholy it produced. Both were part of a demilitarization of gendered behavior, the softening of masculine violence without the loss of its pretensions to power and domination and its potential for abuse. Both suggested a new vibrant sexual femininity but tried to inscribe it and subordinate it to male privilege. Both conquered Mexico through the new mass media, creating languages of popular culture that had little to do with the central government but much to do with the centralization of the recording, radio, and film industries in Mexico City.[45]

With the bolero, Agustín Lara and other composers and lyricists brought the poetry of the Porfirian salon to the twentieth-century brothel, nightclub, movie theater, restaurant, bedroom, kitchen, and patio of the *vecindades*, where immigrants crowded together making new lives in the big city.[46] Carlos Monsiváis has argued that the bolero popularized salon lyricism, but it was this poetry expressed through the Caribbean rhythms and melodies that whispered love and desire over the Mexican airwaves. The palm tree, its branches moving gently in the tropical breeze, became the voluptuous body of woman. Lara wrote and sang:

> In your eyes glistens the emerald of the sea,
> Your mouth is the corral's pink
> In the cadences of your divine voice the rhyme of love and
> In your eyes I see the palm trees swaying in the sun.

In long-distance serenades of longing and unrequited love, Lara sang to his lovers, ex-lovers, and the women who wrote to him.[47] Above all, he sang to prostitutes:

> Every night a different love,
> Every dawn a different vision,
> Every night a different love,
> But in me your love remains.

Lara sang to the modern urban woman. Indeed, he helped to shape her, to liberate her body from corset and confessional. He won hearts, writes Guadalupe Loaeza, because he "treated ladies like prostitutes and prostitutes like ladies."[48]

As Carlos Monsiváis has so eloquently described him, Lara was the stark opposite of the state reformer's and the Catholic's model Mexican. An enraged prostitute had scarred his face.[49] He was married nine times—twice to movie star María Félix. He chain-smoked and was addicted to alcohol and marijuana. He united feminists and Damas Católicas in indignant protest. In 1936, the SEP banned his music from the schools as immoral and degenerate and counseled mothers to keep his music away from their daughters. But young girls heard Lara—often through the *sirvienta* who cleaned house to the sound of radio. Between 1935 and 1945, Agustín Lara became "the minstrel of the national soul." He sang on XEW's wildly popular *Hora azul* and his own show, *La hora última*. Emilio Azcárraga would let no one touch Lara's piano. Fresh bouquets of gladiolas, carnations, and roses graced it each evening as he played to a packed studio.

Lara's music liberated urbanizing Mexico from a stultifying Victorian and Catholic morality. In the burgeoning, dancing, singing city, he helped to legitimize and broaden the public space of pleasure—that had been banished in the Porfiriato to a subterranean bordello culture, frequented by rich men who tried to keep their wives and daughters confined to parlors, salons, and the church. Lara sang to men and women of the necessity and the joy of sensual and bodily pleasure as sources of emotional intimacy. He made such pleasure socially tolerable, but he did not liberate it from sin. Lara's music, as Monsiváis suggests, preserved women as objects of desire, essentially sexualizing the Virgin.[50] His lyrics never transcended a basic, ancient misogyny: women were the source of original sin, the downfall of men, their victimizers. Lara's shaping of a modern Mexican masculinity was certainly as important as his influence on women. In hallowing male sexuality, he also romanticized adultery and irresponsibility, cloaked in the glamour of poetic bohemianism. If Lara spoke to urban women of their sensuality, it is likely that many learned a deeper lesson—to take charge of their bodies, loves, homes, and children for which they would ultimately be responsible.

Fearing that the bolero would dominate the radio at the expense of their own understanding of Mexican popular music, many classicists and folklorists accused Lara of producing a non-Mexican music, far from the "spirit of the people," a weak imitation of that heard in Paris cafés and Harlem clubs.[51] Lara responded: "In twenty years, I have produced more than 600 songs and in all of them, I have been able to do something for Mexico. I don't care if, when my songs are sung in Norway, Sweden or Russia, they mention my name just as long as they know it as Mexican music."[52] In Latin America, the United States, and elsewhere, Lara's music, like that of other Mexican boleristas, became identified as Mexican music. The big bands of Artie Shaw, Jimmy Dorsey, and Glen Miller played them. Frank Sinatra sang Alberto Domínguez's "Frenesí" and "Perfidia," and they soared to the top of the U.S. Hit Parade. In the film *Casablanca*, couples at Rick's café in Morocco danced to "Perfidia." In Argentina, the bolero gained space alongside the tango. Even in Brazil, people liked it, although they preferred the samba.

Above all, in Mexico, the bolero became identified with the new nation. By no means did it stamp out vernacular music, but it enjoyed a wide audience. The writer Salvador Novo told of a visit to Arandas, the heart of Catholic Jalisco:

> We went to the house of the Municipal President who had a radio. . . . While we were eating a fat señor came in and sat down. He was going to sing some songs for us on his guitar. He asked the Minister of Education what he wanted to hear and the Minister said, "A corrido, a local song." The man raised his eyebrows and sang Lara's "Señora Tentación."[53]

Lara celebrated the city and a new modern erotic aesthetic. Ranchero music, which dominated radio in the 1940s and 1950s, celebrated rural Mexico—increasingly as a stylized counterpoint to the city, an evocation of nostalgia, and a unifying nationalist motif. More sexually repressed than Lara's boleros, ranchero music expressed a longing for a mythical countryside devoid of exploitation, want, conflict, and sin, populated by kindhearted hacienda owners, gallant macho lovers, fully clothed virgins, and happy peons. If Lara's music idealized the dangerous, seductive city, ranchero music made the Bajío, the heartland of the antigovernment Cristiada, the nation's "idyllic soul."[54] It iconized the rural subject as morally sincere, loving, trustworthy, and valiant in contrast to the degenerate city slicker. While it affirmed the still-rural character of the country, it was also a music that negotiated the transition to urban life. Perhaps for many (including Lara's listeners), it represented a moral compass in an urban world that seemed to have none.

Ranchero music, particularly ranchera bravía, came to be associated with mariachi bands. Mariachi is an ensemble of *sones* popular in central Jalisco, western Michoacán, and part of Nayarit, and the first mariachis in Mexico City came from central Jalisco. In 1926, the Mariachi Coculense moved to the capital, where they made their first recordings. In 1933 the group performed at the Chicago World's Fair and in the Mexican movie *Santa*. The Mariachi Vargas achieved even greater renown, dominating the airwaves in the 1930s under Silvestre Vargas's direction. In 1937, they made the first of two thousand movies. Originally consisting of vihuelas, violins, harps, and drums, the mariachis acquired their emblematic sounds in the 1930s when they incorporated trumpets. They also adopted charro costume. Although they hailed from a region passionately opposed to the antireligious policies of postrevolutionary governments and never part of the revolutionary upheaval, they were immediately incorporated into the repertoire of an emerging official national culture and memory—performing at political and commemorative events and banquets. President Cárdenas had mariachis accompany him on his political campaign and invited the Mariachis Vargas to play at his inauguration.[55]

The mariachis acquired trumpets in response to the popularity of U.S. big bands, new sound technologies, and public demand. They became interpreters of the ranchera bravía. In the 1930s, Mexican cinema, its composers (Manuel Esperón and Ernesto Cortázar), its singing stars (Tito and Pepe Guízar, Jorge Negrete), and its instrumentalists (mariachi bands) transformed the sweet bucolic ranchera of the 1920s. They mestized it with huapango elements (the falsetto, lyrical duels, and distinct rhythms) and gave it a new sound of triumphalist bravado.[56] The unexpected marketing success of the 1936 film *Allá en el Rancho Grande* in Mexico and Latin America created a new icon, the singing charro, the *galán* clad in tight black pants, silver-embroidered vest, and oversize sombrero, strutting, writes Yolanda Moreno, like something between a fighting cock and an effulgent peacock.[57] While he sang of the joys of the hacienda—courting the modest maiden, raising his pistol at the slightest offense to his honor, downing *copas* of tequila in the cantina filled with singing peons—the charro also celebrated Mexico. Jorge Negrete, star of the 1947 version of *Allá en el Rancho Grande*, gained fame and fans for his "Mexicanidad."

> I am Mexican and my country is brave,
> Word of the macho, there is no land as brave and
>     beautiful as mine.
> I am Mexican and full of pride.

This aggressive, gay, decidedly *machista* music had its female counterpart in the songs of Lucha Reyes. The former member of the all-female Trio Garnica Arsencio lost her voice while touring Europe. She returned singing from the depths of her throat in a style never before heard in Mexico. She "lavished her voice, coughing, moaning, crying, laughing, cursing"—and stopped in the middle of a number to take a drink.[58] Singing of love, abandonment, and torment, she came to personify the temperamental, passionate, strong, and tragic "mujer mexicana bravía."[59] She committed suicide in 1944. Dozens of female vocalists took up her style.

In 1947, *Así es mi tierra*, a program dedicated principally to ranchero music, became XEW's most popular show. Its dominance was fitting to this decade of buoyant demographic growth and urbanization presided over by a conservative official politics that tried to dissolve the sharp class and religious divisions of the recent past in an exuberant fiesta of Mexicanidad. Jorge Negrete brought the ranchera bravía to its heights. He synthesized the modern machismo and ideological mestizaje of the new political class to which he belonged. A former army officer and head of the government-affiliated National Actors' Association, he also sang "Las Mañanitas" to the Virgin of Guadalupe at her shrine on December 12, her birthday. A modern Hispanista and skilled charro horseman, he had also studied to be an opera singer. With his fine baritone voice, he was the ultimate charro—loyal, forever in love, a faithful Catholic son, a brave cowboy-gentleman. He symbolized the compromises of the new ruling class as well as the sense of invigorating triumph Mexicans felt at finally having entered a moment of flourishing modernity—without having sacrificed traditional values, having overcome the revolution's tragedies to enjoy its achievements. When he died in Los Angeles in 1953, his adoring public sang the song he had made famous:

> My beautiful, beloved Mexico
> If I die far away from you
> Tell them I am sleeping
> And ask them to bring me home . . .
> Let them bury me in the sierra

At the foot of the magueys

And cover me with this earth of such perfect men.

When the Mexican president's airplane flew his body home, over ten thousand mourners crowded into the airport to receive it. Many more paid their respects as his body lay in state at the headquarters of the National Actors' Association and later at the Palacio de Bellas Artes.[60]

## Conclusion

In the 1920s and 1930s, music united a severely divided nation. Indeed, it made the nation. It was a medium the Catholic shared with the Jacobin, the entrepreneur with the *ejidatario*, the Dama Católica with the prostitute.[61] In rural communities, music brought together teachers and suspicious townsfolk. It captured the imaginations of thousands of children: if they had to endure the insipid memorization of national wars and presidents, they also became enthusiastic initiates into the nation as they danced the jarabe tapatío and the Yaqui Deer Dance. It was a complex process involving demographic movement, technology, market expansion, and social struggle, as well as artistic technique, performance, and demand, all creatively seized upon by cultural entrepreneurs within and outside the government at a particular moment in the formation of the Mexican nation-state.

Mexican musical nationalism did not begin with the revolution of 1910. It probably began with the secularizing opening of the late eighteenth century that culminated in the wars of independence. Admittedly, we identify it as a process from the perspective of hindsight. It could have taken quite distinct paths, fragmented and died stillborn, or its very elements configured in a distinct manner. It was paradoxically strengthened by foreign invasion, investment, technology, commerce, and aesthetics. It developed in creative tandem with American nationalisms, particularly those of the United States and Cuba. Like them, it drew heavily from Europe but also came to depend on and celebrate a relatively autochthonous creativity. It drew in transnational trends and Mexicanized them, so much so that between 1920 and 1950, they were hardly recognized as anything else.

The revolutionary process, the cultural policies of the postrevolutionary state, and the development of recording, radio, and film affected a maturation in music at all levels. The work of state-supported ethnomusicological research and the attraction of radio, recording, and film had a cascading effect on musical production and performance in regions and communities. In order to conquer Mexico City and at the same time capture local publics, regional musicians broadened, deepened, and defined their repertoires. Urbanization stimulated regional music and performance—in cafes, plazas, nightclubs, and radio stations. It also fostered a music of nostalgia for the *patria chica* left behind. Indicative of the process was José López Alavez's "Canción Mixteca." A band musician from Huajuapán de León, Oaxaca, Alavez went to Mexico City in 1906 to study at the Conservatory. He stayed, playing piano for movies and clarinet in city bands and reportedly introducing the fox-trot to Mexico after President Obregón sent him on a trip to the United States. But he did not forget his native Mixteca:

> How far I am from the land where I was born
> Intense nostalgia invades my heart
> And to see me so alone and sad each leaf I blow
> Wants to cry, to die of feeling.
> Oh, land of sun,
> I long to see you,
> So far away I live without sun, without love.

The canción became Oaxaca's second hymn after the waltz "Dios nunca muere," and the anthem of the entire Mixteca region of Puebla, Oaxaca, and Guerrero. An expression of Alavez's urban nostalgia, it became an expression of regional, local, and ethnic pride, as did the triumphalist mariachi music of Guadalajara and the huapangos of the Huasteca. Musical nationalism did not destroy local and regional identity or dignity. It reconfigured them within new national subjectivities in a mobile world. Today, in the United States, immigrants from all over the Mexican republic sing the "Canción Mixteca." They sing of their longing for home and their pride in being Mexican.

## Notes

1. Juan Jesús Aguilar León, *Los trovadores huastecos en Tamaulipas* (Ciudad Victoria, Mexico: Instituto Tamaulipeco para la Cultura y las Artes, 2000), 106–7.

2. Guy P. C. Thomson, "The Ceremonial and Political Roles of Village Bands, 1846–1974," in *Rituals of Rule, Rituals of Resistance*, ed. William Beezley, Cheryl Martin, and William French (Wilmington: Scholarly Resources, 1994), 300, 309–10.

3. Ibid.; Vaughan, "The Construction of Patriotic Festival in Tecamachalco, Puebla, 1900–1946," in Beezley, Martin, and French, *Rituals of Rule*, 213–21.

4. Information in this paragraph is from Thomson, "Village Bands," 320–36. In Oaxaca and Tlaxcala, bands tended to absorb and displace the chirimía. In the Tzotzil communities of Chiapas, a sharp distinction was made between the bands, which were of nonindigenous, ladino origin, and traditional musical forms that continued to guard village history and secrets.

5. Mario Talavera, *Miguel Lerdo de Tejada: Su pintoresca y anecdótica* (Mexico City: Editorial Compas, n.d.), 69–74.

6. See Ricardo Pérez Monfort, *Estampas del nacionalismo* (Mexico City: SEP/CIESAS, 1994), 82; and Aguilar León, *Los trovadores*, 183–92.

7. Román García Arreola, *La música y el baile de "La Chilena" en la costa oaxaqueña* (Oaxaca: Proveedora Escolar, n.d.).

8. Angel Trejo, *¡Hey, familia danzón dedicado a . . . !* (Mexico City: Olaza y Valdés Editores, 1992), 79–81. See also Jesús Flores y Escalante, *Historia documental y gráfica del danzón en México: Salón México* (Mexico City: Asociación Mexicana de Estudios Fonográficos, 1993); and *Imágenes del danzón: Iconografía del danzón en México* (Mexico City: Asociación Mexicana de Estudios Fonográficos, CONACULTA, 1994).

9. Miguel Civeira Tabeada, *Sensibilidad yucateca en la canción romántica*, vol. 1 (Toluca: Gobierno del Estado de México, 1978), 330; Jerónimo Boqueiro Foster, *La canción popular de Yucatán (1850–1950)* (Mexico City: Editorial de Magisterio, 1970), 319; Juan S. Garrido, *Historia de la música popular en Mexico* (Mexico City: Editorial Extemporáneos, 1974), 58–59.

10. See various articles signed by Estanislao Mejía and Nabor Vázquez on the history of wind bands in *Orientación Musical*, June 1943–June 1944; Juan Pablo García Maldonado (former director of the Banda del Estado de Zacatecas), interview by Marco Velázquez, April 29, 1993; and "Las bandas de música en la revolución," in *Polvos de olvido, Cultura y Revolución* (Mexico City: Instituto Nacional de Bellas Artes and Universidad Autónoma Metropolitana, 1993), 349–79.

11. Nervo: "Ser poeta es una predestinación; es realizar a Dios en el alma; es convertirse en templo del Espiritu Sancto." Carlos Monsiváis, "Agustín Lara: El harem ilusorio (Notas a partir de la memorización de la letra de Farolito)," in *Amor perdido* (Mexico: Era, 1977), 63.

12. Carlos Monsiváis, "El bolero," in *Mexican Postcards*, trans. John Kraniauskas (London: Verso, 1997), 175–76.

13. José Antonio Cahero, "Un mexicano en París," *Heterofonia* (Mexico City) 24, no. 107 (1986): 33; Alba Herrera y Ogazón, *El arte musical* (Mexico City: Departamento Editorial de la Dirección General de Bellas Artes, 1916), 69; and Julio Estrada, "La música Francia y México," *Pauta, Cuadernos de Teoría y Crítica Musical* 2, no. 8 (1983): 5–13.

14. Alejandro L. Madrid, "Modernismo, futurismo, y choque generacional: Las canciones de Átropos según Julián Carrillo y Carlos Chávez," *Heterofonia* 33, no. 132 (2000): 89–110.

15. On Ponce, see Emilio Díaz Cervantes and Dolly R. de Díaz, *Ponce, Genio de*

*México: Vida y época (1882–1948)* (Durango: Gobierno del Estado de Durango, Secretaría de Educación, Cultura, y Deporte, 1992), 75–119.

16. Enrique Alonso, *María Conesa* (Mexico City: Océano, 1987), 85.

17. This is the still relatively unexplored thesis of Carlos Monsiváis in "El bolero," 166–95.

18. Marco Velázquez, "Las bandas de música en la revolución"; Frances Toor, *A Treasury of Mexican Folkways* (New York: Crown, 1947), 310; Ricardo Pérez Monfort, *Estampas del nacionalismo*, 100–106; Marco Velázquez, interview with Ricardo Gutiérrez (director of the band of San Martín Texmelucan, Puebla), San Felipe Teotlalcingo, Puebla, June 1992.

19. See, for example, Ricardo Pérez Monfort, *Estampas del nacionalismo*, 106–20.

20. Luis A. Rodríguez, *El Universal Ilustrado*, March 28, 1919.

21. Leonora Saavedra, "Ourselves and Others: Historiography, Ideology, and the Politics of Modern Mexican Music" (Ph.D. diss., University of Pittsburgh, 2001), 70, 130–33.

22. Alba Herrera y Ogazón, *El arte musical*, 84–101.

23. On the heterogeneity of options, opinions, and factions, see Alejandro L. Madrid, "The Sounds of Nation, Modernity, and Tradition: Mexico's First National Congress of Music as Synecdoche of Discourses," forthcoming in *Hispanic American Historical Review* 86, no. 4 (2006).

24. The following synopsis of Chávez's career is taken from Robert L. Parker, *Carlos Chávez: Mexico's Modern Day Orpheus* (Boston: Twayne, 1983), 1–100; Roberto García Morillo, *Carlos Chávez: Vida y obra* (Mexico City: Fondo de Cultura Económica, 1960), 26–87; Leonora Saavedra, "Ourselves and Others," 137–74, 200–237, 314–20; and Alejandro Madrid, "Modernismo."

25. Carol Oja, *Making Music Modern: New York in the 1920s* (New York: Oxford, 2000), 101–5.

26. Alejandro Madrid, "Modernismo"; Gloria Carmona, *Carlos Chávez, escritos periodísticos (1916–1939)* (Mexico City: El Colegio Nacional, 1997), 60.

27. Critics quoted in Saavedra, "Ourselves and Others," 273; García Morillo, *Carlos Chávez*, 33, 37, 43.

28. Saavedra, "Ourselves and Others," 314.

29. Garcia Morillo, *Carlos Chávez*, 46–56; Parker, *Carlos Chávez*, 100.

30. Ibid.

31. Parker, *Carlos Chávez*, 7.

32. Ibid., 11–12.

33. Saavedra, "Ourselves and Others," 233.

34. Ibid., 247–67.

35. See Patience Schell, " 'The Branch That Grows the Fruit': Contradictory Visions of Womanhood as Seen through Mexico City's Schools for Adults," paper presented at

the conference "Las Olvidadas: Women and Gender in the Mexican Revolution," Yale University, May 2001.

36. Angel Trejo, *¡Hey, familia danzón*, 69–75; see also Jesús Flores Escalante, *Historia documental*.

37. On Yucatecan romantic song, see note 9 above, and Yolando Moreno Rivas, *Historia de la música popular mexicana* (Mexico City: Alianza, CONACULTA, 1979), 99–120.

38. Juan Garrido, *Historia*, 60–61.

39. See, among others, Moreno Rivas, *Historia*, 115–17.

40. Pável Granados Chaparro, *XEW: 70 años en el aire* (Mexico City: Editorial Clío y Sistema Radiópolis, 2000), 15–16, 133, 139.

41. The authors wish to thank Rafael Alcerica for his illuminating insights into this creation of new cultural capital through the mass media in Mexico. See also Granados Chaparro, *XEW*, 199.

42. Granados Chaparro, *XEW*, 99.

43. Interviews with Consuelo Villegas Barrón and Luz María Villegas Barrón, Mexico City, July 16, 2002.

44. Granados Chaparro, *XEW*, 101–4, 119–20.

45. For a fine articulation and development of these ideas, see Mark Pedelty, "The Bolero: The Birth, Life and Decline of Mexican Modernity," *Latin American Music Review* 20, no. 1 (1999): 31–43; and the essays of Monsiváis in *Mexican Postcards* and *Amor perdido*.

46. Monsiváis, *Mexican Postcards*, 176–77; Monsiváis, *Amor perdido*, 61–86; see also Moreno Rivas, *Historia*, 134–53; Granados Chaparro, *XEW*, 71–105; and Pablo Dueñas, *Historia documental del bolero mexicano* (Mexico City: Asociación Mexicana de Estudios Fonográficos, 1990).

47. Granados Chaparro, *XEW*, 78.

48. Cited in Granados Chaparro, *XEW*, 82, 100–106.

49. Information and interpretation in this paragraph are taken from Monsiváis, *Amor perdido*, 61–62, 79–83; Monsiváis, *Mexican Postcards*, 178–83; and Granados Chaparro, *XEW*, 71–105. Quote from *Mexican Postcards*, 183.

50. This argument is first presented in *Amor perdido* and developed in *Mexican Postcards*.

51. Moreno Rivas, *Historia*, 142–45.

52. Ibid., 144–45.

53. Granados Chaparro, *XEW*, 93–94.

54. Moreno Rivas, *Historia*, 181–229; Hugo de Geijertam Grial, *Popular Music in Mexico* (Albuquerque: University of New Mexico Press, 1976); Ricardo Pérez Monfort, *Estampas del nacionalismo*, 127; Joy Hayes, *Radio Nation* (Tucson: University of Arizona Press, 2000), 73–74.

55. On mariachis, see, among others, Moreno Rivas, *Historia*, 182–83.

56. León Aguilar, *Los trovadores*, 171–91.

57. Moreno Rivas, *Historia*, 81.

58. Moreno Rivas, *Historia*, 190; José Ramon Garmabella, *Pedro Vargas* (Mexico: Ediciones de Comunicación, 1984), 178.

59. Moreno Rivas, *Historia*, 190.

60. Moreno, *Historia*, 221.

61. In *Mexican Postcards*, Monsiváis asserts this unification with reference to the bolero. We believe it should be extended to other genres.

PLATE 1. José Clemente Orozco, *The Trench*. Escuela Nacional Preparatoria, Mexico City, 1926. © Clemente Orozco V. Photograph by Desmond Rochfort. Reproduced by permission of Clemente Orozco V. and the Fundación José Clemente Orozco, A.C., and Instituto Nacional de Bellas Artes y Literatura.

PLATE 2. Diego Rivera, *Entry to the Mine*. Secretaría de Educación Pública, Mexico City, 1923. © 2004 Banco de México, Diego Rivera and Frida Kahlo Museums Trust, Mexico City. Photograph by Desmond Rochfort. Reproduced by permission of Banco de México, Diego Rivera and Frida Kahlo Museums Trust, and Instituto Nacional de Bellas Artes y Literatura.

PLATE 3. Diego Rivera, *Partition of the Land* (detail). Secretaría de Educación Pública, Mexico City, 1923. © 2004 Banco de México, Diego Rivera and Frida Kahlo Museums Trust, Mexico City. Photograph by Desmond Rochfort. Reproduced by permission of Banco de México, Diego Rivera and Frida Kahlo Museums Trust, and Instituto Nacional de Bellas Artes y Literatura.

PLATE 4. Diego Rivera, *Mechanization of the Countryside*. Secretaría de Educación Pública, Mexico City, 1926. © 2004 Banco de México, Diego Rivera and Frida Kahlo Museums Trust, Mexico City. Photograph by Desmond Rochfort. Reproduced by permission of Banco de México, Diego Rivera and Frida Kahlo Museums Trust, and Instituto Nacional de Bellas Artes y Literatura.

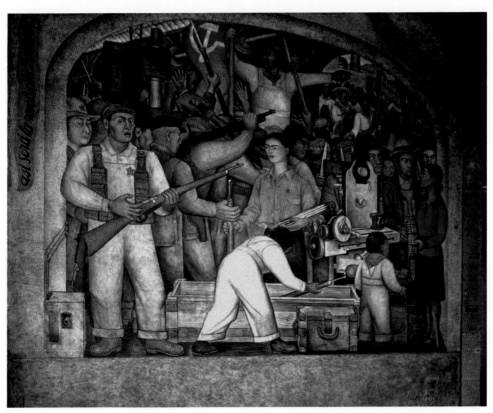

PLATE 5. Diego Rivera, *The Arsenal*. Secretaría de Educación Pública, Mexico City, 1928. © 2004 Banco de México, Diego Rivera and Frida Kahlo Museums Trust, Mexico City. Photograph by Desmond Rochfort. Reproduced by permission of Banco de México, Diego Rivera and Frida Kahlo Museums Trust, and Instituto Nacional de Bellas Artes y Literatura.

PLATE 6. Diego Rivera, central panel of *The History of Mexico*. Palacio Nacional.
© 2004 Banco de México, Diego Rivera and Frida Kahlo Museums Trust, Mexico
City. Photograph courtesy of the Art Archive. Reproduced by permission of Banco
de México, Diego Rivera and Frida Kahlo Museums Trust, and Instituto Nacional de
Bellas Artes y Literatura.

PLATE 7. José Clemente Orozco, *Political and Ideological Exploitation*. Universidad de Guadalajara, 1936. © Clemente Orozco V. Photograph by Desmond Rochfort. Reproduced by permission of Clemente Orozco V. and the Fundación José Clemente Orozco, A.C., and Instituto Nacional de Bellas Artes y Literatura.

PLATE 8. José Clemente Orozco, *Dimensions* (Hernán Cortés). Hospicio Cabañas, Guadalajara, 1938–39. © Clemente Orozco V. Photograph by Desmond Rochfort. Reproduced by permission of Clemente Orozco V. and the Fundación José Clemente Orozco, A.C., and Instituto Nacional de Bellas Artes y Literatura.

PLATE 9. José Clemente Orozco, *The Violence of Conquest* (The Mechanical Horse). Hospicio Cabañas, Guadalajara, 1938–39. © Clemente Orozco V. Photograph by Desmond Rochfort. Reproduced by permission of Clemente Orozco V. and the Fundación José Clemente Orozco, A.C., and Instituto Nacional de Bellas Artes y Literatura.

PLATE 10. David Alfaro Siqueiros, *Portrait of the Bourgeoisie*. Sindicato de Electricistas, Mexico City, 1939–40. © Art Estate of David Alfaro Siqueiros. Photograph by Desmond Rochfort. Reproduced by permission of the Art Estate of David Alfaro Siqueiros/SOMAAP, Mexico/VAGA, New York, and Instituto Nacional de Bellas Artes y Literatura.

PLATE 11. Frida Kahlo, *Pancho Villa and Adelita*, 1927. © 2004 Banco de México, Diego Rivera and Frida Kahlo Museums Trust, Mexico City. Gobierno del Estado de Tlaxcala-Tlaxcalteca de Cultura, Museo de Arte de Tlaxcala, Tlaxcala. Reproduced by permission of Banco de México, Diego Rivera and Frida Kahlo Museums Trust, and Instituto Nacional de Bellas Artes y Literatura.

PLATE 12. Frida Kahlo, *My Birth*, 1932. © 2004 Banco de México, Diego Rivera and Frida Kahlo Museums Trust, Mexico City. Private collection, United States. Reproduced by permission of Banco de México, Diego Rivera and Frida Kahlo Museums Trust, and Instituto Nacional de Bellas Artes y Literatura.

PLATE 14. Frida Kahlo, *A Few Small Nips*, 1935. © 2004 Banco de México, Diego Rivera and Frida Kahlo Museums Trust, Mexico City. Colección Museo Dolores Olmedo. Reproduced by permission of Banco de México, Diego Rivera and Frida Kahlo Museums Trust, and Instituto Nacional de Bellas Artes y Literatura.

PLATE 15. María Izquierdo, *Allegory of Work*, 1936. Collection of Andrés Blaisten. Reproduced by permission of Aurora Posadas Izquierdo and Instituto Nacional de Bellas Artes y Literatura.

PLATE 16. María Izquierdo, *Allegory of Freedom*, 1937. Collection of Andrés Blaisten. Reproduced by permission of Aurora Posadas Izquierdo and Instituto Nacional de Bellas Artes y Literatura.

PLATE 17. María Izquierdo, *Untitled* (*Woman with Horse*), 1938. Davis Museum, Wellesley College, Wellesley, Mass. Reproduced by permission of Aurora Posadas Izquierdo and Instituto Nacional de Bellas Artes y Literatura.

PLATE 18. Marion Greenwood, *Landscape and Economy of Michoacán*. Universidad Michoacana de San Nicolás, Morelia, Michoacán, 1933. Photograph by Elsa Chabaud.

PLATE 19. Marion Greenwood, *The Industrialization of the Countryside*. Abelardo L. Rodríguez Market, Mexico City, 1935. Photograph by Elsa Chabaud.

PLATE 20. Grace Greenwood, *Mining*. Abelardo L. Rodríguez Market, Mexico City, 1935. Photograph by Elsa Chabaud.

# Revolution in the City Streets:
# Changing Nomenclature, Changing Form,
# and the Revision of Public Memory

PATRICE ELIZABETH OLSEN

I SPEAK OF THE CITY

news today and tomorrow a ruin from the past, buried and resurrected every day,

lived together in streets, plazas, taxis, movie houses, theaters,

bars, hotels, pigeon coops and catacombs,

. . . . .

the city that dreams us all, that all of us build and unbuild and rebuild

as we dream,

. . . . .

I speak of the buildings of stone and marble, of cement, glass and

steel, of the people in the lobbies and doorways, . . .

. . . . .

I speak of our public history, and of our secret history, yours and mine.[1]

In his poem "I Speak of the City," Octavio Paz considers the city to be a complex entity, capable of creating dreams and manifesting them, a product of repeated conquests and uneasy coexistence, of varied textures and content. The city is a place where public and private histories intersect, where the latter reveal fundamental flaws within the "official stories" contained in the former. Above all, the city speaks of its change to those who will listen; its buildings and monuments reveal its history, both public and secret, and the stories of its citizens—and expresses the divisions within public memory of the revolutionary nation itself.

From 1928 to 1940, the built environment of Mexico City also speaks of the difficulties in governing and imposing a structure on a revolution, which is, by its nature, against the rules.[2] This city depicts the tensions between those who sought to preserve the city's colonial character as a key element in national identity and those who rejected it as the manifestation of exploitation by an imperial power. Moreover, the city's streets and buildings allow the observer to see what Mexicans chose to retain, and what they discarded. Thus within the city are accounts of a nation and its people attempting to modernize, and searching for a vehicle that would rectify past injustice—and its public memory of that experience. In this period, too, various groups and individuals, notably young socialist architects such as Juan O'Gorman, Juan Legarreta, and Álvaro Aburto, sought the essence of Mexicanidad while attempting to achieve a better society through better design and chose to borrow again from exotic sources, from the Bauhaus functionalists and Le Corbusier.[3] As the city illustrated so clearly, there were few guidelines on how to reconstruct a society following the chaos of prolonged civil war. Evidence of contradictory or incompatible impulses embedded in the revolutionary agenda were visible in nearly every *colonia* or neighborhood and, in particular, the city's Centro Histórico.

This chapter presents a layered examination of the city, beginning with a consideration of the steps taken to "modernize" it—the renaming of certain streets and the commemoration of street names long past. The Centro Histórico experienced several efforts to revise the memories embedded in those streets that continued initiatives made during the final years of the Porfiriato to impose new order on the often chaotic city center. New street names, commemorating the revolutionary heroes Venustiano Carranza, Francisco Madero, and José María Pino Suárez, as well as events such as the commencement of the revolution on November 20, announced the presence of a new power on the site that had served as the locus of authority for centuries. Streets, then, are carriers of meaning, evoking memories of conquest, tragedy, triumph, and burgeoning nationalism (see map of Mexico City's Centro Histórico).

An analysis of the next layer, of what the streets contain, illustrates the problems in consolidating and exercising that power. If the street is considered to be more than a means of providing a corridor for motorized and pedestrian traffic, its significance in the construction of public memory becomes apparent. According to the architectural historian Spiro Kostof, while the street is a public thoroughfare, it is at the same time a "complex civil institution. Its fundamental reality . . . as with all public space, is political. . . . The street, furthermore, structures community. It puts on display the workings of the city, and supplies a backdrop for its common rituals."[4] Streets also contain those work-

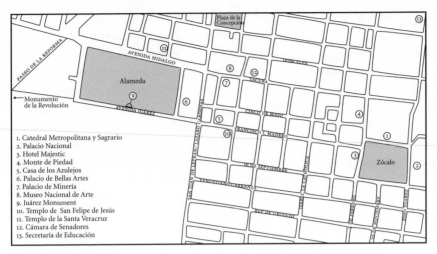

1. Catedral Metropolitana y Sagrario
2. Palacio Nacional
3. Hotel Majestic
4. Monte de Piedad
5. Casa de los Azulejos
6. Palacio de Bellas Artes
7. Palacio de Minería
8. Museo Nacional de Arte
9. Juárez Monument
10. Templo de San Felipe de Jesús
11. Templo de la Santa Veracruz
12. Cámara de Senadores
13. Secretaría de Educación

Mexico City's Centro Histórico, circa 1940. Map by Natalie Hanemann.

ings of the city, in the commercial, governmental, and residential structures that are built on it and thus provide visual cues to the content of public memory of the revolution, and the nature of the society itself. Colonial structures gained a new significance as the Mexican government sought to prevent the encroachment of modernism that might erase elements of national identity that still resonated with many Mexicans. Yet increased population and governmental programs that encouraged capitalist development distanced the city further from the period and culture that had produced those baroque palaces. Buildings thus illustrate the inherent conflict between ideal and reality, between an abstract assembly of elements of national identity and the construction of a functioning nationalism.

In the conclusion to this chapter, the city streets are considered in aggregate, as part of the fabric of revolutionary Mexico. A "revolution" had occurred in its streets in the period from 1928 to 1940. On this occasion, the battle was fought not with the brigantines of Hernán Cortés or the guns of revolutions but with steam shovels and pickaxes. Its impact would be significant, however, just as previous conquests of the city center had been.

"News today and tomorrow a ruin from the past . . ."

On January 11, 1928, *Excélsior* reported the previous evening's actions by Mexico City's Ayuntamiento (City Council) to allocate eight thousand pesos to the

Dirección de Obras Públicas (Bureau of Public Works) for the placement of new colonial-style *azulejo* commemorative plaques on selected streets of "Old Mexico." These plaques would bear the names that the streets carried in 1867. This action did not involve a return to legal usage of the former names. Instead, this was a juxtaposition of names used in the colonial and early national periods with those of the current period. Not every street was to be relabeled; the Ayuntamiento made a noteworthy distinction: "Colonial-style commemorative plaques will be placed on each street that has some history or legend that merits remembrance by means of their old names."[5]

This was hardly front-page news. In the crush of activity during the last year of Plutarco Elías Calles's administration, when the president sought to consolidate power in the central government and to engineer the reelection of Álvaro Obregón, such notice was buried in the newspaper's advertising section, amid other reports of the city council's approval of new street names in other areas of the city, and the naming of the city's new open-air theater after Col. Charles Lindbergh. Yet this was a significant action, indicative of the government's attempts to regulate the content of this rapidly changing city and to direct the public memory of the revolution. With the passage of this seemingly innocuous act, the Ayuntamiento, or bureaus and committees acting on its behalf, would now interpret for the public what was considered worthy of commemoration—which legends, events, and individuals were still relevant, or usable—and which should pass into oblivion. The act also calls attention to the use of street names as a tool to commemorate the contributions of various individuals in the construction of revolutionary Mexico, as well as to remind the public of the martyrdom of Francisco Madero and José María Pino Suárez, assassinated by the usurper Victoriano Huerta in 1913, and to reconcile opposing figures such as the champion of agrarian reform Emiliano Zapata and the bourgeois Venustiano Carranza. Now placed in linear form, they could be reclaimed for the pantheon of revolutionary leaders. Their service to the *patria* would be beyond question.

This contrasted with the historical processes of assigning names to city streets. Residents named streets according to nearby churches and convents, or for a notable person or event. City officials made periodic attempts in the late eighteenth and early nineteenth centuries to bring order to the streets' nomenclature and numbering. Yet disorder continued in the years following Mexico's independence from Spain, amplified by the absence of a government able to dictate order after 1820. As Manuel Orozco y Berra observed in the mid-nineteenth century, "the names of the streets have changed with the times. In few of these times did the authorities intervene; the changes were made by the customs, circumstances, and caprice of the inhabitants."[6]

In 1887 the engineer Roberto Gayol introduced plans to substitute numbers for the Calles de Dios (the so-called Streets of God, named after religious institutions in a given area) and other avenues in the Centro Histórico. Thus residents of streets with lyrical names such as the Calles del Espíritu Santo and San José el Real found themselves living on Sur 3 (Third Street South) or Oriente (East Street). While Porfirian planners may have perceived that the exigencies of modernization required a secularization of street names, resistance to change was sharp, as newspaper editorials commented on the potential loss of tradition and legend, and the difficulty of reconfiguring mental maps of the city in consonance with a new numeric system. Apparently, however, the worst was yet to come. To the historian José L. Cossío, the most serious threat to the integrity of the city center would be posed by revolutionary leaders who attempted to recast the city in their own images. To this point, he saw "nothing had been as prejudicial for the city as the actions of the men of the latest revolution, as due to their limited mentality, all has been changed, in that they claim that the life of the city begins with them, as if to create heroes through a simple azulejo placed on a corner."[7]

Indeed, in 1921, during the celebrations of the centennial of Mexican independence, several streets in the oldest section of the city were recast in the image of the revolution. Notable among these were the conversion of the Calle de Capuchinas into Avenida Venustiano Carranza, the Calles de Plateros and San Francisco into Avenida Francisco I. Madero, and the Calle del Parque del Conde into Avenida José María Pino Suárez. In the following decade, the revolution itself also entered the city's nomenclature as the Cárdenas government terminated work on a new major roadway entering the Plaza de la Constitución, or Zócalo, from the south, Avenida 20 de Noviembre, to commemorate the date Madero began his revolt against Díaz.

With these alterations, the revolutionaries continued a process of revision of public memory that had begun during La Reforma and accelerated under Díaz. Thus the new "revolutionary" streets entered an urban fabric where commemorations of nationalist figures were commonplace and governmental officials recognized the value of representing patriotic events on the landscape. In this respect, then, the luminaries of the revolution joined illustrious nineteenth-century figures such as Benito Juárez, Miguel Hidalgo, Juan Álvarez, Diodoro Carella, Ignacio Allende, Pedro Aranda, José María Morelos, Leona Vicario, Pedro María Anaya, Lucas Balderas, Juan Ruiz de Alarcón, and

Ponciano Arriaga in a seamless web of history, united on the urban grid. Further, governments in the 1920s and 1930s encouraged selective linkages to the precolonial past, with the retention of Aztec names such as Nezahualcóyotl and Xicoténcatl, while others, such as Chiquis, Tizapán, Tlacoaque, Tlaperos, Pipis, and Huacalco, faded from view.[8]

The continuation of the process of historical revision via changing nomenclature of the city's streets in the 1920s and early 1930s indicated the government's perception that the capital city could serve as an element of national unification and as a manifestation of the new revolutionary national identity. The new content of those streets, particularly in the 1930s, would indicate the difficulty of achieving both, as governments pursued strategies of capitalist development and foreign investment while attempting to implement articles of the constitution of 1917 relating to social justice. Mexico City's built environment would manifest conflicts emanating from these diverse goals, as will be shown in the following pages, which offer a tour through a section of the city, assessing these changes in aggregate.

### "Buried and resurrected every day . . ."

In his "Latin Dialogues" published in 1554, Francisco Cervantes de Salazar invited readers to accompany him on a walk through Mexico City, in order to "admire the grandeur of so illustrious a city." The city's character, the author claimed, could not be fully appreciated at a hurried pace from a carriage or other conveyance. Walking through the city allowed the observer to pause and consider it in a new light, literally as well as figuratively, as Charles Flandrau commented in the early twentieth century. Then one could observe "the great, unsympathetic capital" and pause in the Zócalo, "in front of the majestic cathedral, and listen to the echoed sob of history."[9] The Centro Histórico also offered the pedestrian of 1940 a picturesque scene, the equal of any in France, according to the latest guidebook by T. Philip Terry.[10] But it was hardly, as Sydney Clark and so many other writers in this period observed, "the Paris of Mexico."[11] Instead, a brief "walking tour" of the Centro Histórico in 1940 allows the observer to see the streets as part of the fabric of revolutionary Mexico, as well as to understand the cumulative effects of incremental changes on the city—as a product of centuries of negotiation among diverse groups. Its buildings, many of which by 1940 bore scars of the more violent aspects of this process, testify to its uniqueness, as well as to the fact that negotiation does not always have a fair outcome, not even under a revolution. A brief walk, connecting two central symbols of revolutionary governments' power and legitimacy, the Zócalo and the Monument to the Revolution, will illustrate these points.

From the Zócalo, it is possible to reach the Monument to the Revolution by several streets. One could head north along Monte de Piedad to Tacuba, following the ancient path of the Aztecs' Tacuba causeway, crossing the Paseo de la Reforma to follow along the Puente de Alvarado, turning south at Bucareli to watch the hopeful await the drawing of the National Lottery, before turning west along the Avenida de la República to the monument. This path affords the opportunity to see Manuel Tolsá's magnificent classical structures, particularly the Palacio de Minería, at that time home to UNAM's School of Mining Engineering, and the Museo Nacional de Arte, juxtaposed with innumerable market stalls and *vendedores ambulantes* (sidewalk peddlers) selling fresh fruits, vegetables, used clothing, and odd gadgets from worn packs and wooden carts. A beautiful flower market, moved from north of the Zócalo to Avenida Hidalgo above the Alameda, offered another attraction; there was also the opportunity to travel down the same path as the infamous conquistador Pedro de Alvarado, without re-creating his famous causeway leap, tracing history back through the centuries and gaining insights into the changes wrought in the city by the revolution, particularly as one turned the corner to the Paseo de la Reforma. Its new functionalist buildings contrasted sharply with the colonial cityscape just experienced. And here too the pace of city life had quickened: the Paseo de la Reforma, constructed by the erstwhile Austrian emperor of Mexico Maximilian (1863–67) for ease of transit between his palatial residence in Chapultepec Park and the seat of government in the Palacio Nacional, now served as a major corridor for those residing in the new subdivisions of Lomas de Chapultepec and Chapultepec-Polanco.

Another option would be to head west along Avenida Cinco de Mayo until it came to an end at the Palacio de Bellas Artes, then join with Hidalgo to the north, or Juárez to the south, to meet with the Avenida de la Revolución, seeing further evidence of the growing economic penetration by the United States. Railway, steamship, airline, and insurance company offices clustered at its west end; the middle sections of the street from Isabel la Católica to Gante were given to chic restaurants and bars, and the confectionery Dulcería de Celaya, notable for its Day of the Dead skulls artfully crafted in spun sugar. Along Cinco de Mayo one gained the impression of a prosperous, energetic city; poverty and slums were still a few blocks north or south.

In sum, the city contained numerous streets made by the revolution, some bisecting former church lands, or carved from old estates and vacant lands. Their paths, too, represent the course and direction of the revolution and weave their way through many of its signal achievements. Streets such as the Avenida 20 de Noviembre, San Juan de Letrán, and Comonfort, to name a few of the most prominent of such public works during the Cárdenas administration, also manifest the nation's progress and its drive to modernize and industrialize. However, the best path to the Monument to the Revolution lies along Avenida Madero. Other streets might attest more to the city's modernity or to its colonial identity. Avenida Madero, forged from fragments of the former *calles* of San Francisco, Profesa, and Plateros into a unified whole, is less grand than Reforma, but more Mexican. It illustrates the series of conquests and cultural invasions that make up Mexican history, as well as the introspection arising from a decade of violence, as intellectuals and government officials, among others, considered issues of revolutionary and cultural nationalism, and the content of public memory.

The entrance of the neocolonial-style Hotel Majestic, located at Madero 78, affords eastern and western vantage points. To the east is one direction of the revolution: the Zócalo, traditional center of political power with its enormous flag, is the setting for presidential addresses each May 5, September 15, and November 20, speeches that contain official statements about the direction and accomplishments of the revolutionary state. To the west lies another direction of the revolution. Looking straight west past the hotels, storefronts, and offices along Madero, leading into Avenida Juárez, one can distinguish the copper dome of the Monument to the Revolution, a fitting culmination to this revolution-made corridor.

As self-commemoration, it has one of the most visible statements made by governments between 1928 and 1940. But it contained no representations of the revolution's guiding forces, as yet. Images of Francisco Madero, Plutarco Elías Calles, Lázaro Cárdenas, Venustiano Carranza, and Francisco Villa would be added decades later, as would their mortal remains. A somber structure even in a strong morning light, it carried a message not of triumph in war, or of individual glory, but of tenacity. By its sheer weight, it imposed on its viewers the gravity of the recent civil war, and the perception of the permanence of dislocations wrought by the conflict. No garlands or wreaths decorated its facade, as in the case of the Juárez monument—no crowning angel marked its pinnacle, as in the Monument to Independence.

A monument assigns meaning to a particular event and chooses to mark a given interpretation of that event indelibly on the landscape. And this era called for a different iconography than had the Porfiriato. The message imposed by architect Carlos Obregón Santacilia's winning design for the monument was that of permanence. The revolution had been fought for a purpose. The monument's walls provided no friezes that might interpret that purpose, nor were there, as in the case of Diego Rivera's murals, revolutionary slogans that stated government policy emblazoned on the walls. Interpretation of the revolution was left to the individual. Thus the structure could hold an infinite number of meanings and memories.[12]

And in its hollow center, the monument afforded the space to allow observers to confront the intersection of public history — the "official stories" of the experience of consolidating a government from the ruins of civil war and the record of an activist state promoting social justice and equality — with the private history of lives lost, fortunes made, aspirations fulfilled, goals deferred. What happened to the revolution? Was it continuing, "inexorably, to its fulfillment," as Cárdenas stated in a radio address to the nation in 1935?[13] The capital's streets contained some answers, just ahead.

Avenida Francisco I. Madero was considered by many observers to be the most Americanized of the capital's streets. Indeed, extensive services available to the tourist, particularly the new hotels, recalled former treasury secretary Alberto Pani's initiatives to improve tourism in the late 1920s and early 1930s. Further, the street had functioned as a shopping district since the seventeenth century; in 1940 it drew large numbers of tourists given the hundreds of metalsmiths who plied their trades in the arcades that opened onto the street. Other businesses directed toward the foreign visitor included offices of the National City Bank of New York, across the street from La Profesa Church, the American Bookstore at Madero 25, for the latest in maps, guidebooks, and magazines, and the American Photo Supply at Madero 42. Like the hotels, their prices reflected North American rather than Mexican pocketbooks.

If one focused on the neon signs and lavish window displays along the street featuring names such as Norge, RCA, Dodge, and Delaware Punch, it would appear that governments from Calles to Cárdenas had been successful in their pursuit of foreign investment into Mexico. Such investment had left a considerable imprint on the city. But Avenida Madero was not yet a U.S. street, nor was the capital at risk of becoming a caricature of a U.S. city, as some feared. In between the new steel-and-glass functionalist buildings, or the marble-faced Ritz Hotel with its "expres lunch" signboard, there was a city touched by cultural penetration, still retaining some of its historic character. In this respect, one sees the churches La Profesa, San Francisco, and San Felipe de Jesús, and notable private homes from the eighteenth century, such as the Casa del Marqués del Prado Alegre, the Casa Borda, located at Madero 27–33 and 39, respectively, and the Casa del Marqués de Jaral de Berrio (Hotel Iturbide), next to the new "High Life" department store that carried the latest in U.S.-inspired fashions.

This is not to say that these buildings were untouched by the revolution or by decades of urban life and modifications by generations of *capitalinos*. Modernity, albeit an "uncompleted modernity," as Charles Flandrau noted in his observations of the city at the end of the Porfiriato, intruded in unexpected ways. In 1940 it took the form of newspapers stuck in the iron grilles of La Profesa's fence, the product of an organized, enterprising vendor who served hurried travelers without missing a step. And modernity mixed with the timeworn, in the form of beggars and flower vendors already taking up positions early in the morning in front of San Felipe de Jesús Church, a particularly choice spot given its location directly across the street from the august eighteenth-century Casa del Conde del Valle de Orizaba, now housing Sanborn's, or as capitalinos knew it, La Casa de los Azulejos (the House of Tiles), near one of the busiest intersections of the capital.

The House of Tiles provides an interesting point to pause, to consider the survival, or resilience, of certain colonial structures. Many of those that survived in good repair had been converted to new uses, reflecting the needs of a changing society. Private homes and mansions now served as a restaurant and drugstore, in the case of the House of Tiles, and a hotel, as the Casa del Marqués de Jaral de Berrio, closed in 1928 and later converted into a Banamex office, with an art gallery. However, in the midst of change there is continuity. The saints may be missing from upper-story niches, forced disappearances during La Reforma, the Decena Trágica, or another episode of urban violence, but the essence of the old continues in the remaining structure. When it is recycled for new owners and purposes, it carries a distinct message: this cityscape is the product of centuries of competing visions and negotiations. The revolution did not change that fact.

While a constitution begins with a blank piece of paper, the city did not. Architects beginning to design "for the revolution" had no such tabula rasa. They had to work within the existing context, which effectively constrained their actions in several areas. Their protracted battles with more conservative members of the profession indicate that the messages contained within the colonial buildings continued to resonate with many people. Moreover, as Mexicans searched for their national identity in the 1920s and 1930s, these colonial structures served as touchstones to an apparently more civilized, ordered past. The demolition of colonial-era structures, whether for new streets such as 20 de Noviembre, which cut through stone and nostalgia to provide a new entrance to the Zócalo from the south, or for San Juan de Letrán, just ahead after Sanborn's, was fraught with difficulty. Here self-interest collided with abstract notions of the public good, perhaps given the economic climate of the time, in which the nation fought to recover from the devastation of war only to find itself skirting around a global depression. Landowners frequently complained of inadequate compensation offered by the government, but seldom questioned the government's authority to undertake such action, signaling a lasting impact of the revolution as the public accepted and encouraged its more activist role. Further, the replacement of colonial buildings by functionalist structures of reinforced concrete and steel provoked protest for the loss of irreplaceable historic structures.

Ultimately, questions of ownership and vision had to be resolved. Who "owned" the city, particularly in the wake of a revolution fought for social justice? Was the socioeconomic hierarchy of the colonial era that extended through the Porfiriato to be reaffirmed and continued through the cityscape, in allowing the church and wealthy families to retain large urban landholdings, when the public good dictated other uses? And in whose vision would the city be made? Should the people be defined by their past, or by their future? José Vasconcelos's educational and proselytizing efforts aside, Avenida Madero reveals in microcosm the complexities of this struggle, and the difficulties in reaching a satisfactory compromise. Thus in 1940 legislation was in place that protected the facade of the Centro Histórico yet extended little benefit to those who lived and worked within it, as scant capital was reinvested in those deteriorating structures but instead found more fertile ground in the southwestern areas of the city. The "spirit" may have spoken for Vasconcelos's Cosmic Race, but the message delivered may have been less than egalitarian. The outcome certainly was, as revealed in the cityscape.

"I speak of our public history, and of
our secret history, yours and mine"

Avenida Madero ends at the intersection with San Juan de Letrán, widened during the Cárdenas administration to alleviate congestion in the Centro Histórico. In the process of enlarging this street, the Secretaría de Comunicaciones y de Obras Públicas (Ministry of Communications and Public Works) approved the demolition of numerous colonial buildings. Of all of the city's crossroads, this intersection perhaps best summarizes the cultural impulses of the period from 1928 to 1940, as well as the progress made in building technology. As Terry summarized in his popular guidebook, from the steps of the city's first skyscraper, the Edificio La Nacional, a building that represented "the replacing of the obsolescent colonial style with the efficient modern," it was possible to see "beyond the Palacio de las Bellas Artes . . . the street (now the Calle Miguel Hidalgo y Costilla) down which Cortés and his sorely harassed soldiers slowly retreated before Aztec wrath on the memorable Sad Night of July 2, 1520. Facing this *calle* from the North is the old Church of Santa Vera Cruz, founded by Cortés in 1527, hence in the 16th century style. To the right, on the Ave. Madero, glinting in the sunlight, is the famed Casa de los Azulejos, erected in 1596, but in pure Mudejar style. Roundabout are scores of houses in pure Spanish Colonial style, dating from various years in the 18th century." [14]

Here at the corner of San Juan de Letrán and Madero, the Edificio Guardiola, with its sheer mass, art deco bronze trim, and marble-clad facade, effectively balanced the Edificio La Nacional to its diagonal on the southwest corner and formed a counterpoint to the beaux arts Palacio de Bellas Artes (Palace of Fine Arts) at the northeast corner. The palace offered an example of the reclamation of Porfirian excess and the revolutionary popularization of Mexican culture within a shell that had originally carried a distinctly nonegalitarian message. Just two years earlier, the Cárdenas government linked the structure still further to the revolution: following the oil expropriation of March 1938, Cárdenas appealed to citizens to donate whatever they could to defray the cost of the oil expropriation, and to bring their contributions to the palace. The response was overwhelming, according to the city's dailies, which reported Avenida San Juan de Letrán made impassable to vehicular traffic because of the long lines of patriotic citizens "of all classes" waiting to contribute their sewing machines, chickens, wedding rings, and even a child's piggy bank. [15]

La Nacional represented a victory by Mexican engineers over the city's unstable subsoil; it would now be possible for revolutionary governments to build vertically as well as horizontally. Soon thereafter, what the Mexico City chronicler Salvador Novo called the new "crystalline pyramids of aluminum" would appear on the landscape without apology to the viceregal or pre-Hispanic structures below and announce a new process of conquest, this time commercial, in this ancient city, further revising public memory. [16]

Crossing San Juan de Letrán and looking ahead along Avenida Juárez, one would see the immense semicircular monument to Benito Juárez. As interpreted by Brazilian diplomat Erico Verissimo, this "horrifying" structure and "masterpiece of bad taste" did a disservice to the memory of one of Mexico's finest leaders. Verissimo continued his critique: "That Indian, so serious, silent and Spartan, deserved a simpler homage. There he is in the Alameda, sitting in his chair, in a kind of parody of the monument to Lincoln, the *gringo* he so much admired. . . . The chair rests upon a tall pedestal of white marble, much ornamented, and in the centre of a gallery of Doric columns. Mounting guard on the pedestal are two lions, seated but with heads lifted in the alert look of beasts on the point of leaping at any moment to the defense of the statue. The whole seems a rather pompous mausoleum." [17]

Commemorative architecture, as seen in the monument to Juárez, is often less inspired by the actual character of the subject. Rather, it is a product of the time that creates it. This monument was erected in the final year of the Porfiriato, as part of the celebrations of the hundredth anniversary of Mexican independence. [18] Such occasion excuses the grandeur of materials employed and explains this particular stylistic interpretation of Juárez on such a grand scale. By 1910, it was "safe" to commemorate the actions of Mexico's first full-blooded Indian president; memories of the more controversial aspects of La Reforma had faded sufficiently, and what remained had largely been rewritten over the course of a thirty-year dictatorship of Porfirio Díaz. A revolutionary government seeking to remove symbols of the Díaz regime could leave such a monument in place, as it represented another potential source of identity, as well as an exaltation of the Indian, part of the Cosmic Race.

Farther west, Avenida Juárez meets the Paseo de la Reforma. Straight ahead lies the Monument to the Revolution, on the avenue of the same name. If one ascends to the top of the monument's copper dome, some sixty-three meters high, a broader picture of the city is clearly displayed. Its skyline recorded fundamental changes introduced by the revolution and its governments. While ecclesiastical structures still dominated the city's profile, most notably San Francisco, Santo Domingo, and Nuestra Señora de la Encarnación, several of these buildings were religious in facade only. Seventeenth- and eighteenth-century edifices such as San Ildefonso, Santiago Tlatelolco, and the Hospital Real were pressed into service as schools, libraries, offices of revolutionary government departments, and tenements. Governments sought to etch into the public consciousness their achievements under the revolutionary mandate with eponymous structures such as the Mercado Abelardo Rodríguez and the Colonia Plutarco Elías Calles, a housing development for state employees, both completed at the end of 1934. Iconography of the revolution entered the capital in other areas as well, as in sports facilities such as the Centro Deportivo Venustiano Carranza, 18 de Marzo, and Plan Sexenal, and in schools, prominent among them the Centro Escolar Revolución. In the case of these larger projects, the development itself represented the dedication of the government to the revolution and its legitimacy. On smaller projects, such as clinics or primary schools, plaques and signs, not of azulejos but of bronze or steel, heralded the achievement, as well as the dominance of the new civil power.

By 1940, taller commercial buildings had begun to compete for primacy in the Centro Histórico, a sign of a new power configuration emerging in the city and the nation. New architectural styles had also emerged, and with them the development of new construction techniques and materials that allowed architects and governments to reach upward, designing their version of the new Mexico.

The revolution had brought about a new constitution and government, and a new sense of national identity. But presidents during these formative years were faced with a significant problem. How can a revolution, fought against the established rules, be converted into a coherent, positive force? That is, how can a revolution evolve into a government? Mexican officials employed a variety of strategies to do so. They sought unity and tried to bridge gaps among prominent revolutionary leaders: public ceremonies reconciled Carranza, Zapata, and Madero and placed their names on streets, markets, schools, and colonias. The capital city's streets manifested a public memory now full of contradictory elements. Moreover, the city demonstrated that significant differences in perceptions of Mexican reality existed. The street names delineate neat intersections of the revolution and its leaders on the urban grid, recalling those in official histories and public memory derived from the commemoration of that history. However, the content of those streets indicates that this was contested space, and thus contested history.

## Notes

1. From Octavio Paz, "I Speak of the City," in *A Tree Within*, translated from the Spanish by Eliot Weinberger (New York: New Directions Publishing Corporation, 1987), 31–37.

2. Diane Davis, Peter Ward, John Lear, and María del Carmen Collado Herrera discuss tensions among various groups—renters, commercial interests, developers, and government agencies, among others. See Davis, *Urban Leviathan: Mexico City in the*

*Twentieth Century* (Philadelphia: Temple University Press, 1994); Ward, *Mexico City: The Production and Reproduction of an Urban Environment*, 2nd ed. (Chichester, N.Y.: J. Wiley, 1998); Lear, *Workers, Neighbors, and Citizens: The Revolution in Mexico City* (Lincoln: University of Nebraska Press, 2001); and Collado Herrera, *Empresarios y políticos, entre la Restauración y la Revolución, 1920–1924* (Mexico City: Instituto Nacional de Estudios Históricos de la Revolución Mexicana, 1996).

3. For a concise overview of architectural styles from the colonial era to the 1990s and underlying political themes, see Carlos Lira Vázquez, *Para una historia de la arquitectura mexicana* (Mexico City: Universidad Autónoma Metropolitana Azcapotzalco, 1990); and Mauricio Tenorio Trillo, "1910 Mexico City: Space and Nation in the City of the Centenario," *Journal of Latin American Studies* 28 (February 1996): 75–104. Both Valerie Fraser and Enrique X. de Anda provide nuanced discussions of the idealism of young architects in Mexico in the 1920s and 1930s, which sought to direct professional practice toward building to fulfill revolutionary goals of social justice. See Fraser, *Building the New World: Studies in the Modern Architecture of Latin America, 1930–1960* (London: Verso, 2000); and de Anda, *La arquitectura de la Revolución Mexicana: Corrientes y estilos en la década de los veinte* (Mexico City: UNAM, Instituto de Investigaciones Estéticas, 1990). Lilia Gómez and Miguel Angel Quevedo document changes within the architectural community in their collection of oral histories of architects of this era. See *Testimonios vivos, 20 arquitectos*, Cuadernos de Arquitectura y Conservación del Patrimonio Artístico (Mexico City: Instituto Nacional de Bellas Artes, 1981).

4. Spiro Kostof, *The City Assembled: The Elements of Urban Form through History* (Boston: Bulfinch Press, Little, Brown, 1992), 194, 220.

5. "Las calles del México viejo van a ostentar sus antiguos nombres," *Excélsior*, January 11, 1928.

6. Manuel Orozco y Berra, "La Ciudad de México," in *Diccionario universal de geografía y historia* (Mexico City: Imprenta de F. Escalante y Cía., 1854), 633–34.

7. José L. Cossío, *Guía retrospectiva de la Ciudad de México*, 2nd ed. (Mexico City: Espejo de Obsidiana Ediciones, 1990), 125.

8. For a comprehensive examination of the changes in the urban grid and nomenclature since the conquest, see Sonia Lombardo de Ruiz, *Atlas histórico de la Ciudad de México*, 2 vols. (Mexico City: Smurfit Cartón y Papel/CNCA/INAH, 1996–1997).

9. Charles Macomb Flandrau, *Viva México!* ed. C. Harvey Gardiner (Urbana: University of Illinois Press, 1964), 289–90.

10. T. Philip Terry, *Terry's Guide to Mexico: The New Standard Guidebook to the Mexican Republic*, rev. ed. (Boston: Geo. H. Ellis, 1938), 258.

11. Sydney A. Clark, *Mexico's Magnetic Southland* (New York: Dodd, Mead, 1945), 10.

12. For more on the Monument to the Revolution and historical memory, see Thomas Benjamin, *La Revolución: Mexico's Great Revolution as Memory, Myth and History* (Austin: University of Texas Press, 2000), 127–36. For lively commentary by the

monument's architect, see Carlos Obregón Santacilia, *El Monumento a la Revolución, simbolismo e historia* (Mexico City: Secretaría de Educación Pública, Departamento de Divulgación, 1960). View the monument at www.cuauhtemoc.df.gob.mx/turismo/recorridorevolucion or at www.war-memorial.net.

13. Lázaro Cárdenas, "Mensaje radiofónico desde la ciudad de México" (November 2, 1935), in *Lázaro Cárdenas, ideario público*, ed. Leonel Durán (Mexico City: Serie Popular Era, 1972), 20.

14. Terry, *Terry's Guide to Mexico*, 328–29.

15. Ricardo Pérez Montfort, *Estampas del nacionalismo popular mexicano* (Mexico City: CIESAS, 1994), 186–87.

16. Salvador Novo, *México, imagen de una ciudad* (Mexico City: Fondo de Cultura Económica, 1967), 38.

17. Erico Veríssimo, *México*, trans. Linton Barrett (New York: Orion Press, 1960), 72–73.

18. For further discussion see Jerome Monnet, *Usos e imágenes del Centro Histórico de la Ciudad de México* (Mexico City: Centro de Estudios Mexicanos y Centroamericanos, 1995).

# II

Utopian
Projects
of the
State

# Saints, Sinners, and State Formation:
# Local Religion and Cultural Revolution in Mexico

ADRIAN A. BANTJES

What happened that day, November 14, 1921, was, of course, a miracle. Concealed in a bouquet of flowers, a stick of dynamite had been placed under the marble altar beneath the sacred image of Our Lady of Guadalupe in the basilica at Tepeyac. A powerful blast ripped through the sanctuary, shattering the altar and tossing huge brass candelabra into the air. But a panic-stricken priest who arrived at the scene was overwhelmingly relieved to find the image unscathed. Thousands of hysterical believers streamed to the basilica and nearly lynched a suspect, "showering him with terrible curses." Catholics organized a solemn Te Deum in the basilica, closed shops, and staged mass rallies on the Zócalo and throughout Mexico.[1]

How is one to make sense of this seemingly irrational attack against Mexico's most revered religious and national symbol? As David Brading reminds us, even a rabid Reforma anticlerical like Ignacio Manuel Altamirano acknowledged the transcendent significance for Mexicans of the cult of the Virgin of Guadalupe: "It is the national idolatry. . . . In the last extreme, in the most desperate cases, the cult of the Mexican Virgin is the only bond which unites them." Altamirano concluded that the day Our Lady of Guadalupe was not venerated, "the Mexican nationality would have disappeared."[2] The icon of the Virgin lies at the heart of a "Mexican-Guadalupan" national identity.[3] Why seek its destruction?

We cannot dismiss the *bombazo* as an arbitrary, extremist act devoid of significance. In fact, it was just one in a succession of iconoclastic performances that welled up during the Constitutionalist campaigns and continued throughout the revolution. Jacobins incorporated strict anticlerical laws into the 1917 constitution, setting the stage for religious conflict. Radical strongholds such as Tomás Garrido Canabal's Tabasco, Adalberto Tejeda's Veracruz,

Salvador Alvarado's Yucatán, Lázaro Cárdenas's Michoacán, and Rodolfo Elías Calles's Sonora became laboratories of antireligiosity, where caciques experimented with "defanaticization" campaigns involving anticlerical legislation, rationalist education, religious persecution, and systematic iconoclasm. During the late 1920s and 1930s, a faction headed by *Jefe Máximo* Plutarco Elías Calles attempted unsuccessfully to institutionalize defanaticization. Overall, few states escaped the antireligious fury. Yucatán witnessed Mexico's first campaign in 1915, and in Veracruz, services resumed in 1937 after a several-year hiatus. Though implemented regionally and intermittently, defanaticization campaigns were linked to national politics and followed a coherent cultural script aimed at establishing a revolutionary, nationalist civil religion.

Incidents that at first glance might seem exceptional, in reality formed an integral part of the revolutionary process. There was a logic to the antireligious madness. It is harder to fathom the impact of defanaticization on the popular *mentalité*. Defanaticization provoked strong and widespread resistance. This essay attempts to interpret collective responses in order to shed light on the relationship between Mexican popular culture and the revolutionary state. Ultimately, local religion, the cultural matrix many Mexicans used to make sense of the world, survived relatively unscathed and continued to inform everyday life. However, competition from alternative loyalties, in particular revolutionary nationalism, relegated religion to an increasingly constricted realm.

### Tropical Dreams of Modernity

Salvador Alvarado, governor of Yucatán from 1915 to 1918, had a dream of a glorious future for his adopted state and for all Mexico. In his vision, the winged Genio de la Raza (Spirit of the Race) shows an astonished Alvarado the Mexico of tomorrow: a rich land covered with beautiful, modern cities, bustling factories and refineries, and lush agricultural colonies, and populated by an industrious, progressive, and virtuous people. Signs of "Saxon" technology and science, such as trams, trains, and Ford Landaulets, abound. The new temples of modernity are schools and libraries filled with the works of Spencer, Emerson, Le Bon, Darwin, Marx, Ruskin, Taine, and Samuel Smiles. Yucatán has become "a beautiful, dazzling and grand Promised Land."

In Alvarado's brave new world, there is no need for religion, for the clergy "had definitely lost the battle and it would be impossible for fanaticism to take root again in the land where light and truth had blossomed forever. . . . Here and there a church remained open in which entered only an occasional respectable lady." The spirit enjoins Alvarado to assume the titanic task of transforming the *patria* into the marvelous place of his dreams. Awaking, he pledges: "I will do it, despite everything."

Alvarado grasped the opportunity to fulfill his dream and "defanaticize" the "poor, ignorant" Mayan Indians "at all costs." "The practice of religion was . . . purged by the . . . revolution. Defanaticization was completed by the founding of competent lay schools and . . . one hundred libraries."[4] Alvarado also closed churches, expelled priests, and restricted religious freedom. Government-inspired mobs sacked and burned the cathedral of Mérida and vandalized other churches. *Quemasantos* (saint burners) unleashed a furious crusade to incinerate saints' images across the state because "once the idol is dead, the cult is finished." Alvarado was pleased with the results: "All the gods have died and there is no church that hasn't gone to ruin, nor any religion that hasn't vanished."[5]

Alvarado's vision was shared by many revolutionaries. Years later, traveling on the steamboat *Morazán* up the winding Río Grijalva to Mexico's heart of darkness—or "El Dorado," as he called it—the Bolivian revolutionary tourist Roberto Hinojosa arrived in Tabasco, "Land of dreams, riches and hope!" This tropical paradise, "the Bethlehem of the socialist dawn in America," was ruled by the region's Mr. Kurtz, Tomás Garrido Canabal, "academic and farmer, intellectual and rancher, a guide and soldier of socialism; he is the branding iron applied red hot to the back of fanaticism." Hinojosa waxed eloquently on the forced eradication of all religious sentiment and equated Tabasco's "socialism" with antireligiosity:

> Tabascan anticlericalism has not been administered to the people drop by drop, timidly. . . . Garrido has confiscated and nationalized the . . . properties that the friars robbed from the Tabascan natives; and the people have demolished the houses of fanaticism, setting fire to their plaster and wood fetishes. To determine how deeply rooted this systematic anticlerical labor is in the minds of children, I questioned them [and] received these . . . answers: "The saints don't exist, and those made of wood are only good for burning." . . . "The priest and the capitalist steal the bread from our mouths." "Fanaticism is ignorance." . . . "Miracles are fairy-tales, because no *miraculous saint* has ever escaped from the fire."[6]

Garrido believed that the elimination of religiosity was an essential goal of the revolution, which mustered "its materialist philosophy to combat, in the light of reason and proven truth, the farces, dogmas and myths of religion." "All religions are absurd." "There are no gods, nor is there an afterlife." Moreover, religion had always served as the handmaiden of capitalism. "As long as man worships deities and believes in . . . an afterlife, he will remain mentally shackled and the enemy of his own liberation." Garrido realized that the state would have to replace religion with a new moral doctrine "that incorporates radical changes in behavior and in the philosophy of man. . . . Morals instead of religion, work instead of liturgy, self-confidence instead of faith in a deity." Soon there would be "no God but the law, nor any religion but work."[7]

Alvarado's dream of modernity and Garrido's tropical socialism were typical of the Jacobin revolutionary culture found in the scattered laboratories of modernity that flourished from 1915 through the 1930s. These experiments sought not just the destruction of the church as an institution but the disappearance of religion itself.

## Modernity and Religion

The origins of revolutionary defanaticization must be sought in the Enlightenment project of modernity, a totalizing discourse that seeks the triumph of reason and freedom, and the forging of a New Man. Modern revolutionary societies are often characterized by what James Scott has dubbed "high modernism," a quasi-religious belief in the perfectibility of man and society through the rational application of science and technology. The modern state has sought to reshape all aspects of "traditional" culture. This process involves the destruction of "ignorance" and "superstition," that is, of the popular cultures of subordinate groups.[8] The main obstacle to modernity is religion, especially popular religion or "fanaticism." This rationalizing drive entails a process of secularization, the disenchantment of the sacred world and the substitution of the worship of God by the cult of a sacralized humanity. The Enlightenment and the French Revolution profoundly influenced, one might even say invented, modern politics, whether in Europe or Latin America, and provided Mexico with a revolutionary discourse replete with allusions to the French Revolution and its Jacobin *discours déchristianisateur*. Yet Mexicans selectively consumed and reshaped modernity. As Clifford Geertz argues, "Though . . . originally . . . a Western notion . . . the idea of modernity has become the common property of all the world, even more prized and puzzled over in Asia, Africa, and Latin America . . . than in Europe and North America."[9]

## The Cultural Debate

Revolutionary anticlericalism had deep roots in the ancient church-state conflict that had accompanied Mexican state formation since the eighteenth century. In the bloody conflict between liberal and conservative elites that consumed Mexico for much of the nineteenth century, the Catholic hierarchy threw its weight behind conservative regimes and supported the disastrous French intervention. However, the church-state conflict alone fails to explain the intensity of defanaticization. Institutional conflict was accompanied by a deeper cultural conflict. Many anticlericals abhorred popular culture, especially popular religion. During the revolution, we see clear continuities with earlier elite campaigns, both secular and clerical, and dating as far back as the Bourbon reforms, to change campesino culture and religion. Nineteenth-century radical liberals pushed the debate beyond the problem of clerical power and property and criticized Catholic culture itself as an obstacle to the creation of a new, secularized *hombre positivo*, utilitarian, industrious, enlightened, and virtuous. The Reforma dramatically radicalized the debate; a rabid antireligiosity emerged among radical liberals, who, strongly influenced by French thought, sought to establish a patriotic civil religion with Juárez as "high priest."[10]

This trend was interrupted by the *pax porfiriana*. Díaz eschewed extreme anticlericalism and tolerated a church-state détente. Liberal moderates pushed doctrinaire liberals, or *jacobinos*, underground, where they radicalized under the influence of anarchism and mobilized against Díaz. Porfirian noncompliance with Reforma legal restrictions on the clergy and renewed clerical control of education, baptism, and marriage were the focus of their ire.[11] By the early twentieth century, the resurgent church's Second Reconquest had penetrated deeply into the countryside, galvanized by the social Catholicism of the 1891 encyclical *Rerum Novarum*. It established new cults (the Sacred Heart, Christ the King), lay organizations (the Catholic Association of Mexican Youth, Knights of Columbus), political parties, and unions.[12] The most outspoken critic of this revitalized church, and of religion, was Ricardo Flores Magón. In the pages of *Regeneración*, he attacked the clergy for prostituting women, transforming children into fanatics, and exploiting and brutalizing the Mexican people by preaching ignorance and resignation in the face of poverty: "Beneath a cassock rises the lubricity of a satyr. . . . In the shadows of the sacristies the honor of virgins is stained and . . . the head of the Catholic church in Mexico remains impassive when the concupiscence of his libidinous friars, of his lewd fauns, is denounced." Flores Magón dismissed Catholicism and other world religions as "mystical errors": "We revolutionaries are not pursuing a chimera: we are pursuing reality. Nations no longer take up arms to impose a god or a religion; gods moulder in the sacred books; religions dissolve in the shadows of indifference. The Koran, the Vedas, the Bible, no longer sparkle: in their yellowing pages the sad gods are in their death throes like the sun in winter twilight."[13] Revolutionary anticlericalism and antireligiosity were also inspired by "a heterodox nebulosity" of beliefs and *sociétés de pensée*, such as Protestantism, Freemasonry, spiritism, and mutualism, which displayed a fierce anti-Catholicism and coalesced to forge a Jacobin revolutionary sensibility.[14]

The cultural conflict emerged as a central concern of the revolutionary state. The debates of the constitutional convention at Querétaro in 1916–17 would provide radicals with the legislative ammunition to launch an all-out campaign against religion. Many firebrands, such as Francisco J. Mújica, Luis G. Monzón, and Heriberto Jara, were influenced by *magonismo*. They condemned the Vatican-controlled church as a "state within the state," denounced political and social Catholicism, and pledged to end clerical collaboration with "feudal" hacendados and reactionaries like Huerta. They also attacked the religious culture with which the clergy poisoned the minds of rural folk.

The lively discussion on article 24, which addressed religious practice, was conducted in an atmosphere of risqué, boisterous mockery. Amid laughter, whistles, and shouting, one delegate tried to disprove the dogma of the purity of the Virgin. The ancient repugnance of priests resurfaced. Enrique Recio asked delegates to prohibit oral confession and to legislate that priests be Mexican citizens, and married, if younger than fifty years old, because "the laws of nature cannot be broken." Otherwise, "each home [will] be wrecked, . . . each woman [will] be an adulteress, . . . each priest . . . a free satyr in the bosom of society." Monzón lauded the closure of Sonora's churches, "real holes of corruption . . . where . . . girls lose their virginity and the honor of . . . married women is perverted." Debates also focused on religiosity. General Salvador González Torres argued that "religions are perfectly corrupt and . . . have been converted into a plot of stories and legends and aberrations with which [the clergy] attempt to surround the intelligence and . . . heart of . . . children for the purpose of [controlling] them in the future."[15]

Though presidents Venustiano Carranza and Álvaro Obregón tried to restrain Jacobinism and reach a modus vivendi with the church, anticlericalism remained significant in the ranks of the revolutionaries, especially among the followers of Calles and his close ally, the labor boss Luis Morones. Morones's agents were generally deemed responsible for a series of outrageous incidents designed to infuriate Catholics, such as the attack on the Virgin of Guadalupe. Such incidents were met with rising Catholic defiance. The Mexican bishops denounced the anticlerical provisions of the constitution. Clashes between

Catholics and anticlericals turned bloody, and militants of the Liga Nacional de la Defensa de la Libertad Religiosa secretly began to plan for armed resistance. The conflict finally erupted into a full-blown popular uprising, the Cristiada of 1926–29. Tens of thousands of *cristeros* from central-western Mexico battled the federal army and *agrarista* reserves in defense of local culture, religion, and autonomy. The war, one of the bloodiest episodes of the revolution, ended in a stalemate and an inconclusive agreement between church and state, which failed to resolve the profound cultural conflict.

Intellectuals shared the Jacobins' antireligiosity but were ambivalent about popular culture, which they considered both backward and a source for the construction of a new culture. In *Hacia un México Nuevo* (1935), Manuel Gamio, an influential anthropologist and *indigenista*, distinguished between the "popular or folk or anachronistic and deficient culture" of the rural, indigenous, and working-class population, and the "modern, scientific and efficient culture" of the urban population, and advocated uplifting the obsolete rural masses. Speaking of the future of Mexican art, Gamio considered popular, indigenous art richer and more spontaneous than that of Mexicans of European descent. However, Catholicism, with its dogmas, prayers, celebrations, alms, and images, had "disoriented aboriginal thought," diverting it from an indigenous cult of nature. "It is possible to root out religious belief in [this] segment of the population immediately [and] return the Indian to nature."[16] The revolutionary distaste of popular religiosity is also evident in the reports of rural teachers, who were responsible for implementing the cultural revolution locally. Inspector José Vázquez Luna was appalled by the attitudes of campesinos and Tarahumara Indians in the Sinaloan sierra. The villagers of Santiago de los Caballeros celebrated, "saturated with alcohol, [their] fiesta in honor of . . . Santiago, whom they carry on their shoulders through the . . . village to soften the egotistical heart of the 'God of the rains.' " In Santa Cruz, everyone waited "for luck to fall from the skies, to the sound of prayers or the priest's monotonous chants."[17] Popular religiosity was equated with superstition, backwardness, and debauchery, all anathema to the new man of the revolution.

By the 1920s, anticlericalism received renewed inspiration from another off-shoot of Enlightenment thought: Marxism. Politicians, labor leaders, artists, teachers, and soldiers read their Marx, Engels, and Lenin and sought inspiration in Bolshevik culture. However, socialism was generally poorly understood, even by leaders like Cárdenas. Many equated socialism with defanaticization and considered religion a function of capitalist exploitation and class conflict: "All religions . . . divert the action of the oppressed classes by making

[them] trust in an afterlife. . . . Religion is the opium of the people. . . . It is the obligation of all revolutionaries to undertake an indefatigable struggle against it."[18] Such notions pervaded the Secretaría de Educación Pública under Narciso Bassols (1931–34) and Ignacio García Téllez (1934–35). García Téllez called for the "socialization" of Mexican culture through the forging of a new citizen, productive, independent, optimistic, creative, vigorous, progressive, generous, and communitarian. Education was to liberate "our people from . . . all forms of idolatry and superstition."[19] Dissenters remained silent, were purged, or left the profession.[20]

## Popular Anticlericalism

Though revolutionaries often looked down on popular culture, they also drew inspiration from it. To what extent did popular attitudes inform their anticlericalism? Locally there always existed a degree of popular "pious anticlericalism," critical of the clergy yet at the same time profoundly religious.[21] Peasants considered themselves the true guardians of local Catholicism and the often-absent clergy mere purveyors of the sacraments.

This ambivalence arose from the controversial role of the village priest. Since the conquest, the clergy had repeatedly attempted to transform local cultures and impose orthodoxy by banning folk ritual, beliefs, and *curanderismo*. Parish priests wielded considerable authority, often sided with elites, exacted fees, tithes, and personal services, and engaged in business. Conflicts arose over control of communal lands, *cofradía* wealth, and other resources. There was also a sexual logic to popular anticlericalism. Celibacy led males to question the *cura*'s masculinity or denounce his hypocrisy. Revolutionaries torched confessionals, where priests supposedly preyed on women's minds and bodies, to eradicate clerical control symbolically.[22] Yet pious anticlericalism did not make peasants less *religious*. They simply held heterodox ideas about religion, ritual, and morality and vied with the clergy for control of local religion.

Anticlericalism also manifested itself in the popular liberalism that articulated local concepts of community, autonomy, land tenure, and citizenship and often denounced clerical service obligations, fees, and abuses.[23] Yet there was nothing inherently antireligious about popular liberalism. Generally, Jacobinism did not characterize popular revolutionary movements. Zapatista folk liberals coexisted nicely with the clergy, carried religious amulets and banners, and venerated the Virgin of Guadalupe. And while the Villistas initially unleashed a wave of anticlerical terror, they soon came to criticize Constitutionalist iconoclasm and emerged as "protector[s] of the faith."[24] I agree with Alan Knight that the "bulk of anti-clerical sentiment and policy was imported from outside the popular movement, and derived from urban, educated, middle class groups."[25]

## The Defanaticization Campaigns

Encouraged by the rabidly anticlerical Calles, defanaticization became national policy. In 1930 the government moved to enforce compliance of the anti-clerical constitutional article 130, which provided for federal intervention in religious affairs and limited the rights of religious associations and ministers. States responded by sharpening legislation and launching campaigns copied from earlier experiments, albeit with varying degrees of rigor and enthusiasm. Tabasco, Sonora, and Veracruz witnessed extreme campaigns, whereas states where earlier experiments had ended in conflict tried to avoid renewed confrontation. The work of state and local authorities, teachers, PNR branches, officers, popular organizations, Masonic lodges, and anticlerical associations, the campaigns sought to eradicate "religious fanaticism" by means of education, propaganda, iconoclasm, and the prohibition of ritual, and to replace traditional religion with a new, revolutionary civil religion, an intricate symbolic system with its own sacred beliefs, icons, and civic ritual, that is, to effect a "transfer of sacrality."[26]

Revolutionary iconoclasm consisted of a coherent set of practices. Churches were nationalized, closed to organized worship, and often handed over to teachers, workers, and peasants to serve as schools, offices, cultural centers, or warehouses. Many were torched, dynamited, or demolished, sometimes by schoolchildren wielding pickaxes. Some states banned religious nomenclature for towns and streets. The most controversial acts of desecration involved the destruction of religious symbols, especially saints' images, which quemasantos incinerated and smashed, often during obligatory PNR rallies or school festivals. Many states outlawed public rituals such as processions, pilgrimages, fiestas, and bell ringing. Mass became a clandestine activity celebrated in private homes. Priests were persecuted, expelled from seventeen states, severely curtailed elsewhere, and even assassinated. Catholics were purged from the PNR, the civil service, education, unions, and youth groups. "Socialist education" was to "combat fanaticism and prejudices." While Catholic schools were closed or forced underground, socialist schools mustered history and science to attack the clergy and religion and inculcate rationalist, scientific values. In open-air theaters, teachers and schoolchildren treated peasant audiences to plays, poetry, *corridos*, and puppet theater ridiculing the clergy, the faithful, and religion. Schools and public buildings were adorned with revolutionary murals and anticlerical posters.

Defanaticization in itself was not deemed sufficient to create a rational citizen. A revolutionary creed and morality and a new civic ritual would supplant religious beliefs and practices. Calles's pathetic attempt to establish a schismatic national church, the Iglesia Católica Apostólica Mexicana, was a fiasco. Instead, a revolutionary nationalist ritual emerged. New festivals, called Cultural Sundays (Domingos Culturales) or Red Sundays (Domingos Rojos), replaced Mass, holy days, and saints' fiestas, while efforts were made to substitute "socialist" sacraments for church baptisms and weddings. An elaborate Nationalist Calendar challenged the Catholic organization of sacred time. Festivals ranged from obligatory gatherings for bureaucrats and members of revolutionary organizations, featuring antireligious plays and poetry and the ritual incineration of "fetishes," to popular holidays such as Revolution Day.[27] While Mexicans resented the blatant antireligiosity of revolutionary ritual, they welcomed its nationalist aspects and the accompanying sports, parades, dances, and other diversions. Overall, defanaticization was hardly a success. Generally considered a profound threat to local culture and identity, it provoked widespread, often armed, resistance.

## The Significance of Local Religion

Local religion, especially in the indigenous communities of central and southern Mexico, is a syncretic fusion of Mesoamerican and Catholic beliefs. Its central feature is the reciprocal relationship of the individual, the family, and the community with the intermediaries of God, the saints. The saints are not mere symbols but living entities, which move, speak, and cry and reside in home altars and sanctuaries. As "repositories of, and intercessors with, the holy," they are venerated and served with offerings, vows (*mandas*), pilgrimages, and lavish fiestas. In return, saints act as miracle workers and provide protection from storm, drought, flood, plague, and violence. Local religion offers Mexicans a sense of "ontological security," a counterbalance to the "risk, danger, and existential anxiety" of a people constantly threatened by natural disasters, violence, and the supernatural.[28] If neglected or abused, saints may inflict punishment, even death, especially on unbelievers. In local mythology, the saint's image is identified with the locality. It often appears miraculously in a *milpa* (maize field), forest, or grotto or chooses its residence by becoming unbearably heavy during transportation, refusing to budge. Saints disappear when disgruntled or hide when threatened. Thus the village patron saint and sanctuary symbolize community identity and autonomy.[29] This form of local religion was never uniform but characterized many rural and even urban societies and transcended ethnic divides.[30]

Twentieth-century ethnography demonstrates that local religion remained largely intact, despite the profound changes that took place within Mexican Catholicism and society in general. Religion continued to permeate the everyday lives of Mexico's rural population. "Folk Catholicism," argues John Ingham, constituted a "way of life." This "saint system" was a " 'total system' classifying and representing all aspects of worldly existence." "The individual can draw upon, manipulate, and use this comprehensive system of collective ideas to make his own ordinary experiences understandable."[31]

Religion was closely intertwined with local politics and gender relations. Before the revolution, an important but little-studied aspect of local religion, especially in indigenous but also in mestizo communities, was the *cargo* system or civil-religious hierarchy. The system, which emerged during the late colonial era and proliferated in the nineteenth century, can be defined as a "hierarchy of ranked offices that together comprise a community's public civil and religious administration."[32] Those ascending this dual hierarchy attained prestige through the ceremonial sponsorship of the fiestas of patron saints. The system linked religious practices to the local sociopolitical order. Religious sponsorship enabled wealthy men who made a vow to organize and finance a fiesta to join the prestigious ranks of the village elders. Leadership by elders, in turn, allowed villages to maintain a degree of autonomy vis-à-vis the state. John K. Chance and William B. Taylor have found that the nineteenth-century cargo system had a significant leveling function and allowed villages "greater leeway to reconstitute their ceremonial organizations and express religion in their own terms."[33] Most importantly, the system ensured community security through the perpetuation of reciprocal ties with the saints. It would soon become the target of revolutionary scrutiny.

Though it offered women new opportunities, the revolution also infringed on areas of feminine influence, such as local religion. While many female teachers, agraristas, and feminists supported the revolution, including defanaticization, others chose to dissent or faced the difficult prospect of juggling conflicting loyalties. Religion is an important arena for the construction and contestation of gender roles. In the West, the Enlightenment resulted in the (re)feminization of religion. While rationalism became a male domain, women found opportunities for personal perfection, community, and empowerment with the church. New, male-dominated master narratives, such as national-ism, liberalism, and modernity, branded women as superstitious and fanatic.[34] In Mexico, women held a real stake in local religious praxis, which removed them from the confines of domesticity and offered channels for sociability and influence. They played a central role in catechism, church finances, and edu-cation and maintained community contacts with parish priests. Women were more likely than men to attend Mass, confess, and fulfill other religious obliga-tions.[35] *Curanderas* deployed magic to control their partners and protect their children from common forms of witchcraft, such as *mal de ojo* and *espanto*. For young, unmarried women—whose existence was circumscribed by strict gen-der roles—church attendance, fiestas, and membership in Catholic organiza-tions provided opportunities for informal sociability and a space in which to discuss issues such as the choice of a mate. Women often associated Mass with diversion, and adolescents even saw it as an opportunity to flirt. Afterward they visited relatives while men left to drink with their *compadres*.[36]

The feminization of religion was a church-driven process that, moving out-ward from urban centers, penetrated rural areas, establishing successful new devotions, such as the cult of Mary Immaculate, and lay associations such as the Hijas de María, the Asociación de la Vela Perpetua, the Asociación del Apostolado de la Oración, and the Asociación Guadalupana. Members met regularly, wore special medals and ribbons, made collective vows, and par-ticipated in cults and fiestas. In urban areas, thousands joined new Catho-lic mass organizations. By the 1930s, women dominated Acción Católica, ac-counting for 77 percent of its membership. The Unión Femenina Católica Mexicana, Acción Católica's women's branch, had a dues-paying membership of 115,000, who engaged in catechistical, educational, and moralizing activi-ties, supported underground seminaries, combated "socialist education," and engaged in charity.[37] Women resisted the anticlerical state via cristero Brigadas Femeninas. This realm of female influence was directly threatened by the male-dominated state. As Ana Alonso argues, "Because of their [putative] spiritual 'nature,' women commanded a moral authority that they were able to deploy to gain a measure of informal power. . . . The state's attack on the church threat-ened to undermine forms of feminine empowerment."[38]

## Local Responses

How did defanaticization impact local cultures? Which cultural matrixes did Mexicans use to make sense of the burning of beloved saints and the desecration of ancient chapels? Dechristianization threatened ontological security, intricate civil-religious hierarchies, feminine empowerment, and conventional peasant and ethnic identities.

Local saints were crucial to the well-being of individual and community. Believers feared "that something terrible would happen" if they failed to serve them.[39] Saints and crosses were capable of punishing those who neglected their sacred obligations. The Mayos of Sonora expected that the burning of the "Little Children" (the saints) would result in the apocalypse. The Catholics of Tlapacoyan, Veracruz, feared that the incineration of their church and saints' images in 1931 would cause a devastating flood of the Río Alseca. Saints might also abandon the believers. Iconoclasm caused a miraculous image of the Virgin that regularly appeared in a tree near Paxtla, Puebla, to disappear. In Mexico City, a riot almost broke out when rumors spread that the Virgin of Guadalupe had abandoned the basilica and was hiding in a tree.[40]

To avoid being cut off from the sacred, villagers resisted the onslaught or hid the saints' images. In Sonora, the peasants of Batacosa threatened violence to stop police from burning a beloved statue of Saint Bartolo. When Garrido's *milicianos* arrived in Mecatepec to destroy the image of the Cristo de la Salud, Nahua villagers were able to smuggle it north to Veracruz, where Catholics welcomed it in what became a triumphant procession. Garrido reportedly offered a reward of ten thousand pesos for the statue's capture, but it was never found, further enhancing its miraculous reputation. In Sonora, false rumors circulated that the image of San Francisco Xavier was never burned but in fact had been smuggled across the border to a Tohono O'odam reservation in Arizona. Communities were expected to seek revenge for these outrages. In response to the burning of the saints of Tlapacoyan, Catholics besieged the *palacio municipal*, bombarding it with burning chili bombs. A gunfight left thirty wounded and twelve dead, including the mayor, the police chief, and five officers, whose bodies were mutilated.[41] Iconoclasm sparked violence because local ontological security was at stake.

Tales of sacred punishment, such as those collected by Pedro Carrasco in Michoacán, form an important discursive repertoire. For example, a colonel who decapitated the image of the Christ of Carácuaro fell terribly ill but was not granted a peaceful death until he had begged for forgiveness. Workers constructing a movie theater in Pátzcuaro on the site of a demolished church suffered mysterious fatal accidents. In Sonora, the worker who incinerated San Francisco Xavier in the furnace of the Sonora Brewery went mad, or was hit by a truck, while Juan Pacheco, the hated iconoclastic chief of rural police in the

Mayo Valley, lost his son in a shooting or drowning accident. In Mezquitic, San Luis Potosí, holy retribution was swift when individuals stripped the saints of their garments: "Those two didn't last! A thunderstorm came and . . . Juan was carried off by a swollen creek. . . . A punishment from God. . . . And his mama, doña Ventura, also died." Natural disasters befell sacrilegious towns. In Michoacán, the eruption of the Paricutín volcano was attributed to the destruction of a sacred cross, the theft of the Holy Host, and the throwing to the bulls of an image of Christ. The devil, often disguised as a sinister hag, harassed anticlerical agrarista villages but avoided pious settlements.[42]

According to Chance, the period 1920–40, the era of postrevolutionary consolidation, was a watershed in the history of the cargo system in many states, such as Oaxaca, Chiapas, Michoacán, and Guerrero, marking the beginning of its decline or disappearance and the transition to a dual structure in which a purely religious cargo system survived, while civil offices were integrated into a separate state and federal administration. This resulted in a widespread and irreversible loss of power for village *principales* and growing dependency on state and federal politics. This swift and remarkable development was often linked to the anticlerical campaigns. Since 1926, Oaxacan governors and politicians waged an anti-*mayordomía* campaign, portraying the institution as wasteful and financially burdensome. In many villages, the obligatory mayordomía system was abolished. *Juntas vecinales*, which assumed the administration of sealed churches, became the embryo of an alternative village power structure. A new group of young, Spanish-speaking political brokers linked to the state rose to power, challenging the principales. Likewise, in Michoacán towns such as Chilcota, between 1932 and 1940 anticlericals abolished cults and the cargo system, which they considered elaborate excuses for extravagant spending and debauchery, causing a similar split in the civil-religious hierarchy between religious *cabildos* and civil administration. In the highlands of Chiapas, among the Tzeltal and Tzotzil, the situation was more complex. Though the government temporarily undermined the civil-religious hierarchy, from 1936 onward so-called *escribanos*, bilingual *muchachos* who maintained close ties with the state, consolidated their power and came to form a new group of principales by reestablishing the cargo system and assuming cargos themselves. In Chiapas, the entrenchment of Indian "tradition" led to the consolidation of state power.[43]

Other factors, such as increasing contact with the outside world, demographic growth, and socioeconomic change, undoubtedly played a role in the system's decline. Still, Chance convincingly argues that the revolution's attempt to "limit the autonomy of the local community and integrate it in new ways into national society" was a "triggering event." The failure to incorporate new political offices into the civil-religious hierarchies resulted in "a decrease in local level autonomy and an increase in community dependency on state and federal governments."[44]

The anticlerical campaigns placed women in a difficult position. Marjorie Becker argues that women, especially the poor, were torn between religion and land reform and between submission to men and public action.[45] Indeed, revolutionary organizations and practices, such as *ligas femeniles*, school councils, educational programs, and PNR local elections, in which women were allowed to vote, opened new venues for women. However, it is equally clear that community-based religion offered women important opportunities for empowerment. As Mary Kay Vaughan argues, "The Catholic religion gave [women] a propelling self-image, and the symbolism of Mary and the Holy Family, today identified by feminists with female subjugation, were more nourishing images for campesinas than those initially provided by revolutionary schools."[46] Not surprisingly, women launched mass protests that ultimately scuttled defanaticization. To maintain that women were tools of the clergy is to deny them agency. Women distributed flyers, taught in underground Catholic schools, hid priests, organized clandestine masses and school boycotts, and initiated petition drives in support of religious freedom. They occupied churches, stormed schools and government buildings, and attacked, and sometimes killed, rural teachers.[47]

Not all Mexicans actively opposed defanaticization. A passive silent majority chose to ride out the storm, while a minority supported the campaigns for strategic reasons or identified with revolutionary anticlericalism. The latter were primarily agraristas, campesinos allied with the state in hopes of obtaining ejidal lands. Michoacán, where agraristas battled Catholic peasants throughout the 1920s and 1930s, serves as a quintessential case. Many Michoacán peasants embraced not just agrarian reform, but also the wider cultural project, in the process forming new identities. Here defanaticization was primarily a function of local disputes over land and power and allowed a new generation of village leaders to bypass traditional politico-religious hierarchies, landless campesinos to acquire land, and women to take advantage of state-sponsored opportunities for empowerment. Popular religion itself was seldom at the heart of the conflict, and in many agrarista communities, beliefs remained essentially unchanged. Iconoclasm was, argues Chris Boyer, a way for peasants publicly to proclaim their adherence to the revolutionary project. Clearly, the impact

of defanaticization was serious: it sparked violence throughout Michoacán.[48]
However, by the 1940s, conflicts tended to assume a nonreligious discourse.

## Conclusion

The Mexican Revolution involved a cultural revolution, or, to use Theda Skocpol's term, a "metaphysical revolution," which sought to reshape local culture,
identity, and everyday life.[49] Mexico became a laboratory of modernity, where
the Enlightenment dream clashed with the alternative visions that stressed
local culture and religiosity, autonomy, land, and social justice. This clash often
centered on religion.

Communities made use of popular cultural matrixes, especially local religion, to make sense of and influence revolutionary change. Discourses related
to ontological security, gender, autonomy, participation, and identity inter-
sected in the crucial realm of local religion. Catholics resisted dechristianization with the cultural tools at their disposal, ranging from discursive practices
(rumors, tales) that allowed them to interpret otherwise inexplicable events to
methods reflecting the penetration of the state and modern associations, such
as petitions and rallies. Subterfuge was common. Embattled Catholics could
receive the sacraments only by attending clandestine masses. Catholic associations, ranging from Acción Católica to the Sinarquistas, challenged popular
revolutionary organizations. As late as the 1930s, religious unrest and violence
still plagued many regions, from Sonora to Chiapas.

These responses startled Mexico's leaders, who initially countered with
force. However, by 1937, mass campaigns for religious freedom obliged the
government to modify its cultural blueprint and abandon defanaticization.
The violent interaction of rival visions forged Mexico's postrevolutionary political culture. Though Mexicans rebuffed attempts to destroy local religiosity,
the state was still able to penetrate rural communities by abolishing civil-
religious hierarchies and forging new political leadership, in the process bind-
ing local politics to the state. Women, though fiercely defensive of their unique
role in local religion, took advantage of new opportunities in education and
politics. The cultural revolution confronted resistant Mexicans with modern
alternatives to local identities. However, many soon learned to manage plural
identities creatively.

Mexican modernity, though an integral part of revolutionary discourse,
never reached the extremes of "high modernism" because of the absence of two
prerequisites: a strong state and a weak civil society. As late as 1940, the Mexi-

can state remained weak, incapable of imposing its cultural agenda, while civil society, though battered and divided, retained strong resources for resistance in the "cultural idioms" of local culture and religion, idioms that had sparked the revolution to begin with.[50] The state failed to destroy local religiosity but succeeded in penetrating local communities, starting a dialectical process that ultimately forged a new Mexico.

## Notes

1. *Excélsior*, November 15, 18, 19, 1921.

2. D. A. Brading, *The First America: The Spanish Monarchy, Creole Patriots, and the Liberal State, 1492–1867* (Cambridge: Cambridge University Press, 1991), 674.

3. Richard Nebel, *Santa María Tonanztin Virgen de Guadalupe: Continuidad y transformación religiosa en México* (Mexico City: Fondo de Cultura Económica, 1995), 339.

4. Francisco José Paoli Bolio, ed., *Salvador Alvarado: Estadista y pensador (antología)* (Mexico City: Fondo de Cultura Económica, 1994), 70, 82, 96.

5. Franco Savarino Roggero, *Pueblos y nacionalismo, del régimen oligárquico a la sociedad de masas en Yucatán, 1894–1925* (Mexico City: INEHRM, 1997), 360–61.

6. *El Tabasco que yo he visto* (Mexico City: Secretaría de Agricultura y Fomento, 1935), 6, 25–32, 119.

7. Gaveta 35, Garrido Canabal, Tomas, inv. 2312, exp. 140, legs. 5/7, 7/7, Archivo Plutarco Elías Calles (APEC).

8. James C. Scott, *Seeing like a State: How Certain Schemes to Improve the Human Condition Have Failed* (New Haven: Yale University Press, 1998).

9. Clifford Geertz, *After the Fact: Two Countries, Four Decades, One Anthropologist* (Cambridge: Harvard University Press, 1995), 136.

10. Charles A. Hale, *Mexican Liberalism in the Age of Mora, 1821–1853* (New Haven: Yale University Press, 1968), 163–64, 171–73; D. A. Brading, "Liberal Patriotism and the Mexican Reforma," *Journal of Latin American Studies* 20, no. 1 (1988): 30–31, 38.

11. Charles A. Hale, *The Transformation of Liberalism in Late Nineteenth-Century Mexico* (Princeton: Princeton University Press, 1989), 98–99, 132; James D. Cockcroft, *Intellectual Precursors of the Mexican Revolution, 1900–1913* (Austin: University of Texas Press, 1968), 67–68, 95.

12. Jean Meyer, *La cristiada*, vol. 2, *El conflicto entre la iglesia y el estado 1926–1929* (Mexico City: Siglo XXI, 1985), 45; Luis E. Murillo, "Women and the Politics of Local Religious Practices in Porfirian Mexico" (paper, RMCLAS/PCCLAS conference, Santa Fe, 1996).

13. José Miguel Romero de Solís, *El aguijón del espiritu: Historia contemporánea de la Iglesia en México (1895–1990)* (Mexico City: Instituto Mexicano de Doctrina Social Cristiana, 1994), 149, 151.

14. Jean-Pierre Bastián, "Jacobinismo y ruptura revolucionaria durante el porfiriato," *Mexican Studies/Estudios Mexicanos* 7, no. 1 (winter 1991): 30; *Los disidentes: Sociedades protestantes y revolución en México* (Mexico City: El Colegio de México, 1989), 304–5.

15. E. V. Niemeyer Jr., *Revolution at Querétaro: The Mexican Constitutional Convention of 1916–1917* (Austin: University of Texas Press, 1974), 76, 81, 90, 97.

16. *Hacia un México nuevo* (Mexico City: Instituto Nacional Indigenista, 1987), 56–59, 65–67.

17. Report, October 3, 1936, Fondo Dirección General de Educación Primaria, Archivo Histórico, SEP, 318.5.

18. Gaveta 1, Acción Antirreligiosa, inv. 16, exp. 16, fojas 1–2, APEC.

19. Ignacio García Téllez, *Socialización de la cultura* (Mexico City, 1935), 21, 38.

20. Adrian Bantjes, "Idolatry and Iconoclasm in Revolutionary Mexico: the De-Christianization Campaigns, 1929–1940," *Mexican Studies/Estudios Mexicanos* 13, no. 1 (winter 1997): 108.

21. Ruth Behar, "The Struggle for the Church: Popular Anticlericalism and Religiosity in Post-Franco Spain," in *Religious Orthodoxy and Popular Faith in European Society*, ed. Ellen Badone (Princeton: Princeton University Press, 1990), 76–112.

22. Alan Knight, "Popular Culture and the Revolutionary State in Mexico, 1910–1940," *Hispanic American Historical Review* 74, no. 3 (August 1994): 412, 416.

23. Guy P. C. Thomson, "Popular Aspects of Liberalism in Mexico, 1848–1888," *Bulletin of Latin American Research* 10 (1991): 282–83, 289.

24. Meyer, *La cristiada*, 2:95–96; Friedrich Katz, *The Life and Times of Pancho Villa* (Stanford: Stanford University Press, 1998), 446–48.

25. Alan Knight, *The Mexican Revolution*, vol. 2, *Counter-revolution and Reconstruction* (Cambridge: Cambridge University Press, 1986), 184.

26. Mona Ozouf, *La fête révolutionnaire, 1789–1799* (Paris: Gallimard, 1976).

27. David E. Lorey, "The Revolutionary Festival in Mexico: November 20 Celebrations in the 1920s and 1930s," *The Americas* 54, no. 1 (1997).

28. Anthony Giddens, *The Consequences of Modernity* (Stanford: Stanford University Press, 1990), 106–7.

29. William B. Taylor, *Magistrates of the Sacred: Priests and Parishioners in Eighteenth-Century Mexico* (Stanford: Stanford University Press, 1996), chap. 11.

30. Leif Korsbaek, *Introducción al sistema de cargos* (Mexico City: UNAM, 1996), 59.

31. John M. Ingham, *Mary, Michael, and Lucifer: Folk Catholicism in Central Mexico* (Austin: University of Texas Press, 1986), 180; Lynn Stephen and James Dow, introduction to *Class, Politics, and Popular Religion in Mexico and Central America*, ed. Lynn Stephen and James Dow (Washington: Society for Latin American Anthropology, American Anthropological Association, 1990), 1–24; Stephen Gudeman, "Saints, Symbols, and Ceremonies," *American Ethnologist* 3, no. 4 (November 1976): 725–27.

32. John K. Chance, "Changes in Twentieth-Century Mesoamerican Cargo Sys-

tems," in Stephen and Dow, *Class*, 27, see also 28–31; Pedro Carrasco, *El catolicismo popular de los tarascos* (Mexico City: SepSetentas, 1976), 62–63, 76–79.

33. John K. Chance and William B. Taylor, "Cofradías and Cargos: An Historical Perspective on the Mesoamerican Civil-Religious Hierarchy," *American Ethnologist* 12, no. 1 (February 1985): 2, 22.

34. Elisja Schulte van Kessel, "Virgins and Mothers between Heaven and Earth," in *A History of Women*, vol. 3, *Renaissance and Enlightenment Paradoxes*, ed. Natalie Zemon Davis and Arlette Farge (Cambridge: Harvard University Press, 1993), 146–47; Jean Franco, *Plotting Women: Gender and Representation in Mexico* (New York: Columbia University Press, 1989), xii, xviii.

35. Ingham, *Mary*, 161, 175; Oscar Lewis, *Life in a Mexican Village: Tepoztlán Restudied* (Urbana: University of Illinois Press, 1963), 275.

36. Lewis, *Life*, 274–75, 398; Kristina A. Boylan, "They Were Always Doing Something: Catholic Women's Mobilization in Mexico in the 1930s" (paper, St. Antony's College, Oxford, 1998, 28).

37. Lewis, *Life*, 266–67; Guillermo Zermeño P. and Rubén Aguilar V., *Hacia una reinterpretación del Sinarquismo actual* (Mexico City: Universidad Iberoamericana, 1988), 26; Boylan, "They," 17, 26–27.

38. Ana María Alonso, *Thread of Blood: Colonialism, Revolution, and Gender on Mexico's Northern Frontier* (Tucson: University of Arizona Press, 1995), 138.

39. Carrasco, *El catolicismo*, 59–61.

40. N. Ross Crumrine, *The Mayo Indians of Sonora: A People Who Refuse to Die* (Tucson: University of Arizona Press, 1977), 150; John B. Williman, *La Iglesia y el Estado en Veracruz, 1840–1940* (Mexico City: SepSetentas, 1976), 138–41.

41. Adrian A. Bantjes, *As If Jesus Walked on Earth: Cardenismo, Sonora, and the Mexican Revolution* (Wilmington, Del.: SR Books, 1998), 12; Williman, *La Iglesia*, 136–39; James S. Griffith, *Beliefs and Holy Places: A Spiritual Geography of the Pimería Alta* (Tucson: University of Arizona Press, 1992), 51.

42. Carrasco, *El catolicismo*, 119, 130–35; Charles J. Erasmus, *Man Takes Control: Cultural Development and American Aid* (Minneapolis: University of Minnesota Press, 1961), 276–77; David Frye, *Indians into Mexicans: History and Identity in a Mexican Town* (Austin: University of Texas Press, 1996), 112.

43. Stephen and Dow, "Introduction," 10–11; Chance, "Changes," 27–34; Jan Rus, "The 'Comunidad Revolucionaria Institucional': The Subversion of Native Government in Highland Chiapas, 1936–1968," in *Everyday Forms of State Formation: Revolution and the Negotiation of Rule in Modern Mexico*, ed. Gilbert M. Joseph and Daniel Nugent (Durham: Duke University Press, 1994), 265–300; Lynn Stephen, "The Politics of Ritual: The Mexican State and Zapotec Autonomy, 1926 to 1989," in Stephen and Dow, *Class*, 43–49; Carrasco, *El catolicismo*, 80–87.

44. Chance, "Changes," 28, 34–35.

45. Marjorie Becker, "Torching la Purísima, Dancing at the Altar: The Construction of Revolutionary Hegemony in Michoacán, 1934–1940," in Joseph and Nugent, *Everyday Forms*, 262–63.

46. Mary Kay Vaughan, "Rural Women's Literacy and Education during the Mexican Revolution: Subverting a Patriarchal Event?" in *Women of the Mexican Countryside, 1850–1990*, ed. Heather Fowler-Salamini and Mary Kay Vaughan (Tucson: University of Arizona Press, 1992), 115.

47. Salvador Camacho Sandoval, *Controversia entre la ideología y la fe: La educación socialista en la historia de Aguascalientes, 1876–1940* (Mexico City: CONACULTA, 1991), 150–51, 155–58, 172–76, 182–87.

48. Christopher R. Boyer, "Old Loves, New Loyalties: Agrarismo in Michoacán, 1920–1928," *Hispanic American Historical Review* 78, no. 3 (August 1998): 419–55.

49. Theda Skocpol, "Cultural Idioms and Political Ideologies in the Revolutionary Reconstruction of State Power: A Rejoinder to Sewell," *Journal of Modern History* 57, no. 1 (1985): 94–95.

50. Alan Knight, "Cardenismo: Juggernaut or Jalopy?" *Journal of Latin American Studies* 26 (1994): 73–107.

# Nationalizing the Countryside:
# Schools and Rural Communities in the 1930s

MARY KAY VAUGHAN

In 1921, José Vasconcelos, minister of Mexico's new Secretaría de Educación Pública, launched a crusade for schools and national culture that ignited the imagination and energy of teachers, musicians, artists, poets, doctors, archae- ologists, anthropologists, and folklorists. The crusade integrated intellectuals from the capital, Mexico's regions, and towns. It won the applause of cosmo- politan artistic, professional, and political circles. It marked the beginning of one of the most consistent state commitments to the creation of national cul- ture and the expansion of public education in the twentieth century.

In this chapter, I focus on the SEP's rural schools and campesino interaction with them. "Campesino" refers to the rural landless, land-poor, and small property holders. Ethnically, campesinos might be of predominantly Euro- pean extraction, although most were some mixture of European, Indian, and often African heritages. Indigenous communities may also be campesinos. In his companion chapter, Stephen Lewis describes schooling encounters in a wide variety of indigenous communities. However, this chapter focuses on only one type of indigenous community: the central Mexican Mesoamerican community, the indigenous core of the Spanish colonial empire, long accus- tomed to interaction with the dominant society, market, and state—in short, mestizoized. My focus is on the 1930s, when school programs were most robust and controversial. In this decade, highly mobilized local societies negotiated with teachers who promoted social reform, state and nation formation, and the consolidation of the official political party, the PNR (later the PRI).

Contrary to the SEP's claims, schools were not new to rural Mexico. Two of the three regions examined here had ample exposure, one to municipal, secu- lar, liberal schools, and the other to Catholic schools in the Porfiriato. After 1889, a series of congresses sought to nationalize curriculum, ensure its adoption by private Catholic schools, and secure uniform teacher training through a system of normal schools. The singular program would "defanaticize" Mexicans, teaching them a scientific understanding of the universe. It would foster habits of work, punctuality, and thrift and encourage abstinence from alcohol, tobacco, and gambling. Nonetheless, the centralizing thrust was incipient, and results fell far short of goals. According to the 1910 census, only 33 percent of Mexican men and 27 percent of women were literate. Porfirian schools were more important in their production of middle-class talent for the postrevolutionary educational and cultural efforts than they were in transforming popular behavior and eradicating illiteracy.

In continuing Porfirian hopes for behavioral reform, postrevolutionary educators participated in an international milieu of developmentalist thinking and social engineering designed to nationalize citizens in the interest of order, production, and military defense in a competitive global order. Mexican educators were highly creative in their manipulation of the ideas and policies perking in this international milieu. Perhaps no country in the world more faithfully adopted John Dewey's notions of child-centered, "learning by doing" pedagogy. In the SEP's rural Escuela de la Acción, or Action School, learning in principle took place through the cooperative cultivation of gardens and marketing of produce, the raising of animals and bees, and the introduction of modern medicines, first aid, and hygiene. Although they accepted the biologized notion of a diseased social body, Mexican educators linked degeneration to social issues: peasants were sick and lethargic because of rapacious landlords, priests, and an unjust distribution of property and wealth. Redistributive rural policy promoted land reform and the schools' linkage with it. Social policy radicalized during the presidency of Lázaro Cárdenas (1934–40) under conditions of persistent sociopolitical agitation, the massification of politics, and the central state's efforts to establish effective control over a far-flung and highly mobilized society.[1] The educational crusade ignited the enthusiasm of hundreds of rural teachers, who came to see themselves as part of a mystical crusade for the nation, modernity, and social justice. Like the sixteenth-century Spanish missionaries, rural federal schoolteachers became redeemers.

In the 1920s, the SEP pacted with state governments to establish or assume jurisdiction over existing, primarily rural schools. Facilitated by the financial incapacity of state and local governments, the SEP's share of primary school enrollments expanded to 34 percent by 1928 and 54 percent by 1940. A fledgling effort in the 1920s, federal rural education in the 1930s drew strength from its own maturation—from the experiences of policymakers, inspectors, and teachers in the countryside—and its linkage to a policy of economic redistribution (land and labor reforms) and the formation of the official government party, the PNR. By the 1930s, the federal school became the unifying ideological arm of the state. The SEP inscribed the constitution of 1917 in schools and communities—especially in its clauses related to agrarian and worker reform. New national history and reading textbooks turned campesinos and workers into agents in a collective struggle for social justice to be achieved in alliance with the central government. To the pantheon of patriot heroes celebrated in civic festivals (Miguel Hidalgo as father of independence, Benito Juárez as father of the republic, and Francisco I. Madero as initiator of the revolution), teachers introduced new heroes such as Emiliano Zapata, champion of land reform. Local and regional folkloric songs and dances and revolutionary *corridos* were incorporated as "national culture." Action pedagogy expanded to reflect heightened eugenic concern with health, especially in the promotion of anti-alcohol campaigns and team sports.

Unfortunately, the SEP rural school program had deep flaws. Its prescriptions derived from cosmopolitan, urban, and bourgeois notions of science and decorum that were not necessarily compatible with rural needs, practices, and resources. SEP personnel held local culture in contempt and showed little interest in understanding its logic. Under SEP minister Narciso Bassols (1931–34) and culminating with the introduction of "socialist education" in 1934, federal school policy became actively antireligious. Although teacher engagement in antireligious activities varied from place to place, the policy provoked widespread resistance spearheaded by seasoned Catholic social and political organization. Dozens of teachers were killed, and many more were de-eared, assaulted, kidnapped, or simply run out of town. So divisive was this dimension of policy that President Cárdenas officially abandoned it in 1936.

Finally, teachers became actively engaged in the formation of Mexico's official state party. They played a critical role in its massification, in the organization of national worker (CTM) and campesino (CNC) associations that formed the popular base of the Partido de la Revolución Mexicana, the reformed PNR and precursor of the PRI. Thus the federal school, despite its rhetorical commitment to democracy, contributed to the consolidation of an authoritarian, single-party regime. However, within this structure, both teachers and schools frequently functioned to represent and secure local interests and to ensure that local voices were heard within state structures.

## The SEP's Vision of Modernity and Nation in the Countryside

In the 1930s, SEP policy, together with land reform and health programs, aimed at destroying regional, often precapitalist, patriarchal networks of power organized around local hacienda owners and merchants. These would be replaced by national, horizontal, cooperatively organized networks linked to the expanding national market. Policy sought to remake the family in the interests of nation building and development. It sought a restructuring of male productive practices and sociability, the rationalization of domesticity, and a mobilization of children for patriotic development.[2]

Within this vision, the male campesino's production, presumed to be subsistence oriented or dominated by landlord or merchant, would be commercialized and nationalized for the benefit of the campesino family. New, horizontal, state-linked *ejidos* (land reform units), cooperatives, and marketing networks would replace his old reliance on vertical, local networks for resource allocation, provisioning, and trade. His social behavior was to be sanitized—his drinking, gambling, praying, womanizing, and violence curtailed. No longer would a swig of *aguardiente* seal a high-interest loan from the landlord. This act would be replaced by hand shaking and document signing at sober ceremonies in the schoolhouse in which *ejidatarios* received their land titles from government officials or negotiated accords with the government's Ejidal Bank.

The male campesino would read agrarian law and technical manuals and listen to government educational radio rather than to priests. Forsaking blood sports—cockfighting, bullfighting, and boxing—he would join baseball and basketball teams. These would encourage his health and sobriety. They would nurture a proper mix of competitiveness and cooperation appropriate to autonomous, self-disciplined performance in the modern world of anonymity and production.

The rationalization of domesticity focused on mothers in their households. Policymakers urged teachers to promote the civil registration of conjugal unions, births, and deaths—a secularizing process taken over by the state from the church in the nineteenth century. They were to preach against early marriage and to propagate new "scientific" discourses of nutrition, hygiene, and disease prevention. Campesino homes were to be redesigned for health, comfort, and sexual propriety. Windows were to be installed for light and air; animals were to be ejected from the living quarters, and rooms partitioned to prevent "promiscuity." The hearth was to be raised from floor to waist level and a chimney installed to preserve women's backs, eliminate smoke from the house, and reduce accidents. The *molino de nixtamal* (corn-grinding mill) and sewing machine were to be introduced.

Campesina mothers would learn more nutritional ways of feeding their families. Teachers, along with health workers, would fight *curanderas* (healers), "witchcraft," and homespun midwives. They would peddle modern medicines and inoculate against smallpox and other contagious diseases. Sanitation was an urgent matter. Soap should be made and used, latrines built, garbage burned, flies swatted, and water boiled. Integral community development envisaged a new feminine sociability disassociated from the church and linked to civic, secular action. This sociability was an extension of domesticity. Women would gather not to dress the Virgin for festival but to crusade for the moral and physical health of the community in the form of anti-alcohol and sanitation campaigns, participation in the school parents' council, and the organization of patriotic festivals.

The school would mobilize their children for national development. The school's space fell under the state's discursive and normative domination independent of parents and the church. It would be coeducational. Boys and girls would share a common curriculum promoting patriotism and modernity. Girls were as important as boys to the development effort because they would become mothers of citizen workers, consumers, and marginal income earners. Together boys and girls would engage in patriotic learning through cooperative gardening and marketing, competitions in crafts and agriculture, the organization of sports teams, and folkloric performance at patriotic festivals.

### Community Response to Rural Federal Schools

Research to date suggests that community response to the federal program depended on local, historical experiences with schools and with reading and writing. Important as well was how communities had related to processes of state formation: whether or not they had participated in or rejected the liberal patriotic culture of the nineteenth century, and if they had experienced the revolution and the projects of the postrevolutionary state as opportunities to better their lives or as unwanted intrusions. Their response depended on cultural practices and values and their linkage to local configurations of power. Responses varied according to access to economic resources and exposure to the external world.

Also influential in shaping the school encounter was the state's capacity to create the political, material, and cultural conditions for a transformation of

behavior and mentality. The effort of the central government was handicapped
by a lack of resources and technical expertise, and by rivalry and conflict between government agencies, institutions, and authorities at the national, regional, and local levels. State incapacity facilitated the persistence of traditional
practices and values that educators wanted to transform.

To illustrate the diversity of campesino response to the federal school program in the 1930s, this chapter examines encounters in communities representative of three social configurations that played an important role in the
revolution and in the process of postrevolutionary state formation. Communities of Tecamachalco in Puebla were representative of central Mexican peasant
communities forged on a pre-Hispanic Mesoamerican base of communal land-
holding but altered by centuries of interaction with the dominant society. In
the revolution, many, like those led by Emiliano Zapata in Morelos, mobilized
to reclaim lands and water lost to haciendas. Educators viewed these communities as poor, primitive, religiously fanatical, and weakly linked to modernity. While the SEP targeted them for behavioral transformation, in the 1930s
the government did not commit the material resources that would have facilitated such change. The Michoacán town of San José de Gracia is representative
of a second set of communities, western Mexican ranchero settlements that
saw themselves as criollo, or of white European descent, rather than indigenous or mestizo. Smallholders, they identified private property with masculine honor and were suspicious of the government. Devoutly Catholic, their
faith had been fortified by a vigorous Catholic educational and social movement begun in the late nineteenth century. In the 1920s, they became militants
in the Cristero war against the postrevolutionary state's anticlerical policies
and gained fame for their attacks on federal teachers. By contrast, the third
set of communities, newly organized settlements of farmworkers in northern
Mexican agribusiness enterprises, struggled for land reform and trade union
rights in alliance with the central government. Significantly, the government
provided these communities with infrastructural support to transform their
lives in large part because they produced export crops deemed vital to national
development.

## Tecamachalco

In the Porfiriato, the people of Tecamachalco, a district of eight municipalities on Puebla's central plateau, lived in pueblos, *rancherías*, and barrios where
they grew corn, maguey, ixtle fiber, chilies, onions, and beans. They depended

for survival on surrounding haciendas for which they sharecropped, rented, or worked part or full time. Haciendas also provided them with credit and market access. In the revolution, they rose up to reclaim land, power, space, and autonomy. By 1930, one-third of the male population had become ejidatarios, beneficiaries of government land grants. Tecamachalqueños weakened vertical patriarchal networks of hacienda power through their own initiatives, taking advantage of state weakness and periodic offers of support from outside politicians and government agents. In the 1930s, more concerted state efforts to insert them into the national order were complicated by a lack of resources, conflicts between government agencies, and competition among local, regional, and central government authorities.[3] As the Cardenista central government sought to create economic and political linkages through the Confederación Nacional Campesina (CNC) and the Ejidal Bank that would strengthen campesino voices and well-being within a bourgeois order, the state government of Puebla was more conservative and, in alliance with large landowners, sought to end land reform and to curtail *agrarista* power.

Into this thicket of residual agrarista autonomy and competing state agendas for reducing it stepped the federal teachers. Rather than forging an organic alliance with the campesinos, as SEP policy recommended, the school inspector initially sparred with them. He stepped on the newly won rights of Comités Agrarios, organized to petition for land, and the Comisariados Ejidales governing the new ejidos. He challenged their recent conquest of the Comités de Educación, their "unauthorized" use of school space for meetings, and their monopolization of the school parcel, a plot of land set aside for support of the school. He complained that the Ejidal Bank and state agrarian authorities encouraged the production of pulque, the alcoholic source of campesino "decadence." In fact, pulque production was rational. Produced from the maguey plant, which thrived in the dry climate, pulque had a guaranteed regional market, a critically important factor given the weakening of prerevolutionary marketing mechanisms and the still limited formation of new ones.

Religion became a bone of contention. Despite their fledgling loyalty to revolutionary governments for legalizing land reform, few agraristas in Tecamachalco favored the antireligious dimension of socialist education. While the organized Catholic movement was instrumental in generating opposition here, campesinos acted out of their own faith. When villagers of La Portilla were accused of stealing a statue of the Virgin from the hacienda of Santa Rosa, they defended their deed in revolutionary terms. Year after year, they explained, the hacendado had taken corn from each family and from the lands sown by the *cofradía* on the pretext of sustaining the Virgin and building a new chapel for her. The hacendado had sold the corn to build a mezcal factory rather than a chapel. The campesinos had not stolen the Virgin but "liberated her." "The image is now in our hands," they affirmed, "and we want you to take note. After having been so exploited by the *patrones* (bosses), we believe it just to rescue what we made by our own efforts."

Despite these discrepancies, Tecamachalco agraristas found critical support in central government teachers and schools as they confronted the hostile tactics of the conservative Puebla government. Teachers helped to bolster their prestige and to strengthen linkages to the central government for the processing of their claims related to land, water, government abuse, and material resources. Moreover, agraristas valued the public school as a symbol of status and a site of their newly won, but now threatened, power.

From the nineteenth century, the school had formed part of a liberal rearrangement of space that included the town plaza and its bandstand, the municipal palace, and streets that shed the names of Catholic saints to assume those of patriot heroes. This space nurtured a homegrown patriotic civic culture. Schools were locally controlled. Teachers not only taught the rudiments of literacy and patriotic history but organized the civic festival. The latter was particularly meaningful here, for it centered on the fifth of May, the date in 1862 when Puebla's soldiers defeated the French invaders. On the fifth of May, children paraded and teachers waxed eloquent in oratory eulogizing the heroes who had freed the nation from Spanish domination and defended it from foreign aggression. The town band entertained with military marches, Italian arias, and Viennese and Mexican waltzes. Because in the Porfiriato, schools and civic festivals were nominally democratic but in fact confirmed exclusionary hierarchies of power within and between villages, in the revolution they became important to agraristas in their attempts to secure power and place. Thus campesinos worked with teachers to mobilize their communities to build new schools that showcased their prestige and that of their town. They inaugurated them during festivals, whose organization they entrusted to teachers.

The festival created a new fusion between local and national identities. It ranged from the presentation of land titles in the schoolhouse to celebrations of the Cinco de Mayo, Mexican Independence (September 15–16), and the anniversary of the revolution (November 20). Into festival, the SEP injected portions of its paradigm while villagers seized upon ritual to define themselves in the context of changing power relations. The state's democratic messages— the notions of a peasant-made revolution and of class unity, the canonization of Emiliano Zapata, the agrarista hymn, the constitution of 1917 as a document hallowing collective rights to social justice—helped to preserve space for organized campesinos in the midst of a conservative regional consolidation. Local musicians shed their Europeanized repertoire to play love songs from Michoacán, the Marcha de Zacatecas, and their own compositions honoring local culture. Schoolchildren performed the *jarabe tapatío* and the Yaqui Deer Dance.

The height of entertainment was the basketball game. The SEP introduced sports to promote hygiene, sobriety, and productivity. But villagers took to them for reasons, values, and needs of their own. Sports celebrated male physical prowess and dominance, prized in peasant culture. Competitions between communities in festival context acted as a healing mechanism in a region engulfed in competition over land and water within and between villages. Ballgames contributed to forging class unity as they formed part of meetings of the regional branch of the Confederación Nacional Campesina. Moreover, sports, like land reform itself, favored young men and opened for them networks of regional, state, and national competition that expanded opportunities for mobility.

If the federal teachers participated in a reconfiguration of power and development of new sociabilities among campesino men, they were initially less successful among campesina women. The teachers' prescriptions were at odds with local cultural practices, resources, and the organization of power. Violence and deepening poverty had probably reinforced familial patriarchy. The high incidence of kidnapping, assault, and robbery prompted families to seclude women as much as possible. When female teachers visited campesino homes to instruct mothers in proper household management, pediatrics, and hygiene, they often found their entry blocked by women and men who valued the privacy of the hearth and suspected strangers. Official prescriptions encouraged teachers to see local reproductive practices as irrational, ineffective, and ensconced in primitive superstition. However, the teachers had few resources to demonstrate the effectiveness of their own modern "science." Most critically, their recommendations for improving nutrition and sanitizing households and communities ran up against the scarcity of water. Homogenizing peasant women as ignorant, they did not seek out local female specialists whose proven skills and prestige could have brokered in exotic innovations. Instead, campaigns to inoculate against contagious diseases were often tactless. Teachers and Departamento de Salubridad brigades would descend on towns on market days to vaccinate en masse—sometimes accompanied by police and soldiers.

Many Tecamachalco women associated state agents with antireligiosity. This dimension of state policy inhibited women's developing forms of sociability and association that might have empowered them in new ways. Anti-alcohol and community improvement campaigns that engaged women were rare or weak. The strongest schools relied on female support, but for a critical period in the mid-1930s when official anticlericalism was at its height, Tecamachalco women retreated.

The classroom was the state's space for inculcating new notions of citizenship and nationalism in children. However, the classroom was also shaped by parents, Porfirian traditions, and teacher capacity. Throughout the 1930s, parents sent children to school for only a short period of time and irregularly because they needed them for work. Teachers adjusted school hours to allow for work at planting and harvest time. To the Porfirian classroom with its national flag, clock, map of Mexico, and portraits of Hidalgo and Juárez, teachers introduced new textbooks intended to cover in a short period of time and in a rudimentary way a range of materials (science, geography, history, social behavior). Depicting rural life and honoring campesino family, these texts probably assisted cognitive development and worked to offset a persistent devaluing of girls' education. In the 1930s, girls' enrollments were one-half to one-third those of boys.

Within the school, teachers tried to fashion a microcosm of patriotic modernity. The strength of school gardens, animal raising, and crafts varied and depended on teacher initiative and community support. Most teachers organized children into committees for the promotion of hygiene, first aid, antialcoholism, reforestation, and the protection of birds. Participation in these committees became synonymous with service to the *patria*. Festival became the most widespread learning-by-doing activity for schoolchildren. It was a lesson in national culture as they performed ethnic dances, folk songs, and revolutionary corridos. The festival turned into a course in national history as children made altars and recited poems in honor of the patriot heroes. Cleanliness they celebrated in dramas like "The Water Princess and the Soap King." In festivals, they starred as modern producers, exhibiting vegetables, chickens, pottery, straw hats, and artificial flowers.

The work of the school only began to yield fruit in Tecamachalco after 1940. Although the 1940s marked a conservative turn in Mexican politics with the consolidation of a single party and an authoritarian state, they also brought peace, stability, and economic resources to Tecamachalco. Political consolidation, technical maturation, and economic growth enhanced state capacity.

Selectively but in locally meaningful ways, the state provided irrigation and deep-water wells, tractors, plows, seeds, credit, and marketing mechanisms. Completion of a new highway opened possibilities for crop diversification, marketing, migration, and alternative employment. Women and children felt the twin effects of state policies and market growth. The introduction of the molino de nixtamal, the waist-level hearth, water sources closer to home, paved highways, and state-subsidized bus fleets freed female labor and facilitated mobility at a moment when meeting subsistence needs required greater female participation in markets and nonlocal work sites. Mothers saw that vaccinated children survived epidemics, and so asked for shots. Child mortality fell with the introduction of antibiotics. Child nutrition improved with the availability of canned foods, especially sardines. Beer and soft drinks replaced pulque as drinks of choice, and basketball continued its ascendance over blood sports. Girls' literacy began to rise in tandem with boys'.

Women teachers had learned to negotiate. They introduced modern medicines through locally respected practitioners, such as curanderas, and accepted the rationality of many local practices the SEP had condemned as unhygienic and magical. Male teachers became important political negotiators, facilitating campesino access to government resources and often defending them in their negotiations with organizations, authorities, and local elites.

## San José de Gracia

The experience of federal schools in Tecamachalco contrasts with that of the western Mexican community of San José de Gracia, as told by the historian and native son Luis González y González.[4] Here loyalties to Christ the King reduced the possibility for negotiation with federal schools. González's exemplary microhistory of San José does not provide us with in-depth detail about schooling but does give invaluable information about the relationship between community, schooling, and nation. It is likely that the experience of San José was similar to that of other western Mexican ranchero communities that valued their alleged whiteness of skin, private property, autonomy from the state, and religious faith.[5] These communities had been forged by soldiers and pioneers who participated in the colonial state's expansion beyond the central core. In the late nineteenth century, kinsmen living on scattered ranchos of a fractioned hacienda founded San José. They did so with guidance from a renascent Catholic Church opposed to the liberal state and its secular institutions and committed to parish creation and education within the faith. In 1888,

San José became a vicariate in Sahuayo parish. Dedicated to the production of milk, cheese, and beeswax, its men, women, and children related to, and were molded by, ecclesiastical rather than civil authorities. As far as the San Joséans were concerned, civil government stole their wealth in taxes and blasphemed against God and Christ.

The first vicar, Padre Othón, a graduate of a major seminary in Zamora, Michoacán, organized the building of the church, the *curato*, and the school. He introduced theater to entertain and teach Christian doctrine. He brought in the orders of the Hijas de María and the Madres de Asilo to teach literacy and catechism. He solved boundary and family disputes and received visiting bishops and dignitaries. Public officials recognized him as the town's maximum authority. Although the people of San José sold their products via the new railroads to Mexico City and purchased basic necessities from the outside, they had little knowledge of life beyond San José and little sense of Mexico. News of Mexico entered in the final years of the Porfiriato, along with Aspirin and Singer sewing machines, through *El País*, Mexico City's Catholic newspaper.

San José saw itself as a community of hardy, small-scale ranchers despite the fact that the majority of families were landless and worked for a handful of large, often absentee landowners. Unlike the campesinos of Tecamachalco, the landless and land-poor in San José did not mobilize in the revolution. Rather, the town experienced the revolution as an invasion of rapacious armies from northern Mexico. Soldiers looted stores and ranches and seized horses and young women. In their wake followed economic and moral breakdown, poverty, and disease. Many less well-off men turned to violence and banditry, and the young elite men's dreams of progress disintegrated. The landless wanted land but dared not ask the government to expropriate hacienda land because private property was a sacred dimension of male honor in San José. Moreover, no one trusted the government. To provide some land to the needy and to avoid state intervention, the priest Padre Federico González negotiated the sale of a major hacienda. As government anticlericalism intensified, the town's elite young men returned home from their studies at the Zamora seminary to organize the local branch of Catholic Youth. Together with the priest, they led San José into the Cristero rebellion in June 1927. For them, religion was not a matter of class oppression or superstition. It affirmed dignity, autonomy, and faith. It was bound up with patriotism. They fought under the slogan "God, Country, and Liberty."

But the Cristeros were badly defeated. Government-allied forces burned and looted the town. People turned bitter and quarrelsome. Once again, the priest began the community's healing. Once again, religiosity created union. When the government set up its first school in 1931 to defanaticize the population, its teachers were good Catholics who went to mass everyday. Nonetheless, agraristas and schoolteachers in the surrounding region spurred the impoverished male youth of San José's outlying rancherías into petitioning the government for land. Writes Luis Gonzalez, "the old hatred of the poor against the government was now turned against the rich." The local party of property and means strongly objected, but Francisco Melgoza, San José's Cristero schoolteacher, supported the petitioners. He identified Christ with the poor and with agrarianism. Over half the landless benefited from an ejido grant carved from the property of an absentee landlord.

Padre Federico rose to the challenge of uniting the community after the land division. He also shepherded San José's entry into modernity and the Mexican nation-state. Modernity arrived at its own pace in San José: molinos de nixtamal, the radio, and electricity in the 1920s; the movies, cars, and the telephone in the early 1930s. As Padre Federico appropriated these in the interest of community improvement, he imitated the government's program. He promoted the development of small industries, orchards, and agricultural production. He supported the construction of a new bandstand and park for the town's plaza. His program differed from the government's in his preference for private over ejidal property, religious over secular education, and Catholic over civic festival. The town continued to affirm its identity and reconcile its differences through religious ritual: it celebrated its golden wedding anniversary as a vicariate with masses, rodeos, bullfights, and fireworks, all to the music of the town's thirty-five-member band. Padre Federico also sought better relations with government authorities. He invited president Lázaro Cárdenas to visit. The invitation made good strategic sense, as Cárdenas was a native of the municipality of Jiquilpan, to which San José belonged. Like Padre Federico, Cárdenas was a conciliator. Friendly during his stay to both anti-agraristas and agraristas, President Cárdenas helped to reconcile local differences and to dispel San José's suspicions of civil government. Thus did San José enter the postrevolutionary state and nation: firmly on its own terms rather than those of the SEP.

## Northern Mexican Farmworker Communities

In at least two important regions of northern Mexico, the Laguna cotton-producing area in southern Coahuila and eastern Durango and the left bank of the Yaqui River in Sonora, there was an unusual convergence of state capacity and community support for the government's programs in the 1930s. These were new communities of migrant laborers forged through bonds of work and a political struggle for social rights. They were neither deeply rooted communities like those of Tecamachalco nor politically Catholic like San José. Second, from the beginning, state teachers emerged as popular leaders. Teachers assumed moral authority because they lacked religious competitors and identified intimately with the ascendant social struggle. Many Article 123 schools, designed to enforce federal labor law, were created here on agribusiness farms with the objective of not only teaching literacy and patriotism but also securing trade union rights and worker benefits. As part of a mobile labor force exposed to diverse experiences, families here were more open to practices, objects, and forms of modernity than those of Tecamachalco or San José. Further, the organization of production and wealth of agribusiness enterprises in these regions engendered urbanization and new patterns of consumption.

The Cardenista state responded to political organization in these regions with a massive division of land among workers and small farmers and infrastructural support for economic and community development in the form of credit, marketing arrangements, technical assistance, schools, health and sanitation improvements—and in the case of the Laguna, with new housing that conformed with the SEP's and the government's notions of propriety and hygiene. In both regions, notions of Mexicanidad came to be closely bound up with land reform, President Cárdenas, and an ideology of revolutionary nationalism. The land reform, or *reparto*, was interpreted as an assertion of national dignity against foreign owners. Ejidatarios of La Laguna and the Yaqui Valley keenly identified with the struggle of Mexican oil workers against foreign owners and with Cárdenas's nationalization of oil in 1938. Like the Monterrey steelworkers described by Michael Snodgrass later in this volume, they saw themselves as productive, essential participants in a distinctly nationalist project of modern, democratic development.[6]

The reparto in La Laguna in October 1936 received more national attention than the Yaqui reparto of October 1937. The president himself took up residence in La Laguna to oversee the property division and the coordination of a massive, multifaceted development project. His wife, Amalia Solórzano, worked with women teachers in the organization of Ligas Femeniles and provided them with sewing machines and molinos de nixtamal. The Ligas became powerful agents in support of schools and community development.

Yet the story of the Yaqui reparto was no less dramatic.[7] It is congenially related through the eyes of a young girl, Marcelina Saldívar, who came to the Yaqui Valley with her family at the end of the 1920s. The oral histories of valley settlers compiled by Marcelina's son Mayo amplify and contextualize her story. Marcelina's parents, Eulalia and Domingo, had come from Zacatecas via Nayarit to Nogales where Domingo sought work in the United States. He was turned back because he did not know how to read or write. Moving south to the Yaqui Valley, the family wandered like gypsies from agricultural camp to agricultural camp until Eulalia put her foot down in Pueblo Yaqui and said, "Here I stay because the children have to go to school." Domingo went to work in the camps, returning every eight days, and the children attended school in Pueblo Yaqui. Eulalia sent Marcelina to school to give her an opportunity that Eulalia herself had been denied. Her parents had forbidden her to go to school because they believed she would learn to write love letters to her *novios*.

The society on the left bank of the Rio Yaqui was a new one of immigrants, foreigners, and Mexicans who had come to the valley lured by propaganda that touted it as the world's "most fertile land." Together entrepreneurs and campesinos fought rattlesnakes and mosquitoes to clear the cactus and mesquite. They pitched shovels to dig the canals they made flow with the glistening, cool waters of the Yaqui River. On the virgin fields, they planted and picked amazing harvests of lettuce, wheat, rice, beans, and tomatoes. Their heroes of modern morality were entrepreneurial promoters of technology like Mr. McGriffith, who owned a tractor as big as a locomotive, and Mexican president Álvaro Obregón, whose airplane bathed his properties with insecticide. Motorcycles and Model T Fords jauntily plied the roads, honking their way around the mule wagons. Almost overnight in the 1920s, Cajeme, appropriately renamed Ciudad Obregón, became a showplace of modernity. Its stores displayed the latest tools, agricultural machinery, and lubricating oils from the United States, sewing machines, and fashions from Paris—or at least Tucson. Also available for everyone's enjoyment was modern culture. Every weekend, the camps showed the latest films of Hollywood that enshrined new heroes and heroines: King Kong, Clark Gable, Charlie Chaplin, Tom Mix, and Mae West. Every Saturday night there was a dance, neither folkloric nor religious but individualized and secular. Young men and women kicked up their heels to the Charleston and fox-trot. Life in the valley awakened hopes for betterment and dreams of modernity. It made schooling a necessity.[8]

With her mother's support, Marcelina Saldívar committed herself to the school in Pueblo Yaqui. Like those in La Laguna, this school owed much to women for its construction and maintenance. Marcelina adored her teacher,

Rosario Tapia, who typified Sonoran women teachers in her dedication to civilizing the frontier in a spirit similar to that of the U.S. prohibitionists and suffragettes. Doña Rosario organized the adults into the parents' society and mobilized them for improvement crusades. Every two weeks she hosted a patriotic festival to which people came from the surrounding camps. They watched sports competitions and listened to orators celebrate the patria, the revolution, and motherhood. Marcelina, a principal actress in these festivals at the age of nine, remembered:

> We dance the jarabe tapatío. . . . We set up scenery and a curtain in the bandstand in front of Don Pascual Ayon's carpentry shop. In the opening scene, a mother with her children waited for her husband, who arrived drunk with a bottle, wanting to beat her in front of the frightened children. The curtain dropped and another scene opened with a man and a woman seated at a table, waiting for the teacher to show them how to write. . . . For the Twentieth of November, the anniversary of the Revolution, we carried banners against illiteracy and alcohol in parades through the Yaqui. I recited a poem about an orphan dressed in rags. The audience cried and congratulated my parents. The teacher taught us to cry and mimic. She was so very combative (*luchadora*).[9]

The teacher Rosario Tapia was a moral leader here because on the left side of the Yaqui River there was no organized Catholic Church or another competing authority of virtue. The people carried their religious beliefs within them, but religious public life and organization were weak. Hence socialist education caused little controversy.

What was absent in this "promised land" was equality. That came through the efforts of young men like Saturnino Saldívar, Marcelina's uncle, who together with other employees of Campo 65's flour mill—Jacinto López, Machi López, Buki Contreras, Vicente Padilla—began to organize workers. With federal teachers, they formed the Federación Obrera y Campesina del Sur de Sonora, affiliated with the government-backed Confederación de Trabajadores de México (CTM). Teachers in the Article 123 schools in the agricultural camps committed themselves to this organization. As in the Laguna, they introduced federal labor and agrarian laws and worked with Comités Agrarios and union organizations to press for their fulfillment. They formed cooperatives. They taught typing and accounting in night classes. They sponsored patriotic festivals that mixed folkloric dance and song from Mexico's regions with baseball games, and theater that championed sobriety, hygiene, and class struggle. As they commemorated Juárez, they also celebrated the Chicago anarchists martyred in their struggle for the eight-hour day.

Politics were principally the domain of men. Marcelina Saldívar was angry when her uncle Saturnino rejected her offer to help with the organization and he and his friends shooed her away. This hurt her. But she was profoundly moved and excited when the political effort bore fruit in October 1937. President Cárdenas ordered the distribution of lands, owned primarily by North Americans, to more than two thousand campesino families. The agraristas themselves carried out the reparto. "We hardly recognized the peons' faces," recalled Vicente Padilla. "They were transformed by hope. They greeted us with the excitement of children, plain and unschooled, with only their love for the land, their shovels and plows." When Cárdenas came in June 1939, the crowd was so imploring that he got out of his car and rode on an open truck to make better contact with the people. In the official ceremony, the heads of each Comité Agrario paraded before him, turning over their petitions from their ejidos that bore the names of patriot heroes: Cuauhtémoc, José María Morelos, Francisco I. Madero. Thus a national memory with its narrative of insurgency and liberation took shape in this new frontier society. "Viva Cárdenas, muchachos! Viva la Revolución," sang the musicians. The reparto, remembered Marcelina Saldívar, "changed our lives." Cárdenas was "a tremendous god for all of us." "He gave us the pride of knowing that we were equal." In reality, Marcelina was not equal, but she believed in equality and taught it to her students when she became a teacher and to her children when she became a mother. Abandoned by her husband, she worked to give all her children a professional education, and she succeeded.[10]

## Conclusion

The SEP's notions of nation and modernity that emerged in the 1920s were not as revolutionary as official history has portrayed. They had Porfirian roots and drew heavily from an international milieu of social reform and artistic inspiration. Nonetheless, inspired by the revolutionary upheaval, Mexican intellectuals created powerful tools—pedagogical, aesthetic, political, and hygienic—for imagining, integrating, and building the nation. At the same time, their power was subverted by an unconsidered faith in cosmopolitan science; by a spirit of superiority, authoritarianism, and messianism inherent in the still-hierarchical society; by association with a tactless antireligiosity; and by a weak state with limited economic and technical resources. Thus rural communities responded in distinct but thoughtful ways to the SEP's program. While their responses depended on a broad array of historical and conjunctural factors, those examined here—and perhaps many more—had some things in common. Their emerging notions of national identity were strongly rooted in a local sense of identity and newfound pride. Both local and national identities had been forged with and against the government's agents and messages: they had been forged through conflict and negotiation. The process engaged local people as actors and so inscribed in them a new sense of Mexicanidad.

## Notes

1. This discussion of educational policy is drawn from chapters 1 and 2 of my *Cultural Politics in Revolution: Teachers, Peasants and Schools in Mexico, 1930–1940* (Tucson: University of Arizona Press, 1997), 10–11, 25–49.

2. This discussion of rural school policy is drawn from my *Cultural Politics*, 40–44.

3. This description of Tecamachalco is drawn from my *Cultural Politics*, chap. 4, 77–105, and is based on documents from the Archivo Histórico de la Secretaría de Educación Pública, the Archivo General de la Nación (Acervos Presidentes), the Archivo Municipal de Tecamachalco, the Archivo de la Reforma Agraria-Puebla, the Mexican census data from 1895 to 1940, and oral interviews with teachers. My reading of Tecamachalco's school experience owes much to the insights of Elsie Rockwell in her studies of similar communities in Tlaxcala. See Rockwell, "Schools of the Revolution: Enacting and Contesting State Forms (Tlaxcala, 1910–1930)," in *Everyday Forms of State Formation: Revolution and the Negotiation of Rule in Modern Mexico*, ed. Gilbert M. Joseph and Daniel Nugent (Durham: Duke University Press, 1994), 170–208. For other important studies of schooling in central Mexican peasant communities, see Alicia Civera Cerecedo, "Del calzón de manta al overol: La Misión Cultural de Teneria, Estado de México, en 1934," in *Escuela y sociedad en el período cardenista*, ed. Susana Quintanilla and Mary Kay Vaughan (Mexico City: Fondo de Cultura Económica, 1997); and Juan Alfonseca, "Escuela y sociedad en los distritos de Texcoco y Chalco, 1923–40," in *Miradas en torno a la educación de ayer*, ed. Luz E. Galván (Mexico City: COMIE/Universidad de Guadalajara, 1997).

4. The narrative of San José de Gracia is drawn from Luis González y González, *San José de Gracia* (Austin: University of Texas Press, 1974), 102, 198, 116–17, 144, 155, 189–95, and 207–10.

5. For important studies of hostility toward socialist education in western Mexico that include ranchero communities, see Salvador Camacho Sandoval, *Controversia educativa entre la ideología y la fe: La educación socialista en la historia de Aguascalientes* (Mexico City: Consejo Nacional para la Cultura y las Artes, Serie Regiones, 1991); and

Pablo Yankelevich, "La batalla por el dominio de las conciencias: La experiencia de la educación socialista en Jalisco, 1934–1940," in Quintanilla and Vaughan, *Escuela*, 111–40.

6. Information on the educational encounter in La Laguna is from María Candelaria Valdés Silva, "Educación socialista y reparto agrario en la Laguna," in Quintanilla and Vaughan, *Escuela*, 229–50.

7. Descriptions of the Yaqui reparto are drawn from Vaughan, *Cultural Politics*, chap. 7, 163–88. Analysis of the educational encounter on the left bank of the Yaqui River is informed by sources in the Archivo Histórico de la Secretaría de Educación Pública, the Archivo General de la Nación (Acervos Presidentes), the Archivo Administrativo General del Estado de Sonora, United States State Department Records relating to the Internal Affairs of Mexico, 1930–1940, newspapers, many oral histories, and Gerardo Cornejo's autobiographical novel *La sierra y el viento* (Hermosillo: Arte y Libros, 1977). As noted hereafter, I am particularly indebted to Marcelina Saldívar de Murrieta for her long discussions with me about her life in the Yaqui Valley and to her son Mayo Murrieta, who with María Eugenia Graf compiled and imaginatively edited the oral histories of many Yaqui Valley settlers in *Por el milagro de aferrarse: Tierra y vecindad en el Valle del Yaqui* (Hermosillo: Colegio de Sonora, Institute Tecnológico de Sonora, Instituto Sonorense de Cultura, 1992).

8. Information is from Murrieta and Graf, *Por el milagro*, vii–xii, 3–5, 18, 30–33, 39, 86–87, 134.

9. Information is from interview with Marcelina Saldívar de Murrieta, April 7, 1989; Murrieta and Graf, *Por el milagro*, 85.

10. Vincente Padilla in Murrieta and Graf, *Por el milagro*, 114–15; interview with Marcelina Saldívar de Murrieta, April 7, 1989.

# The Nation, Education, and the
# "Indian Problem" in Mexico, 1920–1940

STEPHEN E. LEWIS

For some aspiring postrevolutionary nation builders like Dr. Atl, the isolation and marginalization of much of Mexico's indigenous population was a virtue. Atl, you may recall, wished to conserve the "purity" of indigenous popular arts by shielding artisans from the market and modern ways of life. But for others, especially those involved in education, "unincorporated" indigenous ethnic groups represented a great threat to the nation's future stability and prosperity. Divided into at least sixty distinct ethnic and linguistic groups, most were marginalized politically, economically, and culturally from the national mainstream. So what was to be done with the Indian? While the United States government dealt with its Indian "problem" by further marginalizing them on reservations, Mexican nation builders pursued a different path.

During the critical two decades after 1920, Mexico's most important agent of social engineering, the SEP, launched several remarkable projects aimed at "incorporating" indigenous Mexicans into a single, unified nation. SEP policy evolved as *indigenistas* (nonnative proponents and practitioners of Indian policy) wrestled with political realities, new ideologies, and their own evolving understanding of the nature of indigenous peoples. By 1940, nearly twenty years of SEP *indigenismo* had neither incorporated marginalized Indians nor elevated them in socioeconomic terms. But SEP projects had pushed Mexican anthropologists, educators, and politicians away from biological determinism and toward a more social and material understanding of indigenous realities.[1] Indigenous people themselves also played a role in shaping SEP indigenismo; their resistance to many of its programs forced the SEP and the federal government to recognize the limits of its monolingual monocultural curriculum and endorse (briefly) a more plural vision of the Mexican nation.

## "Indian": The Evolution of a Social Category

Before exploring the trajectory of postrevolutionary indigenous education, we must try to come to terms with what constitutes an "Indian" in Mexico. In pre-Columbian times, what is today Mexico was inhabited by hundreds of ethnically and linguistically distinct states, tribes, and communities, each with its own history, rivalries, and internal divisions. The modern racial and ethnic category "Indian" is, of course, a testimony to Christopher Columbus's geographical miscalculation in 1492. The misnomer stuck, and after the conquest the plurality of indigenous peoples suddenly found themselves lumped into the same subordinate grouping and placed near the bottom of the Spanish colonial caste system. Although subjected to tribute payments and labor obligations, most Indian villages were granted relative autonomy and retained their communal lands.

Although the categories of "Indian" and "mestizo" initially had purely racial or biological meanings, they gradually took on socioeconomic connotations as the colonial caste system slowly gave way to a hierarchy based on class and behavior, and as generations of miscegenation made the caste system too unwieldy. Some indigenous people, both individually and collectively, became well integrated into the life of the colony. Acculturation most typically took place in central Mexico, the administrative, economic, and cultural heart of the colony. Acculturation was much less likely on the geographic, economic, and cultural margins of colonial and nineteenth-century Mexico, places that the late Gonzalo Aguirre Beltrán called "regions of refuge." The indigenous inhabitants of these regions were subjected to some of the SEP's most novel experiments in social engineering in the 1920s and 1930s and are the focus of this essay.

On the eve of the wars for independence, an estimated 60 percent of the population was considered indigenous; one hundred years later, census figures indicate that the percentage had dropped to around one-third. But since the term "Indian" had become a social category based on a range of perceived characteristics, rather than immutable genetic traits, these figures are not firm. The advent of cultural anthropology in Mexico after the revolution did little to clarify matters. Manuel Gamio, the founder of postrevolutionary indigenismo, considered bilingual, Hispanicized central Mexicans (like Zapata's followers) "Indians" and so labeled fully two-thirds of Mexico's population in 1910.[2] As discussed in a previous chapter, cultural promoters Jorge Enciso and Dr. Atl also used the term "Indian" loosely to encompass all impoverished rural Mexicans. Most contemporary observers apply the term much more conservatively based on a combination of characteristics including language, dress, religion, social organization, consciousness, and self-definition. Still, more than five hundred years after Columbus "discovered" Indians, there is confusion today over what exactly constitutes an Indian in Mexico.

## The Origins of Postrevolutionary Indigenismo

The first century of Mexican independence was not kind to Mexico's indigenous populations. Stripped of their colonial-era corporate privileges, most of them lost land in the growth boom later in the century. Although Spencerian positivism and social Darwinism during the Porfiriato reinforced an elite notion of indigenous peoples as backward-looking, vice-ridden impediments to national development, prominent politicians and intellectuals began to advocate their incorporation into the national mainstream through education and hard work. In 1889 a report issued at the first National Congress of Public Education insisted that the intellectual capacity of whites and Indians was the same. By 1900, some Porfirian defenders of the Indian were turning racial determinism on its ear. Dismissing charges that Indians were congenitally lazy and stupid, they instead found them innately hardworking, adaptive, artistic, and resistant. Influential Porfiristas like Justo Sierra, minister of public instruction from 1906 to 1910, argued that the alleged racial inferiority of the Indian was a myth; rather, poor nutrition, low wages, and illiteracy were to blame.[3] Educators and policymakers took note. If cultural and economic rather than racial factors explained the Indians' degeneration, then the Indian could be rehabilitated.

Beyond the heady realm of salon indigenismo, however, the panorama was less uplifting. Despite the Indians' apparent capacity for redemption, most had limited access to schooling in the Porfiriato. Those who resisted Porfirian land policy, such as the Yaquis of Sonora and the Yucatán's rebellious Maya, were subjected to military aggression and forced labor on plantations and haciendas. The true flowering of Mexican indigenismo—and its focus on contemporary indigenous populations—would have to wait until after the dust of the revolution had settled.

Indians were the objects, not the authors, of indigenismo. In the words of Alan Knight, indigenismo was "an elitist, non-Indian construct."[4] It reflected the convergence of several intellectual and cultural trends current among influential Mexicans between 1910 and 1930. Indigenistas attempted to modernize and incorporate the Indian into a new, more egalitarian and just nation. Indigenismo was also a response to more immediate concerns. It was part of the postrevolutionary state's paternalistic attempt to mediate between the various sectors of Mexican society and to correct glaring social imbalances and inequalities. As Alexander Dawson has recently written, "Indigenismo was very much a part of state formation, generating new political actors and channels of communication between the state and local actors, but demanding certain forms of compliance."[5] From a more defensive standpoint, indigenismo (and related campaigns) granted legitimacy to a regime that took power in 1920 by force of arms, intrigue, and assassination. It also aimed to instill loyalty in a population that generally did not identify or sympathize with the nation-state. Empowered by the emerging social sciences, and sanctioned by both the interventionist state and the Mexican cultural renaissance, indigenista anthropologists and educators seized the opportunity to chart the new regime's social policy toward Indians.[6]

Although the SEP's enigmatic founder, José Vasconcelos, could hardly be described as an indigenista, he played a major role in defining Indian education policy during his three-year tenure. Influenced by Andrés Molina Enríquez, whose *Los grandes problemas nacionales* announced in 1908 that Mexico's future lay in the hands of its hardworking, resilient mestizos, Vasconcelos celebrated racial miscegenation in an age when imperialist powers the world over were embracing pure-race racism.[7] Vasconcelos did not refute the racial determinism of earlier decades. He merely appropriated it to prove the superiority of the (Hispanicized) mestizo.

Despite his racial determinism, Vasconcelos's education policies suggested that Indians could, in fact, shed their "Indianness" and join the cosmic race. He and other Latin American thinkers were beholden to Lamarckian eugenics, named after the French biologist who believed that external changes induced on a living organism could become part of that organism's genetic code. In other words, "improvements" could be passed down to future generations.[8] This kinder, gentler, more flexible school of eugenic thought underlies Mexican indigenismo. Vasconcelos believed that living, breathing Indians had no future as Indians, but neither were they a lost cause. Their decadence was not a fixed hereditary characteristic; over time, they could improve themselves through assimilation, or what he called "spiritual eugenics."

For Vasconcelos, the key to indigenous incorporation was the inclusionary Spanish-only national schoolhouse. He explicitly rejected the North American practice of establishing separate schools for the so-called races. Spanish would

be the only language spoken in Mexico's educational "melting pot," partly because SEP pedagogues feared that bilingual teachers would "go native." As
the SEP's director of rural education Rafael Ramírez cautioned Mexico's rural
schoolteachers, "If you speak to [your indigenous students] in their language
. . . you will adopt the customs of their ethnic group, later their inferior ways
of life, and finally you yourself will become the Indian, that is, one more unit
to incorporate."[9]

Implicit in Ramírez's warning was his appreciation of the complex ethnic
makeup of the Mexican population. In rural areas, often language was the
only characteristic distinguishing self-identifying mestizos from Indians. The
wildly divergent estimates of indigenous populations mentioned earlier suggest a profound confusion over what constituted an "Indian," but they also
underscore the subjective nature of ethnic labeling in Mexico. Since virtually
all mainstreamed Mexicans claimed at least some indigenous ancestry, the possibility existed that the remaining Indians could be incorporated. With this in
mind, Vasconcelos embarked on his redemptive mission.


## Missionaries of "Culture"

In 1922, Vasconcelos sowed the seeds for the SEP's network of rural schools.
He sent normal school graduates to rural, often indigenous areas to study
socioeconomic and cultural conditions, to interest community members in
education, and to recruit prospective teachers. These educators were known
as "Missionaries of Indigenous Culture and Public Education." Like the first
Franciscans who had arrived in Mexico almost exactly four hundred years
earlier, these missionaries were expected to impart a message of redemption
to Mexico's indigenous populations while enduring a battery of trials and
tribulations. This time, however, the message was overtly secular, emphasizing
community development, modernization, and incorporation into the mestizo
mainstream.

Hailed in Mexico City as progressive educational and social philosophy, incorporation was not warmly embraced in the indigenous countryside. Most
of Vasconcelos's missionaries were monolingual mestizos. While some were
imbued with a revolutionary missionary spirit, others were downright con-
temptuous of a people they considered uncivilized and barbarous. In many
indigenous villages, the language and cultural barriers were insurmountable.
In certain remote parts of the country, like the Sierra Tarahumara in the North
and the highlands of Chiapas in the South, interethnic relations were so tense

that indigenous people fled at the mere sight of Vasconcelos's missionaries. Uncooperative state and municipal governments, political and social instability, and disease further complicated the missionaries' task.

For these reasons and many others, Vasconcelos's missionaries and teachers had difficulty convincing indigenous children and their parents to attend schools once they were built. Far from the supervisory eye of education officials, teachers sometimes functioned as labor contractors. As one educator in Chiapas explained, students often "formed a platoon of servants who served the teacher in his milpa, his pastures, his orchards, and who looked after his horses, sheep, goats, and other animals."[10] According to another Chiapas missionary in 1923, "Parents frequently approach the local authorities, the teacher, and sometimes the police, offering determined quantities of money, with the object of leaving their children free 'from the punishment' of school. That is, they see the school as a prison."[11] Parents would rather pay the teacher a modest sum than lose their child's labor. Indigenous teachers—the logical answer to indigenous distrust of mestizos—were not trained or hired in many states like Chiapas.

The SEP did enjoy some success in central Mexican villages located near the political and economic heart of the country. In Tlaxcala, where the Spaniards had found allies for their conquest of the Aztec empire, many Nahua-speaking pueblos supported federal education. Some had schools dating from the late colonial period. These had been refurbished in the Porfiriato as part of the liberal project of the education-minded indigenous governor Próspero Cuaumatzín. In the 1920s, communities used federalized schools to enhance their autonomy and status vis-à-vis municipal authorities. However, they refused to be included in the specific SEP program of indigenous incorporation, which they found belittling. The SEP's teachers in these schools—generally well-respected community members—used Nahuatl in the classroom and steered clear of unpopular cultural campaigns.[12]

Xochiapulco, a Nahuatl municipality and town in the remote Sierra Norte of Puebla adjacent to the central plateau, also welcomed federal assistance to bolster schooling. Xochiapulco had received land as compensation for its defense of the nation against the French and Austrians in the 1860s. After these victories, schoolteachers and veteran National Guard officers became community leaders and promoted education to safeguard liberal rights and ideals. In 1923, when Rafael Molina Betancourt introduced the SEP program to Xochiapulco, male literacy rates were already high. Nobody blinked when the SEP created coeducational classrooms. When SEP undersecretary Moisés Sáenz visited

Puebla's Sierra Norte in 1927, he referred to Xochiapulco's main school as the Sierra's "jewel." It was indeed an anomaly for Puebla and most of Mexico, boasting 130 students in five grades, a library, experimental gardens, carpentry shops, chicken coops, beehives, and rabbit hutches.[13] Ignoring the SEP's admonitions against bilingual education, the school taught monolingual Nahuatl speakers in their *lengua materna* (mother tongue) during the first year, then introduced Spanish.

It bears repeating, however, that federal schooling in the 1920s was probably accepted only in indigenous communities that had a tradition of schooling and were already somewhat incorporated into national life. In Xochiapulco, the forces driving social and cultural incorporation were mainly historical and political; in Tlaxcala's Nahua pueblos they were economic as well, since they were located near the transportation and manufacturing corridor linking Mexico City to the Gulf of Mexico. Importantly, too, teachers in both settings were bilingual locals willing to fudge the SEP's directives against bilingual education.

In more remote, peripheral areas where schools had not been built before the revolution, the SEP's monolingual, monocultural curriculum and its mestizo teaching corps failed to take deep root.[14] Hampered by an official Spanish-only language policy, and unable to control some of its teachers and live down its own urban, Western bias, the SEP had little to offer most indigenous people. Triumphant SEP proclamations could barely mask the failure of the missionaries and rural schools in indigenous Mexico. The time had come for a successful and well-publicized experiment in indigenous incorporation, right in the heart of the new nation—Mexico City.

### Incorporation in the City: The Casa del Estudiante Indígena

The stakes were high when the SEP opened the Casa del Estudiante Indígena, a boarding school for indigenous boys, in 1926. As told by Gonzalo Aguirre Beltrán, "The failures of the . . . rural school in monolingual indigenous communities caused many to have serious doubts about [the Indians'] intellectual capacity."[15] Success at the Casa would vindicate SEP policy. Failure, warned Casa director Enrique Corona in 1927, "would damage terribly, profoundly, the SEP's policy of indigenous incorporation in the periphery. It would postpone for dozens of years any new attempt at regeneration by similar institutions."[16]

The Casa's purpose was twofold: it served an important public relations function for the SEP's project of indigenous incorporation, and it trained an indigenous elite which, upon graduation, were to return to their home communities to impart civilization and modernity to their brethren. During its first two years, the school merely aimed to incorporate its students into the urban mestizo mainstream. To this end, it was hugely successful—too successful, in fact. In addition to a core curriculum consisting of Spanish, history, math, and civics, students took courses in auto repair, electrical work, plumbing, metallurgy, and ironworking. Not only did these courses teach skills that lacked practical application in rural, indigenous Mexico in the late 1920s, but they provided students with the means to remain in the urban environment they had come to call home. To counter this tendency, the Casa attempted (in vain) to eliminate course offerings deemed inappropriate and became a rural normal school—in the middle of Mexico's largest city—in February 1928.

Did the Casa prove that Indians were as capable intellectually as mestizos? Official SEP publications took pains to confirm this thesis publicly. Aguirre Beltrán, the patriarch of modern Mexican indigenismo, claimed that the students obtained "brilliant results" compared with mestizo students throughout the republic.[17] While most students received high marks for classes taken at the Casa, internal documents show that Casa students struggled when placed with mestizos in the SEP's neighborhood schools. Casa indigenistas were quick to attribute the scholastic underachievement of Casa students to social and cultural factors rather than intellectual or genetic ones.[18] This fact alone indicates the degree to which Casa indigenistas and the SEP were committed to burying timeworn theories of Indian inferiority based on biological determinism.

Although in practical terms the Casa and its students might have fallen below expectations, politically and symbolically they were extremely useful. The Casa was the clearest example of the postrevolutionary regime's commitment to indigenous Mexico and its claim that Indians could be made useful citizens. For example, in May and September 1929, Casa students and teachers commemorated national holidays by performing honor guards at the Independence Column on Mexico City's principal avenue, the Paseo de la Reforma. On October 12 (Día de la Raza) of that same year, Casa students helped the nation smooth out the rough edges of the Columbian encounter. After first performing an honor guard at the statue of Christopher Columbus, they walked down Reforma to lay wreaths and hold a special commemorative program at the statue of Cuauhtémoc, the last Aztec ruler.[19] A doting national and international press duly covered these events. Finally, every May the Casa hosted sporting and cultural events to honor Mothers' Day. Since the students' mothers could not be expected to attend, mothers from the predominately mestizo Colonia Anáhuac were invited. The only relationship the students could possibly have had with these surrogate mothers was the bond of national community. Unfortunately, it is not known whether women from the neighborhood attended the events or appreciated the political and cultural significance of the invitation.[20]

Although the Casa experiment generally promoted a more social and material understanding of indigenous people, Casa staff occasionally reverted to biological determinism. In 1931 a number of disgruntled students began to make life difficult for Casa director Corona. In order to expel the students and avoid political embarrassment, Corona and his staff suddenly discovered that the "troublemakers" were probably mestizos. In March 1931, Dr. Santiago Ramírez performed a physical examination on eight students, all of whom met the linguistic definition of "Indian." Nevertheless, based solely on a series of physical characteristics, five were determined to be mestizos, including these two from Querétaro:

> Herminio Carbajal, fifteen years of age, from Tolimán, Qro., based on his skin color, his thick hair, the size of his eyelashes, pubic hair, hair on his legs, [and] hairs between his eyebrows, does not correspond to indigenous racial characteristics, but rather appears to be a racial mixture.
>
> Porfirio Hernández, sixteen years of age, from Tolimán, Qro., has silky hair, wavy and thin, with characteristics of the white race. The mouth is finely outlined, with thick lips, the pubis has wavy hair, there are some hairs on the coccyx and the sacrum, the distance between the internal border of the eyes and the width of the eyes are the same, characteristics which, as in the previous case, do not correspond to the indigenous race.[21]

These two "mestizos" and several others were expelled during 1931 and 1932. This arbitrary use of somatic characteristics—to the exclusion of all others—is testimony to the persisting subjective nature of the term "Indian" in postrevolutionary Mexico. When Ramírez asked why they had been allowed to study at the Casa in the first place, Corona tersely replied that some of the "mestizos" spoke an indigenous language; others had traveled too far to be returned to their communities of origin; still others had been recommended by former students. Darío Manzanares, expelled in February 1931, had studied at the Casa because he was related to Emiliano Zapata. Another troublemaker had been admitted because he spoke Mayo and "seemed Indian," but once at the Casa seemed to transform into a mestizo; in Corona's words, "age, the daily routine, the food, and the climate have made apparent some manifestations of *mestizaje*, such as wavy hair."[22]

The Casa was closed in 1932. Part publicity stunt and part proving ground for an indigenous elite, it represented a pivotal moment in the history of Mexican indigenismo and education policy. Although the Casa generally failed to send incorporated young indigenous men back to their home communities as rural schoolteachers and emissaries of civilization, it did prove that Indians could be, and in fact chose to be, incorporated into urban mestizo life under certain extraordinary conditions. Casa students symbolically promoted the SEP's public campaign to refute racial determinism, and SEP spin doctors and nation builders celebrated the Casa's purported success as a vindication of educational policy and nation building.

The Casa also held lessons for its creators. Students at the Casa rapidly assimilated to urban mestizo culture because they had been given the material means and know-how to do so. They proved that true incorporation required more than monolingual cultural campaigns. Results from a second highly touted SEP project pointed to the same conclusion. Shortly before the Casa was closed in 1932, former SEP undersecretary Moisés Sáenz established his own "experimental station of Indian incorporation" at Carapan in rural Michoacán. Sáenz was one of the intellectual progenitors of the federal rural school and had championed its incorporative mission in the mid-1920s. His faith in the Vasconcelista school was shaken after his visit to indigenous communities in Puebla in 1927, when he declared that the traditional language-only incorporative strategy "will not be able to complete the task alone."[23]

Several months at Carapan brought Sáenz's ideological evolution full circle. The empty classrooms, the grinding poverty, and the prevalence of *caciquismo* (bossism) in the area convinced him that the SEP's incorporationist strategy was "simplistic." In place of incorporating the Indian, he proposed "integrating" all of Mexico. And whereas official SEP incorporation generally limited itself to cultural matters, Sáenz reiterated the need for a more holistic political, economic, and social integration involving teachers and various government ministries.[24] The conclusions drawn from the Casa and Sáenz's experimental station were unequivocal. After 1932, the SEP would take a more integral approach to education in indigenous areas. But would Mexico's indigenous people react any more favorably to the SEP's grand designs?

## Socialist Education in Indigenous Mexico

When Lázaro Cárdenas assumed the presidency in December 1934, the SEP adopted socialist education as its official operating philosophy. Socialist edu-

cation used the Marxist rhetoric of class conflict to celebrate and mobilize
Mexico's rural and urban masses. It also placed a new emphasis on the redistribution of resources like land and credit. Ideally, SEP teachers promoted
agrarian reform, enforced federal labor laws, and created federal unions. Actual
implementation of this progressive state-building agenda hinged on local politics, local traditions in education, and whether teachers were skilled in negotiating controversial elements of the official program with their communities.

In spite of its internationalist rhetoric, socialist education was a highly nationalist educational agenda. Teachers were asked to create the new Mexican—
rational, secular, modern, hygienic, and sober. They conducted vaccination
campaigns, built libraries and latrines, and led patriotic festivals. During the
height of the anticlerical campaign in 1935, SEP teachers in some states hosted
secular programs known as "Cultural Sundays" to take the place of Sunday
mass. Naturally, these campaigns put them at odds with peasant women, traditional healers, and staunch Catholics, among others. As a nation-building tool,
socialist education antagonized at least as much as it unified. Its Marxist ori-
entation called attention to the deep socioeconomic divisions within Mexican
society, and its anticlerical campaign opened new wounds. On the other hand,
socialist educators attempted to paper over ethnic divisions, classifying Indians as campesinos with the same material needs and class interests as mestizo
peasants.

Socialist education marks a crucial period in the history of Mexican indigenismo. Before 1934, incorporation was conceived in primarily cultural and
linguistic terms. Under Cárdenas, indigenistas and educators also tackled economic and political matters. They used the rhetoric of class struggle to portray
Indians as victims of a conniving mestizo bourgeoisie, the landed elite, the
church, and foreign capitalists. They saw in indigenous peoples many of the
behavioral traits that they sought to promote in Mexican society, including
honesty, nobility, cooperativism, and a solid work ethic. Cardenistas believed
that once Indians had land, water, tools, markets, and access to credit, and
once their local exploiters were reined in, they could be incorporated into the
national society and economy (which, incidentally, remained capitalist).

How did Mexico's indigenous ethnic groups respond to socialist education?
Reactions were as diverse as indigenous Mexico itself. We begin with highland Chiapas. In 1935, socialist educators launched the first real challenge to
the region's well-honed institutions of indigenous exploitation. The SEP's education inspector in the highlands, Manuel Castellanos, began his work one
month after Cárdenas's inauguration. In a lengthy initial report, Castellanos

wrote that federal education in his zone was still at the mercy of the predominantly ladino (non-Indian) local authorities. The SEP barely had a foothold in
the region, its schools and teachers under siege by those who felt threatened
by federal education's expanded social mandate. As Castellanos noted, "Until
now the Indian problem remains intact and irresolute . . . which is shameful
for our country, and represents a negation of revolutionary principles. Federal
education has done nothing to incorporate the Indian into civilization."[25]

Castellanos and his corps of teachers mobilized communities to build
schools, complete with athletic fields, pit toilets, and experimental gardens.
They also launched the first major social campaigns ever seen in the region,
shaving, delousing, and vaccinating hundreds of Tzotzil and Tzeltal Maya children and their parents and conducting campaigns against typhoid fever and
malaria. All schools had anti-alcohol committees, although Castellanos admitted that little could be done after they had been established, since most of
the municipal authorities in his zone profited from the sale of *aguardiente* (literally "burning water" or rum). As he wrote in one report, "The *alcoholeros*
enjoy more guarantees and official support than the teachers."[26]

Castellanos devoted most of his energy to attacking the institutions that
kept indigenous highlanders in a subjugated state. He struggled to eradicate
the various head taxes that ladino municipal governments levied on Maya communities, and told indigenous men to resist the forced-labor demands issued
by local authorities. He also attempted to enforce state and federal laws against
ladino alcohol manufacturers and sellers in Indian villages. Finally, he attacked
the well-entrenched system of *enganche*, whereby agents of lowland planters
typically used debts and alcohol to compel indigenous laborers to work the
harvest. Ladinos responded vigorously, using every means—legal and illegal,
passive and violent—at their disposal. Schools were burned to the ground, and
teachers were threatened and shot at with such frequency that they were forced
to carry firearms and convert their homes into bunkers.[27]

Sixteen months after assuming his post, Castellanos sounded a note of des-
peration in his bimonthly report to the SEP. Lack of resources, obstructionist
local authorities, enganche, and the Indians themselves conspired against the
success of federal schooling in the highlands:

The education problem of the [Tzotzil Maya] is more complicated than that of
any other *indígena* in the Republic. [I] say this because I have worked with the
Tarahumaras, the Tepehuanes, the Otomís, and other indígenas from Veracruz
and Tabasco, and in no part of the Republic nor in the state are they more brutal-

ized by alcohol, nor is the exploitation of the Indian—through which the greater part of the ladino population lives—so well organized.[28]

In short, the state's economic and political institutions were built on the backs of the highland Maya. Lowland plantations relied on their labor; *enganchadores* and state alcohol interests depended on their consumption of alcohol; and local governments subsisted on their labor and the taxes they paid. Against such powerful local interest groups, socialist education was doomed, especially since it lacked the support of the indigenous communities themselves, who had every reason to distrust monolingual ladino teachers and a curriculum that either ignored or attacked their culture.

In the neighboring state of Oaxaca, Mexico's most ethnically diverse, the scenario was altogether different. In the highland municipality of Villa Hidalgo—home to Zapotecos, Mixes, and Chinantecos—Zapotec elites in the town of Yalalag willingly entered into a partnership with the SEP. They federalized their municipal schools in 1928, believing it would help them consolidate their own political and economic power and dominate local Mixe pueblos. Even after federalization, Yalalag's bilingual indigenous elite retained control over the school and selected its teachers.[29]

In 1932 the school hired Maximiliano Vallejo and Juan Mota, two recent graduates from the regional normal school. Both were members of Yalalag's indigenous elite. Vallejo was the brother of a notorious cacique and was related to the town's powerful priest, Librado Venegas. Mota was the brother of one of the Sierra's most important merchants (*acaparadores*). These men soon turned the school into a work brigade. School recruitment intensified only when workers were needed to build or recondition school buildings, roads, and bridges. Although most of Yalalag's residents wanted their children to learn Spanish as a means of protecting themselves from unscrupulous mestizo merchants, they sent their children to this school only when threatened with fines.[30]

Little changed in late 1934, when this school suddenly became "socialist." Arguably, the school drifted even further from the mobilizing, secularizing, redistributive goals of the SEP. In 1935 school director Vallejo singled out illiterates to provide the mandatory, unpaid labor needed for public works projects. Literates were exempted from such work. As María Bertely writes, "In Yalalag . . . the socialist project was associated with bricks, water, seeds, stones, pipes, doors, boards. . . . It is not known when, how, and for what purpose the Yalateco students used books, pencils, or chalkboards, or whether their teachers taught them Spanish, math, or Mexican history."[31] Appropriation of the socialist education project by the Zapotec elite meant that the school merely reproduced and exploited preexisting inequalities. Monolingual, illiterate Yalatecos remained so. Far from being incorporated into the national mainstream, they were exploited as laborers by their own kind.

Yalalag's socialist school director, Maximiliano Vallejo, met a bloody end after political enemies attacked his family in November 1935. The SEP inspector seized the opportunity to condemn caciquismo and hire "true" socialist outsiders to teach at the school. Soon the so-called true socialists were forced to flee, and Yalalag's indigenous elite regained control of the school and consolidated one of the most powerful and violent *cacicazgos* in the history of the municipality.

Bertely's study highlights the importance of local conditions and personalities in determining the fate of the SEP's ambitious project in the 1930s. In highland Chiapas, local ladinos held political and economic power and lived off Maya labor and consumption. They successfully thwarted the SEP's attempts to "liberate" land-hungry peasants and debt peons. In Yalalag, power was in the hands of an economically savvy indigenous elite who quickly appropriated and deformed the SEP's project. Despite a curriculum designed to mobilize and liberate the masses, preexisting inequalities were reinforced, and local caciques were strengthened. Even the church's power went unchallenged, since one of the teachers was related to the town's priest. We now briefly turn to a third, unique case: the Yaquis of Sonora. In Yaqui territory the SEP was careful not to inflame passions with its extracurricular state- and nation-building program. Still, opposition to the school was undeniable and came principally from restorationist Yaqui who sought to preserve and teach their own language and culture, not learn those of their historic enemies.

No indigenous ethnic group resisted the Porfiriato's modernizing capitalism more than the Yaquis, and no group more egregiously suffered the consequences. The Porfirian army expelled them from their fertile, well-irrigated lands and forced them into diaspora on behalf of Mexican and foreign agricultural interests. During the revolution of 1910–20, the Yaquis fought with the Constitutionalists as part of their campaign to reclaim ancestral lands. In 1926, after postrevolutionary presidents Obregón and Calles failed to honor promises made to them, the Yaquis again rebelled. The federal government unleashed a brutal crackdown that included aerial bombardment. Mindful of the extraordinary resilience of the Yaquis, President Cárdenas realized that he would have to break with SEP precedent in order to incorporate them.

To a greater extent than with other ethnicities, Cárdenas offered the Yaqui tools, trucks, seeds, mules, reapers, and barbed wire. But he also hammered out a series of agreements between 1935 and 1939 that recognized the authority of Yaqui governors and set aside 450,000 hectares as Mexico's only tribal land grant. Cárdenas wagered that economic support and measured political autonomy would create a prosperous and grateful constituency willing to incorporate itself into Mexican society, albeit on its own terms. The Yaqui, however, would use federal support as a means of preserving their own ethnic autonomy.[32]

The SEP moved into Yaqui territory in late 1935. Although socialist teachers conducted a virulent anticlerical campaign elsewhere in the state, complete with the burning of holy images, SEP teachers wisely muted the campaign in Yaqui territory for fear of provoking another rebellion.[33] Even so, it did not take long for the Yaqui to realize that *yori* (non-Yaqui) literacy and schools represented a cultural assault. Most SEP teachers and inspectors—all yoris, and all monolingual in Spanish—were downright racist and denigrated Yaqui culture. Attempts to mix Yaquis and yoris in the same schools were disastrous, as was coeducation. Not surprisingly, schools and patriotic festivals were poorly attended. Though some assimilationist Yaquis did send their children to SEP schools, most restorationist Yaquis did not.

For a brief moment, however, the SEP and the Mexican state showed signs of addressing these problems. When President Cárdenas visited the territory's indigenous boarding school in June 1939, he promised that Yaqui teachers would be trained to teach in Yaqui. The director of the boarding school attempted to incorporate Yaqui history into the school's curriculum. There was some talk of writing textbooks in Yaqui. This innovative, pluralist surge ended abruptly, however, as Cárdenas's own political appointees undermined the project and removed those officials identified with a progressive, pro-Yaqui disposition. Not until 1960 would the Yaquis begin to use SEP schools in large numbers.[34]

As in the 1920s, the SEP's project in the 1930s was accepted by indigenous populations already well on their way toward becoming part of Mexico's political, economic, and cultural mainstream. With or without the SEP's more integral approach toward incorporation in the 1930s, the Yalatecos were becoming Mexicanized. In Oaxaca's Sierra Juárez, indigenous leaders already spoke Spanish, enjoyed political control of their municipality, and worked as middlemen, selling locally grown products like coffee to mestizo outsiders. For them, the SEP's program looked like an opportunity, not a threat. In Yaqui

territory and highland Chiapas, however, the SEP's relatively progressive incorporative project failed completely. In both areas, aggressive ladinos and yoris
had for decades, even centuries, directly exploited the land and labor of indigenous peoples. Ladino and yori greed and brutality had forced both cultures to
turn within as a survival strategy. For both the highland Maya and the Yaqui,
SEP incorporation looked like just another ladino and yori ruse.

## Conclusion

Whatever its shortcomings, the SEP's policy of indigenous incorporation represented a pivotal attempt at inclusive nation building and social engineering
in postrevolutionary Mexico. Its importance and distinctiveness become especially clear when compared with Indian policy and pedagogy in the United
States. Both countries shared the stated goal of Indian assimilation, but to
what end? While the Mexican state sought to pull Indians into the mestizo
mainstream on its own terms and offered a place in the nation for assimilated
Indians, the U.S. government had little faith in Indian students (especially
"purebloods") and kept the door closed to assimilated Indians in larger society.

By the time the SEP was created in 1921, the U.S. government had been running Indian schools for several decades. SEP officials were aware of this experience and took pains not to repeat it. In the mid-1920s, SEP director José
Manuel Puig Casauranc toured U.S. Indian schools and reservations in New
Mexico. He concluded that Indians in the United States "continued to form
a separate social group, absolutely apart from the rest of the components of
the American union." According to Puig, survivors of Indian schools in the
United States "resented that civilization which had instructed them, but which
did not make them an integral part, neither as citizens nor as social subjects,
of the great national family."[35] In a predominately mestizo nation, the idea of
"social separation" was a disturbing one, even if it existed in practice. The celebration of the "cosmic race" may have boded ill for the future of autonomous
indigenous cultures, but it also reflected accurately the sentiments of a society
and a ruling class uncomfortable with the colonial legacy of caste separation.

Between 1920 and 1940, thanks to well-publicized experiments like the Casa
del Estudiante Indígena, Mexican educators convinced themselves and others
that indigenous people owed their subordinate, marginal positions in society
to a host of material and social (and not racial) factors. They also learned, somewhat paradoxically, that the way to alter or eradicate indigenous cultures was

not through imposed cultural campaigns (like Spanish-only school curriculums) but through material means, by providing them with land, water, credit, and equipment.

During the Cárdenas presidency, Indians also entered the political arena. At a host of regional indigenous congresses, indigenous representatives called for special, separate-but-equal Indian schools taught by bilingual, bicultural teachers who resided in their communities.[36] Cardenista educators responded to these challenges in 1939. Under the leadership of Luis Chávez Orozco, the Autonomous Department for Indian Affairs recognized that the problems of indigenous Mexico were not synonymous with those of Mexico's mestizo campesinos. The department stated that Indians had the right to preserve their language and customs and called for bilingual schools taught by indigenous teachers and tailored to local customs and needs. Some months later, delegates at the Interamerican Indigenist Conference in Pátzcuaro, Michoacán, seemingly had the final word on incorporation. Mexico signed on to a declaration stating that "the old theory of the incorporation of the Indian to civilization—a pretext used to better exploit and oppress the aboriginal peoples—has been discarded by the American representatives at Pátzcuaro."[37]

This declaration notwithstanding, the years following the Pátzcuaro conference were disastrous for indigenous education. National priorities shifted to the rapidly industrializing cities, and Mexico's entry into World War II in 1942 resurrected calls for national unity and the dream of a culturally homogeneous nation. After twenty years of slowly evolving toward a curriculum that appreciated difference, the SEP reverted to the failed incorporationist project championed by its founder, Vasconcelos. Although Cárdenas-era pedagogues and anthropologists created the National Indigenous Institute (INI) in 1948 and launched a new program aimed at "integrating" the Indian in ways that allegedly respected indigenous cultures, Indians still constitute Mexico's most marginalized, exploited, and illiterate citizens.

When the Zapatistas of Chiapas took up arms against the Mexican state in 1994, they presented new challenges to the government's incorporationist/integrationist agenda. Deftly employing the nationalist rhetoric and symbolism used by the then ruling party, the PRI, the Zapatistas demanded the same rights ostensibly enjoyed by the Mexican mainstream, namely, land, democracy, justice, health care, and schools. At the same time, however, they insisted on regional and municipal autonomy in political, administrative, and cultural matters (including education) for indigenous peoples.[38] The challenge for the Mexican state today is to create a pluriethnic nation that ensures national unity *and* respects indigenous cultures through autonomy arrangements; in the words of the enigmatic Subcomandante Marcos, the goal is still "un México donde quepan todos" (a Mexico where everyone belongs).

## Notes

For their useful comments on this essay and suggestions for revision, I would like to thank Ben Fallaw and Mary Kay Vaughan. Research funds were provided by a Summer Scholars grant from California State University, Chico, and a Small Research Grant from the Spencer Foundation.

1. Biological or racial determinism is the belief that such factors, rather than material and cultural ones, determine aptitude and character traits.

2. Alan Knight, "Racism, Revolution, and *Indigenismo*: Mexico, 1910–1940," in *The Idea of Race in Latin America*, ed. Richard Graham (Austin: University of Texas Press, 1990), 74.

3. Alexander S. Dawson, *Indian and Nation in Revolutionary Mexico* (Tucson: University of Arizona Press, 2004), 5–6; Charles A. Hale, *The Transformation of Liberalism in Late Nineteenth-Century Mexico* (Princeton: Princeton University Press, 1989), 221, 229–34; and Knight, "Racism," 79–80, 87–88.

4. Knight, "Racism," 82.

5. Dawson, *Indian and Nation*, 6.

6. Alexander S. Dawson, "From Models for the Nation to Model Citizens: Indigenismo and the 'Revindication' of the Mexican Indian, 1920–1940," *Journal of Latin American Studies* 30 (1998): 279.

7. Andrés Molina Enríquez, *Los grandes problemas nacionales* (1908; Mexico City: Ediciones del Instituto Nacional de la Juventud, 1964); Vasconcelos's thoughts on mestizaje are found in his classic *La raza cósmica: Misión de la raza iberoamericana* (1925; Mexico City: Aguilar, S.A. de Ediciones, 1967).

8. Nancy Leys Stepan, *"The Hour of Eugenics": Race, Gender, and Nation in Latin America* (Ithaca: Cornell University Press, 1991), 67–68.

9. Rafael Ramírez, "La incorporación indígena por medio del idioma castellano," *El Maestro Rural* 3, no. 2 (June 15, 1933): 5–6.

10. Marcos E. Becerra, "El Internado Indígena Regional 'Plutarco Elías Calles' establecido recientemente en San Cristóbal L.C.," *Chiapas: Revista Mensual* (Tuxtla Gutiérrez) 1, no. 1 (October 1928): 12–13.

11. Archivo Histórico de la Secretaría de Educación Pública (hereafter AHSEP), 689 (764), Exp. 6, Fo. 54, from Prof. Ernesto Parres, dated from Motozintla, Chis., December 1, 1923.

12. Elsie Rockwell, "Keys to Appropriation: Rural Schooling in Mexico," in *Cultural Production of the Educated Person: Critical Ethnographies of Schooling and Local Practice*, ed. B. Levinson, D. Foley, and D. Hollands (Albany: SUNY Press, 1996), 305–16.

13. Mary Kay Vaughan, *Cultural Politics in Revolution* (Tucson: University of Arizona Press, 1997), 108–12, 118.

14. Gonzalo Aguirre Beltrán, *Teoría y práctica de la educación indígena* (1973; Mexico City: Fondo de Cultura Económica, 1992), 72, 100; *Boletín de la SEP* 3, nos. 5–6 (1924): 598–606; and Moisés Sáenz, *México íntegro* (1939; Mexico City: SepSetentas, 1982), 153, 154.

15. Aguirre Beltrán, *Teoría y práctica*, 100.

16. AHSEP, Secretaría Particular, Caja 4302 (471), Exp. 16, Fo. 71, from Visitador Especial Manuel Mesa A. to *SEP*, dated from Mexico City, June 24, 1932.

17. Aguirre Beltrán, *Teoría y práctica*, 131.

18. SEP, *El esfuerzo educativo en México: La obra del gobierno federal en el ramo de educación pública durante la administración del Presidente Plutarco Elías Calles (1924–1928)* (Mexico City: SEP, 1928), 2:66; AHSEP, Departamento de Psicopedagogía e Higiene, Caja 767 (142), Exp. 83, Fo. 18, from Prof. Angel Miranda B., October 13, 1926.

19. AHSEP, Departamento de Escuelas Rurales (hereafter DER), Caja 6214 (16), Exp. 13, Fo. 26, from Director Enrique Corona to Jefe del DER, SEP, Mexico City, November 11, 1929.

20. AHSEP, DER, La Casa del Estudiante Indígena, Caja 6214 (16), Exp. 4, Fo. 4, dated May 10, 1930; and Alexander Dawson, " 'Wild Indians,' 'Mexican Gentlemen,' and the Lessons Learned in the Casa del Estudiante Indígena, 1926–1932," *The Americas* 57, no. 3 (January 2001): 350.

21. AHSEP, DER, La Casa del Estudiante Indígena, Caja 1474 (849), Exp. 8, Fos. 448–49, from Dr. Santiago Ramírez to Director de la Casa del Estudiante Indígena, March 16, 1931.

22. AHSEP, DER, La Casa del Estudiante Indígena, Caja 1474 (849), Exp. 31, to Jefe del DER from Corona, June 18, 1932.

23. Sáenz, *México íntegro*, 154.

24. Moisés Sáenz, *Carapan: Bosquejo de una experiencia* (1936; Morelia, Michoacán: Talleres Linotipográficos del Gobierno del Estado, 1969), 178.

25. AHSEP, DER, Caja 1332 (191), Exp. 8, Fos. 10–11, from Inspector Manuel Castellanos, April 6, 1935.

26. AHSEP, Dirección General de Educación Primaria en los Estados y Territorios (hereafter DGEPET), Caja 5324 (304), Exp. 20, Fo. 8, from Castellanos, March 12, 1936.

27. Stephen E. Lewis, "A Window to the Recent Past in Chiapas: Federal Education and *Indigenismo* in the Highlands, 1921–1940," *Journal of Latin American Anthropology* 6, no. 1 (2001): 66–71.

28. AHSEP, DGEPET, Caja 5324 (304), Exp. 20, Fo. 19, from Castellanos, May 11, 1936.

29. María Bertely Busquets, "Historia social de la escolarización y uso de castellano escrito en un pueblo zapoteco migrante" (Ph.D. diss., Universidad Autónoma de Aguascalientes, 1998), x–xi, 71.

30. Ibid., 112–15.

31. Ibid., 127.

32. Vaughan, *Cultural Politics in Revolution*, 138, 150–51.

33. Ibid., 137; see also Adrian A. Bantjes, *As If Jesus Walked on Earth: Cardenismo, Sonora, and the Mexican Revolution* (Wilmington, Del.: Scholarly Resources, 1998), 6–36.

34. Vaughan, *Cultural Politics in Revolution*, 138–40, 152–56.

35. SEP, *La Casa del Estudiante Indígena: 16 meses de labor en un experiment psicológico colectivo de indios, Febrero de 1926–junio de 1927* (Mexico City: Talleres Gráficos de la Nación, 1927), 24–26.

36. Departamento de Asuntos Indígenas, *Memoria del Primer Congreso Regional Indígena celebrado en Ixmiquilpan, Hgo. 25 a 26 de septiembre de 1936* (Mexico City: DAAP, 1938), 13; for more on the regional indigenous congresses, see Dawson, *Indian and Nation*.

37. Gonzalo Aguirre Beltrán, *Obra antropológica XII: Lenguas vernáculas* (1983; Mexico City: Fondo de Cultura Económica, 1993), 343–44.

38. On the Zapatistas' drive for autonomy, see Shannan L. Mattiace, *To See with Two Eyes: Peasant Activism and Indian Autonomy in Chiapas, Mexico* (Albuquerque: University of New Mexico Press, 2003).

# For the Health of the Nation:
# Gender and the Cultural Politics of Social Hygiene in
# Revolutionary Mexico

KATHERINE E. BLISS

A 1937 pamphlet produced by the Mexican Departamento de Salubridad Pública warned readers of the perils of contracting the sexually transmitted disease syphilis and detailed the complications that could plague patients who failed to acknowledge or treat their disease symptoms, which included pustules, dermal lesions, pain, and neurological disorders. The text further advised the reader that even graver problems awaited the adult syphilitic who brought a child into the world: "The children of syphilitics carry the disease at birth," the pamphlet read. "They are born horribly deformed. If they are born alive they live only a short time. When they reach seven or eight years old they create great pain because of their human misery. They are mentally incapacitated. For their parents they are a constant reminder. For society they are a useless burden."[1]

Lest readers despair that syphilis infection doomed them for eternity, however, another text urged the afflicted to pursue free and anonymous treatment in public venereal disease treatment clinics. It concluded with the following wisdom: "Conserving one's health is a responsibility one has to oneself, to the family, to the country, and to the race."[2] In a broad interpretation of these health propaganda items, the nation's well-being, not to mention the welfare of the entire race of Mexican people, depended not so much on how the state took care of its citizens but on the very intimate ways in which the individual looked after his own body and ensured that disability—whether his or his child's—did not burden a people anxious to progress.

The syphilis pamphlets' exhortations underpinned both the social hygiene movement and more general developmentalist ideology throughout the years of the "reform phase" of the Mexican Revolution between 1917 and 1940. That the federal government would protect the public's health was a fundamental promise encoded in article 73 of the 1917 constitution. Soldiers and revolutionaries may have taken up arms against Porfirio Díaz to secure land redistribution, promote universal suffrage, and assert domestic control over natural resources, but in the aftermath of constitutional reform, other revolutionaries who styled themselves as "progressives" dedicated themselves to redeeming the Mexican people from the vices they believed the dictatorship had allowed to flourish. Alarmed by high mortality, appalled by the short life span most citizens could expect compared to those of other so-called civilized nations, and dismayed by the extent to which working-age men and women were incapacitated by degenerative diseases that most experts esteemed preventable, physicians, nurses, social workers, and educators joined hands with legislators, activists, and politicians to study ways to improve the collective well-being. Over a decade of investigation and demographic analysis, these reformers determined that preventing the spread of three maladies widely viewed as "social diseases"—tuberculosis, syphilis, and alcoholism—could aid an ailing Mexico. Despite a variety of distinguishing epidemiological characteristics, all three gravely concerned revolutionary health reformers because they disabled adult Mexicans at their most productive ages and because they threatened to endanger the health and productivity of Mexican children, the citizens and workers of the future.[3] Reformers believed that acquiring these intractable diseases was—at least as an adult—voluntary, insofar as infection and addiction could be attributed to personal choices in sexual partners, leisure practices, and domestic space. The campaigns dedicated to preventing their spread were similar in that they challenged the individual's arrangement of his private life in order to promote what reformers construed as the public's interest.

This essay examines the cultural politics of social hygiene in postrevolutionary Mexico by focusing on how competing ideas about gender, progress, individual responsibilities, and collective welfare shaped and challenged the reform agenda. Beginning with an overview of the overlapping influences of developmentalism, anticlericalism, and eugenics, the essay shifts to a discussion of educational programs designed to prevent the spread of tuberculosis, syphilis, and alcoholism between 1920 and 1940. It concludes with a discussion of the public's reception of the state's efforts to regulate their private interests. By the late 1940s, when penal legislation regarding disease transmission replaced regulatory measures and when the introduction of antibiotics rendered bacterial diseases of lesser concern, postrevolutionary hygiene campaigns had nevertheless succeeded in subjecting the individual's domestic and leisure activities to both the state's and the community's scrutiny to promote the health of the nation.

## The Business of Health and Welfare

As they undertook the complex task of developing laws and institutions to put revolutionary social goals into practice, public figures in Mexico's early-twentieth-century social hygiene movement emphasized that improving popular health would, in turn, stimulate national economic health by improving the labor potential of men and women. Revolutionary *higienistas* argued that the new health administration would treat every citizen equally, enhance individual work capacity, and thereby raise the standard of living for all. According to reformist dictates, urban workers, peasants, and poor women and children merited special attention from the revolutionary state because it was they who had languished most under Porfirian economic policies. Within this marginalized population, women and children had experienced the worst social complications associated with alcoholism, tuberculosis, and syphilis-induced disabilities, reformers argued. Left to fend for themselves when their partners' drinking problems interfered with the stability of domestic life, women often bore the brunt of alcohol-induced violence and were vulnerable to a promiscuous spouse's syphilis infection acquired at a local brothel. As Pedro Muro, an associate of the SEP, noted, it was first and foremost important to prevent Mexico's able-bodied men from falling prey to insalubrious lifestyles. Muro emphasized that "to realize the revolutionary goal of redeeming the worker, it is necessary to save him from vice."[4] But in the reformist ideology, until men could be persuaded to forswear drinking alcohol and the womanizing that seemed to accompany male socializing at bars and cantinas, female workers and their children merited society's sympathy and protection because they were so burdened by the disabilities of Mexico's irresponsible men. As an article in the welfare journal *Asistencia* noted, "The Mexican woman needs help. . . . Mothers are obligated to leave home and their children, all day, in order to earn what is necessary for their sustenance [often because they] are abandoned by their husbands who have become alienated from the home and who set a terrible example for their children."[5]

Indeed, the need to reform men and protect women and children was so great that if the revolution did not attack vice and degenerative disease, welfare ideology held, the gains of the ten-year struggle against dictatorial oppression would be overturned. Muro, in a summary of the tenets of the anti-vice campaign in Mexico, noted that alcohol especially was "a traitor to the Revolution, an element of regression, because the drunkard cannot work . . . because of the misery into which he falls because of his drinking, he will basically convert himself into a slave, and with that impede the progress of the entire nation."[6]

Mexican health and education specialists' dedication to promoting hygiene education as an antidote to the problems they associated with addiction and disease drew on their own perceptions of postrevolutionary social reality and their understanding of international health programs. Inspired by the success of North American and European nations in promoting health awareness and disease prevention, reformers emphasized that improving popular health by inculcating the values of personal hygiene could equalize social status and thereby promote the economic development all Mexicans craved.[7] Article 73 of the 1917 constitution granted federal health institutions broad powers to dictate preventative measures "in case of serious epidemics or danger of invasion of the country by exotic diseases."[8] Moreover, the constitution specifically granted the health department "authority over the campaign against alcoholism" and over the sale of substances "which poison the individual and degenerate the race."[9] Reformist legislators transformed these welfare provisions into practical solutions when they authorized the creation of the federal Departamento de Salubridad Pública in 1920. The institutionalization of health reform was followed closely by the consolidation of welfare agencies into the Junta de Beneficencia Pública del Distrito Federal, an institution that was elevated to the federal level and renamed the Secretaría de Asistencia Pública in 1939. The Secretaría de Salubridad y Asistencia, formed by the merger of the Departamento de Salubridad Pública and the Secretaría de Asistencia Pública in 1943, oversaw and coordinated rural and urban social assistance and sanitary services at the federal level.[10]

An assessment of social statistics that health employees collected shortly after the department's inauguration demonstrated that aside from the high mortality associated with revolutionary violence itself, the years of political insecurity and social difficulties had taken their toll on the overall health of the Mexican population. In 1920 tuberculosis ranked just after homicide as among the top fifteen causes of death in the nation. The highly contagious, airborne disease was, moreover, believed to infect as many as fifteen thousand new victims annually in the capital, a city in which poorly ventilated and crowded housing created dense and unpleasant living conditions. The bacterium apparently spread among the metropolis's poorest residents with ease

FIG. 1. The campaign against tuberculosis. Photograph courtesy of the Countway Medical Library, Harvard Medical School.

(see figure 1).[11] To compound this disturbing information, experts discovered soon thereafter that the bacterial infection syphilis, which spread principally via sexual or blood contact, was the leading cause of stillbirth and miscarriage among pregnant women seeking medical care between 1916 and 1920.[12] Although it could not be blamed for as many adult deaths as tuberculosis, syphilis-caused mortality had doubled over the previous decade from .82 to 1.61 per 1,000, suggesting to some that Mexico was in the grip of a sexual promiscuity epidemic. By 1926 the Departamento de Salubridad Pública estimated that 50 percent of *capitolino* men and women were infected with the intractable disease.[13] Syphilis and tuberculosis were worrisome to higienistas both because the diseases reduced life expectancy and because they incapacitated otherwise able men and women, rendering them "economically passive" at a time when the revolutionary nation could ill afford to lose the labor contribution of its youngest and strongest members.

The available information regarding tuberculosis and syphilis infection rates was discouraging, to be sure, but it was alcoholism that caused the greatest concern for sanitation experts in the 1920s. Despite regionally based efforts to curb alcohol production, distribution, and consumption since at least 1915, researchers found that the tendency for men to consume pulque, beer, and *aguardiente* had hardly diminished over the rough years of revolutionary violence and reconstruction. To limit the sale of liquor in the municipality, the Mexico City Ayuntamiento had raised liquor licensing fees in metropolitan entertainment venues over the period between 1918 and the early 1920s, and municipalities in southern states such as Yucatán had outlawed the sale of alcohol outright during the same period.[14] Nevertheless, a 1924 study revealed that in Mexico City alone there were sixty-three bars per ten thousand residents, and specialists warned that the prevalence of alcohol consumption was even more pronounced in impoverished rural areas. Although it was not infectious like tuberculosis or syphilis, alcoholism was associated with contagion and degeneration for several reasons: children saw their parents drink and took up the habit themselves; long-term ingestion of alcohol weakened the body, leading chronic drinkers to shirk their work responsibilities; and frequent intoxication rendered the body more susceptible to graver maladies. Higienistas also worried that people who were frequently under the influence of alcohol were likely to engage in "undesirable" sexual unions. Not only might a drunk man or woman contract a sexually transmitted infection by enjoying an ill-advised encounter with an infected partner, but experts believed that children conceived while the parents were drunk were likely to suffer from a variety of irreversible afflictions. After a 1925 study at a Mexico City elementary school showed that 80 percent of students tested positive for syphilis, a disease they had almost certainly acquired congenitally, some reformers feared that venereal disease infection in the nation had reached epidemic proportions.[15] The grave implications of drinking, sexual promiscuity, and poor sanitation were clear: *Asistencia* proclaimed that "many of our children present hereditary stigmas, morally and physically, and these are from alcoholic, tubercular or syphilitic origin, which naturally incapacitate them for making the most of their situation."[16]

Reformers' alarm over the extent and complexity of the problems associated with social diseases in Mexico inspired a desire to study and assess the reasons why disabling illness flourished in the postrevolutionary context. In the 1920s doctors and nurses interviewed clinic patients regarding their personal habits, social workers made home visits to report on domestic conditions, psychiatrists assessed the institutionalized population's mental state, and legislators toured nightspots, bars, and dance halls to study the intricate pathways of disease transmission in Mexico. After ten years of research and fieldwork, these experts concluded that poverty, gender inequality, and hygiene ignorance played critical roles in the dissemination of disability in Mexico. Inspired by revolutionary anticlericalism, anticapitalism, and a kind of eugenic protectionism, reformers blamed the dictatorship, the clergy, and Mexican men for the nation's sorry state of affairs.[17]

For reformist health investigators in the 1920s, both the Díaz dictatorship and the Catholic Church bore responsibility for most of the Mexican population's current health problems. Arguing that the clergy and the dictatorship had worked hand in hand to steal the people's money and maintain them in poverty and ignorance, health specialists took inspiration from legislators such as Jaliscan federal deputy Arturo Higareda, who in 1917 maintained that "there are three things which have degenerated our poor classes; first, the clergy, which hides the truth and which exploits the poor; second, the government, which, being tyrannical, deprived them of learning, which is the bread of understanding and fountain of spirit; and third, vice, which keeps them from working."[18] Even in 1930 social critics continued to lambaste the Porfirians for the deplorable living conditions that characterized everyday life for most Mexicans. As the Michoacán doctor Arturo Oviedo Mota noted in a personal letter to president Pascual Ortiz Rubio, "The Revolution, in its program to redeem the popular classes, is obligated to combat this 'necessary evil' left over from the Dictatorship. For the Porfirians, the popular classes were despised by Society, and it mattered little or not at all that their children, fodder for the cannon or the brothel, suffered."[19]

If dictatorship and church-induced poverty could be blamed for the undesirable state of popular living conditions, Catholic ideology was directly responsible for the spread of sexually transmitted disease, health authorities reasoned. Indeed, many higienistas pointed to the federal regulation of prostitution, a practice adopted by Conservatives in the 1860s and maintained by the Porfirian regime, for the high rates of syphilis among the population. The Reglamento, which president Plutarco Elías Calles renewed in 1926 despite growing abolitionist pressures, required prostitutes to register with health authorities, report for regular physical examinations to detect signs of infection with a sexually transmitted disease, and work in authorized brothels or *accesorías* in designated urban areas. Revolutionary health ideologues worried that the Reglamento, originally intended to prevent the spread of syphilis, in fact represented a poor way to limit disease insofar as it held a small group of "deviant" women responsible for protecting the health of the rest of the nation. Rather than promote the community's health, they said, the Reglamento instead promoted "Catholic values," including the sexual double standard, by which women were expected to be virginal before marriage and monogamous afterward, while sexual promiscuity was tolerated among men at all ages. As early as the 1915 revolutionary convention, the radical intellectual Antonio Díaz Soto y Gama argued that these Catholic-inspired gender expectations, combined with the legal prohibition against divorce in Mexico, underpinned social toleration of male sexual promiscuity and facilitated syphilis infection. In a fiery speech given at the Convention at Aguascalientes in 1915, Díaz Soto y Gama noted of marriage in Mexico that "after the so-called honeymoon comes fatigue, weariness, and ennui, until society's disgrace begins." When men could no longer tolerate unhappy marriages, he indicated, they were forced to visit prostitutes to seek sexual satisfaction and thus endangered their families with brothel contagion.[20] By the mid-1920s, Dr. Bernardo Gastélum, head of the Department of Public Health, blamed religious prudishness or "false modesty" for the population's secrecy regarding sexual matters and argued that the embarrassment with which men and women associated sexual intercourse frequently prevented them from acknowledging disease symptoms or seeking disease treatment.

Just as health reformers blamed Catholicism for the population's hygiene ignorance and the sexual double standard and the spread of syphilis, so many also felt that the evils of capitalism could be blamed for the alarming spread of disease. Head of the anti-alcohol campaign and later secretary of public education Ignacio García Téllez observed that in rural areas this situation was especially pronounced. "When one leaves the palatial lifestyle of the metropolis to get in contact with the proletarian organizations and poor Indians and others of the country," he wrote, "one discovers the intimate link between the exploiters who foment ignorance and the vices of the oppressed," which he labeled "the favorite arms of the clergy and the capitalists, who try to impede the people's material and spiritual emancipation."[21]

It was not just priests, planters, and hacendados who used alcohol and vice to "enslave" and "degenerate" Mexico's poorest and most vulnerable citizens, however. Revolutionary legislators and administrators also held small business owners such as landlords, madams, and liquor purveyors responsible for the oppression of Mexico's men and women. Brothel proprietors had come under reformist scrutiny when the Mexico City council likened them to slaveholders who oppressed the women who worked there. Although the Reglamento had long enshrined the *matrona* as the mediator between the prostitute and the sanitary inspection service that oversaw women's health care, in 1918 city councilor Dr. Agustín Vidales promoted legislation to bring brothels into compliance with the work protection provisions of constitutional article 123. Stating that "these poor women are eternally locked in those houses, suffering all kinds of humiliations," he sought to undermine the matronas who, he argued "immoderately exploited" *pupilas*, as brothel inmates were called.[22] Moreover, penal legislation progressively restricted the activities of pimps between 1929 and 1931.[23] And in the mid-1930s, municipal legislation subjected Federal District cabarets, where women danced, drank alcohol, and were widely believed to engage in sexual commerce, to regulatory measures.

Penal and regulatory measures limited the profits that pimps, madams, and bar owners enjoyed at the expense of poor men's and women's health, but such measures were protectionist in spirit and reflected the reformers' highly gendered understanding of welfare and national family life. The idea that women were especially vulnerable to the social problems associated with alcoholism infused social legislation during this period and inspired not just anti-alcohol tracts but also the establishment of institutions dedicated to alleviating the economic and child-care burden that working women faced.[24] This protectionist element of health and welfare ideology was certainly consistent with the goals of feminist and abolitionist groups that advocated preventing women from falling into "the life," but it had particular resonance with eugenic thought. Eugenics, the international scientific movement that aimed to promote "good genes" via positive reproduction outcomes, gained a strong following in 1920s Mexico among feminists, socialists, health specialists, and social workers.[25] Although some eugenicists, like their counterparts in North America and Europe, advocated sterilizing chronic alcoholics and criminals, most Mexican adherents advocated a socially "positive eugenics," which held that "communities" or "races" could be improved either by miscegenation with "superior races" or by ensuring that those men and women who did reproduce were free from diseases and other vices.[26] Although both men and women were responsible for maintaining their good health in eugenics thinking, it was women who, as mothers, bore the greatest responsibility to stay disease free, for they gave life to the next generation. As head of the Federal District's Department of Social Prevention and Readaptation, the psychiatrist, socialist, feminist, and prominent eugenicist Dr. Mathilde Rodríguez Cabo emphasized in a speech to social workers that working-class girls suffered doubly in Mexico's postrevolutionary, male-dominated economy. Ill-equipped to secure well-paying employment, they were exposed to sexual abuse and domestic violence, making them vulnerable not just to poverty but to falling into prostitution and to alcoholism as well.[27] As the next generation of mothers, Rodríguez Cabo asserted, they merited the state's full protection and attention.

Eugenics offered both an explanatory model for understanding why Mexican health was so dismal and a solution, for it suggested that the individual could, by adopting good health practices, improve his or her children's hopes for the future. Thus Mexico's problems were collective, but the individual bore responsibility for improving his or her own prospects for the benefit of the whole. Public concerns over private behaviors ultimately met head-on with popular ideas about prevention, health, and well-being, rendering the business of ensuring the nation's health a politically charged enterprise.

## The Morality of Mortality

For the doctors, social workers, and psychologists who studied the problems of morality, mortality, disability, and degenerative disease in postrevolutionary Mexico, the bar, brothel, and home were suspect venues. But whereas bars and brothels could be outlawed or subjected to regulatory surveillance, the home was most difficult to penetrate. In the reformist imagination, the peasant's or worker's domestic space was dark, poorly ventilated, and overcrowded. The social-work student Gustavo Vázquez observed with horror that "given the number of people who out of necessity are compelled to sleep in these rooms, it is easy to understand how they become spaces in which people present themselves with all their passions and defects."[28] In this line of thinking, not only was the poor Mexican's home a defective venue filled with violence and intrigue, but it was apparently so culturally destitute that it drove women to prostitute themselves and men to drink alcohol and waste their hard-earned money. Drunk and sexually promiscuous, men and women contracted syphilis and lost strength, becoming susceptible to a host of other contagions, including tuberculosis. Since hygiene personnel rarely penetrated the citizen's home, the state's capacity to intervene in and correct domestic and intimate affairs in accordance with community health goals was limited. In this context, hygiene education emerged as a way for the state to challenge "unhealthy" private behaviors.

For a variety of reasons, hygiene education offered an opportune way for health specialists to transform individual practices. As the higienista Dr. Alfonso Pruneda noted in a 1934 *Gaceta Médica* editorial expounding the successes of the project, "The school is intimately related to the home" and could "exert a beneficial influence on the entire community." Pruneda, who throughout the 1920s held a variety of posts within the Departamento de Salubridad, emphasized that teachers, students, and visiting doctors and nurses associated with the SEP were key figures in the fight against adult-disabling diseases. Not only could teachers serve as exemplary sanitary role models within the tenements or villages where they lived, he noted, but students could serve a critical revolutionary role, too. As Pruneda opined, "The child is the link between social institutions. . . . He is a vector of the teachings and practices he acquires there such that he can modify domestic conditions." Moreover, "the school is called to do this also through the doctors and nurses associated with it who make home visits." The higienista summarized the benefits of hygiene education, stating that "by converting schools into centers of hygiene activism we can realize different campaigns related to them," such as the "campaigns against alcoholism, tuberculosis and venereal disease."[29]

Although revolutionary reformers were loath to admit it, the classroom had been a critical site of pro-hygiene activities since the late Porfiriato.[30] In the 1920s, revolutionary educators maintained the Porfirian practice of linking ideas about personal hygiene and national well-being in student minds via specific classroom projects. By means of the "Game of Health," for example, teachers encouraged children to report on the family's domestic hygiene and graded students according to their facial and bodily presentation. The teacher marked each child's performance on a special card and rewarded clean students with ribbons in patriotic colors while making dirty children wear black ribbons as punishment. In this game, which clearly linked the child's and family's hygiene to national pride, a green ribbon symbolized hope for Mexico's future, the white represented the child's willingness to follow rules, and red signified pride in Mexico's historic past.[31]

If encouraging children's hygiene awareness was important, higienistas also believed it imperative to directly educate parents with respect to tuberculosis prophylaxis. As Dr. J. Monjaras observed in a 1920 article about domestic hygiene, "If he does not take care to eliminate the dangers to his health, man can encounter numerous dangers in his home."[32] Cleanliness, sunlight, and open space were the tuberculosis bacterium's greatest enemies, preventing it from securing a foothold in the family's domestic space. In poorly ventilated homes, by contrast, "the deadly microbes preserve their virulence indefinitely and conquer more and more victims, as many as are living in the home."[33] To prevent this scenario from undermining the harmony of his own domestic life, the individual was encouraged to visit free tuberculosis clinics, acquire information regarding disease prophylaxis, and assume responsibility for his own health and for the health of his family.

Like domestic hygiene, adult sexual education was a top priority of post-revolutionary health reformers. Although many health specialists, legislators, and doctors believed that religion and capitalism, generally, could be blamed for what appeared to be a promiscuity epidemic in urban centers, they also believed that the citizenry's general failure to recognize disease symptoms and refusal to seek medical attention out of embarrassment or fear of health professionals accounted for the continuing spread of illness via prostitutes to families and children. Rendering sexuality a facet of health science as opposed to religious morality, many felt, was the key to resolving this problem.[34]

To encourage popular awareness of sexual hygiene, in 1927 the Department of Public Health embarked on a propaganda campaign to educate Mexico City's men and women about venereal disease. In that year alone, department employees distributed some 630,000 pamphlets on syphilis, 430,000 on gonorrhea, and 251,000 on personal hygiene. Arguing that this printed and graphic material would "break old, narrow-minded and vicious popular customs and destroy the prejudices and beliefs that ignorance has engendered among the popular classes," reformers were especially anxious to ensure that vulnerable girls and women be made aware of disease symptoms and sexual anatomy. In the 1920s doctors reported that women, especially, had little information about sexual matters and were often surprised when told they were pregnant by an examining physician. Male magazine readers could gain detailed information about human anatomy and sexuality by ordering privately distributed pamphlets such as *Ignorancia Total*, which promised readers current and "scientific" information on sexual practices and pleasures in a language "that will flabbergast you!" However, Mexican women rarely counted on accurate information about reproduction and sexual hygiene. To ensure that the topic of human sexuality became a matter of open discussion, the department underwrote and produced radio programs that transmitted a "moralizing tendency of social renovation" and worked with the SEP to prepare pamphlets, especially for rural and indigenous populations. In addition, higienistas borrowed from the U.S. social hygiene movement and preceded mainstream cinema attractions by screening films such as the American-made *End of the Road*, which shocked audiences with grotesque images of untreated venereal disease acquired over a lifetime of vice. Nurses and doctors gave talks in factories, markets, and public gardens to promote open discussion of issues such as sexual hygiene and how to pick a healthy sexual partner. Social hygienists hoped that by saturating the city's public spaces with graphic images and discourses about sexually transmitted diseases, men and women would be more likely to recognize a problem and seek treatment in the city's free clinics or syphilis treatment hospital before they infected someone else.[35]

A critical perspective on Mexican masculinity permeated the 1920s and 1930s sexual hygiene education material. One prominently displayed magazine announcement, for example, urged women to seek a blood test for syphilis and clearly demonstrated the role that wayward fathers played in spreading the infection. In the foreground of the drawing stood the father, on crutches, with his eyes downcast. Behind him sat the mother with several children, crying, because of the father's — and perhaps her own — venereal disease infection. The text read: "Syphilis is not a secret sickness. If you don't confess it, your children will show it."[36] Another pamphlet warned families of the perils of spreading syphilis to their newborns, who could potentially infect a wet nurse or look like the baby depicted on the pamphlet's cover, a deformed, weak, and miserable child with no hope of a life of his own. Indeed, although syphilitic babies acquired the disease from their mothers through birth, national hygiene campaigns emphasized men's responsibility in disease prophylaxis, stating that "it is necessary to emphasize that for the man who has acquired the vice of visiting prostitutes, it is difficult to avoid contracting syphilis. He who out of habit fails to dominate his sexual instincts cedes easily to temptation."[37] Knowledge and discipline, reformers felt, would remedy this situation.

Although most sex education material was oriented toward redressing the problem of adults' sexual ignorance, reformers judged Mexico's adolescents, who tended to marry young or become sexually active, to also be in desperate need of reliable information about sexuality. However, recognizing that most parents might view the public provision of such information as a violation of privacy, higienistas encouraged parents to talk to their children about sexuality at a young age. Pamphlets distributed to parents, for example, taught them to teach boys how to pick appropriate sexual partners and to look out for signs of venereal disease infection.[38] Others warned that "young men should be prudent and stay away from danger at least until they have reached majority, totally abstaining from any sexual excitement until then."[39]

But the realization that so many parents were themselves ignorant with respect to sexual hygiene or too prudish to impart it inspired some reformers to advocate public sexual education for all students. In 1933 the issue gained national attention when SEP director Narciso Bassols entertained a proposal for incorporating mandatory sex education into the nation's public elementary and secondary institutions.[40] This proposal generated a firestorm of controversy and protest from angry parents' groups for several months after it surfaced, and it was never fully implemented. However, at the Escuela Correccional para Mujeres, which assumed responsibility for educating and rehabilitating delinquent girls, physicians and nurses associated with the Federal District's Sanitary Inspection Service gave frank talks about disease prophylaxis and encouraged the adolescent inmates to take up healthy activities such as volleyball, swimming, and dance.[41]

Because alcoholism was closely associated with tuberculosis and syphilis, addiction prevention occupied a key place in postrevolutionary hygiene education. Regulatory policies, liquor taxes, and even prohibition might limit the production and distribution of alcohol at the regional level, but, as with tuberculosis and syphilis prevention, reformers believed that changing the individual's perspectives on drinking would be the only way to improve society. Not only did the Department of Public Health distribute pamphlets warning readers against alcohol abuse, but health officials worked with teachers to ensure that students and adults understood the deleterious effects of alcohol on domestic life. Like the anti-syphilis campaign, the anti-alcohol propaganda was flavored with the ideology of eugenic protectionism. One pamphlet designed for general distribution proclaimed, for example, that "alcoholism is the gravest obstacle to the tranquillity of the home" and portrayed a drunk father rejecting his distraught wife and young daughter on the cover (see figure 2).[42] The higienista Carlos Jiménez wrote that "effectively the woman and her children are . . . the innocent victims of the husband or alcoholic father who wastes his meager salary to the detriment of their alimentation and provision of clothing." Jiménez warned that children who grew up in such a household were likely to form the next generation of alcoholics.[43] Nationally, public officials took advantage of the protectionist bent of anti-alcohol campaigns to authorize the establishment of locally based women's temperance and prohibition organizations, seeking to harness women's incipient political activism and their experience with the ill effects of alcoholism to promote social change.[44]

Teachers, too, assumed responsibility for encouraging youths to become involved in anti-alcohol campaigns via poetry and song in the classroom. As Yucatecan Dr. Ayuso O'Horibe noted in a published speech: "When someone has one, two or three glasses of aguardiente, he feels that his face is on fire, he turns red, he gets congested, his brain no longer thinks well, he loses his sense of voluntary movement. When he drinks even more, his brain thinks even

FIG. 2. The campaign
against alcoholism.
Photograph courtesy of
the Countway Medical
Library, Harvard
Medical School.

worse and he no longer knows what he is doing or saying, he loses himself completely."[45] Lest they succumb to the seductive powers of drink and turn into such horrible specimens of humanity, O'Horibe suggested that children recite the anti-alcoholic oath on a regular basis and teach simple slogans to family and friends, like "We will never go to the taverns" and "Whiskey is vile and degrading."[46] Higienistas hoped that the active participation of mothers and children in hygiene promotion and alcoholism prevention would lead Mexico's wayward men into a bright and productive future.

### Individual Choices, Public Outcries

Hygiene education campaigns exhorted men, women, and children to protect their own health and that of their families against degenerative diseases that limited the productive capacities of able-bodied people and—by extension—the nation. But although educational materials couched their instructions in terms of individual, familial, and community benefits, Mexican citizens did not always respond to the state's intrusion into their bodily practices, leisure activities, and domestic life. Between 1920 and 1940, the targets of campaigns repeatedly challenged and protested the nature and gender implications of federal hygiene propaganda. Moreover, men and women applied the logic of sanitation and hygiene to their own lives and developed their own sense of "well-being" that often clashed with the state's definition.

Doctors' warnings that crowded living conditions encouraged the spread of tuberculosis went largely unheeded, at least in crowded cities like the capital, where the threat of bacterial infection was greatest. Throughout the 1920s and 1930s, the city became home to thousands of rural migrants who settled in newly converted inner-city tenements or installed temporary housing in unimproved areas on the outskirts of town.[47] With low-paying jobs and recently arrived relatives joining them, many migrant families pooled resources and shared domestic space, often sleeping several people to a bed and sometimes even enclosing domestic animals in the one-room apartment at night. Moreover, long shifts or the necessity of holding down numerous jobs left few poor men and women enough time to perform the household cleansing and ventilation that health authorities encouraged on a regular basis. Indeed, what appeared to higienistas to be stubborn peasant resistance to hygiene was instead a practical if unpleasant lifestyle shaped by poverty, migration, low skills, and inadequate urban employment opportunities. It was not until the 1950s that the government began to tackle the problem of inadequate housing.

Like the antituberculosis campaign, the effort to dissuade women from engaging in prostitution failed in the sense that many urban women encountered great difficulty earning a living through the often degrading and low-paying factory jobs that were available to them. On their own in the city or responsible for children and elderly dependents, working women increasingly turned to prostitution. By 1938, experts estimated that there were some forty thousand women in the capital engaged in sexual commerce. Although it was dangerous, degrading, and unreliable work, many prostitutes reported that sexual commerce offered them more independence and better wages than the jobs for which uneducated and illiterate women were qualified. Poverty and single parenthood pushed many women into sexual commerce. For example, in a letter to President Calles, prostitutes who called themselves the "daughters of disgrace" stated that they could not find work in the countryside or in factories and insisted that most of them worked in sexual commerce "out of necessity" and not "because of vices." Prostitutes who were forcibly hospitalized at the Hospital Morelos for syphilis treatment advanced a critical protest of health administration policies that centered around gender claims. Stating that they were mothers who had been abandoned by men and who worked to support their children, they demanded the right to have their children stay with them in the hospital while they recovered, and demanded the state accord them the respect it offered all mothers who bore and raised children.[48]

The campaign to promote openness with respect to sexuality and sexual education met with protest from men, who perceived the state's effort to teach women about sexuality as undermining men's masculine prerogatives. When word of the Bassols sexual education plan was leaked to the press, for example, not only did organized Catholic groups mount considerable opposition, but teenage boys offended by the idea that their female peers might be exposed to "immoral" anatomical information staged a protest at a downtown movie theater.[49] In Morelia, Michoacán, five thousand Catholic petitioners protested the state's sexual education plan, calling it an attempt to introduce "pornography in the schools." These protests were so vehement that they ultimately helped produce Bassols's resignation within a few months.[50] In Mexico City, neighborhood groups protested the Department of Public Health's effort to locate a sexual tolerance zone in an outlying working-class neighborhood during the same period. Citing the poor impression that women of "the life" would give their wives and daughters, they begged health officials to locate vice elsewhere in the city.[51]

In rural Mexico, planters and alcohol merchants worked hand in hand to protest the anti-alcohol campaigns. In Chiapas, for example, federal teachers encouraged the governor and local officials to enforce prohibition, which was officially implemented in 1935. Nevertheless, this failed to stem the flow of alcohol for a variety of reasons. In the first place, local government officials actually depended on liquor taxes as a source of municipal (and sometimes personal) revenue in this impoverished state. Second, in the areas where prohibition was ostensibly enforced, wealthy distributors bribed local officials to look the other way when their goods moved through town. Third, alcohol was a critical element of local labor-contracting practices, insofar as lowland planters' agents often offered aguardiente (rum) on credit to highland Indians, who were later forced to pay their debts through agricultural work. Finally, liquor "played a pivotal role in the civil and religious life of indigenous communities, since religious cargo holders profited from its sale, and everything from court hearings to marriage transactions involved its ritual exchange."[52] Even where prohibition was officially enforced, clandestine stills proliferated, satisfying local demand. The complex relationship between alcohol, community relations, and individual ambitions undermined anti-alcohol initiatives in other states, too. In Michoacán in 1936, local women complained to the Morelia municipal president that the city's tax collector, an inveterate gambler, was also "actively engaged in the clandestine sale of alcohol."[53]

But besides directly contesting or subverting education campaigns, individuals selectively adopted hygiene information as they found it to be useful to their own lives. The state's emphasis on new leisure activities sometimes had unanticipated consequences. Adult education programs frequently emphasized sports as a useful social substitute for popular male pastimes such as drinking and womanizing with friends. The popular media joined the hygiene campaign. The magazine *Mujeres y Deportes* emphasized the importance of replacing vices with hygienic and health practices. In an article entitled "More Sports, Fewer Vices," the author proudly proclaimed that "vice has been attacked from every direction by sports, and it is wonderful to note the number of people who now dedicate themselves to the practices of athleticism instead of destroying their bodies in the centers of vice."[54] However, researchers who investigated male social practices were discouraged to learn that sports teams often went to brothels or bars after sports games were over.[55] Women who participated in the state's anti-alcohol activities found a similar sense of community in their endeavors; indeed, their membership in the Ligas exposed them to political allies and like-minded women, with whom they joined in other activist efforts to advance a variety of feminist and radical reforms well outside the state's official program.[56]

Finally, men and women adopted their own ideas about personal hygiene and individual welfare in ways that blatantly clashed with reformers' views of how to ensure the health of the nation. In protesting the dissolution of the Mexico City zone of tolerance in 1938, prostitutes invoked their need to earn a living, their right to protection from the state, and their desire to enjoy well-being as they understood the term: freedom from police exploitation and physical abuse. Similarly, male clients were dismayed by the disappearance of the district and invoked their right to enjoy transitory sexual encounters as essential to the "health of the body."[57]

While the introduction of antibiotics in the 1940s reduced the incidence of bacterial diseases and fostered a demand for pills, the importance of hygiene made its way into popular culture. Women's magazines ran stories that emphasized the power of hygiene with respect to beauty and the ability to attract men. For example, *Nosotras*, a monthly magazine associated with the Partido Nacional Revolucionario's women's auxiliary, sought to appeal to a broad spectrum and ran frequent articles on sports, beauty, fashion, and health. In an ongoing serialized story entitled "Juanita Tenoria: The History of a Beautiful Woman," a feminine version of the Don Juan parable, Juanita declares that her state of "physical, moral and hygienic" integrity has helped her time and again in the pursuit of love.[58] In an article entitled "The Charms of the Lips," an anonymous author instructed women with respect to hygienic methods for preserving this "great seductive attribute."[59] Beauty salons such as the Salón de Belleza "Medal" wooed readers with advertisements that promoted their "hygiene and courtesy."[60] But it was not just mainstream advertisers who understood that discriminating customers sought hygienic guarantees: even brothel madams realized the popular currency of hygiene and promoted the sanitary nature of their establishments in men's guidebooks to nightlife in Mexico City.[61]

Revolutionary hygiene campaigns that sought to promote Mexican men's and women's concerns for their own health and the well-being of their families were largely successful by the 1940s, at least in the sense that individuals developed a sense of the meanings of hygiene and welfare for their own lives. Convincing the individual citizen to consider that personal hygiene was also a responsibility he or she had to "the country and to the race," however, was a different matter. Throughout the 1920s and 1930s, hygiene propaganda successfully infiltrated print media, radio, advertising, popular literature, and graphic design. Men and women demanded hygienic conditions from the businesses they patronized, but they developed their own ideas about the ways in which they might model their domestic lives, intimate relations, and leisure activities to accommodate the state's exhortations.

## Notes

1. Departamento de Salubridad Pública, *Sífilis* (Mexico City: Departamento de Salubridad Pública, 1937), 3.

2. Departamento de Salubridad Pública, *Consejos higiénicos para evitar el contagio de las enfermedades venéreas* (Mexico City: Departamento de Salubridad Pública, Oficina General de la Campaña Antivenérea/Talleres Gráficos de la Nación, 1940), 1.

3. Investigators referred to health-induced disability as "economic passivity" and

likened its status to that of childhood or old-age dependence. See "La función social de la beneficencia pública," *Asistencia*, August 15, 1934, 28.

4. Pedro M. Muro, *La campaña antialcohólica* (Mexico City: Silbarios de la Secretaría de Educación Pública, n.d.), 29. The concept that providing sanitary services to rural peasants could function as an aspect of revolutionary wealth redistribution is discussed in Ana María Poppi, "The Mexican Ejidal Services: A Program Born in Morelia, Michoacán" (paper presented at the Conference on Latin American History, Boston, January 2001).

5. "Casa Amiga de la Obrera," *Asistencia*, August 15, 1934, 21.

6. Muro, *La campaña antialcohólica*, 21.

7. Jeffrey Weeks discusses similar tensions between moral and health reform projects in late Victorian England in his *Sex, Politics and Society: The Regulation of Sexuality since 1800* (Essex, England: Longman Press, 1981); see also Theodor Rosebury, *Microbes and Morals: The Strange Story of Venereal Disease* (New York: Viking Press, 1971); and the collection of articles in Arien Mack, ed., *In Time of Plague: The History and Social Consequences of Lethal Disease* (New York: New York University Press, 1991).

8. Article 73, section 16, *Constitución Política de los Estados Unidos Mexicanos*, 1917.

9. Ibid.

10. "Ojeada sobre las enfermedades dominantes en la República Mexicana," *Gaceta Médica de México* 65, nos. 7–8 (1934): 198–99. See also the "Reglamentos de salubridad pública," in *Diario Oficial: Órgano del Gobierno Constitucional de los Estados Unidos Mexicanos* (Mexico City: Palacio Nacional del Poder Ejecutivo en México, December 19, 1924), 3–18; Anthony Mazzaferri, "Public Health and Social Revolution in Mexico" (Ph.D. diss., Kent State University, 1968), 217; and Gustavo Baz Prada, *Historia de la salud en Oaxaca, 1943–1993* (Oaxaca: Secretaría de Salud del Gobierno del Estado de Oaxaca, 1994).

11. "Ojeada sobre las enfermedades dominantes," 188.

12. "Causas de muerte intrauterina de enero 1916 a la fecha," *Boletín de Salubridad Pública*, no. 4 (1925): 91.

13. Bernardo Gastélum, "La persecución de la sífilis desde el punto de vista de la garantía social," *Boletín de Salubridad Pública* (1926): 8.

14. Archivo Histórico de la Ciudad de México (AHCM), Sanidad, vol. 3891, various files; Ben Fallaw, "Dry Law, Wet Politics: Drinking and Prohibition in Revolutionary Yucatán, 1915–1935," *Latin American Research Review* 37, no. 2 (2002): 37–64.

15. Archivo Histórico de la Secretaría de Salubridad y Asistencia (AHSSA), Salubridad Pública (SP), Inspección Anti-venérea (IAV), box 5, file 1, 35.

16. "Casa Amiga de la Obrera," *Asistencia*, August 15, 1934, 21. Fear of degeneration and the fatal links between alcoholism, tuberculosis, and syphilis were not limited to postrevolutionary Mexican higienistas. In Argentina doctors and reformers similarly worried about the implications of disabling disease for the nation's economic progress.

See Diego Armus, "Salud y anarquismo: La tuberculosis en el discurso literario argentino, 1890–1940," in *Política, médicos y enfermedades: Lecturas de historia de la salud en la Argentina*, ed. Mirta Zaida Lobato (Buenos Aires: Ediciones Biblios, 1996), 93–116.

17. Archivo General de la Nación (AGN), Administración Pública de la República (APR), Presidentes Obregón/Calles, file 242-MI-H-I.

18. Mexico, Congreso, Cámara de Diputados, Diario de los debates de la H. Cámara de Diputados, XXVII Legislature, Ordinary session, año 2, no. 3 (September 4, 1917), 24.

19. Alberto Oviedo Mota, "El problema social de la prostitución," letter to Pascual Ortiz Rubio, 1930, AHSSA, SP, Servicio Jurídico (SJ), box 20, file 10.

20. *Crónicas y debates de la Soberana Convención Revolucionaria*, vol. 3 (Mexico City: Bibliografía del Instituto Nacional de Estudios Históricos Revolucionarios Mexicanos, 1965), 548–49.

21. Ignacio García Téllez, "Los estragos que causa el alcoholismo," *Asistencia*, September 15, 1934, 39.

22. Ordinary session of *cabildo*, February 21, 1918, *Boletín Municipal: Órgano del Ayuntamiento de la Ciudad de México* 3, no. 5 (March 12, 1918).

23. Katherine Elaine Bliss, *Compromised Positions: Prostitution, Public Health and Gender Politics in Revolutionary Mexico City* (University Park: Pennsylvania State University Press, 2001), 127–51.

24. Ibid., chap. 5.

25. For a comprehensive analysis of the goals and politics of the Mexican Eugenics Society, see Alexandra Minna Stern, "Responsible Mothers and Normal Children: Eugenics, Nationalism and Welfare in Post-revolutionary Mexico, 1920–1940," *Journal of Historical Sociology* 12, no. 4 (December 1999).

26. Nancy Leys Stepan, *The Hour of Eugenics*: *Race, Gender and Nation in Latin America* (Ithaca: Cornell University Press, 1991).

27. Mathilde Rodríguez Cabo, "El problema sexual de las menores mujeres y su repercusión en la delincuencia juvenil femenina," *Criminalia* 6, no. 10 (1940).

28. Gustavo Vázquez, *Etiología de la delincuencia infantil en México*: *Ideología que debe sostener el órgano que conozca de las faltas cometidas por menores* (Lic. thesis, Facultad de Derechos y Ciencias Sociales, Universidad Nacional Autónoma de México, 1940).

29. Alfonso Pruneda, "Cooperación de los maestros de educación primaria en la educación higiénica," *Gaceta Médica de México* 61, no. 6 (June 1930): 313–15.

30. Mary Kay Vaughan, *The State, Education and Social Class in Mexico, 1880–1928* (Dekalb: Northern Illinois University Press, 1982); Patience Schell, "Working Bodies, Revolutionary Minds: Public Health in Mexico City's Primary Schools, 1896–1928" (paper presented at the Conference on Latin American History, Boston, 2001); and Stephen E. Lewis, "Revolution and the Rural Schoolhouse: Forging State and Nation in Chiapas, Mexico, 1913–1948" (Ph.D. diss., University of California, San Diego, 1997).

31. Archivo Histórico de la Secretaría de Educación Pública (AHSEP), Departamento de Psicopedagogía e Higiene, Educación Higiénica de los Niños/Proyectos, file 142.27.

32. J. M. Monjaras, "La higienización de las casas desde el punto de vista del desarrollo y propagación de algunas enfermedades transmisibles," *Gaceta Médica de México* I, no. 5 (1920): 133.

33. G. Mendizábal, "Algunas consideraciones acerca de la profilaxis de la tuberculosis," *Gaceta Médica de México* 5, no. 8 (August 1910): 335.

34. Gastélum, "La persecución de la sífilis," 5–25.

35. Katherine Bliss, "The Science of Redemption: Syphilis, Sexual Promiscuity and Reformism in Revolutionary Mexico City," *Hispanic American Historical Review*, no. I (February 1999): 1–40.

36. Advertisement, *Mujer: Para la elevación moral e intelectual de la mujer mexicana*, March 1927, back cover.

37. Departamento de Salubridad Pública, *Sífilis*, 3.

38. Juan Soto, *La educación sexual en la escuela mexicana: Libro para los padres y los maestros* (Mexico City: Ediciones Patria, 1933).

39. Departamento de Salubridad Pública, *Sífilis*, 3.

40. See Lewis, "Revolution and the Rural Schoolhouse"; Anne Rubenstein, "Raised Voices in the Cine Montecarlo: Sex Education, Mass Media and Oppositional Politics," *Journal of Family History*, July 1998; and John W. Sherman, *The Mexican Right: The End of Revolutionary Reform, 1929–1940* (Westport, Conn.: Praeger, 1996), 38.

41. Bliss, "Science of Redemption."

42. Departamento de Salubridad Pública, *El alcoholismo es el más grave obstáculo para la tranquilidad del hogar* (Mexico City: Departamento de Salubridad Pública, 1937), front cover.

43. Carlos S. Jiménez, "Asistencia Pública y Medicina Social," *Gaceta Médica de México*, October 31, 1938, 442.

44. Fallaw, "Dry Land, Wet Politics"; Jocelyn Olcott, "All the Benefits of the Revolution: State Sponsored Women's Organizing in Mexico" (manuscript); Mary Kay Vaughan, *Cultural Politics in Revolution: Teachers, Peasants and Schools in Mexico, 1930–1940* (Tucson: University of Arizona Press, 1997), 56.

45. H. Ayuso O'Horibe, "Juramento anti-alcohólico en las escuelas," *Gaceta Médica de México* 61, no. I (January 1930): 3–4.

46. Ibid., 4.

47. AGN, Secretaría de Fomento, Censo de 1921, Distrito Federal, unclassified.

48. Katherine Elaine Bliss, "'Guided by an Imperious, Moral Need': Prostitutes, Mothers and Nationalists in Revolutionary Mexico City," in *Reconstructing Criminality in Latin America*, ed. Carlos Aguirre and Robert Buffington (Wilmington, Del.: Scholarly Resources, 2000).

49. See Rubenstein, "Raised Voices in the Cine Montecarlo."

50. Sherman, *The Mexican Right*, 38.

51. Katherine Bliss, "Paternity Tests: Fatherhood on Trial in Mexico's Revolution of the Family," *Journal of Family History*, July 1999.

52. Stephen E. Lewis, *The Ambivalent Revolution: Forging State and Nation in Chiapas, 1910–1945* (Albuquerque: University of New Mexico Press, 2005), 100–106.

53. Stephanie Mitchell, "Por la liberación integral de la mujer: Women and the Anti-alcohol Campaign" (paper presented at Las Olvidadas: Gender and Women's History in Postrevolutionary Mexico, Yale University, May 11–13, 2001), 7. On the anti-alcohol agenda in Tabasco, see Kristin A. Harper, "Reforming the Familia Tabasqueña: The Politics of Everyday Life in Revolutionary Tabasco," from the same conference.

54. "Más deportes, menos vicios," *Mujeres y Deportes*, August 11, 1934, 4.

55. Armando Jiménez, *Cabarets de antes y de ahora de la ciudad de México* (Mexico City: Plaza y Valdés, 1992).

56. Olcott, "All the Benefits of the Revolution."

57. Katherine Elaine Bliss, "Between Risk and Confession: The Popularization of Syphilis Prophylaxis in Revolutionary Mexico," in *Disease in Modern Latin American History*, ed. Diego Armus (Durham, N.C.: Duke University Press, 2003).

58. J. Octavio Picón, "Juanita Tenorio: Las memorias de una mujer hermosa," *Nosotras: revista para la mujer que lucha* 1, no. 1 (1934): 40.

59. "Los encantos de los labios," *Nosotras* 1, no. 1 (1934): 33.

60. Advertisement, *Nosotras*, July 1934, 21.

61. *México de noche: Guía para el hombre que quiera divertirse*, 1933, 1937.

# III

Mass
Communications
and
Nation
Building

# Remapping Identities:
# Road Construction and Nation Building in
# Postrevolutionary Mexico

WENDY WATERS

In 1925, the postrevolutionary government of Plutarco Elías Calles promoted roads as the foundation on which the goals and dreams of the government could be realized. The Calles administration insisted that a road network would boost the country's economic strength by providing transport for its agricultural and mineral products. The administration also believed that roads would be crucial to its goal of creating the new Mexican—a modern producer and consumer, active in national social, economic, and political life. Such a transformation did, in fact, occur, although unevenly and not always in anticipated ways. This chapter shows how the construction of roads and, subsequently, the goods, people, and ideas that traveled along them helped individuals and communities to incorporate new notions of Mexicanidad.

## Postrevolutionary Road Building: A General Overview

Postrevolutionary road construction began in earnest in 1925 when President Calles created the National Road Commission. The commission's mandate included not only coordinating road construction throughout Mexico but also providing employment opportunities to Mexicans and offering empowering lessons for the country. One important purpose was to demonstrate that Mexicans were capable of developing and modernizing their country themselves. The commission gave Mexican engineers opportunities to direct road construction and offered ordinary citizens the chance to do unskilled labor on the roads. Funding for road construction initially came from gasoline and alcohol taxes in addition to other money granted by the national treasury. Foreign loans were not part of this initial picture. Later, in the 1930s, the government raised more money by selling road bonds to foreign and domestic investors.

Mexican control over road construction contrasted with the building of the railroads during the Porfiriato. Crucial to nation and state building in the late nineteenth century, the railroads had required enormous capital investment and obliged the government of Porfirio Díaz to offer numerous concessions to foreign financiers. It could be said that foreigners benefited as much from the making of Mexico's railroad network as Mexicans did. Foreign interests came to own the railroads, extracted huge mining and land grants in connection with them, and directed the lines from centers of mineral and agricultural production to ports and the northern border for shipment abroad. Mexican railroad workers faced harsh conditions and could only hope for the most menial jobs. Skilled work usually went to foreigners (mostly from the United States). When an educated Mexican managed to obtain a high-end job, he was almost always paid less for the same work than his foreign counterpart. For these reasons, working conditions on the railroads provided some of the grievances that launched the revolution in 1910.[1]

Twentieth-century roads suited Mexico and its needs far better than had nineteenth-century railroads. As the Mexico City newspaper *Excélsior* frequently trumpeted, roads were better adapted to Mexico's rugged terrain than railroads. While trains could not climb grades steeper than 2 percent, motor vehicles using roads could climb grades exceeding 10 percent, thereby reaching more of the countryside. Furthermore, road transport in buses and trucks suited the smaller-scale family farming that characterized much of rural Mexico, especially as government decrees returned lands to peasants after the revolution. Finally, roads could be built inexpensively and gradually by a combination of local, state, and national efforts, which fit Mexico's need for a project that could begin slowly, while the economy was weak and recovering from years of civil war, and then expand as resources became available. Constructing roads autonomously and within Mexico's financial means was a key component of the initial road program. When it launched the National Road Commission, the Calles government explained that roads would only be built at the rate the country could afford on the basis of its own resources. Rather than compromise on quality, the government decided initially to limit the number of kilometers constructed. The first plan of the Road Commission in 1925 was to build a network with a hub in Mexico City. Highways from there would spread out to the Gulf Coast port of Veracruz, to Nuevo Laredo at the U.S. border, and to the West Coast port of Acapulco. Within this master plan, four main sections began in 1925: Mexico City to Cuernavaca (on the road to Acapulco), to Puebla (on the road to Veracruz), and to Pachuca (on the road to Nuevo Laredo), as well as from the northern industrial city of Monterrey to Nuevo Laredo (also on the Mexico City–Nuevo Laredo route).

Although it was a nationalist project, the government was forced to admit that there were not enough Mexican engineers with experience building roads and bridges to direct all these projects. Mexicans with skills and experience did receive contracts for smaller works, such as the international bridge between Piedras Negras and Eagle Pass. But the first large contract, formally signed in September 1925, went to a U.S. firm, Byrne Brothers Construction of Chicago. In addition to doing engineering, the firm advised the National Road Commission on priorities for road construction and on the purchase of equipment, most of which came initially from the United States.

The contract with Byrne Brothers stipulated that Mexican workers and engineers would learn and benefit from the deal. Seventy-five percent of technical personnel working on any Byrne Brothers–directed road had to be Mexican; 85 percent of administrative employees had to be Mexican; and Mexicans were to do all manual labor.[2] As the years passed, subsequent contracts included more roles for Mexicans. This gave them the practical experience necessary to direct future construction projects themselves. By the 1930s, many Mexicans were making money on roads. Contracting company owners did particularly well, owing to their political connections and their business savvy.

Among the most successful Mexican contractors was General Juan Andreu Almazán. This politically connected individual became involved in road building as head of the military in the state of Nuevo León in 1925. Almazán was so effective at directing his troops in road construction around Monterrey that President Calles suggested to him that he form his own road contracting company. This he did. His firm, the Anáhuac Construction Company, prided itself in hiring Mexican engineers and workers, offering proof that the nationalist ideals behind the road-building program could work in practice. In recognition of his success, in 1930 Almazán was named national communications secretary and given the task of overseeing broader infrastructure building policy and practice around the country. While he served in public office, Almazán resigned as president of Anáhuac, although he retained ownership. His company continued to thrive and receive road-building contracts, as did other companies started by Mexican entrepreneurs.[3] Almazán and many of those he favored were representative of a new class of buccaneering capitalists closely associated with government-sponsored development projects. The capital they accumu-

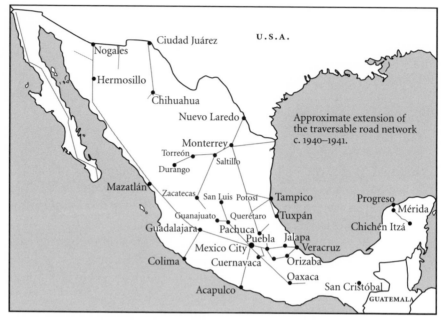

Mexican highways. Map by Wendy Waters and Natalie Hanemann.

lated, especially through road construction, served to underwrite an expansive industrialization of the country after 1940.

By and large, the initial Mexican-made plan for road building worked. Between 1925 and 1940, Mexicans constructed over ten thousand kilometers of roads (see map of Mexican highways).[4] These connected the country, increasingly linking people from different regions and towns to national political, economic, and cultural life. By 1934, when Lázaro Cárdenas became president, many began to feel they could and should talk to federal politicians. The first postrevolutionary president to campaign personally across the nation, Cárdenas used new roads to meet thousands of Mexicans in their own communities during and after his campaign. Cárdenas not only supported the ongoing construction of highways but also made executive decisions to add smaller roads connecting one or two small communities—including the road to Tepoztlán discussed later in the chapter—to the national road network.

When Cárdenas nationalized the oil industry in 1938, he did so for a range of economic and political reasons not directly related to roads. Yet national control of oil provided a final ingredient to the process of making road construction and transport a symbol of Mexico's nationalist path to development. Just as Mexicans controlled the building and planning of highways, so they now also controlled oil—the key ingredient for making highways and driving along them. Soon PEMEX stations (gas stations belonging to Petróleos Mexicanos, the state-owned corporation that managed the oil industry) painted in patriotic red, white, and green dotted the nation's roads and streets as the exclusive gasoline vendor. They provided a constant reminder of the message begun by Calles and furthered by Cárdenas—that Mexicans could develop their own country.

Involving individuals and communities in the road-building effort—a financial necessity in these resource-scarce years—opened opportunities for patriotic participation and the development of a sense of shared national pride. In 1925 the communications secretary urged communities to form their own road brigades. Hundreds, perhaps thousands, of communities around the country answered the call and did their best to build roads or upgrade existing tracks to suit motor vehicles. In the beginning, ordinary Mexicans who joined in road construction did so for reasons that appear to have been pragmatic. Workers, for example, were often grateful for an opportunity to work on construction crews and, in most cases, to earn more than the national minimum wage. Others thought more broadly. A road could offer multiple economic opportunities for the community generally, and for individuals personally. Or a road might offer social and cultural enrichment, such as a link to a beach, a religious shrine, a commercial center, or an educational institution. Some also considered the tourist potential of their region, noting what foreign and national travelers could find to admire and enjoy in their communities.

Not everyone wanted roads, of course. Some feared the unknown that roads would bring or were uncertain as to whether the machinery used in road building had sinister connections. In Tepoztlán various elders believed that the road to their town was constructed with such speed that the devil had made a pact with the engineers to make heavy boulders more easily movable in exchange for 245 souls. The legend insisted that the devil subsequently hid in a cave along the roadside at kilometer 15, taking the souls of those who perished in motor vehicle crashes.[5] In San Juan Chamula, Chiapas, in the 1940s, roads were opposed by Tzotzil Maya villagers who feared that improved communications between their municipality and the ladino commercial and administrative center of San Cristóbal de Las Casas would make it easier for ladinos (non-Indians) to exploit them. Many also believed that numerous Ik'al (Negroid giants—

likely a legend enduring from the colonial era) roamed the region, capturing and selling Indians to ladino road crew chiefs who turned them into grease to lubricate their road-building machinery.[6]

For other Mexican villagers, politics played a key role in determining whether or not their town obtained a road. Powerful families sometimes objected to the new roads because they threatened their control over the populations of isolated regions. Other towns refused to build them out of fear they would benefit rival communities. In still other cases, communities were too divided, too poor, or too isolated to build roads. Others wanted roads and did not get them because more politically connected groups routed them in other directions. Many, like the Chamulans, had historically grounded reasons to shun outsiders and preferred not to integrate themselves. Thus it is important to keep in mind that roads did not reach everyone. They did, however, connect many Mexicans in unforeseen ways.

## Roads and Community in Veracruz

Initially, Mexicans in Veracruz responded to the road-building programs of regional governments more than to national initiatives. Because Veracruz was a relatively rich state—home to Mexico's largest commercial port and a producer of oil and agriculture—its state government could afford to assist in road construction. At first, the Calles government accepted this effort, since the end result was desirable—roads. But the federal government also recognized that regional power and control had been an obstacle to national unity since the nineteenth century and had become so once again as the revolution empowered the regions at the expense of the central government. In both the Calles and Cárdenas eras (1925–40), federal governments saw road construction as something that could help bring Mexicans together if controlled by the national government. By the 1930s, the central state gained strength over regional governments, in part through politics and in part through economics, as the federal government had greater access to financial resources and was better able to survive the Depression than its regional counterparts.

In the 1920s, Veracruz underwent a radical agrarian experiment of land reform and political mobilization. Agrarian community interests were the focus of several successive state governments, especially that of governor Adalberto Tejeda (1928–32),[7] who had been the national communications secretary in the Calles government in 1925. Tejeda saw roads as integral to his effort to support the interests of peasants and to bring about broader development in the state. The road construction program he supervised as governor built partnerships with communities, especially agrarian towns. These partnerships in turn strengthened allegiances to the state government.

One of Tejeda's first moves in 1929 was to expand the number of community road associations. Writing to all municipal presidents, he stated that he wanted to intensify the construction of roads but needed their help. He asked them to create municipal road associations that would promote new routes and conserve existing ones. They would apply for funds and tools from the state. Tejeda made people and villages aware that other communities shared their interest in roads, and the accompanying commercial and social opportunities united people in Veracruz behind a common cause, distinct from the national road project.

Community-organized road building was not new to Veracruz or to other parts of Mexico. Constructing public works—whether roads or a community building or fixing the plaza—often depended on a voluntary labor system, the *faena*. In it adult male villagers agreed to work a certain number of days per month (usually four to eight) for the community without pay. Using this long-established system to build roads bridged the gap between old and new and allowed people to identify with, and participate in, the new project under familiar terms. While towns such as Vela de Alatorre donated labor, others raised funds. For example, the residents of Nautla gave $5,000 (pesos), Misantla $11,000, and Colipa $13,000.[8] In Veracruz and much of central Mexico, the process of road construction fit within existing patterns of village life and organization. Over time, requests grew for assistance, and more was forthcoming, which helped villagers to forge more regular and concrete links with those beyond the village.

Obliging individuals to work on the road, however, was a sensitive issue. Before the revolution, rural people were not only often coerced into working on plantations and haciendas but also obliged to perform faena labor for municipal improvement—road and bridge building, street paving, ditch digging, and park construction—frequently for interests not their own. At the end of the Porfiriato, when increasingly elaborate municipal modernizing projects ran up against a deteriorating income base, communal labor obligations became particularly onerous in certain regions. Thus the constitution of 1917 outlawed all forms of obligatory unpaid labor. In the 1920s, some villagers expressed their concern to the state government that they might be forced to labor on the roads in violation of new national laws and principles.[9] Zealous about the revolution's new constitution, politicians often responded with sympathy and concern. However, given that faena was a deeply rooted custom that predated the Spanish conquest, it seems that, if they were not coerced outright, many villagers in Veracruz and elsewhere believed this labor was appropriate, especially when road construction offered new opportunities for empowerment and improvement.

Over time, the source of road construction efforts at the local level shifted from the faena and voluntary efforts of the late 1920s to government projects that used professional crews or paid villagers for their efforts. Villagers no longer asked for tools and supplies, but for roads themselves. For example, the president of the Material Improvements Group in Acayucán, Veracruz, wrote to the state governor asking for a road, explaining that it would give "immense agricultural enrichment to this region that currently cannot produce for export owing to a lack of means of communications. . . . Constructing a road, which represents the beauty of the modern world, would require some help from your government, along with the most indispensable efforts from our community."[10] As costs went up and local economic capacity declined, responsibility for constructing roads fell to the national government. There was also a political dimension to this shift. The regional focus of Tejeda's development policy in Veracruz was eventually perceived as a threat to the federal government's state- and nation-building program, and strong central government opposition to Tejeda forced him from office in 1932.

In the 1930s, roads and the promise of their construction came to tie people to the national capital. The nationalization of politics advanced with the election of President Cárdenas in 1934. His approach to road construction, like other policies, reflected his special interest in making workers and peasants prosperous, enthusiastic contributors to Mexico. Letters addressed to him about roads show that their authors at least discursively identified with national issues emanating from the revolution. As one writer explained, with their promise of rapid communication, economic opportunity, and educational and cultural improvement, roads embodied "the pure principles of the Revolution."[11] Peasants professing loyalty to revolutionary governments considered themselves entitled to roads. Petitioners from Veracruz argued that "easy communication is one of the benefits of the Revolution."[12] Whether or not the letter writers believed their rhetoric, they were discursively and practically participating in a Mexican national experience beyond the confines of their towns. Moreover, the notion that roads were part of a revolutionary promise and legacy was to endure. In 1994, the EZLN (Zapatista Army for National Liberation) demanded that the revolution finally reach Chiapas in the form of land, education, justice—and roads.

The revolutionary rhetoric embellishing road requests also bespoke an enthusiasm for becoming modern and a view of the revolution as a modernizing process. The secretary general of the Auto Transport Company of Huatusco, Veracruz, suggested that the revolution should mean "progress," and he concluded his letter, "Communication [roads] is progress." He also demonstrated the ability to imagine new, politically favored national groups—the agrarian and working classes—in his argument that roads, like the revolution, would benefit them. Somewhat disingenuously, he included himself in the working class. "In the region of Huatusco," he wrote, "we belong to the genuine working class, and because of this we feel that this [road] work is a necessity; we are disposed to make the greatest sacrifices in order to obtain a motor road for Huatusco that will incorporate the town into the progressive direction that other places . . . are following." [13] Letters written in the 1930s increasingly show Mexicans identifying with abstractions such as the revolution, progress, and "imagined communities" of workers, peasants, and Mexicans.

## Tourism and Roads

Thinking about Mexico and Mexicans in ways that transcended individuals' direct experiences also happened when many villagers considered the tourist potential of their areas. Envisioning one's community as a tourist attraction —and therefore in need of a road—was part of the process of recognizing the town's place in national and international contexts and seeing it from the viewpoint of an outsider. Beginning in 1930, the national government showed its interest in tourism by hosting tourist congresses alongside national road-building conventions. The SEP urged teachers to interest their communities in developing tourist facilities. Presenting one's region as a tourist destination allowed people to show pride in their region and to recognize what distinguished it from other potential tourist destinations nationally and internationally. Such a process often implied the creation of national as well as local pride.

Local people found themselves forging new subjective and national identities as they imagined "the other"—fellow Mexicans or foreigners. They also had help from the government and national newspapers, which stressed four aspects of Mexico that would be of interest to tourists. First, its scenic beauty —from beaches to snowcapped volcanoes and the varied countryside in be-

tween—was considered unmatched in the world. Second, the colonial Spanish heritage offered a unique and older European past to showcase for tourists from North America who lacked such a legacy. Indigenous cultures of the
past and present offered another attraction—living Indians became folkloric
in their dress, dance, music, and artistic production, while past civilizations
had built pyramids and empires before the age of European expansion. Finally,
Mexico's new, modern, and industrial infrastructure was expected to impress
foreign tourists.

In their letters to government officials asking for roads, citizens frequently
used these themes to explain the value of their community for tourism. Consider a letter to President Cárdenas from Juan Lenshin C. Vista of the customs
house in Tuxpán, Veracruz, asking the president to finish highway connections
to Tuxpán and Tampico. He referred to the area as a "rich and beautiful zone"
of "magnificent rivers, such as the Pánuco, Chucarles, the Tuxpán, and others
of less importance but no less breathtaking." The area, he said, would receive
a "new flood of tourists" with a road connecting the region to the rest of the
republic. He also suggested that tourists might want to look at the modern
man-made sights such as the large banana, chicle, and exotic fruit plantations
and the oil fields.[14] Today these are not considered tourist attractions, but in the
1930s they represented the new modern Mexico that the government wanted
to showcase to the world.

In Tepoztlán, Morelos (approximately ninety kilometers south of Mexico
City), tourism also became a factor in road promotion. Villager Jesús Condé
and a group of cohorts, including two teachers, actively promoted the idea of
a road to link their town (of approximately five thousand) with Cuernavaca,
Morelos's state capital, situated on the Mexico City–Acapulco highway. In
1930 he wrote a series of articles in the Mexico City newspaper *Universal* that
expressed how Tepoztlán and surrounding villages were worse off economically than before the revolution and needed additional sources of livelihood.
Condé explained that with the road, "the region will become one of the favorite recreation and tourist locations, as it is close to the Republic's capital and
its attractions are much superior to those offered by the paradise of the south,
Cuernavaca."[15] Condé highlighted as a crowd drawer the small preconquest
pyramid dedicated to the god Tepozcatl, located about an hour's hike up a hill
just outside town. He also wrote about the village's natural beauty, located
on a ledge with a spectacular view over many valleys below. Moreover, tourists would want to visit the town's sixteenth-century Dominican convent, a
symbol of its colonial heritage.

Condé recalled the comments made by an unnamed German traveler who proclaimed that if this scenic region were in Europe it would fill with visitors every weekend. Condé demonstrated familiarity with both Mexico and the world. Indeed, he had lived in Mexico City during the revolution, when fighting had made Tepoztlán dangerous. He had also worked as an assistant to the American anthropologist Robert Redfield, who studied Tepoztlán in his first Mexican community study, published in 1927. Such exposure made him think beyond the confines of his hometown—though he still took pride in it— to see Mexico's national potential in new ways.

## The Road to Tepoztlán

There were two rival factions in Tepoztlán, and Condé was influential among the group interested in modernizing their town. This group received support from the Colonia Tepozteca, a community of civic-minded, relatively well-off ranchers and merchants native to Tepoztlán but residing in Mexico City. Condé's desire to "modernize" is fitting, since he had worked closely with Redfield, one of the first anthropologists to theorize about modernization. The opposing group, for its part, wanted to restore and enhance agrarian life; many of its members had actively supported Emiliano Zapata's land reform struggle in the revolution. However, when faced with adverse economic, climatic, and social conditions in 1930, both factions agreed that the town's problems could be solved by a road connecting Tepoztlán to the state capital of Cuernavaca, eighteen kilometers away. While the modernizers anticipated more trade, tourism, and the opportunity to visit the city for work or pleasure, the agrarian group believed the road would bring seasonal employment and greater access to markets.

In building the road, each side worked independently of the other, as they could not get along. One side began in Tepoztlán, and the other started construction from Cuernavaca. Most work was done as voluntary, rotating labor (called *cuatequitl* labor, similar to faena in Veracruz). Turning their factionalism to creative use, the villagers succeeded in building a rough road. When the road washed out after two years, *vecinos* led by Jesús Condé appealed to the federal government for help in building a more enduring highway. In their letters, they reminded the government of the town's initiative, as well as its beauty and heritage. Villagers argued that the road demonstrated their revolutionary commitment and allegiance and made them worthy of President Cárdenas's help.

In 1935 Cárdenas responded and visited the town, reaching it by rail and horseback. The president's visit made being Mexican more real to villagers. Still today in Tepoztlán, people speak of Cárdenas's visit. (Cárdenas made even more frequent visits to towns with roads.) On this visit he was particularly impressed with the region's beauty and its archaeological importance, so much so that he declared the surrounding hills a national park. Tepoztecos who had formerly logged and extracted coal from these hills were henceforth forced to look outside the village for employment.[16] Cárdenas also promised to have the National Road Directorate (formerly the National Road Commission) rebuild the road according to modern engineering specifications. Within a month, engineers from the road directorate arrived and began surveying and initiating construction. Over the next eight months, between eight hundred and nine hundred men worked on the road. They completed it in January 1936.

## Road Openings

The opening of the Tepoztlán road exemplifies the ideas, images, and rituals seen in other road inaugurations. Government officials (including communications secretary Francisco Múgica) and the media formed a motorcade that paraded from Mexico City to Cuernavaca to Tepoztlán to symbolize the town's new link to the national capital. Other inaugurations of roads within a few hundred kilometers of the national capital adopted the same ritual, with motorcades of government officials, representatives of the press, and private citizens fanning out from Mexico City to the town where the road began. Asphalt spokes came to link the country's towns to the hub of Mexico City, connecting increasing numbers of Mexicans to the nation's capital.

In the ritual opening of the new road, residents of towns along the route lined the road to welcome the guests. As the motorcade traveled the eighteen kilometers of new highway to Tepoztlán from Cuernavaca, it passed under banners and arches prepared by the villagers of Tepoztlán. Their slogans read: "The Revolution Has Succeeded in Morelos," "Cárdenas Means Honor: The Revolution Is Guaranteed," and "Paso al progreso" (Gateway to Progress). Once in town, the politicians, bureaucrats, journalists, and villagers celebrated the opening with special festivities. In Tepoztlán, Jesús Condé shook Secretary Múgica's hand. Together they cut a ceremonial ribbon. Schoolchildren performed for the guests (see figures 1–3). Half of them were barefoot and in traditional dress, while the other half wore store-bought clothing and shoes. Their parents, similarly distinguished by types of clothing, attended the celebration and welcomed the road for their own reasons. One citizen gave a speech

FIG. 1. "Gateway to Progress," Tepoztlán. Photograph courtesy of Archivo General de la Nación.

FIG. 2. Secretary Mújica and Jesús Condé cut the ribbon, Tepoztlán. Photograph courtesy of Archivo General de la Nación.

FIG. 3. Schoolchildren welcome guests, Tepoztlán. Photograph courtesy of Archivo General de la Nación.

in Nahuatl and Spanish addressed to Cárdenas himself, who was expected but did not appear. The speech celebrated indigenous Mexico in the making of a modern nation. In Nahuatl, he said:

> In the name of municipal authorities, commercial leaders, campesinos, workers, and tradespeople of Tepoztlán, I have the gracious task of extending a cordial greeting and humble welcome to you and those who accompany you. . . . You are the first president to visit our village and the first to be interested in the well-being of Mexican towns and the needs of the humble people. Like a doctor you have identified the cause of our illness and administered the right medicine to alleviate it—roads and tourism.[17]

Beyond Tepoztlán, the ceremonies and pageantry that marked the opening of roads furthered the making of a national identity and created new sources of national pride. Road openings always received coverage—often quite extensive—in the country's newspapers, the readership of which expanded greatly as the road network and literacy rates grew. Exemplary was the opening of the Pan-American Highway from Nuevo Laredo to Mexico City. Its four-day inauguration festivities included a motorcade from the U.S. border to Mexico

City. Delegates stopped at numerous points to admire the scenery, villages, and new economic and industrial developments. The local residents served as proud hosts for these occasions. In an *Excélsior* article describing the section of the highway between Tamazunchale and Ciudad Valles (in San Luis Potosí), the author wrote of the "magnificent rivers" and "majestic mountains" they passed. Numerous tourists had already arrived in the area, and Tamazunchale residents had been working hard to receive them. They had built modern tourist facilities (hotels and restaurants) and put in a new drainage system to improve sanitation. Both the villagers and the article showcased the modernity and scenic beauty of the region for a Mexican and a foreign audience.

These rituals of inauguration showcased nationalist messages. The highway from Mexico City to Nuevo Laredo was designed in part to bring Americans into the country as tourists and investors. Yet Mexicans had built it on their own terms. Although a few U.S. contractors had worked on the road (Byrne Brothers Construction being the most prominent), they had been paid by the Mexican government and had transferred knowledge and expertise to Mexicans who eventually took over and completed the highways. The construction and opening of this road symbolically changed the nature of American involvement, putting Mexicans in control and creating a new context for national development. Mexican government and business owners invited Americans to the opening festivities. As noted, road construction served as a powerful source for Mexican capital accumulation, launching a new era of industrialization after 1940.

## Post–Road Changes

Many Mexican towns experienced change after becoming linked to the national road network. Jesús Condé of Tepoztlán never saw the results. Ironically, he died in 1939 in a motor vehicle crash at kilometer 15 of the new road to his village. But others in his community and around Mexico had to face and negotiate the ideas, products, opportunities, and experiences introduced by roads.

Tepoztlán was hardly an isolated village before the arrival of the road. Tepoztecos frequently rode or walked to Cuernavaca and Mexico City. They made use of the train station located in their municipality. Nevertheless, evidence suggests that with the advent of the road, individuals in Tepoztlán and elsewhere forged new personal identities in tandem with a broader process of Mexicanization. Roads also seem to have accelerated the processes by which individuals freed themselves from local hacendado control and came into more direct contact with market forces and the institutions of the state and federal government. The following analysis is based on data from Tepoztlán and Hueyapán in Morelos, Xalatlaco in the state of Mexico, Tecamachalco and Atlixco in central Puebla, and San José de Gracia in Michoacán.

Roads facilitated the introduction of urban fashions and trends that entered via newspapers, visitors, and residents who returned from work experiences in other parts of Mexico and the United States. The exchange created new desires and tastes for manufactured goods such as packaged bread, Coca-Cola, canned foods, and shoes. Becoming a consumer required income, and the roads created employment opportunities. Many men abandoned agricultural work to take up traditional professions such as baking, carpentry, shopkeeping, and bricklaying. Others entered newer areas of work making shoes, milling corn, teaching school, driving buses, and repairing vehicles.

Despite the risks inherent in the cash economy, many people sought the new professions. Jobs associated with buses and other motor vehicles were desirable to many because they were at once "modern" and an outlet for masculine prowess. Driving buses, servicing them as a mechanic, and working around them in other ways became popular professions. In Tepoztlán, a man gave up his post as the religious *mayordomo*, responsible for care of a chapel and sponsorship of religious festival, to work for the bus company. The religious charge may have been prestigious, but it took time and offered comparatively little remuneration.[18] The bus job became a source of status and prestige, and it symbolized a modern masculinity. By the mid-1940s, Tepoztlán's two competing bus lines had become political actors and a new source of friction in the community. Not only did the directors of both companies become increasingly influential, but Tepoztlán's road facilitated the export of plums, tomatoes, and gladiolas to regional markets and made it easier for Tepoztecos to work and study outside the town. This diversity of economic activity made it harder for Tepoztlán's rural-based caciques to economically dominate the town as they had before 1930.[19]

While men most often took advantage of new job opportunities, women's lives changed, as well as did notions of femininity. In Tepoztlán, women had remained close to the house, grinding corn for tortillas for as many as six hours a day. The act of grinding corn and shaping tortillas was intricately intertwined with being female—it kept women within the protected confines of the household—and feminine: the most desirable wife made the finest-tasting tortillas.

The introduction of the corn mill in 1925 challenged prevailing notions of gender.

Men, who saw the mill as a threat to their control over their wives and daughters, organized a boycott against it and shut it down. It should be noted that the mill owner himself was not originally from Tepoztlán. His lack of status in town likely contributed to the mill's rejection.[20] Women often resisted the mill for fear of being called lazy, not wanting to hand-grind corn. It was also said that machine-ground *masa* made less-savory tortillas; the woman who used it became less desirable as a wife. Two years later, a local entrepreneur installed a second mill, which enjoyed more success. Oscar Lewis attributed that success to "the revolution of the women against the authority of the men."[21] Yet acceptance was not a simple issue of women challenging their subordination to men. More complex forces were at play.

The corn mill in Tepoztlán was not broadly accepted or used until the arrival of the road.[22] Lewis wrote that villagers were quick to see that the families who gained materially after the introduction of the road did so because women used it to take advantage of expanding market opportunities.[23] If a Tepoztecan woman used the corn mill, she could go to Cuernavaca on a forty-five-minute bus ride, sell the products she cultivated and cared for in the household compound—fruit, vegetables, herbs, eggs, chickens—and return home in time to prepare tortillas and take them to her husband in the fields in the midafternoon.

Buses made women's travel far safer than it had been in the past, especially given the period of revolutionary violence that in many places stretched into the 1940s. Nevertheless, travel also opened a new threat (or perceived threat) to female honor and by extension the honor of a woman's male protector, if she had one. Families took care to guard women's chastity. Few women ventured to the city on their own without taking a sister, children, or female neighbor along as a chaperone. Women traveling alone were considered suspect by "decent families." In Luis Buñuel's 1952 film *Subida al cielo* (shown in the United States as *Mexican Bus Ride*), a particularly glamorous young woman travels alone, provocative in her tight-fitting clothing and exposed flesh, flirting with the men and almost seducing the "good boy," a young, newly married man who is dutifully running an errand for his dying mother. The film depicts travel for unaccompanied men and women as both risky and risqué, accurately portraying a popular notion. The sight of a young female schoolteacher heading off alone to a job filled some Tepoztecans with concern and derision in the 1930s. They were certain she would soon return—pregnant and unmarried.[24]

But if traveling on the road could lure individuals away from the moral safety of their families, it could also bring them back. In *Mexican Bus Ride*, although tempted by the flirtatious single woman, the young man remains faithful to his wife and his mother and returns to his hometown after visiting the city.

Choosing to travel by bus did not necessarily imply an abandonment of traditional values. Many families who appropriated certain consumer goods and modern services did so to strengthen long-standing practices rather than to replace them. More money could mean finer dresses to wear to church or more candles to burn at the home altar. Far from abandoning religion, as postrevolutionary governments had hoped, Tepoztecan women attended church more often once the corn mill and the road had lessened their household burdens. A consequence of the postrevolutionary negotiation of the old and the new in the countryside appears to have been a sharper awareness and respect for tradition combined with an ambivalent, selective, but nonetheless real embrace of modernity. Again, Buñuel's *Mexican Bus Ride* is illustrative. When the bus gets stuck in a river, one of the passengers, a PRI politician who is a fanatical enthusiast of modernity, hails a farmer on his tractor to pull the bus out. The tractor becomes irrevocably stuck in the mud along with the bus. Finally, a pair of hefty oxen led by a young girl rescues these emblems of modern technology from the forces of nature.

Roads probably had the greatest impact on children, many of whom had only recently been liberated from the task of helping their mothers grind corn or complete other household chores.[25] School enrollments often increased after a road reached a town, in large part because roads and the greater contact they brought with the outside world demonstrated to parents the advantages they might obtain through educating their children.[26] Ideologically, economically, and socially, roads encouraged the use of schools, and vice versa. According to Oscar Lewis, "The school became the symbol of modernity (*lo nuevo*) in Tepoztlán, and fostered a greater identification with the nation," while "breaking down the localism of Tepoztlán's neighborhoods."[27]

At a regional level, schools used roads because they facilitated the shared celebration of festivities and sports competitions between towns and at the regional and national levels. In these events, participating youths could recognize shared values, activities, and desires as Mexicans. The new sociability encouraged consumerism on a modest scale—buying athletic uniforms and shoes, soft drinks, and factory-made clothing. Adolescence became defined as a separate stage of life, a time when young people increasingly identified national identity with modernity. Young people in San José de Gracia, Michoacán, and in Tepoztlán, Morelos, expressed a greater interest in appearing modern by wearing fashionable shoes and urban-style clothing and pursuing "city habits," including smoking.[28] In Tepoztlán, they preferred to speak Spanish rather than the indigenous languages of their parents.

San José de Gracia and Tepoztlán are very different towns. San José was traditionally Catholic, non-Indian, ranchero, and antirevolutionary. Tepoztlán was an originally indigenous community of equally religious, corn-cultivating peasants, many of whom identified with the agrarian struggle of Emiliano Zapata in the Mexican Revolution. Despite their differences, several years after the road had arrived in each town, many young people in both places felt bored with their lives.[29] Many wanted the excitement and advancement associated with the cities. Schooling, travel, and the information these brought nurtured a culture of mobility. For adventure, education, economic opportunity, and material gain, the "revolution generation" took to the roads. They headed for cities—most of all, but not exclusively, Mexico City—or, in the case of San José de Gracia and other towns in western Mexico, for the United States.

## Conclusion

Road building in Mexico between 1925 and 1940 was a nationalist project that through its discourses and practices contributed to forging national identity. Trumpeted as a distinctly Mexican project independent of foreign assistance and models, road building provided Mexicans with jobs, capital, and economic opportunity, all bound together in a rhetoric linking revolution with modernity, material improvement, expanding knowledge, pride in the Mexican past, and confidence in a common national future. Roads contributed to revitalizing many local economies, to enhancing the distinctiveness of particular communities within the national cultural patrimony, and to familiarizing people with their country beyond the bounds of the *patria chica*. Roads also contributed to the centralization of national life and power. The capital became not only the political and economic center of the country but the cultural center as well. In the following decades, Mexico City supplied the most influential newspapers, comic books, magazines, school programs, radio broadcasts, and films.

While road construction contributed to nation building, it was also eminently transnational. Roads were designed to lure foreign tourists to a land of pyramids, baroque churches, and sixteenth-century convents, *chinas poblanas*, *charro* cowboys, and mariachi musicians. They were also intended to transport Mexican goods to foreign markets in exchange for foreign products. As much as roads led to Mexico City, the principal highways led as well to the northern border with the United States and to the nation's major ports.

Road building created the infrastructure and the capital that laid the groundwork for an accelerated wave of industrialization after 1940. Although U.S. capital would increasingly dominate Mexican economic growth, this influence was neither as one-sided nor as unidirectional as standard analyses of imperialism often depict. Thanks in great measure to Mexican roads, the combined symbolic, cultural, and demographic power of Mexico has also made over the longer term for an ever-deepening Mexicanization of U.S. culture and society. In short, national identities are forged and reforged in a complex, ever-changing transnational milieu. In the case of Mexico and the United States, roads have been central to mutual, yet very distinct, processes of national identity formation.

## Notes

This chapter is based on my master's thesis, "Roads, the Carnivalesque, and the Mexican Revolution: Transforming Modernity in Tepoztlán, 1928–1944" (Texas Christian University, 1994), and my doctoral dissertation, "Re-mapping the Nation: Road Building as State Formation in Post-revolutionary Mexico" (University of Arizona, 1999).

1. John H. Coatsworth, *Growth against Development: The Economic Impact of Railroads in Porfirian Mexico* (De Kalb: Northern Illinois University Press, 1981); John M. Hart, *Revolutionary Mexico: The Coming and Process of the Mexican Revolution* (Berkeley: University of California Press, 1987).

2. *Excélsior*, August 12, 1925, 1.

3. U.S. National Archives, Military Intelligence Division 2064-543, Major H. E. Marshburn, "Visit of Military Attaché to Certain Mexican Military Headquarters" (June 19, 1934), 3–4; Archivo General de la Nación (hereafter AGN), Fondo Administración Pública, Comunicaciones y Transportes, Caja 17, 535/14, Acuerdo 176; UCLA Program on Mexico, Almazán Collection, unpublished transcript of Almazán interview with James Wilkie, 86–88; AGN, Ortiz Rubio, Exp. 13/7319.

4. Following the outbreak of World War II, and especially following the U.S. entry into it in 1941, the U.S. government became concerned about possible German or Japanese invasion through Mexico. To shore up North American defense, the U.S. government and military began a program of assisting Mexico with transportation infrastructure, including airports and roads. Because of the heightened nationalist sentiment in Mexico, the U.S. role in various projects was often kept quite secret. Stephen Niblo, *War, Diplomacy and Development: The United States and Mexico, 1938–1954* (Wilmington, Del.: Scholarly Resources, 1995), 229–31; Friedrich E. Schuler, "Foreign Policy, 1910–1946," *Encyclopedia of Mexico*, 509.

5. Florence Muller, *Folktales of Tepoztlán in Morelos, Mexico*, ed. Henry Field (Miami: Field Research Projects, 1973).

6. Henri Favre, *Cambio y continuidad entre los Mayas de México* (1971; Mexico City: INI, 1984), 95; Ricardo Pozas, *Chamula, un pueblo indio de los Altos de Chiapas* (Mexico City: INI, 1959), 193.

7. Tejeda also served as Veracruz governor from 1922 to 1925, before roads became a national or state priority.

8. Archivo General del Estado de Veracruz (hereafter AGEV), Fondo Fomento, Sección Comunicaciones y Transportes, Caja 110, folder "Misantla, Carretera a Nautla"; letters dated April 27, 1925, June 6, 1925, and May 15, 1925; *Excélsior*, January 24, 1926, sec. 2, p. 7.

9. AGEV, Fondo Fomento, Sección Communicaciones y Transportes, Caja 116, letters dated May 5, 1928, August 30, 1929, August 30, 1929, May 17, 1928, June 28, 1929, and September 18, 1929.

10. AGEV, Fondo Fomento, Sección Communicaciones y Transportes, Caja 103, letter dated July 6, 1929.

11. AGEV, Fondo Fomento, Sección Communicaciones y Transportes, Archivo Clasificado, 1936, Caja 200, 317/25, letter dated March 13, 1936.

12. Archivo Francisco J. Múgica, Jiquilpan, Michoacán, vol. 156, doc. 195.

13. AGEV, Archivo Clasificado, 1936, 317/52, November 21, 1936.

14. AGN, Cárdenas, Exp. 515.1/104.

15. University of Chicago Special Collections, Robert Redfield Papers, box 43, folder 3, booklet published from the articles by Jesús Condé entitled *Tepoztlán: Tierra de Promisión*.

16. Claudio Lomnitz-Adler, *Evolución de una sociedad rural* (Mexico City: Fondo de Cultura Económica, 1982), 104–5.

17. AGN, Cárdenas, 515.1/76; letter to Cárdenas, July 17, 1936.

18. Oscar Lewis, "Social and Economic Changes in a Mexican Village," *América Indígena* 4, no. 4 (1944): 291.

19. Oscar Lewis, *Tepoztlán: Village in Mexico* (New York: Holt, Rinehart and Winston, 1960), 37; Lomnitz-Adler, *Evolución*, 177.

20. Lewis, *Tepoztlán*, 77; Lomnitz-Adler, *Evolución*, 102.

21. Lewis, *Tepoztlán*, 77.

22. Oscar Lewis, *Life in a Mexican Village: Tepoztlán Restudied* (Urbana: University of Illinois Press, 1963), 108; Lewis, *Tepoztlán*, 22; Lewis, "Changes in a Mexican Village," 304; Robert Redfield, *Tepoztlán—a Mexican Village* (Chicago: University of Chicago Press, 1930), 155.

23. Oscar Lewis Papers, box 112, "Datos Sobre el Molino."

24. Lewis Papers, box 118, folder "Family Fragments," document "The Story of My Life," 19.

25. Lomnitz-Adler, *Evolución*, 102–3.

26. Mary Kay Vaughan, *Cultural Politics in Revolution: Teachers, Peasants and Schools in Mexico, 1930–1940* (Tucson: University of Arizona Press, 1997), 104.

27. Lewis, *Tepoztlán*, 37, 43.

28. Lewis Papers, box 118, "Family Fragments," "Sujeto Investigado C.," 1; Manuel Ávila, *Tradition and Growth: A Study of Four Mexican Villages* (Chicago: University of Chicago Press, 1969), 374; Luis González y González, *San José de Gracia* (Austin: University of Texas Press, 1974), 225; George Foster, *Tzintzuntzan: Mexican Peasants in a Changing World* (Boston: Little Brown, 1967), 247.

29. González, *San José de Gracia*, 225.

# National Imaginings on the Air:
# Radio in Mexico, 1920–1950

JOY ELIZABETH HAYES

During the spring and summer of 1933, the Department of Rural Instruction inspected dozens of village schools in Mexico's Central Valley, where, months earlier, the Ministry of Public Education (SEP) had donated radios. SEP officials were anxious to learn how this new tool was being used. Radio, they hoped, would strengthen the ties between the central government and the rural schools by allowing the SEP to broadcast instructional and cultural programs throughout the country over its own station, Radio XFX.[1] The donated radios, seventy-five in all, were relatively inexpensive Atwater Kent receivers that operated on AC electric current. Before distribution, the radios' tuning devices had been set to receive only the XFX radio signal and locked to prevent tampering. In this way, SEP officials hoped to ensure that the radios were used only for the government's intended goals of education and cultural unification.

The government inspector, Luis F. Rodríguez Lomelí, encountered considerable support and enthusiasm for the donated radios in the communities he visited. Although several villages lacked electricity and could not operate their radios, villagers objected when he attempted to remove their unused or broken radio sets. In one Tlaxcala village, the townspeople argued that they should be allowed to keep their radio in the hope of getting a contract with the power company in the next couple of months. In another, villagers told the inspector that they had sent someone to Puebla to buy a new tube for their radio, and that they were planning to install it in a community social building currently under construction.[2]

This enthusiasm for the SEP radios, however, did not reflect an equal interest in the government's radio programs. Although all the radios had been preset to receive only the SEP station, the inspector found that in almost every case the seals had been broken to unlock the radio's tuning device. In village after village, Rodríguez Lomelí reported, people were listening to everything but station xfx. When he tried to interest members of one Puebla village in xfx programs, they informed him that "they frequently get together at the school, but they do not dedicate themselves to listening to [the sep's] programs."[3] After visiting a Tlaxcala village, he reported that the people "regularly get together to listen to musical numbers, talks and in general the programs of other radio stations."[4] One village in the state of Mexico had taken the liberty of moving the radio from the school to a local theater where campesinos congregated to listen to the programs of other radio stations.

Rodríguez Lomelí explored a number of reasons for this general lack of interest in xfx broadcasts. He noted one teacher's comment that the musical format of xfx would not interest rural listeners because for them the music "must be popular and the songs, *rancheras*, since only in that form can they attract campesinos."[5] In Hidalgo the inspector reported that "there are teachers who . . . insist that the radio not be tuned exclusively to the sep station, alleging that they find the music of Agustín Lara or something equally frivolous more interesting."[6] Although he emphasized the "corrupting" influence of teachers, Rodríguez Lomelí also noted another reason for listener apathy: xfx programs failed to address listeners' local and regional interests. In Puebla, for example, villagers specifically requested "accounts of regional history," along with programs on animal care, agriculture, and health and hygiene.[7]

This early experiment in rural broadcasting highlights three defining features of Mexican radio during the period 1920–50. First, the sep radio project indicates the extent to which the government invested in radio as a powerful new medium for building national identity and allegiance. Radio's birth and development coincided precisely with the rise of the postrevolutionary state, so it is not surprising that the government gave particular attention to radio as a means of national unification and political consolidation. Government intervention in radio took two major forms during this period: the creation and dissemination of radio programming, as in the case of xfx, and the establishment of national radio regulations. Both practices promoted an official version of national culture over the airwaves and gave the central government privileged access to the medium.

Second, the story of xfx reveals the dominant role that commercial broadcasters played in Mexican radio beginning in the early 1930s. Guided by talented entrepreneurs and powered by Mexican and North American capital, commercial broadcasters produced standardized forms of popular music designed to attract audiences on a national scale. This national market, however, was not conceived in a vacuum. Nationalistic radio regulations, together with government broadcasting projects like XFX, both inspired and limited Mexico's commercial broadcasters. Over the course of the 1930s, radio entrepreneurs discovered that their own brand of musical nationalism could satisfy government imperatives while building a vigorous broadcasting industry in Mexico. Their "Mexican formula" continued to thrive in the 1940s and 1950s as the industry benefited from U.S. investment during World War II and the growth of transnational advertising in the postwar years.[8]

Third, the XFX experiment shows the unique role that radio broadcasting played in a country of historically isolated localities and regions. Given Mexico's difficult terrain, limited means of transportation, and low literacy rates, radio was poised to play a central role in connecting these dispersed communities and promoting national politics and culture. For the first time, oral culture, drama, and music could be centrally produced and distributed to much of the nation. Although national transmission did not guarantee uniform reception or interpretation, broadcasters worked to standardize a set of cultural practices for national consumption. This chapter examines each of these features—the unique capacities of the medium, the state's investment in radio, and the dominance of commercial broadcasters—in order to show how radio shaped national identity and memory in Mexico.

## The Radio Medium and Mexican Culture

As a means of point-to-mass communication, radio had the ability to reach widely dispersed listeners from a single location and create a "virtual common space" in which listeners could experience the same media messages simultaneously. In principle, this virtual meeting ground could be as big or as small as the audience reached by a single broadcasting station or network, but in practice it tended to be coterminous with the national territory.[9] As will be explored hereafter, this was largely due to the explicit efforts of government and commercial interests to build a broadcasting system that would help integrate the national market and polity.

As the case of XFX makes clear, however, all broadcasts were subject to local practices of selection and interpretation that could not be controlled at the national level. Nonetheless, broadcasters developed communicative strategies to work against the cultural pluralism of the national space and engage listeners in a unifying national discourse. First, they relied on repetition, standardization, and simplification as means of strengthening their radio messages against the centripetal force of local contexts and customs. "National" cultural practices were reduced to simple narratives, icons, and symbols that could be circulated to millions of people across great distances. For example, folk melodies and rhythms evoking the noble *charro*, the beautiful *china poblana*, and the picturesque Mexican countryside became increasingly recognizable over the airwaves. Second, broadcasters exploited the sense of intimacy that many listeners experienced when a radio signal obliterated the distance between the broadcaster and the audience. Radio's simultaneous and immediate mode of communication made nationally dispersed messages an intimate part of local experience.[10]

Radio's character as a medium of pure sound also influenced its relationship with Mexican culture. As an aural medium, radio was forced to draw on cultural practices that could be translated into sound and speech, such as storytelling, humor, theater, and music. Music, as a highly flexible, portable, and easily reproducible art form, became a particularly rich source of radio sound. From the beginning, broadcasters perceived music as "a necessity of human life and primary material of radio."[11] By relying on music and spoken language rather than print, radio became one of the first mass media to communicate across the social lines of race, class, and gender. As Mexico's oral and literate cultures merged and mingled during the 1920s and 1930s, radio was perfectly positioned to disseminate the new cultural forms they created.

## Government Radio Broadcasting Regulations

Although the audience for radio remained tiny during the 1920s, with an estimated twenty-five thousand sets in operation in 1926, it was a critical decade for the establishment of radio regulations in Mexico. Following the path of most other countries, the Mexican government asserted control over radio communication as a strategic public resource and medium of national commerce. In the years following World War I, however, the Mexican government's control was directly challenged by a partnership of U.S. government and private interests. These interests, including the newly formed Radio Corporation of America (RCA), aimed to open Latin American radio systems to development by U.S. corporations with minimal government oversight. Latin American opposition to this initiative took shape at the Inter-American Conference on Electrical Communications held in Mexico City in 1924. Against protest from the United States, the delegates resolved that electronic communication media were public services over which national governments held direct control. These resolutions became the basis for Mexico's first radio law of 1926.[12]

The 1926 Law of Electrical Communications (LCE) and the 1931 and 1932 revisions of the Law of General Means of Communication (LVGC) established a mixed system of commercial and government broadcasting. The 1926 LCE declared the airwaves to be a national resource, allowed only Mexican citizens to own or operate radio stations, and prohibited any transmissions that attacked state security, public order, or the established government. The LVGC required commercial broadcasters to carry all government announcements free of charge at the same time as it prohibited them from transmitting programs of a political or religious nature. Further regulations, established in "defense of the national culture," required stations to broadcast only in Spanish and prohibited radio studios from being located on foreign soil.[13]

By the mid-1930s there were seventy radio stations operating in Mexico and approximately 250,000 receivers. Under the activist Cárdenas administration, the Radio Law of 1936 increased the amount of government programming that all stations were required to carry and demanded that all stations include at least 25 percent "typical Mexican music" (*música típica*) in each radio program. "Typical Mexican music" was defined as music of mestizo or Indian origins. Several powerful broadcasters protested the law and suggested that they be given more flexibility in presenting music of Mexican authorship. The Communications Ministry rejected their petition and noted that such a change would destroy the specific aim of the law, which was "none other than that of diffusing our typical music with greater intensity, as this constitutes one of the most fertile manifestations of our popular art."[14]

By the late 1930s there were 120 radio stations broadcasting in Mexico and over 450,000 radio sets in operation. As the business of broadcasting took off, an increasingly organized and proactive broadcasting industry was able to block most of the government's regulatory initiatives. For example, radio industry lobbyists defeated a proposal by the Communication Ministry to create a national network of government broadcasting stations financed by a European-style subscription system. In addition, efforts to increase industry taxes were derailed, and the industry's tax burden was actually decreased.[15] Although regulatory activism declined rapidly after 1939 as the influence of commercial broadcasting organizations grew, most of the nationalistic regulations established during the Calles and Cárdenas regimes—including the Mexican music requirement—remained in place throughout the 1940s and 1950s.

## Government Broadcasting

Along with radio regulations, the Mexican state shaped the medium through its own broadcasting activities. These activities were of two main kinds: broadcasts over commercial stations and broadcasting projects like the SEP station XFX. Broadcasts over commercial stations included speeches by government officials, reports issued by state agencies, and a small number of educational and cultural programs disseminated over private stations. Presidential speeches, which were usually broadcast over both government and commercial stations, played a major role in building a national radio audience and evoking national allegiance during times of crisis.[16] One of the most important stations for disseminating presidential speeches and government propaganda was station XEFO, operated by the government's official party, the Partido Nacional Revolucionario. Along with station XEFO, the SEP station XFX was one of the earliest and most influential government outlets. A closer look at the organization and programming strategies of station XFX offers insights into the Mexican state's efforts to construct national culture and identity over the air.

Founded in 1924 by María Luisa Ross under the original call letters CZE, radio station XFX was part of the first wave of government and commercial stations authorized by the Ministry of Communications and Public Works beginning in 1923. XFX did not begin regular daily broadcasts until the early 1930s, when Narciso Bassols took over the directorship of the SEP. In an effort to build a national, unified system of education, Bassols developed radio broadcasting as a central tool for the SEP's rural education programs.[17] Although the SEP radio project had a national vision, the actual reach of the station was constrained by its low-power transmitter (five hundred watts) and limited financial resources. Because of the low level of radio interference during these early years, however, the station's weak Mexico City transmitter was able to cover most of the country's central valley by day and much of the republic by night. While XFX drew only a fraction of the audience reached by high-powered commercial stations, it probably received the particular attention of educators, government bureaucrats, and other prominent citizens. Radio reached professionals and the upper class, as well as urban dwellers of all classes in public places such as bars, restaurants, community centers, and schools. In addition, XFX was able to increase its potential audience by broadcasting important programs in network with more powerful stations, and, as discussed earlier, by distributing radios to rural schools.

Under the direction of the writer Agustín Yáñez and the Office of Cultural Radiotelephony, station XFX developed two broad program types: educational programs aimed primarily at schoolchildren and more broadly cultural programs aimed at the general public. The XFX daytime schedule included courses in language, history, geography, and hygiene, as well as a news program and *The Home Hour* (*La hora del hogar*), a program aimed primarily at Mexico City housewives. Station XFX became an important channel for promoting state health and hygiene campaigns to fight what Katherine Bliss has defined in her chapter here as the major diseases crippling Mexican development: tuberculosis, syphilis, and alcoholism. Educators saw radio as an effective way to penetrate the home: to consolidate an alliance between the modern, secular housewife and mother and the developmentalist state. *La hora del hogar* addressed homemakers as "priestesses ruling over blessed sanctuaries," tending "the sacred fires" of the home. Programs covered child rearing and child psychology, the organization of the home, etiquette, health and hygiene, and proper dinner conversation. Although XFX programs spoke to women primarily as vehicles for socializing and educating men, SEP records indicate that women took advantage of the free education offered over station XFX in order to better their own lives. The most popular programs offered practical instruction and graduated some thirty students a month.[18]

The evening schedule was devoted predominantly to musical programs but also included lectures, literature readings, and radio theater. One evening program, *Antena campesina*, targeted rural women with similar sorts of hygienic, homemaking, and puericultural information as *La hora del hogar*.[19] In addition, XFX was a general outlet for government bulletins ranging from health campaigns to reports on economic development and public works. Through a programming schedule designed both to educate and to entertain, station officials planned a "moral, economic and material coming together of the people of the country."[20] As one station announcement proclaimed, the objective of XFX cultural programs was to build "direct relations between the whole of the Mexican family and the educational leaders in whom the government of the republic has placed the standard of national culture."[21] Overall, XFX cultural programs aimed to build national unity and extend the social influence of the SEP into the everyday lives of Mexican citizens.

The SEP's cultural policy was most clearly elaborated in the case of musical programming, which filled the bulk of the prime broadcasting hours on station XFX. SEP officials viewed music as one of Mexico's most vibrant and deeply rooted art forms and hoped that XFX musical programs would carry the joy and nostalgia of popular songs directly into the private lives of the listening audience.[22] In their view, music's emotional power promised to build "currents of sympathy" in the national collectivity and channel emotional longing toward a government-sanctioned model of national culture.[23]

A closer look at XFX musical programming reveals two key strategies used by SEP officials to build this model of national culture. First, XFX concerts sought to demonstrate the connection between exemplary strands of Mexican popular music and the European art music tradition. Following Mexican thinkers like José Vasconcelos, SEP intellectuals aimed to show that Mexico had a "legitimate" national culture capable of meeting the standards of Western civilization. Second, by drawing on the country's regional musical genres, from the *huapangos* of the Huasteca region to the *jarabes* of the Bajío, SEP officials worked to create a national "panorama" of musical traditions. Regional songs were positioned as inspired examples of a larger body of Mexican national music and were used to authenticate the SEP's official version of national culture.

Broadcasts of classical and modern art music dominated XFX evening hours, making up over 60 percent of all musical programs. "Art music" is used here to describe symphonic and chamber music composed in a predominantly European harmonic and rhythmic style. These broadcasts included daily piano concerts, performances by the XFX Radio Orchestra, and concert series by the National Classical Quartet, the Popular Evening School of Music, the National Conservatory, and the Mexican Symphony Orchestra. Under the direction of Carlos Chávez, the Mexican Symphony began broadcasting over station XFX and XEFO during the early 1930s as part of an effort to popularize symphonic music among Mexico's peasants.[24]

While XFX concerts were filled with European music, the overall focus of the station's art music was on the creation of a modern, pan-Hispanic musical culture. For example, Spanish art music inspired by folk and popular tunes (such as Ravel's "Bolero") was repeatedly featured in XFX concerts. This music was presented together with compositions by Mexico's own composers, most notably Silvestre Revueltas, Carlos Chávez, and Manuel Ponce, who integrated elements of mestizo and indigenous music into their modernist compositions. Program listings included Ponce's "Balada Mexicana," Revueltas's "8 x radio," and Chávez's "Vals elegía" and "Antigona." Weekly concert series combined the music of Beethoven, Chopin, and Debussy with the works of Spanish composers Enrique Granados and Manuel de Falla, and Mexican composers Ponce and Revueltas. These concerts were often conducted by Revueltas or Chávez,

and their works were usually situated at the climax of the program as the culmination of a pan-Hispanic musical tradition.[25]

Together with art music, concerts labeled as "popular" or "Mexican" were
featured prominently during prime-time listening hours, making up almost 20
percent of evening musical broadcasts. The Office of Cultural Radiotelephony
used two very different formats for presenting popular music: an "official"
musical format and a "vernacular" musical format. The "official" format featured mestizo and indigenous tunes performed by trained musicians and professional orchestras.[26] For example, one concert series entitled the "National
Encounter for Education and Culture" was transmitted directly from various
states in the republic as part of official ceremonies honoring the states' educational achievements. These concerts were intended to popularize music from
each state in order to build what OCR officials characterized as a "strengthening panorama of national life."[27] In this way, XFX broadcasters highlighted
and celebrated the popular culture of individual states while mapping these
regional cultures onto the national domain.

The "vernacular" musical format broadcast by station XFX presented popular music in more or less its original form; that is, performed by regional groups
and instrumentalists rather than institutionally trained orchestras and musicians. One program by musicians from the states of Jalisco and Michoacán
offered traditional mariachi music that XFX directors claimed was, until then,
"completely unknown in the city."[28] In general, these programs went to great
lengths to present popular music as a kind of "authentic" specimen of Mexico's
ethnic roots. One station advertisement claimed that these broadcasts "offer
all cultured people who worry about the expressions of our vernacular art, the
best opportunity to appreciate the rich and varied nuances of the panorama of
our national folklore."[29] According to this ad, some XFX broadcasts were specifically designed to teach Mexico City's privileged classes how to overcome
their presumed discomfort with popular culture and learn to appreciate the
vernacular arts.

Through these musical programs, SEP officials created what Raymond Williams has called a "selective tradition" that chooses and reinterprets practices
of popular culture in terms of the cultural system of dominant social groups.[30]
However, it must be stressed that their efforts were part of a struggle for hegemony and dominance not yet achieved. In this struggle, they fought particular
demons. They wanted to elevate Mexico's ethnic culture to European standards, counteracting deformed stereotypes of Mexicans prevalent in Europe
and the United States. They sought to transform regional popular culture into

an authentic, civilized, respectable national culture, removing it from "backward" settings of popular pleasure, grief, and violence: cantinas, *pulquerías*, religious fiestas, bullfights, brothels, and battlefields. They also sought to offset the "corrupting" influence of commercial popular radio and foreign rhythms, for which American jazz became the code word.[31] In giving airtime to a wide array of popular musicians and music, they preserved, celebrated, and disseminated particular expressions of popular culture scorned by the traditional cultural elites and threatened by the inroads of foreign commerce.

Indeed, the SEP archive holds evidence that some educated, urban listeners responded positively to the SEP's construction of musical nationalism. A small group of twenty-five fan letters provides access to the direct, personal expressions of these Mexico City listeners. Their letters were written in response to an International Popular Music program featuring jarabes, *sones*, and indigenous songs from the state of Michoacán. As a group, the letters suggest that some listeners experienced XFX broadcasts as building a shared memory and nostalgia with other Mexicans. One listener wrote to thank the station for a musical broadcast that "spiritually transported" him to his native region. Another listener wrote to congratulate the station for "making known the regional music of all parts of the Republic, and in this way touching the sentiments of everyone who more or less relive the memory of their hours of youth upon hearing the sounds of regional music, of country music that to some is bound to be so familiar." This writer continued, "One must imagine that here [in Mexico City] there are peoples from all parts of the Republic and that each one will remember his native region upon listening to these village songs."[32] Although this nostalgia was based on the listeners' individual childhood memories of different regions and states, it could be recognized as "Mexican" and shared in common through the simultaneity of the radio medium.

Overall, station XFX played a significant part in the government's efforts to use radio to build national cultural and political unity. Despite its limited impact on radio audiences, the musical nationalism developed by XFX broadcasters became an influential model of radio programming. The Education Ministry's station was the first major testing ground for government-sponsored cultural broadcasts that expanded greatly under the Cárdenas administration. In 1936, the president created the Autonomous Department of Press and Publicity (DAPP) to coordinate government broadcasting, regulate media content, and organize government information activities. In 1937, radio station XFX was transferred to the DAPP, where its call letters were changed to XEDP, and the station became the state's primary radio outlet.[33]

One of the DAPP's most ambitious efforts was *The National Hour* (*La hora nacional*), a one-hour weekly program of music, drama, history, and government reports that debuted in 1937 and can still be heard today. The program, which originated from station XEDP, was broadcast nationally by the powerful transmitters of commercial station XEW. By government decree, every station in the country was required to rebroadcast the program. After the DAPP disbanded in 1939, production of *La hora nacional* continued under the direction of the Ministry of the Interior.

A look at *La hora nacional* reveals numerous continuities with XFX programming. Of the many prominent educators and intellectuals who planned and participated in XFX cultural programs, Rodolfo Usigli and Mauricio Magdaleno went on to play important roles in developing *La hora nacional* and other DAPP programs. In 1936 Usigli became director of the DAPP, while Magdaleno went on to coordinate the production of the show between 1943 and 1950. In addition, the main objective of the program was similar to that of earlier XFX broadcasts: to expose a national audience to an officially sanctioned version of Mexican culture. In pursuit of this goal, *La hora nacional* continued the SEP's project of musical nationalism, with a focus on Mexican art music that incorporated popular musical themes. For example, the program for October 10, 1937, highlighted the composition "Danzas Mayas," written and directed by Efrain Pérez and performed by the DAPP Symphony Orchestra. In this program and others, *La hora nacional* drew liberally on the model of a "national musical panorama" first developed by SEP officials at station XFX.[34]

## Commercial Broadcasting

Over the course of the 1930s, state broadcasting activities sent a clear signal to commercial broadcasters: maintain the favorable opinion of the central government by promoting "typical Mexican music," transmitting government messages, and avoiding political and religious discourse. As private concessionaires on the public airwaves, commercial broadcasters had to address the demands of the state. On the other hand, as commercial enterprises dependent on North American technology and capital, they also had to serve the interests of U.S. media corporations and transnational advertisers. Mexican radio entrepreneurs learned to move deftly between the Mexican state and U.S. corporations, seeking the support of each in order to gain their own creative space, markets, profits, and institutional dominance. In the space they carved out, Mexican broadcasters imported program formulas and production practices from the United States but transformed and adapted them to suit the aesthetics of Mexican culture and the political economy of Mexican broadcasting.

Such was clearly the case with Emilio Azcárraga, one of a small group of entrepreneurs who began broadcasting in Mexico during the 1920s. Like other station owners, he financed his radio ventures with a combination of foreign capital and capital accumulated in domestic industries such as publishing, electronics, and retail sales. Azcárraga started station XEW in Mexico City in 1930 with support from RCA. His station, known as the "Voice of Latin America from Mexico," soon became the most powerful station in the Western Hemisphere, with two hundred kilowatts of power. By 1938 Azcárraga controlled two national networks loosely affiliated with NBC (XEW) and CBS (XEQ). In 1941 he entered a partnership with Clemente Serna Martínez, owner of Monterrey's most important radio station, and created Radio Programas de México (RPM) to manage his radio empire. By 1942, RPM had sixty Mexican affiliates—almost half of all radio stations in Mexico—and had begun to establish a regional presence in Central America and the Caribbean.[35] By the early 1940s, Mexico had a half dozen radio networks and a commercial broadcasting industry that was organized and coordinated through the National Chamber of the Radio Broadcasting Industry (CIR, later CIRT).

Over the course of the 1930s, broadcasters like Azcárraga found that Mexican singers and musicians performing popular Mexican tunes provided an ideal radio content—a content that both satisfied government demands and helped define a distinctive national broadcasting market. During the mid- to late 1930s, station XEW devoted as much as 90 percent of its prime-time schedule to musical programming, with typical Mexican orchestras (*orquestas típicas*) dominating the scene.[36] These orchestras, featuring performers like Jorge Negrete, Agustín Lara, Pedro Vargas, and Toña la Negra, were conducted by Mexican composers such as Tata Nacho and Alfonso Esparza Oteo. Hit songs included Mexican boleros, corridos, sones, huapangos, and rancheras. Ranchera music, in particular, grew in popularity beginning in the late 1930s. The commercial ranchera was an urban musical form that romanticized prerevolutionary social relations and idealized the countryside. Mexico's Bajío region —comprised of Michoacán, Jalisco, Querétaro, Aguascalientes, and Guanajuato—particularly came to embody the idyllic "soul" of the nation in ranchera songs and films.[37] Although ranchera music became increasingly "urbanized" by the late 1940s—emphasizing the working-class cantina rather than the rural countryside—the music continued to evoke nostalgia for a popular, paternalist utopia.[38] Thus the musical content that built and sustained the nation's broadcasting market also provided a medium for national memory and nostalgia.

Although music continued to be the primary material of commercial radio in Mexico, nonmusical programs became increasingly audible during the 1940s and 1950s. An analysis of station XEB for the period 1938–48 shows that the percentage of musical programming in prime time dropped from almost 90 percent in 1938 to a low of 60 percent in 1944. In large part, this drop in musical programming can be explained by the increase in news, government reports, and propaganda programs during World War II. Indeed, by 1948, music made up 75 percent of the evening schedule. However, this trend also indicates an increase in serial drama programs (*radionovelas*), game shows, children's programs, and sports broadcasts over the course of the 1940s. Although musical programs returned to their dominant position in the years after the war, the percentage of news, serials, and other nonmusical programs did not drop to prewar levels but remained a significant component of the evening schedule.[39] News reports, which became a regular part of radio listening during the war years, became an important site in which commercial broadcasters evoked the national market as a community of shared memories and mutual interests.

## Conclusion

Over the course of the 1930s and 1940s, a combination of government activism, commercial innovation, and audience demand produced a unique national radio content. Government radio policy played an early and formative role in shaping the broadcasting system into an effective tool for state and nation building. In the case of radio, the project took the form of a musical nationalism designed to incorporate citizens into a shared national culture. This national culture was constructed as both a "legitimate" expression of the Hispanic-European tradition and an "authentic" product of Mexico's mestizo-Indian roots. Musical nationalism was promoted over government broadcasting stations like XFX and through radio regulations like the 1936 law requiring commercial broadcasters to include 25 percent "typical Mexican music" in every broadcast. Commercial broadcasters, for their part, embraced musical nationalism as a means of defining a national radio market that they were uniquely positioned to serve.

By 1940, the central government had largely stepped out of radio as a broadcaster in its own right, leaving the medium in the hands of Azcárraga and other commercial broadcasters whose interests were closely allied with those of the state. At the outbreak of World War II, Azcárraga's position was strong enough to ensure that his organization would control and direct much of the U.S. government's wartime investment in Mexican broadcasting. By the end of the war, the Azcárraga organization was poised to dominate the development of the next broadcasting medium—television—and continue its production of a distinctly Mexican, and often explicitly nationalist, programming content.

## Notes

This chapter draws heavily on my book *Radio Nation: Communication, Popular Culture and Nationalism in Mexico, 1920–1950* (Tucson: University of Arizona Press, 2000). It also reflects editorial suggestions made by Mary Kay Vaughan.

1. The official call letters were XEFX, but all SEP documents give them as XFX.

2. Archivo Histórico de la Secretaría de Educación Pública (hereafter AHSEP), Oficina Cultural Radiotelefónica (hereafter OCR), Caja 1311, Exp. 76, "Informe . . . Estado de Tlaxcala," from Luis F. Rodríguez Lomelí (hereafter RL), March 25, 1933.

3. AHSEP, OCR, Caja 1311, Exp. 76, "Informe . . . Estado de Puebla," from RL, March 18, 1933.

4. "Informe . . . Estado de Tlaxcala," 1–2.

5. AHSEP, OCR, Caja 1311, Exp. 76, "Informe . . . Zona de Tlalnepantla, Estado de México," from RL, April 24, 1933.

6. AHSEP, OCR, Caja 1311, Exp. 76, "Informe . . . Estado de Hidalgo," from RL, April 22, 1933.

7. "Informe . . . Estado de Puebla."

8. John Sinclair, "Dependent Development and Broadcasting: 'The Mexican Formula,'" *Media, Culture and Society* 8, no. 1 (1986): 81–101.

9. Rudolf Arnheim, *Radio*, trans. Margaret Ludwig and Herbert Read (London: Faber and Faber, 1936), 238.

10. For more on the role of mass communication in nation formation, see Benedict Anderson, *Imagined Communities: Reflections on the Origin and Spread of Nationalism*, 2nd ed. (London: Verso, 1991); Eric J. Hobsbawm, *Nations and Nationalism since 1780: Programme, Myth, Reality* (Cambridge: Cambridge University Press, 1990); and Jesús Martín-Barbero, "Communication from Culture: The Crisis of the National and the Emergence of the Popular," *Media, Culture, and Society* 10 (1988): 447–65.

11. AHSEP, OCR, Caja 1310, Exp. 37, "Oficina Cultural Radiotelefónica," undated report, 1933.

12. Hayes, *Radio Nation*, 27–28, 37. For more on the conference's role in shaping Mexican broadcasting, see James Schwoch, *The American Radio Industry and Its Latin American Activities, 1900–1939* (Urbana: University of Illinois Press, 1990); and Fer-

nando Mejía Barquera, *La industria de la radio y televisión y la política del Estado mexicano (1920–1960)* (Mexico City: Fundación Manuel Buendía, 1989).

13. Paul L. Barbour, "Commercial and Cultural Broadcasting in Mexico," *Annals of the American Academy of Political and Social Sciences* 108 (March 1940): 101.

14. Ibid., 101.

15. Mejía Barquera, *La industria*, 93.

16. Hayes, *Radio Nation*, 80–86.

17. John A. Britton, "The Mexican Ministry of Education, 1931–1940: Radical and Institutional Development" (Ph.D. diss., Tulane University, 1971), 51–52.

18. Ageeth Sluis, "Revolution and the Rhetoric of Representation: Gender Construction in Mexican Radio and Cinema, 1920–1940" (M.A. thesis, University of Wyoming, 1997).

19. Ibid.

20. AHSEP, Radio Educación, Exp. 1068, Department of Bellas Artes (hereafter BA), "Ideas para la reorganización de la Dirección de Radio de la SEP," by Agustin Yáñez, February 28, 1932.

21. AHSEP, OCR, Caja 1313, Exp. 20, "Rumbos Nuevos," undated, 1933.

22. AHSEP, OCR, Caja 1313, Exp. 20, "[Quarto] Concierto de música popular internacional," segunda parte, March 11, 1933.

23. Mary Kay Vaughan, *The State, Education, and Social Class in Mexico, 1880–1920* (De Kalb: Northern Illinois University Press, 1982), 258.

24. Carlos Chávez, "Music in a Mexican Test Tube," *New York Times Magazine* 7, no. 2 (July 1945): 8; and Hayes, *Radio Nation*, 53.

25. AHSEP, OCR, Caja 1315, Exp. 33, "Actividades diarias, horario general," March–December 1933. For more on the pan-Hispanic vision that guided XFX programming strategies, see Hayes, *Radio Nation*, 46–55.

26. AHSEP, OCR, Caja 1315, Exp. 33, letter from Agustin Yáñez to the Dir. de Ed. Fed., Estado de Jalisco, May 31, 1933.

27. AHSEP, OCR, Caja 1310, Exp. 37, "Oficina Cultural Radiotelefónica," undated report, 1933.

28. AHSEP, OCR, Caja 1313, Exp. 20, "Hora de música popular internacional," February 18 and June 3, 1933.

29. AHSEP, OCR, Caja 1316, Exp. 32, "Nuestra música aborigen actual . . . ," May 28, 1933.

30. Raymond Williams, *Marxism and Literature* (Oxford: Oxford University Press, 1977).

31. AHSEP, Radio Educación, Exp. 1068, BA, "Obra de extensión por radio," undated report, 1932; OCR, Caja 1310, Exp. 37, letter from A. Badillo to Narciso Bassols, April 29, 1933; and Radio Educación, Exp. 1068, BA, "Obra de extensión por radio," undated report, 1932.

32. AHSEP, OCR, Caja 1315, Exp. 33, "Reportes . . . relativos a los conciertos de música michoacana y araucana," February–March, 1933; letter from Julio Moto, March 6, 1933.

33. Sluis, "Revolution and the Rhetoric of Representation."

34. "Mauricio Magdaleno" and "Rudolfo Usigli," *Enciclopedia de México* (Mexico City: SEP, 1987); R. C. Norris, "A History of *La Hora Nacional*: Government Broadcasting via Privately Owned Radio Stations in Mexico" (Ph.D. diss., University of Michigan, 1962), 13; and "Danzas Mayas en *La Hora Nacional*," *Excélsior*, October 9, 1937, 8.

35. For more on the rise of the Azcárraga broadcasting empire, see Pablo Arredondo Ramírez and Enrique E. Sánchez Ruíz, *Comunicación social, poder y democracia en México* (Guadalajara: Universidad de Guadalajara, 1986); Miriam Delal Baer, "Television and Political Control in Mexico" (Ph.D. diss., University of Michigan, 1991); and Claudia Fernández and Andrew Paxman, *El Tigre: Emilio Azcárraga y su imperio* (Mexico City: Televisa, 2000).

36. Hayes, *Radio Nation*, 71.

37. Caes af Geijerstam, *Popular Music in Mexico* (Albuquerque: University of New Mexico Press, 1976), 43.

38. William Grandante, "Mexican Popular Music at Mid-century: The Role of José Alfredo Jiménez and the Canción Ranchera," *Studies in Latin American Popular Culture* 2 (1983): 99–114; Yolanda Moreno Rivas, *Historia de la música popular mexicana* (1979; Mexico City: Alianza Editorial Mexicana, Consejo Nacional para la Cultura y las Artes, 1989), 171.

39. Hayes, *Radio Nation*, 72.

# Screening the Nation

JOANNE HERSHFIELD

During the golden age of Mexican cinema between 1930 and 1955, film took part in the postrevolutionary state's *campaña nacionalista* (nationalist campaign). This campaign involved a concerted political and cultural effort to mold a national "sentiment" that could unite a diverse and divided population.[1] This sentiment came to be known as Mexicanidad, a set of discourses that identified an "essential" Mexican identity. In the following discussion, I examine how competing ideologies about national identity were narrated and visually represented in the movies of the 1930s, when Mexican filmmakers and their audiences transformed an industry long dominated by Hollywood into a "national" one operating in a global marketplace.

The postrevolutionary nation and the new Mexican citizen were formed through a set of discourses, stereotypes, and memories of national identity that circulated in public through official mandates and productions as well as through popular culture, the mass media, and interpersonal relations. Throughout the 1920s and 1930s, the state, with the support of intellectuals and artists, instituted numerous cultural projects to instill and legitimize its ideals linked to the Mexican Revolution and to national history. These included painting huge murals in public places, building monuments to revolutionary heroes, and nationalizing public education. At the same time, the state's ideological hegemony was never absolute. Public discourse about the meaning of the nation and national identity was not restricted to official edicts and school programs but emerged through other kinds of popular-culture practices and genres such as jokes, gossip, comic books, songs, musical reviews, popular theater, and film. A variety of competing conceptions of national identity circulated in oral and written histories, in popular culture, and in the burgeoning mass media. These alternative conceptions struggled with official discourses for recognition and legitimacy and were often successfully incorporated into the discourse of Mexicanidad.

Alan Knight finds that ultimately the state failed to "transform and homoge-
nize the Mexican population." Instead, he suggests that a "different kind" of
transformation ensued, one that "emanated not from the state but from the
market. In other words, cultural transformation and homogenization were
basically socioeconomic, not political, processes."[2] One powerful site for the
negotiation of nationalism in Mexico was the cinema, the preeminent form of
mass media in the twentieth century. Through film's melodramatic language,
often conflicting understandings of Mexicanidad reached film audiences. The
cinema addressed concerns such as urbanization and modernization, changing relations between women and men, between family members, between the
individual and the state, and between Mexico and the world. It provided possible solutions to questions about how one could retain traditions that honored
family and religion and still take part in the economic project of urbanization
and industrialization that challenged those traditions.

## The Development of a National Cinema

Film production in Mexico at the turn of the century began as a series of
private ventures by a few visionary entrepreneurs who became movie producers, distributors, and exhibitors. They used cameras to document and celebrate Mexico's landscapes, its indigenous cultures, and the political pomp
and circumstance of president Porfirio Díaz's extended reign (1876–1911). Between 1898 and 1928, Mexico produced over one hundred silent documentaries
and feature films.[3] Other entrepreneurs bought French, Italian, and American
films and entered the exhibition business with an inventory of several dozen
movies. Initially, Mexico's film audience was composed of the new urban proletariat. Porfirian industrialization drew disenfranchised peasants into the cities
in search of work and a better life for their families. The cheap price of entertainment drew a largely illiterate viewing public into theaters and *carpas*, the
tented amusement shows that traveled across the country bringing vaudeville
and musical acts to small towns and isolated villages. By the turn of the century
there were over twenty-two venues for motion pictures in Mexico City, and
new theaters devoted exclusively to film projection were under construction.
By 1911 the number of motion picture theaters in Mexico City had jumped
to forty.[4]

Narrative filmmaking came to a virtual standstill during the revolution, although filmmakers continued to produce documentaries that captured the encounters between revolutionary forces and the *Federales*. These films proved to

be very popular.[5] Whether these productions of roving cameramen satisfied a taste for violence, horror, and adventure or a desire to follow contemporary events, watching them was a nationalizing experience. The end of the military phase of the revolution marked the beginning of a studio system and feature-film production, primarily backed by private initiative and investment. Cinema received minimal support from Venustiano Carranza's administration, which was mostly interested in educational or propagandistic films.

From its inception, Mexican narrative cinema was transnational in terms of themes, stories, and cinematic style. Filmmakers were inspired by a number of influences, borrowing from Hollywood, French and Italian cinema, and their own theatrical, literary, and artistic traditions. The content of silent films ranged from adaptations of classic and modern European literature and theater to films that explicitly showcased Mexico's own history, its landscape, myths, cultural practices, and traditions. *El grito de Dolores* (1908, Felipe de Jesús Haro), for example, was a nationalistic piece that narrated the Mexican War of Independence against Spain (1810–21). It provided a model for subsequent cinematic epics celebrating Mexican history, a theme that would remain prominent for fifty years.

Following *El grito de Dolores*, filmmakers took inspiration from an emerging populist nationalism that celebrated national histories, regional customs, and indigenous peoples. This new genre is exemplified by historical dramas such as the earliest known Mexican feature-length fictional film, *¡1810 o los libertadores!* (1916, Manuel Cirerol Sansores), a romance; and *Tepeyac* (1917, Carlos E. González and José Manuel Ramos), one of the earliest films about the national devotion to the Virgin of Guadalupe. Films like *Cuauhtémoc* (1918, Manuel de la Bandera) and *De raza azteca* (1922, Fernando Martorel) presented cinematic histories of the pre-Columbian era. *El caporal* (The Boss, 1921, Juan Canals de Homs and Rafael Bermúdez Zataraín) anticipated the emergence of what was to become Mexican cinema's most popular genre in the golden age, the *comedia ranchera*. *El caporal* took place in northern Mexico along the U.S. border. The film historian Aurelio de los Reyes writes that the film, like the subsequent comedia ranchera, was not a historical narrative of the hacienda system but one that constructed it in an idyllic imaginary that ignored the brutal system of peasant exploitation.[6]

If there was an explicitly "Mexican" cinema genre during these early years, it was epitomized by films inspired by Mexican popular theater genres: *zarzuelas* (musical farces), *géneros chicos* (melodramatic short plays that drew on folkloric and popular themes), and *revistas* (parodic musicals based on newspaper articles about dramatic events in Mexican social and political life). A number of films including *Don Juan Tenorio* (1898, Salvador Toscano), *El amor que triunfa* (Love That Triumphs, 1917, Manuel Cirerol Sansores), and *Viaje redondo* (The Circular Journey, 1919, José Manuel Ramos) were either adapted from, or aesthetically inspired by, popular theatrical works. *Don Juan Tenorio*, a condensed filmed version of the play, consisted of a number of brief one-shot tableaux that traced the longer narrative of the original theatrical production. Toscano's film was typical of early fictional films in that it not only was an adaptation of a play but also modeled the linear structure and the spectacle of stage play presentation.

In 1919, a revista-inspired film, *El automóvil gris* (The Gray Automobile, Enrique Rosas), was released to enthusiastic audiences.[7] Based on a famous public incident, *El automóvil gris* dramatized the activities of a gang of thieves who, disguised in uniforms of Carranza's Constitutionalist Army, carried out numerous robberies, murders, and kidnappings in Mexico City in 1915 using search warrants stolen from police headquarters. Advertised as "authentic," a "transcription of the truth,"[8] *El automóvil gris* combined the realism of Mexican documentary, the chronological narrative structure introduced in earlier narrative films, elements of melodrama borrowed from Italian and French films, and a number of new cinematic techniques introduced by the American filmmaker D. W. Griffith, such as cross-cutting between two simultaneously occurring scenes.

Mexican audiences (as well as most audiences around the world) were educated in how to watch films by Hollywood. These audiences approached films with certain expectations in relation to film stories and film style. By the 1920s, the characteristics that defined a "good" film were those that Hollywood had conventionalized. These included technical factors—lighting conventions, acting styles, camera techniques—as well as formal considerations such as narrative structures, plot, themes, and content. Thus, for the Mexican cinema to succeed as a national cinema, it had to largely model itself on the Hollywood version of what a film should look like and what kinds of stories it should tell. As the Mexican cultural critic Carlos Monsiváis puts it, "The founding project of the Mexican cinema was the 'nationalization' of Hollywood."[9]

The classic Hollywood films were character-centered narratives. These narratives were structured through a chain of cause and effect driven by the protagonist's desire to achieve a goal. The narrative moved forward through a series of conflicts that arose to inhibit the protagonist's realization of the goal until some kind of resolution or closure was achieved. The Hollywood film style favored a realist aesthetic. That is, lighting, acting style, editing, and sound were subordinated to the advancement of the narrative and functioned to disguise the artifice of moviemaking.

Hollywood was also responsible for the initial creation of the "cinematic Mexico" and the "cinematic Mexican," and thus Mexican audiences (as well as European audiences) first saw themselves represented on-screen through the lens of American filmmakers. These images materialized in the United States in early American travel literature and in popular "dime" novels of the late nineteenth century. The political and ideological effects of the Spanish-American War of 1898 were also visible in the United States' earliest cinematic representations of Mexico and Mexicans, intensifying existing racist perceptions. Stereotypical images relied on the appeal of spectacle in folk costumes and settings and ethnic and racial performers employed to authenticate Hollywood's vision of an "exotic" Mexico populated by swarthy, mustached *bandidos* and pretty *señoritas*. An early Thomas A. Edison Kinetoscope travelogue, *Pedro Esquirel and Dionecio Gonzales: Mexican Duel* (1898), was one of the first films that featured Hollywood's Mexican stereotypes. These stereotypes proliferated in films such as *The Greaser's Gauntlet* (1908, D. W. Griffith), *The Mexican's Jealousy* (1910), *On the Border* (1913), *Bronco Billy and the Greaser* (1914), *The Greaser* (1915), and *Scarlet Days* (1919, D. W. Griffith).

Mexican officials objected to the "greaser" stereotypes that pervaded through the 1920s and finally resorted to banning all the films of offending production companies in 1922.[10] *The Dove* (1927), a film set in Tijuana, was one of several banned in Mexico. In the case of this film, the Mexican consul general G. S. Seguin accused Hollywood of "using grossly exaggerated and very negative Mexican characterizations."[11] The Mexican government instituted an embargo against the film's producer, Famous Players and Metro. However, that embargo proved difficult to enforce and relatively ineffective. Mexican exhibitors rallied against it, arguing that it hurt their business, which, at the time, was dependent on screening Hollywood films.[12]

Despite creative and economic risk taking, Mexican filmmakers could not compete with a booming U.S. film industry that was already looking to expand its global reach. U.S. investors had realized the opportunities of a rapidly expanding audience south of its border and began investing in Mexican distribution and exhibition. Pressured by filmmakers and local investors, the state finally began to implement protectionist legislation in the form of quotas and subsidies in an attempt to nurture the growing domestic film industry. However, these policies did little to shift the balance of power with Hollywood

because of an inadequate supply of local product and because audiences preferred Hollywood films. By 1928, 90 percent of all films exhibited throughout
Mexico (as in the rest of Latin America) were made in the United States.[13]

While the postrevolutionary regime of President Álvaro Obregón and his
minister of education José Vasconcelos lent its patronage to painting and crafts,
filmmakers did not enjoy much support. Although Obregón's administration
made some attempt to stabilize the young industry, the government exhibited
little interest in taking an active part in filmmaking's economic, ideological, or
aesthetic development. State film production was spread out under the aegis of
the Ministries of War and Marines, of Education, and of Agriculture Development. According to the historian Federico Dávalos Orozco, "At best, the state
conceived of the cinema as a useful pedagogical tool for mass education."[14] The
state sponsored scientific, historical, and ethnographic documentaries rather
than narrative features.

The introduction of sound and the ensuing development of well-equipped
film production studios in the 1930s (bankrolled by private investment, government loans, and U.S. money) fostered the expansion of the industry and
gave filmmakers a chance to develop an economically viable national cinematic vision. This was not an easy task. Film sound technology required an
enormous input of scarce capital. The small production entities that produced
early sound films were often forced to disband after the release of a single
film. Secondly, after a decade of Hollywood's monopoly of Mexican screens,
audiences (and filmmakers) preferred Hollywood's narrative and technological standards. However, sound introduced language barriers that, in the final
analysis, probably did the most to encourage the growth of national film industries in Latin America. Hollywood studios attempted to counter this threat
by producing Spanish-language versions of certain films. Ultimately, however,
Latin American audiences rejected Hollywood's "Spanish" sound films with
their mixture of Latin American and Andalusian accents.

The economic viability of the Mexican film industry was ultimately made
possible with the support of President Cárdenas (1934–40). He established a
protectionist policy that included tax exemptions for domestic film production and created the Financiadora de Películas, a state institution charged with
finding private financing for films. He instituted a system of loans for the establishment of major film studios. During his administration, the first modern
studio, Clasa (Cinematográfica Latino Americana, S.A.), was built with private
money and outfitted with the most modern production equipment available.[15]
Cárdenas's policies succeeded in strengthening all aspects of the industry. Film

production grew from six films in 1932 to fifty-seven films by 1938, and more importantly, Mexico's share of its domestic market grew significantly.[16]

There were now five motion picture studios in Mexico City: the Compañía Nacional Productora de Películas, Universidad Cinematográfica, México-Films de Jorge Stahl, Industrial Cinematográfica, and Estudios Clasa. Thirty-seven movie theaters screened first- and second-run film in Mexico City alone.[17] However, there was not yet a consolidated industry, nor were there any generic formulas in place. There was no agreement or even sense of what a "Mexican" film was, and there was no public discourse that defined the films as "national." Some films adapted Mexican novels, dealt with Mexican historical events, or borrowed their stories from current events. Others adapted European novels and plays. Still others were unabashedly replicas of Hollywood films.

The success of *Allá en el Rancho Grande* (Fernando de Fuentes) in 1936 proved that there was now a large enough market to sustain an industry dependent on box office receipts. Once it was obvious that work was available in Mexico, Mexican film actors and technicians working in Hollywood returned to their native country, bringing with them the skills and cinematic conventions they had learned. They provided a ready-made technical and artistic force for the emerging industry.

According to de los Reyes, two strands of nationalist cinema developed in the 1930s: "un nacionalismo conservador" and "un nacionalismo liberal."[18] The conservative discourse of cinematic nationalism celebrated colorful indigenous traditions, practices, and clothing, and traditional familial and religious values. Liberal nationalism, conversely, cinematically celebrated the modern aspects of postrevolutionary Mexico, specifically its growing urbanity and modernity. Although these strands may have been motivated by the political or ideological leanings of film directors and producers, ultimately both were successful at the box office because they corresponded to the two already circulating dominant discourses of nationalism, identity, and change.[19]

Three major types of films emerged: a state-supported cinema, an independent experimental cinema, and films made primarily for commercial reasons that resembled the Hollywood model in narrative strategies, cinematic aesthetics, and mode of production. Public figures and intellectuals called on the government to take part in *el cine educativo*.[20] However, the film industry never enjoyed the same level of governmental commitment as did education, the fine arts, and other cultural practices. A few films were produced that were commissioned by the state and specifically formulated as educational tools.

*Sendas del destino* (1939, Juan J. Ortega), for example, produced for the Comisión Nacional de Irrigación, was a melodrama about the problems encountered in the construction of the Angostura dam in Sonora.[21] Other state-supported narrative productions such as *Redes* (Nets, 1934) and *¡Vámanos con Pancho Villa!* (Let's Go with Pancho Villa, 1935) promoted the populist nationalism celebrated by Cárdenas and his supporters and projected an "official aesthetic" that privileged *indigenismo*.

Indigenismo was a network of intellectual, political, and artistic ideas that argued, among other things, that the roots of Mexican national identity could be found in Mexico's Indian cultures. Advocates of this project had two primary goals: to "rehabilitate" the Indian so that he could be incorporated into the national project, and to "blend" indigenismo with nationalism.[22] Artists adapted elements from popular culture as well as Mayan and Aztec influences into their work as a political statement about the nature of Mexican national culture. Indigenismo became entrenched in popular conceptions of national identity through powerful, popular symbolic transformations such as cinema. At the same time, many proponents of indigenismo, particularly those engaged in film, failed to acknowledge the linguistic, historical, and cultural differences among the diverse groups that made up Mexico's indigenous populations: they stereotyped "the Indian."

In 1935 two state-funded films were released that promoted a cinematic version of indigenismo: *Redes* (Nets), codirected by Fred Zinnemann, the American photographer Paul Strand, Agustín Velázquez Chávez, and Emilio Gómez Muriel; and *Janitzio*, directed by Carlos Navarro. Postrevolutionary nationalist theater, painting, and folklore inspired the genre's aesthetics. So did foreign pseudoethnographic films such as Robert Flaherty's *Moana: A Romance of the Golden Age* (1926), F. W. Murnau's *Tabu* (1931), and Basil Wright's *Song of Ceylon* (1934). While these documentaries purported to be "realistic" portrayals of primitive peoples, they employed certain cinematic techniques developed in avant-garde filmmaking that belied their professed concern with realism: an interest in formal composition, a lyrical editing style, and the development of a poetic rather than narrative structure. *Moana*, which depicts the daily life of a Samoan boy, was lauded as an "intensely lyrical poem on the theme of the last paradise."[23] Lyrical timelessness and the unity of nature, culture, and the agentless, primordial human being characterize this genre, recalling early-twentieth-century modernism and the artistic indigenismo examined by Rick López in this volume.

The principal cinematic influence on the *indigenista* genre, however, emerged from an unexpected source. In 1930, the Soviet filmmaker Sergei Eisenstein arrived in Mexico to make a film about the history and people of Mexico with financial support from the American writer Upton Sinclair. De los Reyes argues that before Eisenstein, "cinematic nationalism had been a strongly conservative and moralistic movement that aimed at preserving the past, holding fast to it, negating and avoiding the changes that the Revolution had operated in society and defending the established order."[24]

While the cinematic strategies of Eisenstein's film owe much to his earlier work in the Soviet Union, the images and ideas foregrounded in *¡Que viva Mexico!* are also inspired by the nationalistic intellectual and artistic fervor he observed and participated in during his sojourn in Mexico, specifically, indigenismo. According to Eisenstein, *¡Que viva Mexico!* would be "a rhythmic and musical construction and an unrolling of the Mexican spirit."[25] Charles Ramírez Berg points to two primary characteristics of Eisenstein's cinematic style that influenced Mexican filmmakers and cinematographers such as Emilio Fernández and Gabriel Figueroa: Eisenstein's "exaltation of native imagery . . . [and] his appropriation of the work of Mexican artists to inform his visual style."[26] As I discuss elsewhere, the opening montage of pre-Columbian images in Fernández's 1943 film *María Candelaria* includes a shot of a young Indian woman standing next to the stone figure of an Aztec woman. This shot is almost identical to the one composed by Eisenstein for his prologue.[27] Fernández and Figueroa also repeatedly made use of Eisenstein's low-angle camera framing to set characters against the Mexican landscape.

Eisenstein's *¡Que viva Mexico!* turned contemporary rural people into Indians and represented them as figures of tropical exoticism—as in the sensual, graceful movement of Zapotec women of Tehuantepec—but it also portrayed them as brutally exploited workers. In contrast to commercial films that would depict hacienda life as secure, abundant, and jolly under the kindly rule of the prerevolutionary hacendado, Eisenstein's hacendado is an abusive tyrant who sanctions the rape of peasant women, enforces a backbreaking work schedule, and punishes a peon by burying him in the desert sand, where he is eaten by insects and baked by the sun.

*Redes*, Mexico's first sound film sponsored by the government's Secretaría de Educación Pública (SEP), tells the story of a village of poor Indian fishermen who go on strike against the greedy agent who exploits their labor and buys their fish. Like Eisenstein's *¡Que Viva Mexico!* and the murals of Rivera and

Siqueiros, the film is an epic of class struggle. *Redes* had two official purposes: it would "educate" Mexicans on Mexicanidad while countering the aesthetics of commercial Hollywood and Mexican films. Shot on location in Veracruz, the film featured local inhabitants as the "stars." If the film's story focused on the fishermen's poverty and exploitation and on their resistance, the cinematography, inspired by Eisenstein, romanticizes their lives by emphasizing the beauty of the landscape and the people and promoting an "intimate" and mythical connection between people and nature.

*Janitzio* narrates the story of an Indian girl, Eréndira, who becomes the mistress of a criollo engineer to keep her fiancé out of jail.[28] She is murdered by her people for breaching the sexual mores of the village. Unlike *Redes*, *Janitzio* was conceived as a commercial film and is presented as a love story rather than as social criticism. The film is set in an unnamed period before the revolution and thus avoids overt political commentary. However, at another level, *Janitzio* updates Mexico's foundational myth: the La Malinche/Cortés union, the famous first interracial romance in Mexican myth and history. When the Spanish conquerors arrived in Mexico in the early sixteenth century, they appropriated Indian women as servants to cook, clean, and provide sexual services for their armies as they marched across Mesoamerica. The most famous of these women was Malinalli—or La Malinche, as she became known in Spanish—who eventually became Cortés's mistress and interpreter. Despite the fact that La Malinche was a slave, she is remembered as the woman who betrayed her people. *Janitzio* repeats the legend by punishing an Indian woman for the sins of a white male, but also for her alleged betrayal of her own people.

The indigenista genre continued throughout the 1930s with commercially produced films such as *El indio* (The Indian, 1938), *La india bonita* (The Pretty Indian Girl, 1938), and *La noche de los Mayas* (The Night of the Mayas, 1939). The latter was promoted as a film about "the last remaining descendants of the race, secluded in an undefined region with invisible but closed boundaries," and was lauded by journalists for its "intelligent preoccupation with authenticity."[29] Like *Redes* and *Janitzio*, *La noche de los Mayas* reinforced stereotypical representations of racial and ethnic divisions that defined Mexico's social strata. These films were acclaimed by U.S. and European critics and several Mexican critics and helped to place Mexican cinema on the world map. Mexican leftist intellectuals and cinephiles praised the indigenista genre, arguing that such filmmaking would "elevate" the individual and group consciousness of the proletariat while contributing to the construction of a national cinema practice.[30] Like the Indians in the "national art" of Rivera and Siqueiros, the indigenista films portrayed Mexico's indigenous peoples as pure and simple, like children who had to be led to social (and revolutionary) consciousness by the intellectual elite.

The indigenista genre was not the only attempt to define Mexican cinema. Intellectuals and artists familiar with European experimental forms of cinema wanted Mexican films to proceed in that direction. These filmmakers drew on Mexican theatrical traditions and European avant-garde cinematic practices such as German expressionism and surrealism. In 1934, the Cinema Club of Mexico was founded by a group of filmmakers committed to educational and artistic filmmaking and to countering "the detestable spirit of Hollywood and its false and commercial motion picture industry."[31] A number of young Mexican directors had first been involved in alternative artistic and theatrical practices. Julio Bracho (1909–78), for example, who made twenty films over a period of thirty years, began his career in Mexican theater and was a founding member of a number of experimental theater groups including Escolares del Teatro (which was state supported) and Trabajadores del Teatro. Juan Bustillo Oro, who became one of the most respected film directors of the golden age, and Mauricio Magdaleno, a prolific screenwriter in the 1930s, 1940s, and 1950s, were the founders of the Teatro de Ahora, a leftist group committed to interrogating Mexico's social and political problems. Initially, these and other theater groups produced a few works by Mexican playwrights, but the majority were adaptations of the classics of Shakespeare, Sophocles, and Molière or of contemporary European or American works by writers such as Eugene O'Neill or George Bernard Shaw. By the early 1930s, however, this independent theater was primarily producing plays with Mexican historical or political themes by young Mexican writers.[32]

Another young director who came out of theater was Adela Sequeyro, who wrote and directed three films in the 1930s: *La mujer de nadie* (1937), *Más allá de la muerte* (Beyond Death, 1935), and *Diablillos del arrabal* (Little Devils of the Slums, 1937). Her films were inspired by French cinema, primarily the work of director Jean Renoir, one of the leading practitioners of a cinematic movement called "poetic realism," a fusion of documentary realism and poetic lyricism. *La mujer de nadie* tells the story of Ana María, who is banished from her home by her violent father and finds refuge with three young provincial artists, a painter, a poet, and a musician, who transform her into their inspirational muse. The film opened to rave critical reviews that heralded the film for its aesthetic and stylistic innovations. One journalist noted that the film was the first to challenge the Hollywood style of Mexican filmmaking, and another suggested that "its ancestry transcended what had been attempted so far."[33] Sequeyro's film, however, did not fare well at the box office. Dávalos Orozco observes that "the artistic value" of films such as *La mujer de nadie* "seemed to be in direct opposition to the needs of the film industry and the public" in the 1930s.[34] It was the commercial cinema, which made up a majority of films released during the first decade of sound, that was ultimately embraced by the public as their national cinema. Measured in terms of attendance and box office receipts, these were the films that emerged as "popular" in the 1930s. Although these films also drew on Mexican literature, theatrical traditions, and contemporary Mexican themes, the commercial films were patterned on Hollywood's cinematic strategies. Whether they were set in historical or contemporary contexts, these films exalted traditional values of patriarchy, the family, the macho hero, and virtuous, submissive femininity. This cinema exemplified conservative nationalism as outlined by de los Reyes. For example, *Madre querida* (Beloved Mother, 1935, Juan Orol) introduced the melodramatic genre exalting the Mexican mother who sacrificed all for her family. *La Adelita* (1937, Guillermo Hernández Gómez), a melodrama that took place during the revolution, looked back fondly on the prerevolutionary Porfirian regime, on the patriarchal hacienda, and on the centrality of the family and the Catholic Church in public and private life.

While many producers were politically conservative, they saw the development of the industry as an economic venture rather than an ideological one. Ultimately they were businessmen, and it was the box office success of these commercial films that ensured their continuity. Producers discovered very quickly that the most popular films drew on shared cultural histories and traditions. Familiar national stereotypical characters from popular theater and music such as the *macho*, the patriarchal father, the abnegating mother, and the prostitute with the heart of gold were deployed to tell contemporary stories. These traditional characters had a role in the renarrativization and representation of a "modern" Mexican national identity.[35] They were ready-made symbols, archetypes whose meanings were transformed to make sense of changing social and personal relations.

The first successful Mexican sound film, *Santa* (Saint, 1931, Antonio Moreno), explored the nation's insecurity about changing gendered social roles. Based on a nineteenth-century novel by Federico Gamboa, *Santa* narrates the story of a young country girl who is seduced by a soldier, ejected from her home by her angry brothers, and compelled to seek refuge and employment as a prostitute in a Mexican City *cabaretera* (dance hall). Santa's departure from

her agrarian village—deliberately portrayed as peaceful in this antiurban film—
paralleled the real-life journey of thousands of men and women from what was
in fact a more tumultuous countryside wracked by violence, hunger, and conflicts over land (see figures 1, 2, and 3).

*Santa* was one of the first films in the new genre of urban melodramas
that pictured workers struggling to support their families, neighborhoods
fraught with violence and petty crime, and a nightlife of cantinas and cabare-
teras. The film envisioned the city as an anonymous space where peasants and
workers crowded into hastily erected *arrabalas*, or neighborhoods. There were
no families: Santa lived in the cabaretera with the other "hostesses." Jarameño,
a famous bullfighter and Santa's lover, lived in a mansion with his servants.
Hipólito, a blind piano player who worked in the brothel, lived in a one-room
tenement with his young son.

Abandoned by Jarameño, Santa died from the effects of poverty, alcoholism,
and an unnamed venereal disease. Santa's downfall paints a critical picture of
postrevolutionary industrialization and urbanization that encouraged women
to exchange the safety of the rural home, family, and the church for the empty
promises of the modern city. The film affirmed the conservative discourse that
idealized tradition, championed religion, and criticized the modern paradigm
of progress.

In 1936 the wildly successful film by Fernando de Fuentes, *Allá en el Rancho
Grande*, placed Mexican cinema on the international map. It marked the second or "industrial" period of national filmmaking and the emergence of Mexican cinema in the global marketplace. It signaled a profound change in the
direction of the industry and in the cinematic representation of nationalism.
Its overwhelming success instituted the popular genre of comedia ranchera, a
kind of cowboy musical that incorporated elements of comedy, tragedy, popular music, and folkloric or nationalistic themes.

Its producers were aiming for two markets: the domestic and the international. Because the Mexican audience was still limited in numbers, economic survival depended on success in other Spanish-speaking countries and
in Spanish-language theaters in the United States. For those audiences, Mexican films had to acknowledge the historical perceptions about Mexico and confirm the expectations of an international market that understood Mexicans
through a set of recognizable customs, characters, music, and landscapes.

The comedia ranchera romanticized the political-cultural discourse of Hispanismo, a conservative ideology that defined Mexican identity and culture
in terms of a Catholic Spanish heritage. The "cult" of Hispanismo emerged

FIG. 1. The seduction of Santa. Photograph courtesy of Dirección General de Actividades Cinematográficas de la Universidad Nacional Autónoma de México.

FIG. 2. Santa in the *cabaretera*. Photograph courtesy of Dirección General de Actividades Cinematográficas de la Universidad Nacional Autónoma de México.

FIG. 3. Santa and Jarameño. Photograph courtesy of Dirección General de Actividades Cinematográficas de la Universidad Nacional Autónoma de México.

through an alliance of Catholic peasants and wealthy, conservative landowners in the central-western region of Mexico (principally Jalisco, Guanajuato, and Michoacán) that opposed official agrarian reform and anticlericalism. This alliance led armed resistance in the Cristero revolt (1926–29), a bloody guerrilla war that cost at least eighty thousand lives. *Allá en el Rancho Grande* invents and celebrates the prerevolutionary hacienda system and turns it into a utopian paradise.

The hero of de Fuentes's film was the singing *charro*, as exemplified by Tito Guízar and, later, by Jorge Negrete, the aspiring opera singer who became the first Mexican superstar when he premiered in the comedia ranchera *¡Ay, Jalisco, no te rajes!* The charro was a symbol of Hispanic masculinity—light-skinned, handsome, and respectful of the "inherent" divisions within Mexican society. He personified a specific kind of Mexican machismo. Although only a ranch hand on the hacienda, his role was to be what the cultural critic Gustavo García defines as the "mediator," the protector of the peons against the powerful hacendados.[36] At the same time, the charro's role was to maintain the patriarchal system that kept classes, races, and genders in their places. In *Allá en el Rancho Grande*, José Francisco (Tito Guízar) defends the reputation of his fiancée, Eulalia, from the attentions of his childhood friend Felipe, who has become the hacendado. Through various displays of virility, the two men eventually resolve their quarrel, José and Eulalia are reunited, everyone resumes his or her social and gendered place, and everything returns to normal. The hacendado tells his son that he is the "father, mother, judge, and, ultimately, the grave-digger of his workers."[37] Ironically, the hacendado could be interpreted as a metaphor for the consolidating postrevolutionary state, the charro hero, meta-phor for the many caciques or intermediaries who facilitated its functioning.

This singularly Mexican film genre glorified the machismo of the Mexican nation, drawing a link among the just hacendado, the charro, and the pater-nalistic state. At the same time, the comedia ranchera may be read as a thinly disguised challenge, in the form of a musical love story, to Cárdenas's social and economic reforms, his land redistribution, nationalization of private industry, and promotion of women's rights.

The mixed reception of this film in Mexico reveals the public debates about national identity that circulated in popular discourse. If audiences applauded the genre, journalists and intellectuals criticized it. Many writers and other intellectuals argued that films like *Allá en el Rancho Grande* confirmed what the world already knew about Mexico, that the nation was a "country of cow-boy dandies, peasant girls wearing colorful shawls, combs, and castanets." Filmmakers were accused of pandering to foreign impressions of Mexico by perpetuating existing stereotypes. A writer for the weekly journal *Todo* sum-marized what he believed to be an "irrefutable fact" for foreign audiences: in Mexico, it is only *el pueblo*, the lower strata of society, that have a "suffi-ciently vigorous personality" to express in artistic endeavors. The aristocracy and bourgeoisie, conversely, are "colorless."[38]

How could reactionary films like *Allá en el Rancho Grande*, *Bajo el cielo de México* (de Fuentes), *La Zandunga* (de Fuentes, starring Lupe Vélez), *Nobleza ranchera* (1938, Alfredo de Diestro), and *La tierra del mariachi* (Raúl de Anda) be released during the presidency of Cárdenas? According to the Mexican film historian Emilio García Riera, the industry was not at all concerned with these criticisms because Mexican producers "wanted no risks and sought maximum profits at minimal effort." For the industry, "innovation and intelligence [were] poison at the box-office."[39] The domestic and international success of *Allá en el Rancho Grande* convinced the industry that they had discovered the formula of a national Mexican cinema, and the government did not openly disagree. The film's cinematography (it was photographed by Gabriel Figueroa, who would go on to become the premier cinematographer in Mexico), its cast of characters, its acting style, its use of popular songs, its rural settings and cos-tumes, its director, and its stars set the standards for the immediate future of the Mexican film industry.

For a few years, the comedia ranchera was the most recognizable, and thus most exportable, Mexican film genre. García Riera, for example, argues that these films were popular because Mexican and Latin American audiences adored characters with "humble origins, big peasant-style skirts and hair bows, and virile workers as mates."[40] Perhaps audiences appreciated such representations of the hacienda films as "realistic." De los Reyes wonders if the public identified with the idealization of the characters in these films, who were all "good and knew how to dress and wear national costumes with dignity."[41] And finally, Carlos Monsiváis suggests that de Fuentes's film was popular because it "idealized everything." He writes that the genre proliferated because audiences were enchanted with "comedies and dramas that revolved around the idea of a paradise lost located in an indefinite time where men were strictly male and women definitely female."[42]

## Conclusion

Ultimately, Mexican cinema in the 1930s may be defined as a national cinema because its audiences perceived it as such. By incorporating competing discourses of national identity into a singular category of Mexicanidad, films addressed Mexican spectators as national subjects who found illustrations and explanations that resonated with their experiences, their newly formulated desires, and personal and public memories. The multiple discourses of a cinematic Mexicanidad—the conservative and the modern—fused into a set of characters and backdrops that populated the screen for more than twenty years.

The golden age of Mexican cinema flourished throughout the 1940s. The industry's growth was encouraged by governmental economic policies, by Latin America's continued demand for Mexico's Spanish-language films, by the technological and financial support of the U.S. government during World War II, and by the recognition by Mexican producers and directors that their prosperity depended on maintaining a loyal audience. This audience was, first and foremost, interested in being entertained by genres, stories, and stars they recognized as "Mexican." Through the performance and dramatization of Mexican history and contemporary life and the incorporation of regional and ethnic habits and practices, Mexican films proved to be one of the primary sites through which Mexican audiences worked through these public debates and ultimately came to recognize themselves as subjects of the nation. Through their participation as audiences, Mexicans made their voices heard at the box office and confirmed that this diverse cinema was, in essence, a national one. Until the end of the 1950s, Mexican national cinema thrived on its popularity in the theaters of Mexico City and small towns spread out across a vast territory that had, only recently, been made into a nation.

# Notes

1. Arjun Appadurai defines national subjects as "a community of sentiment . . . a group that begins to imagine and feel things together." Arjun Appadurai, *Modernity at Large: Cultural Dimensions of Globalization* (Minneapolis: University of Minnesota Press, 1996), 8.

2. Alan Knight, "Revolutionary Project, Recalcitrant People: Mexico, 1910–40," in *The Revolutionary Process in Mexico: Essays on Political and Social Change, 1880–1940*, ed. Jaime E. Rodríguez O. (Los Angeles: UCLA Latin American Center Publications, 1990), 230.

3. The nonfiction genre dominated early Mexican cinema. Out of more than 230 films produced in 1896 and 1906, approximately 200 of those were classified as *reportajes* or *documentales*. See Juan Felipe Leal, Eduardo Barraza, and Alenadra Jablonska, *Vistas que no se ven: Filmografía mexicana, 1896–1910* (Mexico City: Universidad Nacional Autónoma de México, 1993), 11.

4. Alexandra Pineda and Paulo Antonio Paranaguá, "Mexico and Its Cinema," in *Mexican Cinema*, ed. Paulo Antonio Paranaguá, trans. Ana López (London: British Film Institute, 1995), 15–18.

5. Aurelio de los Reyes, "The Silent Cinema," in Paranaguá, *Mexican Cinema*, 67.

6. Aurelio de los Reyes, *Medio siglo de cine mexicano (1896–1947)* (Mexico City: Editorial Trillas, 1987), 112.

7. The serial was reedited, sound was added, and *El automóvil gris* was rereleased in 1933.

8. De los Reyes, *Medio siglo*, 76.

9. Carlos Monsiváis, "Mythologies," in Paranaguá, *Mexican Cinema*, 117.

10. Ruth Vasey, *The World According to Hollywood, 1918–1939* (Madison: University of Wisconsin Press, 1997), 19.

11. Allen L. Woll, *The Latin Image in American Film* (Los Angeles: UCLA Latin American Center Publications, 1980), xxvii.

12. For a discussion of this incident, see Helen Delpar, "Goodbye to the Greaser: Mexico, the MPPDA, and Derogatory Films, 1922–1926," *Journal of Popular Film and Television*, spring 1984.

13. Jorge Schnitman, *Film Industries in Latin America: Dependency and Development* (Norwood, N.J.: Ablex, 1984), 16–17.

14. Federico Dávalos Orozco, "The Birth of the Film Industry and the Emergence of Sound," in *Mexico's Cinema: A Century of Film and Filmmakers*, ed. Joanne Hershfield and David R. Maciel (Wilmington, Del.: SR Books, 1999), 18.

15. Although Clasa was forced to declare bankruptcy after the production of its first film, *¡Vámanos con Pancho Villa!*, the studio was bailed out with government support.

16. Emilio García Riera, *El cine mexicano* (Mexico City: ERA, 1963), 25.

17. Pineda and Paranaguá, "Mexico and Its Cinema," 30.

18. De los Reyes, *Medio siglo*, 186.

19. Anne Rubenstein, *Bad Language, Naked Ladies, and Other Threats to the Nation: A Political History of Comic Books in Mexico* (Durham, N.C.: Duke University Press, 1998).

20. Eduardo de la Vega Alfaro, "Origins, Development and Crisis of the Sound Cinema (1929–64)," in Paranaguá, *Mexican Cinema*, 82; "El cine educativo," *Todo*, October 3, 1933.

21. Emilio García Riera, *Historia del cine mexicano* (Mexico City: SEP, 1985), 107.

22. Alan Knight, "Weapons and Arches in the Mexican Revolutionary Landscape," in *Everyday Forms of State Formation: Revolution and the Negotiation of Rule in Modern Mexico*, ed. Gilbert M. Joseph and Daniel Nugent (Durham, N.C.: Duke University Press, 1994), 59–60.

23. Herman G. Weinberg, quoted in David A. Cook, *A History of Narrative Film*, 2nd ed. (New York: W. W. Norton, 1990), 236.

24. De los Reyes, *Medio siglo*, 186.

25. Sergei Eisenstein, *Immoral Memories: An Autobiography*, trans. Herbert Marshall (Boston: Houghton Mifflin, 1983), 180. For an extended discussion of this film, see Joanne Hershfield, "Paradise Regained: Sergei Eisenstein's *¡Que viva México!* as Ethnography," in *Documenting the Documentary: Close Readings of Documentary Film and Videos*. Barry Keith Grant and Jeanette Sloniowski, editors (Detroit: Wayne Sate University Press, 1998), 55–69.

26. Charles Ramírez Berg, "Figueroa's Skies and Oblique Perspective: Notes on the Development of the Classical Mexican Style," *Spectator* 13, no. 1 (fall 1992): 31.

27. Joanne Hershfield, *Mexican Cinema/Mexican Woman, 1940–1950* (Tucson: University of Arizona Press, 1996), 55.

28. *Janitzio* would be revised in 1943 as *María Candelaria*, which starred the preeminent Mexican cinematic couple, Dolores del Río and Pedro Armendáriz, and was directed by "el indio" Fernández.

29. Carlos Pinedo, "¡Qué dura es la vida para los indios mayas!" *Todo*, August 24, 1939, 49.

30. Agustín Aragón Leiva, "Divulgación científica por la cinematografía," *El Nacional*, October 9, 1932, 3. Quoted in de los Reyes, *Medio siglo*, 187.

31. Rodolfo Usigli, *Mexico in the Theater*, trans. Wilder P. Scott (Jackson: University Press of Mississippi, 1976), 147–48.

32. Guillermo Schmidhuber, *El teatro mexicano en cierne, 1922–1938* (New York: Peter Lang, 1992), 103–4; and Marcela del Río Reyes, *Perfil y muestra del teatro de la Revolución Mexicana* (Mexico City: Fondo de Cultura Económica, 1997).

33. Quoted in de la Vega Alfaro, "Origins, Development and Crisis," 35.

34. Dávalos Orozco, "Birth of the Film Industry," 21.

35. For a discussion of the creation of national stereotypes between 1920 and 1940,

see Ricardo Pérez Montfort, "Indigenismo, hispanismo, y panamericanismo en la cultura popular mexicana de 1920 a 1940," in *Cultura e identidad nacional*, ed. Roberto Blancarte (Mexico City: Consejo Nacional para la Cultura y las Artes), 343–83.

36. Gustavo García, "Melodrama: The Passion Machine," in Paranaguá, *Mexican Cinema*, 156.

37. Quoted in de los Reyes, *Medio siglo*, 145.

38. *Todo*, January 9, 1934.

39. García Riera, "The Impact of *Rancho Grande*," in Paranaguá, *Mexican Cinema*, 130–31.

40. Ibid.

41. De los Reyes, *Medio siglo*, 152.

42. Monsiváis, "Mythologies," 118.

# IV

## Social
## Constructions
## of
## Nation

# An Idea of Mexico:
# Catholics in the Revolution

JEAN MEYER

In Mexico, the Catholic Church belongs to the culture of the people and shapes it. For many people, it is the guarantee of mental survival, of dignity, and of hope. It can be an element of ethnic as well as national identity and a form of patriotism. It can also inspire rebellion. In a world of suffering and misery, it is at once comfort for the afflicted and luxury for the poor. The church is collective property, and the religious fiesta is the embodiment of community.

Since the Enlightenment, our time has wanted to individualize and privatize religion, depriving it of its social dimension and roots. This project has been especially visible in politics and particularly in relations between the state and the church. Challenged by this new reality, the Catholic Church has fought a lengthy, defensive, rearguard, and apparently desperate action. Despite its political defeats, the church in Mexico has shown an amazing capacity to digest, change, and innovate because it has always conserved its popular base. This essay will explore the diversity of the Mexican Catholic Church and some of the ways that hierarchy and social base have responded to its challengers, namely, anticlericalism and revolutionary atheism.

## The Catholic Awakening and the First Mexican Revolution

From the presidency of Benito Juárez (1857–72) until 2000, all Mexican governments have been officially anticlerical and many overtly Jacobin. There has been one exception: that of Francisco I. Madero, who led the revolution against the dictator Porfirio Díaz. On May 24, 1911, Madero greeted the formation of the National Catholic Party with the following words:

> I consider the organization of the Partido Católico Nacional (National Catholic Party, or PCN) as the first fruit of the liberties we have conquered. Its program

reveals advanced ideas and the desire to collaborate in the progress of the Patria in a serious way and within the boundaries of the Constitution of 1857. Its modern ideas . . . are included in the program of the new government. . . . All political parties are welcome: they are the best guarantee of our liberties.[1]

Madero's attitude did not come from his being Catholic. He was a spiritualist who believed in the possibility of communicating with the dead. It came from his essentially democratic position and his development of a united political front, essential to his defeat of the old regime. Madero looked for and got Catholic support despite the fact that many Maderistas continued to view Catholics with Jacobin mistrust.

Vanguard Catholics—the poet Ramón López Velarde, the philosopher Antonio Caso, the historian Angel María Garibay, the writer Eduardo J. Correa, and so many others—were abreast of the advances of social Catholicism and the Catholic labor movement and press in Europe. These were inspired by Pope Leo XIII's 1891 encyclical *Rerum Novarum* addressing the living conditions of working people. Criticizing both the crude reality of "savage" capitalism and the new ideology of socialism, the encyclical proposed an alternative, third path: an economy based on small and medium-sized family properties. Social Catholicism developed first in the north of Catholic Europe (in Germany, Belgium, and the Netherlands), then in France, North America, and Latin America. In Mexico it grew after 1900 and accelerated after 1910 with the rise of the Catholic Party, a Catholic trade union movement, and Acción Católica. The latter sought to organize all sectors of society according to age (La Juventud Católica), gender (Damas Católicas), and occupation (unions) under the direction of bishops and priests.

The official newspaper of the Catholic Party, *La Nación*, represented the opinion of these illustrious men, who were Maderistas to the end. Certainly, the vanguard did not represent all Catholics. They were an advanced sector that would clash bitterly with the second revolution, that of the Constitutionalists—Carranza, Calles, and Cárdenas. Gabriel Zaid has written: "In 1911, the Catholic Party produced a surprise comparable to that of the coalition of Cuauhtémoc Cárdenas in 1988, and with similar problems that ended up destroying it."[2] The Catholic resurgence, long dreamed of and worked for by so many, did not perceive the problems inherent in its own success. It was enthusiastic about the historic opportunity of being openly Catholic in the public sphere and revindicating this right. Dozens of Catholic deputies, senators, and governors won elections during the Maderista presidency (1911–13). A renowned Catholic writer, José López Portillo, became governor of Jalisco. He wrote the "Guadalupana Hymn," which became the anthem of the Catholic movement:

> ¡Mexicanos, fly quickly
> in pursuit of the banner of the Virgin,
> and in the struggle you will be victorious
> defending the Patria and God!

During the governorship of López Portillo, Jalisco's PCN adopted three legislative measures representative of the Catholic platform. First, they voted on an electoral reform that would ensure the representation of minority parties through proportional representation. Second, they changed laws to ease government recognition of professional degrees granted by private (Catholic) institutions. Most importantly, they attempted to insure small property holdings, rural and urban, against the depredations of usurers and the vicissitudes of weather and economic crisis. They intended to tie this insurance to the development of credit cooperatives for small producers through which they could create their own safety net and free themselves from dependence on high-interest loans.[3]

Unfortunately, these proposals went by the board when General Victoriano Huerta ended the "Maderista spring" in the winter of 1913. He and his Porfirian military cronies assassinated the president and took power in a brutal coup. Those who led the rebellion against Huerta, the Constitutionalists, were anticlericals. They later defeated the peasant leaders Emiliano Zapata and Francisco Villa and renewed the old struggle between Catholics and liberals. Their constitution of 1917 limited the church's institutional role in society. Article 3 prohibited religious instruction in all schools; article 5 equated religious vows with slavery; article 13 denied legal status to religious organizations; article 27 nationalized all church property; and article 130 established the state's right to limit religious worship and delegated this responsibility to the local congresses.

Catholics against the Second Revolution:
The Civic Struggle (1918–26)

Catholic clergy and laity immediately protested these clauses. It is not my intention to recount the history of this movement from 1918 to 1938 but to capture the sense of its people. First I turn to a popular provincial leader, Anacleto González Flores. From Tepatitlán in the Altos de Jalisco, the heartland of militant Catholicism, González Flores was trained as a weaver of *rebozos* (women's shawls). He studied at the Catholic seminary in San Juan de los Lagos but was forced to repeat both his high school and legal studies in official schools in Guadalajara because the government would not recognize the seminary's degrees. More than a lawyer, he was a brilliant orator and polemicist; organizer and moral leader of Guadalajara's youth wing of Catholic Action, the Asociación Católica de la Juventud Mexicana, or ACJM; and founder of the powerful Unión Popular, modeled after similar groups in Germany and Belgium. The name itself, Unión Popular, came from the German Volksbund, after the group that opposed Bismarck's campaign to curb the power of the Catholic Church. Formed in 1925 to oppose the anticlerical policies of the Calles government, the UP organized through a network of trade unions, cooperatives, and parish organizations that had surged in west central Mexico—especially in Jalisco, Colima, part of Michoacán, Nayarit, Zacatecas, and Aguascalientes. Its strength explains why the Cristero rebellion later surged in this region.

In 1918, González Flores and Catholics of Jalisco confronted the rabidly anticlerical policies of the government of the Carrancista General Manuel M. Diéguez. Applying article 130 of the constitution in highly restrictive terms, the legislature voted to restrict the number of priests to one per every five thousand faithful and the number of churches to one per priest; all priests had to register with the government in order to preach. The city of Guadalajara threatened to expropriate 60 percent of the city's Catholic churches and turn them into schools and museums. At the same time, Diéguez's subordinates arrested the archbishop of Guadalajara and sent him into exile in the United States.

Against these measures, Guadalajaran Catholics organized a massive and sustained protest campaign, petitioning the government for repeal of its measures, closing their churches rather than complying with the law, and gathering in the streets and parks to pray and celebrate Mass. Wearing black as a sign of mourning, they boycotted public transportation, theater, movies, dances, and parties. They boycotted the pro-government daily newspapers and those who advertised in them. González Flores led young Catholic men and women in protest marches that ended in jail. Young women were generally released with a scolding, but the men ritually refused to post bond and served their sentences, using the time to organize prayer and study circles among the other inmates. Demanding repeal of the anti-Catholic legislation and the return of their spiritual leader, by 1919, they had won both.

More than any other Catholic leader, González Flores was able to articulate a broad, incisive, and sophisticated critique of the revolution and its leadership.

Following the confrontation with the Diéguez government, González Flores described the revolution as "essentially a destructive movement."[4] He held the Porfirian dictatorship responsible for the dissolution of public conscience that led to the revolution:

> The religious persecution stems from the enormous dose of secularism that the dictatorship injected into the body of the belittled Patria. It worked tenaciously to destroy in the intimacy of society the Evangelist's redemptive theses, through positivism in the institutes of higher education, through the press, through schoolteachers, and in public spectacles. A generation was formed that by instinct wanted to hear the famous Jacobin cry of the Italian Gambetta: "Clericalism: that is the enemy."[5]

At the end of the Obregón presidency, González Flores prepared the Catholics of western Mexico for passive resistance. He counseled civil disobedience and individual sacrifice. He systematically repudiated the use of violence. González Flores followed the example of Gandhi, who had transformed the Indian National Congress from a narrow, middle-class society into a mass organization. For his activism, Gandhi was jailed from 1922 to 1924. Once released, he launched a huge movement of nonviolent civil disobedience against English rule. González Flores cited Gandhi in his speeches and articles and adopted his tactics, organizing an effective boycott across Jalisco in 1926 through the UP organizational network:

> The difference between the crusades of yesterday and those of today is clear: the crusades of yesterday drove their spurs into the sides of the steeds of war and avenged the mutilation of their rights with the sword. The new crusades know that the triumph over tyranny does not come through violence, but through the word, the idea, organization and the sovereignty of opinion. They know that force begets force, blood begets blood, and despotism, despotism. People who need violence to recover their freedom are condemned to suffer the tyranny of many or the tyranny of one until a slow, disinterested, and enthusiastic labor succeeds in forging and molding the soul of the masses. Today when we are asked to use arms as weapons against tyranny, we respond with this word that is synonymous with victory: organization.[6]

The UP, like the National League of Religious Defense in Mexico City and elsewhere, was initially formed to fight against the schismatic church, an attempt launched by the federal government and the official trade union, the CROM, to found a Mexican Church in 1925 loyal to the revolution and opposed to Rome. Successful in this struggle, the UP turned to focus on the Ley Calles, a presidential decree introduced in summer 1926 that required priests to register with civil authorities. This law, which tightened article 130 of the constitution, was designed to force the subordination of the church to the state.[7]

Shortly before he was killed in April 1927, González Flores introduced the concept of the "plebiscite of the martyrs." He wrote: "To vote against Caesars, democracy needs to dress itself not in the white toga of the citizen of Athens or Rome, but in the martyr's bloodied vestments."[8] For González Flores, these two related concepts were the key to defeating tyranny. "Plebiscite" was the democracy of mass mobilization, cutting across lines of class, age, and gender. Jalisco's Catholic lay organizations successfully used mass pilgrimages, economic boycotts, public marches, and civil disobedience to force the state government not to apply article 130. Second, "martyrdom" was the logical extension of his teaching of individual sacrifice. Public protest could also provoke police violence, such as the July 22, 1918, gathering of tens of thousands in Guadalajara to protest article 130 and the archbishop's exile. In this case, mounted police rushed the large crowd, beating many and killing at least six.[9]

This was the context in which González Flores called for the martyr's plebiscite. It was also the personal decision he took in his own life, one that would end in his torture and execution. Driven by his obsession with martyrdom, González Flores openly challenged the civil authorities. He concluded with a prophecy:

> The Revolution is afraid. It has a demolishing grip over the living, but it cannot touch the dead. As in *Macbeth*, as the murders multiply, so do the ghosts and the terror. It is haunted by the procession of the dead. Our grandchildren will be present at the funeral of the Revolution in our Patria. The gravediggers will be Hernán Cortés and Bartolomé de Las Casas.[10]

A Catholic Hispanist notion of Mexican history underlay this vision and made heroes out of the Spanish conqueror, Hernán Cortés, and Bartolomé de Las Casas, the priest who insisted on the Indians' humanity and the need for crown and church to protect them from the abuses of the conquistadors.

The peaceful struggle of the Catholics could not sustain itself against the suspension of public worship and the closing of the churches in the summer of 1926. Spontaneous uprisings in the countryside and riots in the city convinced the young men of the National League of Religious Defense (the "Liga") and Catholic Youth Action (ACJM) that armed struggle would bring a quick victory. With their violence, they began to imitate the revolutionaries.

## Catholics against the Second Revolution:
## The Armed Struggle (1926–29 and 1932–38)

As the historian José C. Valadés has written, until 1926 the bishops had re-strained the rebellious impulses of their flock, fearing the mounting humilia-tions to which the church would be exposed if the Liga were unleashed.[11] Yet this attitude of Christian pacifism could not last forever, especially in the face of the new and increasingly fervent signs of government anticlericalism. The Ley Calles provoked the Catholic vanguard to take up the revolutionary violence they abhorred. The religious dimension of the conflict put them in contact with the people, rural and urban. From this encounter surged the great war of the Cristiada (1926–29), resuming in 1932 with what has been called "la Segunda" or the Second Cristiada.

The *cristeros*, rural guerrillas, did not have a sociopolitical program. They re-acted in legitimate defense of what they considered to be the aggression of "bad government." The Cristiada surprised everyone—people and institutions, the army, the government, the church, and even the insurgents who launched it. What stands out is the glaring contradiction between the slowness and stagna-tion of the political conflict between the church and the state and the sudden launching of the popular uprising, unforeseen, unscripted, unexpected, and unorganized.

When the state cornered the church in the summer of 1926, the church doubled the bet: it decided to suspend worship. The bells stopped ringing, chapels were emptied, the liturgy was suspended, and sacramental life went underground. The government responded to the suspension of public worship with a prohibition of private worship. The people found themselves cut off from the sacraments; they could neither marry, confess, nor take communion. They had to die without the last rites. As many Catholics said, "It is better to die fighting." "There is no evil that lasts more than a hundred years," and "he who spits at heaven gets it back in his face."

The armed movement was a rural, multiclass coalition that lacked only the rich and the *agraristas*, the recipients of land through government agrarian reform. It was impossible to suppose in such people a common or uniform economic motivation. Many historians think that campesinos logically have to support an agrarista government that provides them with land, although it is well known that agrarian reform is rarely made for and by campesinos. These historians explain Cristero campesino behavior as "deviant" owing to a lack of class consciousness or because of their petit bourgeois consciousness or their simple idiocy, fanaticism, and obscurantism. Yet one has to insist on the exceptional social participation of the Cristiada—exceptional because it did not respect such notions of class or barriers of age or gender, convenience or prudence.

Women joined minors, children, and old people in the war, and in a certain way had the greatest responsibility in it. They provoked the men, young and old. "If you are a man," they said, "you won't tolerate this humiliation. If you are a man, you cannot abide what they are doing to the Church, to the Virgin, to us, your mother, your wife, your sister, your sweetheart, who are defending the Church." Just as women had had a decisive role in the civic conflict, so they did in the armed struggle. For this, the Cristero Plan de los Altos de Jalisco issued on October 28, 1928, affirmed: "The Mexican woman . . . has been a powerful and decided agent in this struggle. She has the full right to continue vigorous and resolved in her redemptive activities in the hour or national reconstruction. . . . For this . . . it is just that women have the right to vote in elections." Having done the same reading of contemporary history and of Mexican women as pawns of priests, the revolutionary ruling class postponed women's right to vote for thirty years.

It would be difficult to find a moment like this in Mexican history, a moment so inclusive in character. Groups defined by their nonparticipation in a history that did not belong to them, that was made against them, groups that normally mobilized for strictly local reasons, joined this movement. The cristeros recruited from all these groups, all the rural classes, except the hacendados and the agraristas, who were seen by the Catholics as the state's hostage, client, and instrument. Such cross-class appeal revealed the seriousness of a crisis that moved all segments of rural society, but especially those in west central Mexico. Each segment obeyed different variables and had divergent interests according to indicators of race, *mestizaje*, population density, and modernization. But what was the common variable and, at the same time, the most spectacular contradiction posed by the government to the rural people? Religion, without a doubt.

The Cristero insurgents never thought about taking power or becoming the state. Poorly instructed in the history of Mexico as well as in the history of the church, they freely invented the present and allowed themselves the luxury of indiscretion. In their own way, they were nationalists and patriots. They manifested their faith in Mexico and in Christianity. The use of flags and banners, of symbols with figurative meaning, meant a great deal to these people. They were profoundly scandalized by the lack of national flags carried by the federal army. The agraristas' red banners seemed to them no more than "little butcher's pennants," because even today the red flag still marks the butcher's shop. They spoke indignantly of the betrayal of the army that abandoned the red, white, and green banner for the red one, the black one, the red and black flag, and other emblems that to the cristeros were blasphemous and even diabolic.

The cristeros themselves carried the oldest national standard, the flag of the independence struggle, red, white, and green, which had at its center an image of the Virgin of Guadalupe on one side and, on the other, the eagle perched on the cactus eating a serpent. The Virgin of Guadalupe blazed in the banners of Hidalgo and Morelos, the priests who had led the people's armies to liberate the nation from Spain. The cristeros especially saw in Morelos the defender of Mexico and religion against the heretic French who invaded Spain in 1808 with the intention of destroying the faith. A son of rural, southern Michoacán, Morelos was of mixed ethnicity: African, European, and Indian. A military genius, he led a guerrilla war against the Spanish Royalist army from 1811 until his execution in 1815. Servant of the Virgin of Guadalupe, he became an enduring symbol uniting popular democracy with Catholic nationalism. For the Cristeros who saw themselves as his heirs, the "Turk" Calles represented the foreign invader. As far as they were concerned, this enemy was bent on de-Catholicizing the country, completing their destructive adventure begun with the U.S. annexation of one-half of Mexican territory in 1848.

The cristeros had a vision of the world that led them to contest the state's attempt to root out so-called irrational resistances to modernity. Chinese Marxists described these resistances as "psychological vestiges"; Lenin dismissed them as "a child's illness" typical of peasants. The postrevolutionary state, being much more ideological than its classically liberal nineteenth-century predecessor, also entertained a much more ambitious project. It wanted to take up the old dreams of unification and dominion over the truth and turn them into a totalizing orthodoxy. It wanted to capture souls. This campaign marred the otherwise positive activity of the SEP.

The conflict between the state and the cristeros revealed the uprootedness that accompanied industrialism and urbanization. The urban intelligentsia and the workers, in good part, became "rational," a rationalism that functioned as a new secular religion. Even a well-educated priest could not hope to enter intellectual circles in those years. The attempt to establish a schismatic church, and the violent persecution of Catholics between 1926 and 1929, and 1932 and 1936, showed that this official "ideaocracy" could not be tolerant; it had to accelerate the decay of the faith and traditional culture. The ideology was the product of scientific knowledge, of rationality. Thus the government embraced socialist education, inspired by the Escuela Racionalista of the Spanish anarchist Francisco Ferrer Guardia.

In December 1933, the PNR reformed article 3 of the constitution to declare the "socialist," antireligious character of teaching. The minister of education at the time, Narciso Bassols, was a self-proclaimed Marxist who believed, like Lenin, that religion was the opiate of the masses. He recommended abandoning efforts to "enlighten" adult generations too profoundly diseased by the religious cancer. Instead, the state should attempt to instill in youth a "rational" vision of the world. In July 1934 from Guadalajara, the heart of Mexican Catholicism, President Calles issued his famous "Grito de Guadalajara." The revolution has not ended, he said. It was entering a "psychological" stage because its eternal enemies still threatened it.

> We cannot surrender the future of the Patria and the Revolution to the enemy. With what treachery the reactionaries and the clergy claim the children for the home and youth for the family. This is an egotistical doctrine, since children and youth belong to the community, the collectivity and the Revolution has the essential duty to attack this sector, appropriate consciences, destroy all those prejudices and form a new national soul.[12]

A series of violent attacks against the church and new reductions in the number of authorized priests followed. After Cárdenas's election, the reformed article 3 of the constitution was approved. Not content with excluding religious doctrine, it would combat "fanaticism" and "prejudices." Confused in the public mind with Bassols's earlier proposal to implement a mild form of sexual education, the reform of article 3 provoked uprisings in 1935, unleashing such hostility among campesinos and in the middle classes that the government had to retreat. In many parts of Mexico, this rationalist school was the source of many sterile struggles that destroyed the confidence of the people in public education for a long time.

In the battle for the school, the church acted with cold and determined resolve. "These señores," wrote the apostolic delegate to Mexico's archbishop in 1934, "want to distract and provoke: they would like to see us tear out our nails."[13] This time around, the church had the support of urban sectors, the universities, many agraristas, and finally American and world opinion through the Catholic and Protestant churches. But once again, as in 1926, the hierarchy was unable to control the fury of the flock in western Mexico. The renewal of the guerrilla war (an estimated 7,500 cristeros had taken up arms in 1935) and the terrorism against teachers persuaded the government to back down. In three years, Cristeros assassinated 100 teachers, lacerated 200 (often by cutting off their ears), and burned numerous schools to the ground.

When Cárdenas wrested political control from Jefe Máximo Calles in June 1935, a year after his election, he initiated a gradual anticlerical thaw. At the time, only 305 priests were authorized to preach in the entire country. Anxious to mend fences with the Cárdenas administration, the apostolic delegate exiled in the United States called for tranquillity. He condemned the Catholic rebels and called on all Mexicans to pray for religious liberty. His words were premature, because peace did not come until 1938. By this time, in west central Mexico, there had surged a mass political organization of Catholics, the Unión Nacional Sinarquista.

## A Vision of the Nation

Sinarquismo emerges at the end of our period as one of its fruits. It offers a global and coherent vision integrating elements of social Catholicism, intense nationalism, and international human rights. The Unión Nacional Sinarquista was founded in 1937 in León, Guanajuato, by the local section of La Base, a powerful, clandestine movement formed in 1934 by militant Catholics, Jesuits, and the church hierarchy to coordinate civil resistance to the antireligious politics of the government and the Mexican Left. La Base in turn came out of Las Legiones, a resistance movement organized in Guadalajara in 1931 to struggle for a Christian social order that would be anticommunist, antirevolutionary, and nationalist. In the 1930s it operated in west central Mexico through clandestine cells. In contrast to the underground nature of Las Legiones and La Base, Sinarquismo was an open social movement, pressing for civic and religious liberty. Like them, it was strong in the states of Guanajuato, Michoacán, Jalisco, Querétaro, Aguascalientes, and Zacatecas. Here it became a mass, multiclass movement engaging campesinos, workers, artisans, small merchants, teachers, and lawyers. On the eve of the Mexican elections in 1940, Sinarquismo claimed 100,000 militants.[14]

The name "Sinarquista" was forged on the model of "sindicato" or union (*syn dike*) from the Greek (*syn arke*), meaning "with authority, with power, with order." Theirs was an ideology of obedience and conquest, a mystique of leadership and hierarchy, an exaltation of nationalism, a condemnation of the Bolshevik revolution, the Masons, the Protestants, and capitalism. These elements all suggest a fascism that meshed with extreme nationalism in a utopian program of justice for all social classes. The Catholic component of the movement advocated a corporativism opposed to class struggle. It dreamed of a state that would regulate conflicts while protecting the nation, the church, and society.

This movement that refused to become a political party struggled to restore an ancient order destroyed by antipatriotic Mexicans, governments, and foreigners. Flags and banners marked the organization, which called for sacrifice and exalted nonviolence, poverty, and asceticism. It proposed to "save" Mexico. Nationalism was an essential element in its ideology: the cult of its uniformed soldiers, of the flag, of religion, of the imperial and Hispanic past, of the militants who had fallen in defense of the *patria*. It professed hatred for the United States and evoked the time when the land from Florida to Oregon was Spanish. It sought to defend Mexicans subjugated in the United States. The "Sixteen Basic Points of Sinarquismo" began with an exaltation of the patria, culminating in the affirmation that "Mexico reclaims, for its own salvation, the permanent union of all its sons and only establishes one division: Mexicans and anti-Mexicans." Dogmatically anti-Marxist, Sinarquismo also decried unbridled capitalism and claimed to offer, through the social doctrine of the church, a "third way," a "new attitude toward Mexico."[15]

For Sinarquistas, Catholicism had to be "integral." Religion had to penetrate every aspect of life. The social reign of Christ had to be installed. Corresponding to the neo-Thomism of theologians, the movement foresaw a return to the Middle Ages and embraced its social organization and notion of "the common good." This search for a third way between liberalism and socialism constituted all the ambiguity of these ideologies, from which Sinarquismo could not free itself. It was at once a movement, a quasi party, and a vast "Christian social order" that resembled the Carlist populism of social Catholic legitimists in early-nineteenth-century Spain, and at the same time found itself, by force of circumstances, in the ideological camp of contemporary fascism, particularly that of the Iberian Peninsula. Sinarquismo could be defined as a Catholic lay movement, corresponding to a Catholic revival that drew on other movements. However, its character was essentially Mexican.

The Sinarquistas gained the sympathies of North American Catholics. The Catholic sector favorable to the European strongmen Mussolini in Italy, Salazar in Portugal, and Franco in Spain defended the UNS, as did the Jesuits and the National Catholic Welfare Conference. The majority of North American Catholics were conservative and looked favorably on the Sinarquista social program in line with the encyclicals *Rerum Novarum* (1891) and *Quadra-*

*gesimo Anno* (1931). The religious fervor of this mass movement, of enthusiastic youth and disinterested leaders, their preoccupation with the poor and for-gotten masses, made the North American Catholics compare it with Catholic Action. It alarmed them much less than had the cristeros, those incomprehen-sible impoverished pilgrims of a holy war totally alien to the North American mentality.

The UNS rejected violence and helped to disarm the last cristeros. It struggled against article 3 and for the reopening of churches through boy-cotts, school strikes, petitions, mass demonstrations, and the organization of schools with women teachers who had been fired or demoted. Agitation and propaganda were part of its nonviolent direct action. This nonviolence, in-fused with millenarian elements, did not mean passive conduct: it internalized and channeled aggression in ways that impressed observers. A political pariah, the UNS identified with Mexico, a pariah nation that had to liberate itself from the United States. All the strategies of civil resistance (going to jail, not pay-ing fines, etc.) were rooted in the ethic of the pariah. The ethic went hand in hand with a reverence of power. Its political style combined firmness and respect.

Somewhat like Italian fascism, the UNS brought together both conservative elite and popular forces. They spoke two languages and belonged to two dif-ferent political universes. Until 1944, paternalistic and authoritarian leaders of the old style linked to La Base coexisted with young chiefs of a modern move-ment who violently attacked liberalism and democracy, as well as the unjust economic order. The difference between the conservatives and the rebels was social. The conservatives belonged to the old oligarchy, and the new leader-ship to the middle classes. A generation also divided them. The young, angry leaders violently attacked the historic Left (the Cardenistas) and their class war, but not their social objectives. They even recruited from sectors claimed by the Left: students, industrial workers, poor campesinos, and Indians. This version of Sinarquismo was born in the halls of the universities (young jurists of Gua-najuato) and was initially propagated by nationalist youth who found nothing in the litanies of an overly conformist Left. It then spread through the historic heart of the Mexican nation, in the agrarian Bajío with its great densities of people, and then to indigenous communities and workers crushed by misery. This populist movement appeared to be the carrier of radical revindications. It was feared by some of its own leaders and taken into consideration by the government, especially as official nationalism became more vehemently linked to anticommunism after 1940. The UNS in its greater statistical dimension was agrarian, but it functioned as well as a "revolution" of the middle classes, as a reappearance of what the revolution had repressed or mismanaged.

## Cultural Revolutions

The Catholic world is made up of the ecclesiastical institution in its Roman and Mexican dimensions, the faithful, numerous lay organizations, diverse social classes, regional modalities, different age groups, and both sexes. I cannot give a voice to all these groups. Perhaps a solution to the problem is to present Father Federico González (1889–1969), whom you have met in Mary Kay Vaughan's chapter earlier in this book. I knew him personally during the last five years of his life. This lucid, intelligent man had the advantage of covering much social and mental space: as the provincial son of a ranchero of Michoacán, he had his feet firmly on the ground, in his native land of San José de Gracia. As a priest, seminary professor, and parish vicar, he belonged to the Catholic Church and had national and international contacts. As a priest, ranchero, and leader of his pueblo, he related to the local and national state, including the president of the republic. He lived all the revolutionary stages from Maderismo to Cardenismo. He organized a successful agrarian reform in San José in 1924. Despite his horror of violence, after long reflection and theological consultation, he decided that it was necessary to participate in the Cristiada. Later, he led the process of reconciling with the state presided over by General Cárdenas. On a visit to San José in 1940, Cárdenas praised Padre Federico "for his elevated character, his understanding of the social problems of the country and for his dedication to improving the lives of the people of San José." In the thirty years that followed, Padre Federico dedicated himself to fomenting agriculture and education and to what his nephew Luis González called "agrarismo parvifundista," or cooperative forms of work between small private landowners. He lived his life justifying an observation the fervent liberal Lorenzo de Zavala had made a century before: "It is noteworthy how the Mexican clergy in general has embraced the interests of the people as their own."[16]

## Conclusion

The Mexican Revolution was, in the words of Luis González, "thirty years of penitence." At least in the countryside, those who lived it did not much appreciate the "fiesta of bullets." After a few years of breathing space between 1920 and 1925 came the terrible period of religious conflict, the Cristiada, the

Segunda, and socialist education. At last came the agrarian reform, hoped for and feared.

In no previous period had there been so many changes: the hacienda disappeared, leaving the countryside with the *ejido* and the tiny family farm (the *minifundio*). At the same time, modernization accelerated, bringing the highway, electricity, the telephone, cars, the radio, and the *molino de nixtamal*. It was the end of one world and the beginning of another. The cultural revolution (better said in the plural) undertaken by successive governments and contested by Catholics completed the change. In the eye of the storm, their violent passions and sentiments in full play, peoples, regions, social classes, and genders formed a nation. Ironically, as Mexico became more nationalist, it may also have become more Catholic. Today no one challenges the idea that Catholicism is still an essential element of national identity. Even Mexicans who claim not to be Catholic will often assert that they are "Guadalupanos."

In July 2000, the official party of the revolution was finally voted out of power by a Catholic party of the center right, the PAN (National Action Party). On inauguration day, newly elected president Vicente Fox broke with precedent and went to the Basílica of the Virgin of Guadalupe to pray.[17] In July 2002, Pope John Paul II canonized the Indian Juan Diego, to whom the Virgin had appeared in 1531. Millions of Mexicans at long last felt vindicated.

## Notes

The author and editors would like to thank Robert Curley for his assistance with this chapter. It has been translated from Spanish by the editors.

1. Jean Meyer, *La Cristiada*, vol. 2 (1973; Mexico City: Siglo XXI Editores, 2000), 60.

2. Gabriel Zaid, *Obras de Gabriel Zaid II: Muerte y resurrección de la cultura católica* (Mexico City: Colegio Nacional, 1993), 328–29.

3. Meyer, *La Cristiada*, vol. 2, 61.

4. Demetrio Loza, *Anacleto González Flores, el Maestro* (Guadalajara: Editorial Xalisco, 1937), 82.

5. Ibid., 83–84.

6. Ibid., 86.

7. Meyer, *La Cristiada*, vol. 2, 243; J. M. Puig Casauranc, *La cuestión religiosa en relación con la educación pública en México* (Mexico City: Talleres Gráficos de la Nación, 1928), 11–12.

8. Loza, *Anacleto González Flores*, 149.

9. Biblioteca Nacional, Fondo Palomar y Vizcarra, 41/297/3206-3207, Álvarez Tostado to Palomar y Vizcarra, July 22–23, 1918; Robert Curley, "Slouching towards Beth-

lehem: Catholics and the Political Sphere in Revolutionary Mexico" (Ph.D. diss., University of Chicago, 2001), 271–72.

10. Loza, *Anacleto González Flores*, 150.

11. José C. Valadés, *La revolución mexicana*, vol. 8 (Cuernavaca: Editorial Quesada, 1967), 16.

12. *El Nacional*, July 21, 1934.

13. Jean Meyer, *La Cristiada*, vol. 1, 362.

14. Jean Meyer, *El Sinarquismo ¿un fascismo mexicano?* (Mexico City: Mortiz, 1979), 46. In October 1943 there were 310,000 registered Sinarquistas. On Sinarquismo, see also Rubén Aguilar V. and Guillermo Zermeño P., eds., *Religión, política y sociedad: el Sinarquismo y la Iglesia en México: nuevos ensayos* (Mexico City: Universidad Iberoamericana, 1993); and Pablo Serrano Álvarez, *La batalla del espíritu: el movimiento sinarquista en el Bajío, 1932–1952* (Mexico City: Consejo Nacional para la Cultura y las Artes, 1992).

15. Ibid., 113–29.

16. Lorenzo de Zavala, *Ensayo histórico de las revoluciones de México*, vol. 1 (1831; Mexico City: MN de la Vega, 1845), 276.

17. "Oró el guanajuatense ante la imagen de la tilma de Juan Diego," *La Jornada*, December 2, 2000.

# Guadalajaran Women and the
# Construction of National Identity

MARÍA TERESA FERNÁNDEZ ACEVES

The Catholic loyalties of Guadalajara have been well noted by historians and revolutionary *caudillos* alike. The rabid anticlerical president (1924–28) and Jefe Máximo (1928–35) Plutarco Elías Calles called the city the "henhouse," a slur against both women and Catholics.[1] What is less discussed is Guadalajara's liberal, secular tradition. This essay on women's civic cultures in Mexico's second city shows the radicalization of both the Catholic and liberal traditions through the revolution. This is the story of Guadalupe Martínez, daughter of a liberal working-class family who became a schoolteacher and a leader of the radical Círculo Feminista de Occidente in the 1920s and 1930s. She went on to head the female section of the state branch of the Confederación de Trabajadores de Mexico (CTM, or Confederation of Mexican Workers) and the Partido Revolucionario Institucional (PRI, or Institutional Revolutionary Party), the official workers' organization and party of the postrevolutionary state. It is also the story of Julia Fernández, daughter of an upper-class family that lost much of its wealth in the revolution. A Catholic activist in defense of religious liberty, in the late 1930s Fernández founded a Catholic girls' school, the Colegio Aquiles Serdán.

These oral histories are more than isolated reconstructions of individual experiences. Rather, their narratives, combined with other primary and secondary sources, open a window onto the multiple and complex political, social, religious, and gender relationships and identities in flux throughout the revolutionary period. These women introduce us to Guadalajara's working-class and Catholic cultural symbols, meanings, and practices. Their lives detail how women played a central role in the construction of national identity and corroborate Mary Kay Vaughan's thesis that "the real cultural revolution of the 1930s lay not in the state's project but in the dialogue between the state and society that took place around that project."[2] These two women's stories speak of what inspired them to create and appropriate representations of national culture as they participated in the regional incorporation of three neglected groups—workers, women, and Catholics—into the national narrative. Although these women were leaders, they did what many women did in this tumultuous and creative period. In rhetoric and in practice, they went beyond the gendered discourses of the revolution and the church, both of which restricted women to the private sphere and perceived them exclusively as mothers and moralizers of society. Martínez's and Fernández's challenges to official discourses brought female rhetoric and practice into the public sphere even in the absence of women's full rights as voting citizens. This chapter discusses their construction and expression of patriotism and national identity and tells the story of a divided city that, despite the conflicts of revolutionary upheaval and postrevolutionary state building, became integrated into the modern Mexican nation.

Neither the state of Jalisco nor its capital, Guadalajara, experienced homegrown revolutionary movements such as the Zapatista agrarian revolt in central Mexico, Pancho Villa's popular mobilization in Chihuahua, or the more middle-class Constitutionalist rebellion of Venustiano Carranza, Álvaro Obregón, and Calles in northern Mexico. Rather, Jalisco remained relatively calm, and in 1912 the National Catholic Party, backed by an emerging Catholic social movement, won the state governorship.[3] In mid-1914, the Constitutionalist general Manuel M. Diéguez entered the state with his army. Making himself governor, Diéguez imposed a series of anticlerical restrictions to punish the "reactionary Catholic party" for its recognition of General Victoriano Huerta's military coup against Francisco I. Madero in 1913 and to implement the constitution of 1917. Diéguez introduced important social reforms in church, labor, and educational matters. He sent bishops and foreign priests into exile, closed Catholic newspapers, repressed lay religious organizations, and forced them to go underground. He also confiscated properties of the clergy and upper class. To build a regional mass base for the Constitutionalist cause, he promised to improve the conditions of urban and rural workers and encouraged them to organize and strike. In the educational realm, Diéguez created the basis for a completely secular public school system and closed Catholic institutions of learning.[4]

As Jean Meyer's essay in this volume indicates, Catholics responded to Diéguez in powerful and effective multiclass, multiorganizational forms. However, a secular movement involving workers and schoolteachers also emerged in the city of Guadalajara. Nurtured in nineteenth-century anticlerical liberalism and radicalized through the introduction of anarchist ideas and the revolutionary process, this movement opposed the Catholic mobilization on the grounds that it was illegal in its objection to clauses of the Mexican Constitution of 1917 and backward in its social program and ideology. The radicals also denounced it for supporting class hierarchies and identifying with capitalist owners of industry and land. They welcomed the new social rights promised to workers in article 123 of the constitution and looked to postrevolutionary governments to implement those rights. In the early 1920s, Catholic and secular organizations competed vigorously in the city for public space, recognition, and political rights. Under anticlerical governors José Guadalupe Zuno Hernández (1924–26) and Margarito Ramírez (1927–29), secular organizations of workers, campesinos, and women gained political strength and numbers, while the Catholic civic movement was weakened by repression, the Cristiada (1926–29), and the accords signed between the church hierarchy and the national government in 1929.

Nonetheless, persistent government anticlerical measures in the 1930s moved Catholics to develop new forms of organization and resistance. In response to the reform of constitutional article 3 and the introduction of socialist education in 1934, *cristero* general Lauro Rocha announced the renewal of the Cristero war. Violence erupted in much of Jalisco's countryside. Education officials initiated massive firings of public schoolteachers who were known to be proactively Catholic or refused to accept the reform.[5] A major battle involving students, professors, and popular organizations ensued over control of the university and resulted in the creation of a conservative university separate from the state institution. In response to widespread Catholic hostility, the Cárdenas government curbed its Jacobinism, and by the end of the 1930s, church and state had negotiated a coexistence that implied the subordination of popular organizations to both hierarchies.

Recent historiography has shown that women were intimately involved as Catholics and seculars in civic struggle and mass organization in Guadalajara.[6] In their campaigns for the rights of women, workers, and Catholics, they shaped processes of state building. Women like Guadalupe Martínez and Julia Fernández learned to negotiate skillfully within the respective hierarchies of state and church that eventually subordinated them. As their stories show, women also contributed significantly to nation building, creatively appropriating and shaping symbols, memories, and narratives of national identity that they in turn inculcated in Mexican youth.

### Guadalupe Martínez (1906–2002)

Guadalupe Martínez's father, David Martínez, came from the textile town of Juanacatlán, Jalisco. He was an electrical worker and painter. Her mother, María Villanueva, grew up and worked in the textile factory town of La Escoba in the municipality of Zapopan, Jalisco. The Martínez Villanueva family had five children, all of whom eventually became schoolteachers. Guadalupe, the oldest, was born in Guadalajara in 1906.

David Martínez was a liberal. He deeply admired the heroes who had liberated Mexico from Spain between 1810 and 1821 and Benito Juárez, the liberal president (1858–72) who had defended the *patria* against the French invaders and their reactionary Catholic allies while upholding the constitution of 1857 and its principles of secular education and separation of church and state. In 1910, Martínez was a member of Guadalajara's anti-reelectionist circle organized by the tailor Enrique Calleros in support of Francisco I. Madero's electoral challenge to the dictator Porfirio Díaz.[7] Martínez turned his principles into living and plastic paintings (*tableaux vivants*) illustrating "La Patria y el Pueblo" (The Patria and the Masses), Benito Juárez, and the principles of liberalism. The Martínez children were active participants in these creations. In the presentation of "La Patria y el Pueblo," Guadalupe posed as the patria and her brother David represented the pueblo. In the background a sign read "Sufragio Efectivo, No Re-elección" (Effective Suffrage, No Reelection), the slogan of the Maderista revolutionary movement.[8] In another live tableau that became a painting, Guadalupe personified the law, and her sister Isabel, justice. Dolores appeared as an angel crowning Benito Juárez. As Juárez, her sister Belén unfurled the constitution.[9] In this way, the Martínez Villanueva children learned their liberal values.

Guadalupe Martínez attended grammar school at the Escuela Superior No. 6 "Doña Josefa Ortiz de Domínguez," named for the only recognized female conspirator in the Mexican wars of independence. At the same time, she attended the "iconoclast school" run by the radical liberal teachers Laura Apodaca and Carmen and Trinidad Hernández, precursors of the Guadalajaran feminist movement and committed anticlerics.[10] The school formed part of the activities of the Guadalajara branch of the Casa del Obrero Mundial (House of the World Worker), an organization of artisans and skilled workers that sought to "liberate" children from religious beliefs while promoting worker unionization, rights, and support for the Mexican Revolution.[11] The Casa preached solidarity with workers of the world and advocated an anarchist overthrow of the capitalist order and what the workers saw as its principal arm of support, the Catholic Church. These ideals were brought to the interior of the Martínez family when the father, a member of the Casa, asked his children and wife to stop going to Mass because the Catholic Church was not helping the Guadalajaran working class. David Martínez wanted his children to become the future teachers and organic intellectuals of the working class, liberating them from exploitation and religious enslavement. He sought an active, revolutionary role for both his female and male children in the public sphere.

The new revolutionary state, however, envisioned a more passive role for women. For the state, women were mothers who belonged mainly in the private sphere and entered the public sphere only to campaign for education, health, morality, temperance, and the protection of children. The state aspired to transform traditional gender roles through civil and labor reforms that gave more rights to women in the household and the workplace, but without upsetting patriarchy.[12] These reforms sought to control women in both private and public spheres in the interests of national development.

However, revolutionary upheaval, the conflict between church and state, and the process of postrevolutionary state formation politicized secular-minded women and led many to new roles in the state bureaucracy and labor movement, where they attempted to shape social policy related to women, children, education, and labor. The female secular discourse argued that women were not only in the service of others; rather, they should also be granted roles as citizens, professionals, and workers. For secular-minded women, the public sphere could not be an exclusively male domain but required the inclusion of female voices in the creation of a new patria. Guadalupe Martínez was one of these agitating women.

In 1927, Guadalupe Martínez graduated from Normal School and became director of the Escuela Primaria Urbana No. 47 (Urban Grammar School Number 47). Sometime before, she had met María Díaz, the militant textile worker organizer and her mother's relative, who schooled her in the ongoing activities and principles of the secular trade union movement. In 1927, Díaz and Martínez helped to form the Círculo Feminista de Occidente.[13] The organization brought together middle-class (primarily teachers) and working-class women to push for women's education and political and social rights, particularly for working women. State governors Zuno and Ramírez supported this organization in their efforts to build a popular, secular movement. No doubt their interest in the Círculo stemmed from their interest in countering the potent Catholic oppositional movement, in which women so actively participated. In these years, Díaz and Martínez worked with seamstresses, domestic servants, women shoemakers, and food-processing workers to form unions. The Círculo Feminista was particularly effective in organizing strong, radical female tortilla worker unions.[14]

In the 1930s, Martínez struggled for women's rights within the emerging official party of the revolution, the PNR, and in the Confederación Obrera de Jalisco (COJ, or Confederation of Jaliscan Workers), which in 1936 became the Federación de Trabajadores de Jalisco (FTJ, or Federation of Jaliscan Workers), the local branch of the state-supported Confederación de Trabajadores de Mexico (CTM). In 1934, she participated in the Third Congress of Women Peasants and Workers, where she spoke in favor of socialist education, a position she firmly upheld as a schoolteacher and political activist in the bitter battles sparked by this reform in Guadalajara. Together with María Díaz, Irene Robledo, and Concha Robledo, she created the female section of the PNR in Jalisco and shaped its militant platform in favor of women's civil, political, and social rights.[15] She became the general secretary of the Frente Único Pro Derechos de la Mujer, which pressured Cárdenas to grant women the right to vote. She was an active member of the Federación de Grupos Culturales (Federation of Cultural Groups) of the COJ and founder of the first evening secondary school for workers, an important initiative opening postelementary education to workers.

In 1940, she became secretary of the Jaliscan women's section of the PNR. In 1949, she married Heliodoro Hernández Loza, head of the Jalisco trade union movement, the FTJ, affiliate of the national CTM. Although in the 1920s and 1930s Martínez and Hernández were pioneering radicals organizing labor and political movements, after 1940 their behavior became more conservative and subordinate to the hierarchical interests and modes of the state, official party, and labor movement. Like the official hierarchies to which they belonged, Guadalupe Martínez's husband was patriarchal. He asked her to stop teaching school. Martínez recalled: "I could not even teach my Universal Geography and Calligraphy classes at the Normal."[16] However, Hernández let her continue her political work in the Círculo Feminista, the CTM, and the PRI. While her rhetoric adapted to the moderate and institutional discourse of the official trade union movement, she also learned how to use traditional gender roles and hierarchical networks to gain space and attention for women. In 1953, she participated in the founding of the Comité Pro Derechos de la Mujer and fought for women's right to vote, which was granted in that year by the Ruiz Cortines government.[17] She tried to organize female home workers in the textile industry's putting-out system, a particularly vulnerable workforce that emerged after 1940 as employers tried to evade labor laws. She served as a deputy in the state and federal congress on three occasions and as a substitute federal senator between 1958 and 1977.

### Guadalupe Martínez and the Construction of National Identity: The Route of the Insurgency (1954–98)

Guadalupe Martínez's civic field trip, "La Ruta de la Insurgencia," was a sort of mobile version of her father's patriotic live tableau. The idea for it occurred to her and Heliodoro Hernández when, during an International Labor Organization meeting in Geneva, Switzerland, they saw tours of French and Italian schoolchildren selected to travel because of their school achievements. Martínez and Hernández resolved to do the same for workers' children in Mexico, with the purpose of teaching them about their country's history and the role of workers in it.[18] Beginning in 1954, they sponsored the annual Ruta de la Insurgencia for children of members of the Sindicato Único de Trabajadores Automovilistas de Jalisco, the union Hernández founded in the 1920s.[19] Forty children from the third to the sixth grade participated in the monthlong trip. Selected for academic performance and responsible behavior, the children practiced principles of duty and discipline, hygiene, teamwork, mutual service, and collaboration in the course of the trip. A teacher and nurse accompanied them.[20] Viewed by Martínez and Hernández as a "civilizing" device, the trips were also intended to promote the children's interest in higher education and professional careers. They took pride, for instance, in Gilberto Acosta, who as a child took the trip and as an adult became an attorney and federal deputy "serving the working class."[21]

The trips' primary purpose was patriotic: children learned about Mexico's history, heroes, and natural beauty by visiting physical sites. As they visited them, they sang the songs and recited the poetry and oratory that inscribed their importance and meaning in individual memory. Children visited the states of Jalisco, Guanajuato, Querétaro, Hidalgo, México, Puebla, Oaxaca, Morelos, Guerrero, and Michoacán. Although the trip was called the Route of the Insurgency with reference to the independence struggle in 1810, over time it included sites of pre-Hispanic civilization, those where liberal soldiers defended the nation against foreign invaders, and those commemorating working-class leaders of the revolution. What was especially important about these trips and distinguished them from patriotic celebrations in public schools was the way in which they celebrated working-class struggle and integrated it into the official national narrative.

Trips through Jalisco and to Puebla became moving, speaking, and musical stories of national memory and identity. In Jalisco, children sang "Allá en el Rancho Grande," typical of the popular ranchero culture of western Mexico. They honored the priest Miguel Hidalgo, "Father of the Patria," whose insurgent armies marched from Guanajuato to Guadalajara in 1810. They visited the bridge of Zapotlanejo, where the Indian rebel Juan Terríquez killed the Spanish count of la Cadena in the struggle against Spain. The children visited the town of Tepatitlán, the birthplace of Heliodoro Hernández, and learned his life story as a lesson in modern values and moral aspirations. They were told he was born on a small ranch and studied at the local grammar school. As an adolescent, he migrated to the United States, where he worked at different jobs and learned to drive. Returning to La Barca, Jalisco, he taught people how to drive tractors and, in Guadalajara, became a bus driver and organizer of the first drivers' union. Here, the narrative went, he became committed to sacrificing himself to help other people. At the end of Hernández's story, teachers asked the children: "What can be learned from this man who gives everything without expecting anything in return?" "Through Heliodoro Hernández," the teachers told the students, "we see the sunshine that sheds light on the difficult path that workers must constantly travel."[22] Thus was this local labor leader elevated to the status of patriot hero, fighter for and creator of the nation—not to mention that of revered cacique.

In Puebla, students sang the popular song "Qué chula es Puebla" (Puebla Is Beautiful). They visited the cathedral, symbol of the aesthetic achievements of the Spanish colony. They explored the forts of Loreto and Martínez, where Mexican soldiers valiantly triumphed over the French invaders at the battle of the Fifth of May in 1862. They paid homage to the tomb of General Zaragoza, who led the heroic defense. They went to the house of Aquiles Serdán, shoemaker and leader of a revolutionary conspiracy of workers and schoolteachers to overthrow the dictator Porfirio Díaz in 1910. They honored this martyr shot by Díaz's henchmen. They visited the tomb of Evangelina Osorio, a female teacher who started a school attended by Fernando Amilpa, an important founder and leader of the regional and national trade union movement. The students also met the leaders of the Puebla workers' organization, the mayor of the city of Puebla, and the governor.

This civic field trip was the lasting legacy of a woman who devoted her professional career to furthering an agenda of what became official working-class revolutionary nationalism. Ironically, though Martínez was a lifelong advocate of women's interests and rights, the civic field trip served the children of an all-male union.

## Julia Fernández (1912–97)

Like Guadalupe Martínez, Julia Fernández was a schoolteacher. Unlike Martínez, Fernández was strongly identified with the Catholic movement of resistance against the antireligious policies of the postrevolutionary governments. Although she was too young to have participated in the demonstrations of Catholic women's organizations in their struggle for political and social rights against the Diéguez government and those of the 1920s, she shared their sentiments. As the founder of an important Catholic girls' school, she learned to negotiate with both the church hierarchy and the postrevolutionary state in such a way as to preserve the integrity of Catholic education and to open new social space for Catholic women. In the process, she, her fellow teachers, and their students created a distinct notion of patriotic history and national identity.

Julia Fernández was born in 1912 in Hostotipaquillo, Jalisco, to a well-to-do family.[23] Her father, Juan Fernández Leal, was a businessman who owned a hotel, a bakery, and two stores. Her mother, María del Pilar Ruiz Acosta, was a housewife. Fernández was the oldest of twelve children. Revolutionary violence forced the family to flee to Guadalajara in 1913. In this move, they lost both wealth and status. Although they bought a house in the middle-class neighborhood of Jesús and employed servants, they were beset with economic problems.

Fernández attended the Catholic grammar school of El Calvario and studied for a year at a private normal school before entering the public Escuela Preparatoria para Señoritas y Normal Mixta (Female High School and Coed Normal School). In part, Fernández sought a career in teaching because there were few other professional options for women in that period. She also loved to study and saw teaching as a high-status profession. In addition, she had role models in several of her mother's relatives who had become teachers. Like other graduates of the Normal, she expected a job when she finished. However, she and her sister Esperanza graduated in 1933 just as the introduction of socialist education splintered Guadalajaran society. Teachers lined up for and against the reform. Fernández recalled that her fellow student María Luisa Ruiz had organized the Liga de Maestras Revolucionarias. Many of the members of this organization were able to keep their jobs, but the Fernández sisters were refused admission because as devout Catholics they were barred from teaching in public schools.

In the early 1930s, Fernández worked at the Colegio Independencia, a private school run by the Salesian order. Here she earned twenty pesos monthly compared to the seventy pesos earned by public schoolteachers. In 1933, governor Sebastián Allende closed all private schools and accelerated the crackdown against nonrevolutionary public schoolteachers. Many Catholic teachers resigned from their positions, were fired, or left without jobs upon the closing of Catholic schools. Several of the teachers at the Colegio Independencia went to work in a cracker factory to support themselves. At the advice of different Jesuits, many, including the Fernández sisters, sought a clandestine space to continue teaching. Some taught middle- and upper-class children in their own homes. They also taught reading and writing to their siblings and neighbors.

Under these conditions of repression, the Fernández sisters and other female colleagues from the Colegio Independencia, including Carmen Aceves Navarro, began working on the idea of creating a new private school for girls. Carmen Aceves Navarro was a member of the Unión Femenina Católica Mexicana (UFCM, or Mexican Catholic Feminine Union).[24] The UFCM was part of the Acción Católica Mexicana (Mexican Catholic Action) that was created after the Cristero war and the signing of the 1929 accords between church and state to subordinate lay activities to the control of the church.[25] The Mexican Catholic Action organized lay Catholics according to their gender and age.[26] As part of the Mexican Catholic Action, the Unión Femenina helped the church in its missions, raised money for clandestine schools and seminaries, and sponsored religious education and catechism classes in parishes.[27]

The Fernández sisters, Carmen Aceves Navarro, and their colleagues envisaged a girls' school based on the philosophies of Saint Francis de Sales (1567–1622) and Saint John Bosco (1814–86), both of whom had educated poor and middle-class children and emphasized teachings about Christ and devotion to the Virgin María Auxiliadora. Saint John Bosco had founded the Salesian Society in Italy in the mid-nineteenth century to combat the anticlerical and antireligious thought emanating from the French Revolution.[28] Fernández and Aceves also decided to adopt his pedagogy because it emphasized a constant, affective interaction between teacher and student rather than relations of authoritarian distance and intimidation. Unlike de Sales and Bosco, these teachers were going to teach mainly middle- and upper-class girls. In choosing a name for the school, they could not select one of the saints but were forced by official conditions to choose a revolutionary hero. They chose Aquiles Serdán, the Puebla shoemaker and Maderista organizer revered on Guadalupe Martínez's Ruta de la Insurgencia. Organized Catholics had supported the Maderista struggle against Díaz, and Fernández judged that Aquiles Serdán had been "an honest and good revolutionary." Moreover, these young women were good tacticians: Aquiles was the birth name of the current pope, Pius XI.

Like Guadalupe Martínez, the Catholic women could advance their project only through negotiation with a male institutional hierarchy. Julia Fernández and Carmen Aceves discussed their project with José Garibi Rivera, who became archbishop in 1936. He had befriended Fernández earlier as auxiliary bishop and had noted her excellent skills as a catechist in the parish of Dulce Nombre de Jesús. The archbishop agreed to help negotiate the project with the government while the parish of Dulce Nombre de Jesús donated used furniture for the new school. Simultaneously, these teachers obtained a loan from Aceves Navarro's mother and presented their project to the SEP at the state and federal levels.[29] While the archbishop was negotiating the opening of the school, president Lázaro Cárdenas initiated an anticlerical thaw in 1936 that was followed at the local and regional levels.

With the quieting of tensions between church and state in 1937, the women opened the Colegio Aquiles Serdán. The school's slogan was "Science, Work, and Virtue." The motto accommodated the state's notion of instructing citizens for a modern patria, but the teachers also made it part of their own civic culture that blended the state's principles of duty and modernity with Catholic values. They chose the motto because "science referred to the knowledge of things. In order to have scientific knowledge, one had to work, and work is a virtue."[30] For these women, virtue embraced the Catholic cardinal virtues of prudence, justice, fortitude, and temperance, and the theological virtues of faith, hope, and charity. It offered instruction from kindergarten through secondary school and included courses in business and home economics. In astute negotiation with the state, they established a lay school and incorporated the state curriculum, including instruction in music, sports, and later English. Of these, sports represented a particularly significant, novel addition to the Catholic women's curriculum, since Damas Católicas had protested women's sports in the 1920s. At the same time, at a fundamental level, the Colegio Aquiles Serdán surreptitiously preserved a Catholic curriculum.

The teachers agreed among themselves that only women would run the school. They pledged that if one of them married, she had to leave the organization. The meddling of husbands or male authority figures in school affairs was prohibited, although the teachers listened to the advice of priests. Fernández regarded her long teaching career at the Colegio Aquiles Serdán as her own apostolate. From its inception, she was also part of the Marian Congregation of the Colegio Aquiles Serdán and filial of the temple San Felipe Neri. The congregation was devoted to the Virgin Mary and included most of the school's students. Led by a Jesuit, women members had different appointments from president to treasurer and did charitable work at hospital and parochial schools.

### Julia Fernández, the Colegio Aquiles Serdán, and Patriotic Parades

Students of the Colegio Aquiles Serdán became enthusiastic participants in the civic parades that took place in the Parque de la Revolución in Guadalajara. The parades of the 1940s were much more peaceful than those of the 1920s and 1930s. During the 1920s when Zuno governed, upper-class and "Red" working-class groups would come to blows on Independence Day. The rich drove their automobiles in the parade and threw flowers. It was a prerevolutionary custom of the privileged known as the Flower Wars.[31] In 1933, the still influential Zuno asked the Confederación Obrera de Jalisco to sponsor a float representing the Motherland in the Independence Day parade. The union selected Laura Rosales, a Normalista graduate and supporter of socialist education, to represent the Motherland because of her indigenous features. She dressed in the Mexican flag. Conservative and Catholic groups opposed to socialist education pelted her with stones.[32]

By contrast, the patriotic parades of the 1940s were much more consensual and integrated. Colegio Aquiles Serdán students marched in five different civic parades: Independence Day, the Día de la Raza, Mexican Revolution Day, Flag Day, and the Cinco de Mayo. As with all schools, they had a drum corps, wore uniforms, and marched in step. One student carried the Mexican flag with the school's name emblazoned in the center. Teachers and girls from Guadalajara's middle and upper classes were proud to show Tapatía society that they too were part of the construction of a modern nation and commemorators of Mexican history. In the Día de la Raza parade of 1940, children from public and private schools carried their banners along with twenty-one other flags from Latin American countries. Mexican Revolution Day and the Cinco de Mayo featured athletic demonstrations. Flag Day was a solemn ceremony in which three students from the Colegio Aquiles Serdán joined those of other schools in pledging allegiance to the flag. Aquiles Serdán student Alicia Shelly wrote in her diary: "The patriotic festival has several purposes. First, it is patriotic and makes you feel proud to be Mexican. Second, it is physical. It helps us exercise and strengthen our muscles. The third is moral because discipline builds character."[33] Every year, she noted, the parades got better as sports and military organizations competed with one another for the best presentation.

In the Independence Day parade of 1941, the Colegio Aquiles Serdán made a float representing Sor Juana Inés de la Cruz, the seventeenth-century Mexican nun who was a major poet and scholar of the baroque period.[34] With this gesture, teachers and students rescued from the Mexican past the woman who has come to be known as Mexico's greatest female heroine and one of its most brilliant intellectuals. By elevating Sor Juana to the pantheon of patriot heroes, the Colegio told Tapatía society that it was schooling women who could be enlightened and religious at the same time. Without referring directly to God or to feminism, they advanced their religious, social, and political goals. Catholic teachers wanted to be modern. For them, being patriotic was a dimension of modernity. Selecting elements from the Mexican past that were compatible with their values but did not provoke liberals and revolutionaries, they saw themselves moving forward with their students as participating members of a modern nation.

## Conclusion

Guadalupe Martínez and Julia Fernández each formed a part of two distinct female communities that reflected political and social divisions in revolutionary Guadalajara. The revolution made them both part of the middle class: Martínez rose into it, and Fernández fell down to it. They came from families with different notions of Mexican history and social and political values, differences that became more acute with the conflicts unleashed by the revolution. Yet the revolutionary process gave each the opportunity to expand her orbit of sociopolitical action and to hone professional and political skills that in turn opened opportunities for other women.

Martínez came from a class culture rooted in nineteenth-century Mexican liberalism and working-class community and family values. In the 1920s, she embraced the radical revolutionary discourse against the powerful Catholic movement. Both of her parents came from two textile factory towns and were related to the most radical female political leader of the 1920s: María A. Díaz. Martínez's nationalism came from her liberal, working-class background, which glorified the heroes of the independence, honored Juárez, and celebrated Mexico's defeat of the French invaders in 1862. Martínez's civic

leadership illustrates how nineteenth-century working-class tradition radicalized in the course of the revolution only to be domesticated by official politics
and unionism after 1940. Its traditions and radical expressions were not eliminated, but they were tamed and subjected to institutional regulation, much as
Martínez submitted to her husband but did not, for this, fall silent.

In contrast, the case of Fernández presents a rural upper-class culture based
on deep Catholicism and very conservative family values. The armed movement of 1910 weakened the family's economic position. Forced to migrate to
Guadalajara, they became middle class in an urban environment. The implementation of socialist education in 1933 closed Julia Fernández's possibilities
to work in the expanding public school system. Fernández and other Catholic teachers accommodated institutional Catholicism and revolutionary state
policies into their educational project. They played an important role in the
education of upper- and middle-class women and the maintenance of Catholic
values in a modernizing setting.

To a degree, both Martínez and Fernández held radical positions on women.
In the Círculo Feminista del Occidente, Martínez sought full political, social,
and civil rights, particularly for working women. Fernández and her colleagues
probably saw the Círculo's promotion of women's rights as fundamentally
linked to an anti-Catholic agenda. But the teachers of the Colegio Aquiles Serdán were radical in their own way. They wanted no male interference in the running of their school. Underwriting their convictions was doubtless the stead-
fast and highly significant participation of women in Guadalajara's Catholic
movement. On the other hand, just as the teachers of the Colegio accepted the
counsel of priests and bishops, so Martínez and many of her *compañeras* were
obliged to subordinate themselves and their program to the male hierarchies
of Mexican politics, unionism, and state institutions.

Interviewed at the end of their lives, Martínez and Fernández, in their selective narration and interpretation of selves and events, emphasized how they
had learned to negotiate skillfully with male leaders they admired and respected. Above all, they were conscious that they had opened spaces for female
interests and voices within both the state and the church. Silent about their
own submission to patriarchy, they preferred to highlight their creativity in
expanding social, economic, and civic opportunities for women within and
despite these male-dominated structures.

As teachers they sought to forge notions of national identity and history
and to pass these on to new generations of Mexican children. The Route of
the Insurgency contributed to the success of the state's cultural project by re-

inforcing the teaching of the skills, attitudes, and behaviors it championed: academic achievement, discipline and order, productivity, patriotism, and social service. But it also incorporated into national history the heroism of the workers' movement and its leaders, an incorporation not originally anticipated by SEP educators. Similarly, the patriotic project of the Aquiles Serdán school shows how Catholic women educators used the rapprochement between church and state to consolidate their religious values within an officially secular national project. In the long run, the state did not erase Guadalajara's Catholic tradition, nor did Catholic Action eliminate liberal thinking in Jalisco. While Martínez's and Fernández's projects of national memory and culture were at odds with each other, both incorporated new, aspiring social groups into a national, modernizing process. Both women participated actively in the dialogue between state and society around a cultural project that through its very negotiation came to respect regional diversity and include workers, women, and Catholics.

## Notes

1. Jean Meyer, *La guerra de los cristeros*, vol. 1 of *La Cristiada* (Mexico City: Siglo XXI Editores, 1973), 7, 9.

2. Mary Kay Vaughan, *Cultural Politics in Revolution: Teachers, Peasants, and Schools in Mexico, 1930–1940* (Tucson: University of Arizona Press, 1997), 20.

3. Laura O'Dogherthy Madrazo, *De urnas y sotanas: El Partido Católico en Jalisco* (Mexico City: CONACULTA, 2001), 195–284.

4. Friedrich Katz, *The Life and Times of Pancho Villa* (Stanford: Stanford University Press, 1998), 480–81; Zenaido Michel Pimienta, *Episodios históricos de la educación en Jalisco* (Guadalajara: Talleres Vera, 1960), 9–10, 25–36; José María Murià, *Historia de Jalisco*, vol. 4 (Guadalajara: UNED, 1981), 237–40.

5. Pablo Yankelevich, "La batalla por el dominio de las conciencias: La experiencia de la educación socialista en Jalisco, 1934–1940," in *Escuela y sociedad en el periodo cardenista*, ed. Susana Quintanilla and Mary Kay Vaughan (Mexico City: Fondo de Cultura Económica, 1997), 115–39; Alma Dorantes, *El conflicto universitario en Guadalajara, 1933–1937* (Guadalajara: Secretaría de Cultura and Instituto Nacional de Antropología e Historia, 1993), 230; Jacinta Curiel, interview by author, Guadalajara, Jalisco, December 2, 1998.

6. Although most of the literature on the Mexican Revolution and the Cristero rebellion mentions that women were important in resisting anticlerical revolutionary policies, recent studies have documented Catholic women's participation in more detail. See Agustín Vaca, *Los silencios de la historia: Las cristeras* (Guadalajara: El Colegio de

Jalisco, 1998); María Teresa Fernández Aceves, "The Political Mobilization of Women in Revolutionary Guadalajara, 1910–1940" (Ph.D. diss., University of Illinois, Chicago, 2000); and Kristina Boylan, "Mexican Catholic Women's Activism, 1929–1940" (Ph.D. diss., Oxford University, 2001).

7. Enrique Calleros was a *jefe antireeleccionista* and a tailor. In his shop, he held secret meetings to plan the rebellion against the Porfirian regime. On July 14, 1910, Calleros received an order from the Maderista Roque Estrada to start the Maderista rebellion in Jalisco. Calleros led the Club Antireeleccionista de Jalisco and the Junta de Conspiración Armada in 1910. See Instituto Nacional de Estudios Históricos de la Revolución Mexicana, *Diccionario histórico de la Revolución Mexicana*, vol. 4 (Mexico City: INEHRM, 1991), 63.

8. Dolores Martínez, "Una mujer y su destino" (manuscript, 1975), 1:21, 2:264.

9. Ibid., 1:20.

10. Rosendo Salazar, *Las pugnas de la gleba: Los albores del movimiento obrero en México* (Mexico City: Partido Revolucionario Institucional, 1972), 215–16; Fernández Aceves, "The Political Mobilization of Women," 96–98.

11. Margarita Castro Palmeros et al., "Indicios de la historia de las relaciones laborales en Jalisco, 1900–1936," in *IV Concurso sobre Derecho Laboral Manuel M. Diéguez* (Guadalajara: UNED, 1982).

12. Several historians have called this policy the modernization of patriarchy. See Vaughan, *Cultural Politics in Revolution*; Susan Besse, *Restructuring Patriarchy: The Modernization of Gender Inequality in Brazil, 1914–1940* (Chapel Hill: University of North Carolina Press, 1996); and Victoria de Grazia, *How Fascism Ruled Women: Italy, 1922–1945* (Berkeley: University of California Press, 1992). For a discussion of the concept of patriarchy, see Ann Farnsworth-Alvear, *Dulcinea in the Factory: Myths, Morals, Men and Women in Colombia's Industrial Experiment, 1905–1960* (Durham: Duke University Press, 2000), 31–33; Thomas Miller Klubock, "Writing the History of Women and Gender in Twentieth-Century Chile," *Hispanic American Historical Review* 81 (August–November 2001): 510–18; Heidi Tinsman, *Partners in Conflict: The Politics of Gender, Sexuality, and Labor in the Chilean Agrarian Reform, 1950–1973* (Durham: Duke University Press, 2002), 11–13.

13. Archivo Histórico de Jalisco, Ramo de Trabajo, T-7-927, Caja T-101, Exp. 2470.

14. Fernández Aceves, "The Political Mobilization of Women," 188–202, 243–46, 254–59.

15. Ibid., 272–74, 277–81.

16. Guadalupe Martínez, interview by author, Guadalajara, Jalisco, August 15, 1996.

17. Esperanza Tuñón Pablos, *Mujeres que se organizan: El Frente Único Pro Derechos de la Mujer, 1935–1938* (Mexico City: UNAM and Miguel Angel Porrúa Grupo Editorial, 1992), 158.

18. Guadalupe Martínez, interview by author, Guadalajara, Jalisco, July 19, 1998.

19. *Gente*, Año 1, special number, July 3, 1998, 7.

20. Dolores Martínez, Guadalupe Martínez's sister, went on most of the trips as a teacher in charge of the children.

21. Dolores Martínez, "Plan de trabajo de la excursión la 'Ruta de la Insurgencia'" (manuscript, 1978), 2.

22. Ibid., 4.

23. Her biography is based on an interview. Julia Fernández Ruiz, interview by author, tape recording, Guadalajara, Jalisco, August 14, 1996.

24. Archivo de la Unión Femenina Católica Mexicana, Comité Diocesano de Guadalajara, Libro 1, 1930–35.

25. Peter L. Reich, *Mexico's Hidden Revolution: The Catholic Church in Law and Politics since 1929* (Notre Dame: University of Notre Dame Press, 1995), 99.

26. The Unión Católica Mexicana (Mexican Catholic Union) included married men; the Unión Femenina Católica Mexicana (Mexican Catholic Feminine Union) organized married women; the Juventud Católica Femenina Mexicana (Mexican Catholic Female Youth) focused on single women, and the Asociación Católica de la Juventud Mexicana (Mexican Catholic Male Youth) was created for young men. See Francisco Barbosa, *La iglesia y el gobierno civil*, vol. 6 of *Jalisco desde la revolución*, ed. Mario Aldana Rendón (Guadalajara: Gobierno del Estado de Jalisco and Universidad de Guadalajara, 1987), 456–57.

27. Kristina Boylan, "They Were Always Doing Something: Catholic Women's Activism and Activity in Jalisco, Mexico, in the 1930s" (paper presented at LASA 1998, Chicago), 7.

28. See Charles George Hebermann et al., *Catholic Encyclopedia: An International Work of Reference on the Constitution, Doctrine, Discipline, and History of the Catholic Church* (New York: Encyclopedia Press, 1913).

29. Consuelo Aceves Navarro, interview by author, Guadalajara, Jalisco, September 20, 2000.

30. Concha González, interview by Rosa Elena Fernández, Guadalajara, Jalisco, tape recording, August 14, 1999.

31. Laura Rosales, interview by author, Guadalajara, Jalisco, tape recording, August 15, 1996. William H. Beezley, "The Porfirian Smart Set Anticipates Thorstein Veblen in Guadalajara," in *Rituals of Rule, Rituals of Resistance: Public Celebration and Popular Culture in Mexico*, ed. William Beezley, Cheryl English Martin, and William E. French (Wilmington, Del.: Scholarly Resources, 1994), 177.

32. Laura Rosales, interview by author, Guadalajara, Jalisco, tape recording, August 15, 1996.

33. Alicia Shelly, "Desfilando," in *Colegio Aquiles Serdán: Curso Escolar, 1940–1941* (Guadalajara: Tipografía y Litografía Yguiniz, 1941), 22.

34. *Colegio Aquiles Serdán: Curso Escolar, 1941–1942* (Guadalajara: Tipografía y Litografía, 1942), 64.

# "We Are All Mexicans Here":
# Workers, Patriotism, and Union Struggles in Monterrey

### MICHAEL SNODGRASS

On a Saturday morning in January 1936, some three thousand steelworkers in the northern industrial city of Monterrey crowded into a downtown auditorium to celebrate the first union election in the mill's thirty-five-year history. The moment marked a key juncture in the annals of Mexican labor. One year earlier, president Lázaro Cárdenas had been inaugurated amid unprecedented numbers of strikes. Although it alarmed employers, Cárdenas stuck to his pro-union policies, which emboldened militant workers like those at Monterrey's Fundidora Steel Mill. Motivated by long-standing grievances, they launched an organizing drive that secured unanimous rank-and-file support for what became Local 67 of Mexico's Miner-Metalworkers Union. Upon signing their first collective contract, the steelworkers jubilantly broke into a recently penned ballad that fused worker patriotism with union struggle:

> We are the Miners Union, an organization of brothers
> In which we are united, ninety thousand Mexicanos
> Ninety thousand Mexicanos, wearing sandals, shoes, and boots
> Who, without sounding boastful, are among the greatest patriots of all.[1]

While Local 67 became the vanguard of militant unionism in Monterrey, not all workers subscribed to the union cause. Operatives at the city's Cuauhtémoc Brewery sided with their employers, who happened to be the most powerful industrialists in Mexico. These businessmen blamed the city's rash of labor conflicts on the federal government. In response, they organized a conservative resistance movement to protest its labor policy. On February 5, 1936, just days after Local 67's victory, Monterrey's streets teemed with some fifty thousand antigovernment protesters. The issue of unionism had polarized Mexico's industrial capital, pitting the industrialists against the state and workers against one another. Both sides adopted patriotic discourses to defend their positions.

This chapter focuses on Monterrey, Nuevo León, to explore the languages of patriotism that became ubiquitous in Mexico's factories, plazas, and union halls. Beginning in the 1920s, Mexico's revolutionary government tapped into and attempted to channel working-class patriotism as part of its shifting project of economic reconstruction, political integration, and cultural engineering. I will examine how state labor policy evolved, why it met resistance, and how it achieved mixed results. The working men of Monterrey's brewery and steel mill are the story's principal blue-collar protagonists. They exemplified the divergent responses that state labor policy generated among Mexican workers. The brewery operatives joined their employers in a multiclass movement of opposition to the state's revolutionary project. They evoked a conservative patriotism that fused discourses of regionalism, masculinity, and anticommunism. The steelworkers, on the other hand, used the government's language of revolutionary nationalism and their own understanding of machismo in their embrace of militant unionism. Like many other Mexican unions, their Local 67 become an active member of Mexico's "revolutionary family" and performed an important role in the state's cultural project in the decades to come.

### "We Lack Neither Discipline Nor Love for the Homeland"

By the onset of Mexico's 1910 revolution, workers of diverse social backgrounds, regional loyalties, and occupations had come to share a national identity. The artisans and operatives of Porfirian Mexico had imbibed patriotism in their schools, political clubs, and mutual aid societies. Civic festivals, street theater, and the penny press furthered their identification with the nation. Those native-born workers who suffered discrimination in Mexico's foreign-owned mining camps, oil fields, and railroad yards linked their offended dignity to their Mexicanness, as did those who went north to labor in the factories and fields of the United States. There, a Mexican anthropologist observed in the 1920s, the immigrants "learn immediately what their mother country means, and they think of it and speak [of it] with love."[2]

The identities shared by the workers of Monterrey reflected their hometown's unique character. By 1910, the northern Mexican railroad hub was known as "Mexico's Chicago," a symbol of industrial progress and urban modernity in an overwhelmingly agrarian society. Mexico's industrial capital developed a concentration and diversity of industry exceptional by Latin

American standards. Local workers produced an array of consumer goods, from furniture and work clothes to cigarettes and beer. Others labored in heavy industries such as smelting, cement, glass, and steel. Industrial labor engendered patriotic pride, for Monterrey's workers understood that the products of their labor helped liberate Mexico from its historic dependence on foreign imports. Furthermore, unlike in Mexico's other industrial centers, where foreign capital predominated, native capitalists owned and operated the majority of Monterrey's factories. That earned the industrialists a respected place in Mexican society and politics, especially among *regiomontanos*, as the locals are known. Civic boosters lauded the captains of industry for their entrepreneurial spirit, dedication to Mexico's economic development, and benevolent treatment of their workers.

The regiomontanos also ascribed their hometown's prosperity to the unique character of local workers, who achieved renown for being industrious, disciplined, and orderly. Taking pride in the mastery of their trades and their high literacy rates, the workers considered themselves "more cultured" than workers elsewhere.[3] Like many other northerners, they subscribed to the values of independence, hard work, and resistance to central government authority that were common to the frontier region. This regional identity built on the *norteños'* critical view of central and southern Mexico: lethargic, submissive, and economically backward societies weighed down by an oppressive colonial heritage. Monterrey's civic and business leaders would use the notion of northern superiority for their own interests—to create regional loyalties between workers and employers and to foster local working-class enmity toward radical labor activists, especially those tied to Mexico City-based unions.

It was precisely the militancy of Mexican workers provoked by the revolution that these industrialists sought to repress. The revolution had an ambivalent impact on Monterrey's workers. The hardships caused by civil war generated a collective desire for the stability and security of prerevolutionary times. At the same time, it recast popular consciousness, motivating many to challenge customary labor relations. The militants developed a keen understanding of the labor rights bequeathed by the 1917 constitution. They believed that the labor code established the government's obligation to mediate industrial disputes on the workers' behalf. Its passage sparked an explosion of labor militancy in Monterrey and elsewhere as workers organized and struck to secure long-term aspirations such as improved working conditions and union recognition. In Monterrey, the strikes achieved mixed results. Some secured the eight-hour day and higher wages, but few won union recognition. Nonetheless, the struggle honed a new generation of union activists who would evoke labor's constitutional rights to secure their vision of industrial democracy. In the meantime, the industrial strife prompted Monterrey's entrepreneurs to institute the systems of company paternalism for which the city earned renown.

Managers at the Cuauhtémoc Brewery and Fundidora Steel developed an impressive range of welfare benefits and recreational programs meant to foster company loyalty, stifle militant unionism, and promote the "moral and cultural elevation of the working class."[4] Employees and their families gained access to company housing, food commissaries, and medical clinics. Company schools offered vocational training and physical education. Veteran workers steeped in a working-class tradition of mutual aid collaborated with management in the administration of cooperative societies, the primary vehicles through which fringe benefits were channeled. The cooperatives also sponsored cultural activities to promote healthy lifestyles and integrate workers into common company cultures. Working-class families spent recreational time at employer-sponsored barbecues, fiestas, and countryside excursions. Organized sports figured prominently in paternalistic practices. Like the social reformers of the federal government, local boosters believed that the "moral influence of modern sports" enhanced labor productivity, diverted working men from the cantina, and nurtured a "sincere identification with one's native soil." Monterrey's brewers and steelworkers saw through these designs to "call us to order" and "eliminate our vices."[5] But they astutely capitalized on the fringe benefits and cultural programs that remained largely unavailable to people of their class. Company paternalism helped quell militant unionism by offering working-class families the social security to which they aspired after the civil war.

At the same time, an organized labor movement, led primarily by railroad workers, flourished in Monterrey in the 1920s. These self-described "anarcho-communists" challenged employer paternalism and promoted unionization by advocating ideals of class solidarity, constitutional rights, and industrial democracy. They castigated Monterrey's employers for "violating the democratic principles of our revolution." In this turbulent decade, neither the brewery nor the steel mill was free of union organizers. The local industrialists therefore maneuvered to subvert the labor law and fire troublesome workers. The benevolent face of the paternalistic coin masked a coercive underside. The steel and brewery workers learned to forsake their constitutional right to union representation not only for the promises of paternalism but out of fear of dismissal.[6] By the end of the decade, Communist labor activists who scorned the industrialists had become equally critical of the nation's political leaders owing to the latter's perceived failure to defend workers' rights.

In many ways, these corporate labor policies neatly complemented the revolutionary project of the federal government in the 1920s. Monterrey's industrialists endeavored to shape their employees into hardworking, clean-living, and productive citizens (see figure 1). They built hygienic housing, promoted sports, and trained workers and their children in the industrial arts. As the federal government's commitment to economic reconstruction and the "modernization" of the Mexican masses trumped its support for state-sponsored syndicalism in these years, the Monterrey elite's well-publicized commitment to the "moral and cultural elevation" of workers earned them praise from visiting political dignitaries like José Vasconcelos.[7] Indeed, by the early 1930s, local government authorities were administering their own housing, sports, and vocational training programs as they competed with employers for the hearts and minds of workers. The industrialists, however, retained advantages in their greater financial resources and everyday access to workers. Most importantly, they enjoyed the collaboration of the loyal employees who acted as their agents in cultural engineering.

No firm shaped a more loyal workforce than the Cuauhtémoc Brewery. Nor did any local company more effectively cultivate popular conservatism among its 1,500 workers. Veteran operatives came to share their employer's sense of "business patriotism," the notion that Cuauhtémoc contributed to the national interest by promoting industrial progress and human development. They boasted of their bosses' native roots, the brewery's vocational training programs, and the company's commitment to industrial diversification. By the 1920s, the owners of Mexico's largest brewery also produced malt, bottle tops, packaging materials, and a host of glass products that had once been imported from abroad. Longtime employees took pride in working for what they considered "the most integrated and thoroughly Mexican enterprise in the Republic." Loyal workers imparted their political ideas and cultural values to fellow workers. In the pages of *Work and Savings*, the company's popular magazine, they preached class harmony and editorialized against communism, labor laws, and the revolutionary government. They particularly disdained Monterrey's radical labor activists. One editorial published in *Work and Savings* decried organized labor's "unjust petitions and violent strikes" as an obstacle to "industrial progress." These workers refused to sympathize with such unionists "because we lack neither discipline nor love of the Patria." Instead, they concluded, "the best proof we can give of our culture is the respect we share toward our ally, Capital."[8]

FIG. 1. "Trabajo y Ahorro" (Work and Savings) promotes modern virtues.
Photograph courtesy of Archivo General del Estado de Nuevo León.

Organizing drives at the brewery ran aground on the shoals of company loyalty in part because the discourse of class harmony reflected a lived workplace experience. Theirs was an industry characterized by light tasks and a cool atmosphere during long, sweltering summers. Such conditions encouraged congeniality between workers and bosses. Frequent and surprise appearances by the firm's upper hierarchy enhanced the "family-like" atmosphere and "camaraderie" as managers greeted workers, asked about their families, and lent a hand in the work.[9] The brewery's cultural programs reinforced amicable bonds between managers and operatives. Supervisors taught night classes, coached athletic teams, and presided over community improvement boards in neighborhoods surrounding the plant (see figure 2). These social interactions facilitated management's capacity to shape the workers' political outlook.

The Fundidora Steel Mill also tried to shape its workers' culture and identities. Echoing the ideals of the revolutionary government, management vowed to "forge the Patria" by shaping the "men of steel" into exemplary workers and model citizens. More than the exchange of labor for wages, steel production became a patriotic mission. Few companies played a more significant role in Mexico's economic development than the Fundidora, then the only integrated steel mill in all Latin America. Much like Mexico's oil or railroad industries, steel proved indispensable to the nation's industrial progress. The fruit of steelworkers' labor would build the railroads, schools, and industry of the new Mexico. From this sense of mission—and the great dangers they faced at work—a unique culture of work, patriotism, and machismo developed among the "men of steel." They sang a popular *corrido* that celebrated colleagues who lost their lives at the mill as having "died for the homeland."[10] They took immense pride in their work and their legendary status as Monterrey's finest athletes.

As at the brewery, company paternalism integrated workers and families of diverse backgrounds into a common company culture known as the "Great Steel Family." Yet key variables differentiated the firms. The Fundidora depended on the state as the primary consumer of Monterrey steel. The mill's administrators resided in Mexico City and adjusted their labor policy to shifting political tides. Despite their promotion of working-class patriotism, the firm's principal directors were of European birth. That may explain their reputedly "liberal" managerial philosophy. They neither espoused the Monterrey elite's disdain for central government authority nor repressed the workers' right to union representation. Indeed, the mill's Monterrey director publicly advocated their "right to organize in any way they pleased," a philosophy that the steel-

FIG. 2. "Trabajo y Ahorro" (Work and Savings) celebrates its baseball team. Photograph courtesy of Archivo General del Estado de Nuevo León.

workers later appropriated to their own ends.[11] In the meantime, the mill negotiated exclusively with the Federated Steel Unions, a company union established by veteran workers and plant supervisors. By the early 1930s, militant workers labeled the Steel Unions a *sindicato blanco*, a "white union" beholden to the dictates of management.

Rank-and-file workers came to agree as they chafed at the plant's "arrogant and despotic" foremen. Indeed, at the Fundidora Steel Mill, the benevolent promises of industrial paternalism met their limits on the shop floor. The steelworkers suffered Monterrey's highest accident rates owing to unchecked occupational health and safety hazards. Those who dissented faced punitive dismissals at the insistence of company union leaders. Workplace conditions bred a generalized sense of powerlessness. Looking back on the 1920s, one worker recalled that "in order to keep one's job . . . we had to do whatever the bosses said." These affronts to manly dignity cut across the benevolent grains of paternalism. But rather than undercut their loyalty toward a company in which they took great pride, workers blamed the abuses on the Steel Unions' leaders.[12] The "democratic promises of our revolution" championed by radical labor activists came to resonate powerfully among them. President Cárdenas's political opening would embolden them to act.

### "The Legitimate Interests of the Working Class"

When General Cárdenas assumed the presidency in 1934, he inherited a nation-wide labor insurgency prompted by the Great Depression. By then, the moderate labor confederation backed by the governments of the 1920s (the CROM) had virtually disintegrated. From this context of renewed organizing drives, strikes, and violent protest emerged a new Mexican labor movement, better organized, more militant in tactics, and more radical in its demands. Cárdenas's labor policy responded to and further galvanized worker mobilization. His government established two basic objectives: the unification of workers into a single labor central, the Confederation of Mexican Workers (CTM), and the negotiation of government-arbitrated collective contracts that guaranteed labor's constitutional rights. Once realized, working-class unification would end years of interunion squabbles. Labor peace would then promote national industrial development and thus diminish Mexico's dependence on foreign capital and imported goods.

Cardenista labor policy continued promoting the government's cultural and political goals as well. The "revolutionary unions" would serve as schools for the making of a new Mexican working class—hardworking, clean-living, and loyal to the state and its new official party. As many workers came to believe, a genuine humanism also motivated General Cárdenas. He believed it his patriotic duty and paternalistic obligation to protect workers' rights and raise their families' living standards. His labor department defended striking workers and mediated disputes on labor's behalf. But government policy and working-class militancy provoked a conservative backlash. Both Cardenistas and conservatives appropriated patriotic language to sanction their opposing positions.

Monterrey exemplified these tumultuous times in Mexican labor history. The Great Depression had shattered the city's reputation for class harmony. Workers struck and launched organizing drives at unprecedented levels. Union organizers made solid inroads in railroad yards, smelters, and many factories, including the steel mill and the brewery's sister company, Monterrey Glass-works. The local Communist Party soon boasted one of the largest blue-collar memberships in Mexico.[13] Renewed militancy prompted Monterrey's industrialists to sign collective contracts with company unions led by loyal, more compliant workers. By recognizing the so-called white unions, they ostensibly obeyed the labor law while also shielding their workers from militant union organizers. In 1932, the sindicatos blancos federated as the Independent Unions of Nuevo León, adopting a moniker that celebrated the regiomontanos' staunch independence and historic autonomy from Mexico's national labor federations. However, as local industry rebounded, Communist and pro-government activists—known collectively as "reds"—launched dissident movements against, and often from within, white unions.

The process began at the steel mill in 1935 when dissident workers challenged their union bosses. Enlisting the aid of the Mexico City–based Miner-Metalworkers Union, the dissidents built rank-and-file support by fashioning a pro-union discourse that highlighted constitutional rights and industrial democracy. They promised doubled wage rates, seniority recognition, and, most importantly, the right to elect their own leaders and secure a strong union voice on the factory floor. While the steelworkers respected the benefits derived from company paternalism, their long-standing conflicts with the plant's foremen left them open to these promises. The mill's old-guard leaders countered the insurgency with appeals to the workers' regional and masculine identities. They juxtaposed the "honor and virility with which [they had] defended the workers' interests" to the "deceitful and disorienting claims of the timid scab herders from Mexico City." They warned that the "violence" characteristic of the Miner-Metalworkers Union "in no way meshes with the culture and sincerity of the regiomontano worker." "They will poison your consciousness," the conservatives warned, "overturning twenty years of living and working together peacefully." Their pleas proved futile. In January 1936, the steelworkers elected unanimously to become Local 67 of the national Miner-Metalworkers Union.[14]

The emergence of Local 67 galvanized union activists in Monterrey. One week later, militants at Monterrey Glassworks penned a manifesto and plastered the broadside throughout the sprawling plant. It began: "Monterrey's proletariat celebrates tonight because the Steel Unions abandoned their old ideology and transformed themselves into a revolutionary organization." The dissidents reminded their fellow glassworkers that *their* white union neither filed grievances, protested layoffs, nor pressed for higher wages because "they fear the company's wrath." "They have essentially renounced the freedoms that belong to workers in a democratic country like our own," the militants concluded.[15] When the company fired the manifesto's authors, the reds declared a strike to force representation elections and allow the plant's 1,600 workers to choose their own union leaders.

This conflict focused the country's attention on Monterrey. National labor leaders saw the union election as an opportunity to score against the glass factory's owners, Mexico's most powerful industrialists. They celebrated when a narrow decision handed the red union a victory on February 1. The controversial outcome came only after government officials nullified the ballots of 144 office workers, who were considered ineligible to vote by Mexican labor law. In contrast to the steel mill, the glassworks' labor force divided on the issue of unionism. Moreover, whereas the Fundidora's Mexico City–based directors acquiesced to the change in union leadership, the regiomontano industrialists blamed their setback on the sinister designs of Cardenista labor authorities. They fought back with a conservative resistance movement that transformed the labor dispute into a showdown with the federal government.

Convening hours after the election, Monterrey's businessmen announced their sponsorship of a "grand, patriotic" demonstration for February 5, which just happened to be Mexico's Constitution Day. They enveloped the movement in a red-baiting, flag-waving discourse that drew nationwide attention.[16] The rally's organizers mobilized local support through propaganda meant to resonate with the regiomontanos' national and regional loyalties. Press releases highlighted the fact that Monterrey's industrialists were "100 percent Mexican." The march would protest "the preconceived and highly dangerous intrusion of professional communist agitators from Mexico City." These outsiders, regiomontanos were reminded, "have subverted the local order and overturned the rhythm of cooperation and hard work that has been the base of Monterrey's prosperity." To punctuate the protest and display their economic might, the businessmen resolved to couple the march with a two-day lockout of local industry and commerce.

Monterrey's white unions cast their patriotic pride with the industrialists. Early reports even portrayed the movement as a labor-led initiative. Union leaders proudly informed a Mexico City reporter that "in contrast to workers elsewhere in the Republic," the regiomontanos would put down their tools "to defend their place of work . . . [and] support their employers." The industrialists' protest thus became a "loyalty strike" to safeguard "the legitimate interests of the working class." While the local radio airwaves buzzed with anticommunist diatribes, loyal workers distributed flags emblazoned with the slogan "México Sí, Rusia No!" They adorned plant gates and city walls with flyers appealing to the regiomontanos' regional, masculine, and Christian identities. "REGIOMONTANO!" one proclaimed, "Now is the time to stand erect —the hour when the virile, independent worker protects his home, mother, children, and workplace from Stalin's slaves." The Communists would spread "class hatred . . . dedicate your daughters to free love . . . [and] turn your sons into slaves." Another handbill exhorted: "WORKERS OF MONTERREY! Fight the Communists who reject God. . . . Down with the Communist government of Mexico."[17] Thus did the march's organizers envelop their resistance in the language of conservative patriotism while obscuring the protest's original motivation: the struggle against Cardenista labor policy.

The rhetoric of regionalism, anticommunism, and manly independence was familiar to blue-collar regiomontanos. That of Christianity was not, at least as a political discourse. Religious doctrine had long infused labor relations in central and western Mexico, where church and lay leaders mobilized workers into Catholic labor unions in the 1920s.[18] However, consistent with the North's more secular leanings, Catholic unions never materialized in Monterrey. Nor had Christianity entered into the discourse and practices of company paternalism, as it would in coming years. One labor activist later recalled that although "the priests were always on the employers' side . . . they did not have the influence to carry out their anti-union propaganda [among workers]." Significantly, the conservative Catholicism with which Mexicans currently identify Monterrey first emerged publicly in the mid-1930s as one facet of an antigovernment discourse designed to mobilize local resistance to state labor policy, much as Christian doctrine was then being employed by central Mexican Catholics opposed to the state policy of socialist education. In the meantime, Monterrey's conservatives had converted organized labor's setback at the glassworks into an anticommunist crusade in defense of the *patria*.

On February 5, 1936, an estimated sixty thousand regiomontanos marched in the largest antigovernment demonstration in Mexican history at the time. As the parade progressed, the marchers alternated choruses of the national anthem with defiant cries of "Death to the Communists!" Over their heads sailed slick banners produced by the event's organizers: "Juárez or Stalin?" "Defend the Embattled Patria!" and "Down with Russian Traitors!" Observers were struck by the diversity of the crowd. At the forefront paraded prominent industrialists and workers from forty-two white unions. Behind them followed the workers' families, merchants and Rotarians, and farmers trucked in from the countryside. People of all ages and walks of life wove through the narrow downtown streets. But the enthusiastic participation of thousands of local workers proved the most conspicuous feature of the day. Finding a ready explanation for this display of popular conservatism, Mexico City labor leaders asserted that since "the regiomontano workers are unaccustomed to struggle, their class consciousness remains weak." Union activists in Monterrey, whose own struggles disproved these presumptions, cited other factors to explain the mobilization. They credited the "subversive role" of Monterrey's print and radio media, which business leaders used to "carry out their anti-union campaign under the guise of fighting communism." They also pointed to the industrialists' threats of economic sanctions. Indeed, the Cuauhtémoc Brewery, whose operatives were the rally's largest blue-collar contingent, threatened to fine workers who played hooky on the day of the march.[19]

On the other hand, Constitution Day represented but a single, dramatic, and well-publicized moment in the history of popular conservatism in Monterrey. Leaders of the independent unions certainly sympathized with the anticommunist propaganda, and rank and filers shared the expressions of patriotism heard on that day. Moreover, the protracted labor conflicts that threatened to paralyze local industry frightened and angered many workers, who endorsed a banner proclaiming, "We Demand the Right to Work!" Communist labor militants, many workers believed, threatened their accustomed way of life and endangered their families' livelihoods. The workers marched to defend these.

President Cárdenas himself arrived in Monterrey two days later. He spent the following week listening to rival labor leaders, touring blue-collar neighborhoods, and meeting with industrialists. The latter reminded him of their patriotic contributions to Mexican progress. They decried the "artificiality" of local strikes, noting that "no real disequilibrium" existed between workers and employers, since "we are all Mexicans here." They blamed the discord on CTM leader Lombardo Toledano, who they claimed was "sent [to Monterrey] on instructions from Moscow." Cárdenas agreed with the industrialists on the need to "combat bad labor leaders . . . who sell out the workers' just cause to enrich themselves." But he restated his policy of national labor unification and reminded the businessmen that the government was now "arbiter and regulator of social problems." The president then got to the point on Monterrey: "On the question of communism, you can all be *tranquilos*. . . . Your workers are fighting for a better standard of living and nothing else." Cárdenas ended his visit with his historic "Fourteen Points" speech clarifying his government's labor policy. He concluded the speech with the threat for which it gained fame: "The businessmen who have wearied of the social struggle can hand their industries over to the workers or the government." "That would be patriotic," he declared, "the industrial lockout is not."[20] General Lázaro Cárdenas then departed Monterrey, never to return again as president.

The Spirit of Cardenismo

Events in Monterrey galvanized Mexico's revolutionary and conservative forces alike. The president's pugnacious rhetoric did little to promote industrial peace. Rather, it emboldened union activists in key industries like oil and mining to assert new and more radical demands. Two years later, in 1938, Cárdenas responded to the pressure of striking workers by nationalizing Mexico's foreign-owned oil companies.[21] His bold move aroused unprecedented displays of national solidarity. But the patriotic euphoria endured only briefly. Labor agitation and a brief economic recession (1937–38) provoked a conservative backlash across northern and central Mexico. Businessmen, old-guard politicos, and conservative union bosses united to protest Cardenismo and resist CTM organizing drives. As in Monterrey, they fashioned a discourse of regionalism, patriotism, and anticommunism to mobilize both working- and middle-class supporters. Prompted by these and other conservative pressures, the Cárdenas regime would consolidate its gains and moderate its policies.

Up north, Monterrey's industrialists sustained the struggle against red unions despite the president's threat of industrial expropriation. The local elite consolidated the social movement they had launched in February 1936 with the formation of Nationalist Civic Action (ACN), a conservative alliance that soon counted branches throughout northern Mexico. According to its statutes, the ACN appealed to "regiomontanos who cherish order and progress" and pledged to "foster respect for the flag, dignify the home, and preserve the family." Its spirited rallies attracted upward of twenty thousand locals "of all social classes" to Monterrey's Cuauhtémoc Park, where members sang patriotic Mexican songs and reaffirmed the class harmony that in their view had fostered prosperity. The ACN's festive public face contrasted with the coercive underside of the antiunion crusade. In July 1936, federal officials ordered the ACN's dissolution after its members opened fire on a Communist-led labor rally, killing three local workers.[22]

The industrialists nonetheless sustained their strategies to drive militant unions from their factories. At plants like Monterrey Glassworks, management fired worker-activists, violated the collective contract, and intimidated union sympathizers. As a result, walkouts, fatal interunion violence, and general strikes further polarized Monterrey. But the aggressive tactics begot results. Shortly after two protest strikes paralyzed the glassworks, the rank and file elected to reinstate the company union in two of the plant's three divisions. Many did so for reasons articulated by one white union supporter: "We will now earn better salaries through the incentives granted by the company and dedicate to our families the time stolen from us by the reds to attend their meetings, marches, and riots." As the reds themselves admitted, the open-shop victories owed as much to coercion as to "a strong and very large faction of *obreros blancos*," the loyal workers who ensured that "in Nuevo León the bourgeoisie is stronger than the proletariat."[23]

Few workers remained more loyal to their employer than those of the Cuauhtémoc Brewery. The company responded to Cardenista labor policy and union drives by refining its paternalistic regime and setting local precedents that persist to this day. Like the city's other nonunion factories, management continually matched the wage hikes and benefits secured by the revolutionary unions. Cuauhtémoc's cooperative society oversaw the development of new worker housing, modern medical facilities, and a handsome sports and recreation complex. The Cuauhtémoc Workers Union took credit for having "resolved the workers' problems . . . without resort to violent confrontations and useless proclamations." By doing so, the white union's leaders claimed to defend "the basic principles of the Revolution . . . [and] to serve as an example, such that the well-being of all Mexicans becomes a reality." Meanwhile, company managers devised new means of shielding the workers from organized labor. Female operatives were forbidden to date union workers. A network of spies watched the men in their cantinas and on the shop floor. The firm even extended its promotion of antiunion sentiments into workers' homes. Company officials visited mothers and wives to warn of the dangers of unionism and distribute literature explaining the church's opposition to communism. Of greatest long-term significance, both the brewery and its increasingly diversified subsidiaries refined their hiring practices to screen out applicants from local union households. The kin of Monterrey's union workers were denied employment in what became Mexico's largest industrial empire.[24]

The Cárdenas years consolidated Monterrey's reputation as a city of recalcitrant industrialists and company unions. Yet the period also gave birth to revolutionary unionism. The city's unique economic development ensured that national industrial unions of electrical, railroad, and metal workers established a strong presence there. These were the blue-collar regiomontanos who embraced Cardenismo. They capitalized on state labor policy to secure union recognition and built their unions into durable institutions that challenged the hegemonic pretensions of Monterrey's elite for decades to come. In return for government support, union leaders were expected to transform the revolutionary unions into vehicles of cultural engineering and political integration. Over time, Monterrey's red unions achieved the state's objective of establishing labor discipline and delivering rank-and-file votes for the ruling party, but they did so on their own terms, legitimizing their actions in languages of revolutionary nationalism and the regiomontano spirit of independence.

The steelworkers' Local 67 exemplifies the early history of such revolutionary unions. Leaders responded to the antiunion ambience of their hometown by building enduring rank-and-file loyalties.[25] The Fundidora's acquiescence to unionization facilitated the process. Indeed, the company's historic promotion of working-class patriotism—a discourse that linked steel making to nation building—inadvertently sanctioned the workers' own endorsement of revolutionary nationalism. Thereafter, the practices of militant unionism built on those of company paternalism. Local 67 worked jointly with management to administer the mill's welfare benefits, from worker housing to consumer cooperative to a company school. The union also took charge of the cultural programs that had originated in the 1920s. Its secretary of education and cultural affairs oversaw sports teams, the union press, and a women's group and youth association that integrated male workers' wives and children into the new union culture.

The rank and file's early allegiance to Local 67 reflected the conquests secured in their first collective contract, from higher wages to seniority rights. The contract also established the closed shop, the most controversial prerogative of Mexico's red unions. That clause gave the union the right to dismiss dissident workers and nominate all new hires. The so-called exclusion clause later became the basis of union boss corruption, most notoriously in the petroleum industry. But Monterrey's unionists saw the closed shop as their right to dismiss troublesome workers in order to preserve unity in the ranks. The union hiring hall also protected workers' families from the discriminatory hiring practices instituted by the local elite. Equally important, the "democratic promises" of the revolution became a reality in both the workplace and the union hall. The institution of shop committees, elected by workers in each department, gave Local 67 a strong voice on the factory floor. Weekly union assemblies helped workers to hold leaders accountable to rank-and-file interests.

Retired steelworkers therefore remember 1936 as a year of "emancipation."

For Salvador Solís, the moment signaled the end of "tyrannical foremen" and "self-appointed leaders who did nothing in defense of the workers." Antonio Quiroga cherished his newfound "right to protest all transgressions without fear of reprisal." Salvador Castañeda speaks in reverential terms of "Don Lázaro" Cárdenas, the president "who provided an impulse to the labor movement in Monterrey . . . and liberated workers from years of ignorance and misery." Such testimonies reveal a historical memory that was as much a product of lived experience as of Local 67's efforts and capacity to preserve the spirit of Cardenismo. In mandatory union assemblies, leaders narrated a history of pre-1936 labor relations, one in which despotic foremen and "sold-out" union leaders suppressed the workers' constitutional rights. By contrasting this neo-Porfirian past to the conquests won by Local 67, they aimed at teaching younger workers "to care for and protect their union."[26]

Labor leaders promoted Local 67's "social value" not only as a bargaining agent but also as a union dedicated to political causes. In the 1930s, the latter ranged from extending solidarity to striking Mexican workers to supporting the Republican side in the Spanish Civil War, a hallmark of Cardenista foreign policy. At times, rank-and-file workers betrayed their own sense of nationalism by protesting the use of union funds. Resolutions to contribute one day's wages toward the Republican cause provoked the greatest discontent, for Mexico's popular classes shared a historical disdain for the Spanish. Labor leaders countered such sentiments by explaining the difference between heroic Republicans and *gachupines*, the "bad Spaniards who only come [to Mexico] to enrich themselves." In the meantime, dissenting workers proposed more "patriotic" alternatives, from Christmas gifts for the local poor to aid for victims of a Coahuila mine blast. Their union affiliation also incorporated Monterrey's red workers into the Mexican Revolutionary Party (today's PRI). Theirs was a conflictive and negotiated integration. Guided by a tradition of political independence, the regiomontano workers persistently defied Mexico City's imposition of outside candidates and presented their own slates of left-independent aspirants. As a result, Local 67 earned its "quotas of power," or the right to appoint one union member to the city council and another to state congress.[27]

Union membership introduced the steelworkers to the tumultuous world of labor politics. Personal, political, and generational rivalries spilled over into Local 67's weekly meetings. So did the workers' sense of manliness. Steelworkers remember the union assemblies as "muy pesadas"—heavy, raucous affairs attended by exhausted, sometimes inebriated, and often armed steelworkers. Violent and fatal melees could result. Workers therefore elected union officials who, as one leader recalled, "had the balls to fight against management and discipline the workers . . . less with reason than bravado." Just as Monterrey's nonunion workers articulated a sense of manly independence in resisting organized labor, so did the reds uphold militant unionism as a macho endeavor. The brewery's male operatives became regular targets of the steelworkers' barbs on the streets and baseball fields of Monterrey. Veteran Cuauhtémoc workers readily admit that they earned reputations as *tibios*, "softies" who acquiesced to their own subordination by abstaining from union activism.[28] For the steelworkers, machismo fused with the languages of patriotism and industrial democracy as enduring features of their union identity. To be sure, all these Monterrey workers shared a presumption that unionism was a male prerogative. But their divergent uses of gender ideology demonstrate how discourses may be appropriated selectively and fashioned to sanction diverse behaviors.

Unity proved indispensable for the defense of union prerogatives. Throughout the late 1930s, the "men of steel" staged *paros locos*—swift, unannounced work stoppages—to protest production speedups or contract violations. Such wildcat strikes enraged supervisors but caused few economic losses. However, with each biannual contract negotiation came the threat of more serious strikes. The steelworkers refrained from striking when the recession of 1937–38 led President Cárdenas to demand patriotic, belt-tightening sacrifices from all Mexican workers. With the onset of recovery, the steelworkers appropriated the president's language of revolutionary nationalism to justify militancy. With a strike looming in 1939, Local 67's leaders wrote to Cárdenas that "our members only aspire to reap a minimum part of the copious profits obtained at the expense of our noble, sincere, and patriotic efforts." They expressed their pride in manufacturing steel for constructive, nation-building ends. They reminded Don Lázaro of Monterrey's union struggles and of "that memorable occasion when you harshly reprimanded [the local industrialists] for their failure to cooperate in Mexico's progress." "Our Local 67 emerged from that formidable battle," they wrote, "and placed itself at the vanguard of the working masses, setting a living example of unity, brotherhood, and the collective strength of labor."[29] Although Cárdenas never responded, federal authorities intervened in the dispute, and management acquiesced to worker demands. The president whom Monterrey's steelworkers credited for their "emancipation" left office shortly afterward, but the spirit of Cardenismo lived on in the workshops, union halls, and neighborhoods inhabited by the men of steel.

## Conclusion

General Cárdenas ceded the presidency to a more conservative, pro-business successor in 1940. By then, the government's cultural project had achieved a good many of its nation-building objectives in labor relations and working-class formation. Monterrey's industrialists responded to the revolutionary insurgency by developing systems of company paternalism that helped promote the "moral and cultural elevation" of Mexican workers. The antiunion policies masked by paternalistic benevolence ensured that the Cardenista vision of national labor solidarity met its limits in Monterrey. There, as elsewhere in Mexico, the federal government's opponents astutely enveloped their conservative resistance in the language of patriotism.

Workers in Mexico's strategic oil, mining, railroad, and metallurgical industries—among many others—capitalized on state labor policy to organize powerful industrial unions. For Monterrey's steelworkers, the benevolent promises of paternalism contradicted their workplace experience, and they mobilized to secure the "democratic promises" of revolutionary nationalism. Local 67's leaders transformed the steelworkers' union into an enduring institution that preserved rank-and-file unity, defended labor's prerogatives, and kept the spirit of Cardenismo alive for future generations. In contrast, the Cuauhtémoc Brewery workers evoked their conservative patriotism and regional loyalties to resist state-sponsored syndicalism. Their enthusiastic resistance did not pass unnoticed by the Cárdenas regime. The government yielded to popular pressures and abandoned its project of working-class unification in Monterrey. Monterrey's brewery workers thereafter assumed key leadership roles in the Independent Unions of Nuevo León, upholding their autonomy from national labor federations and precluding their integration into Mexico's ruling party.

Ironically, both revolutionary unionism and company paternalism served to discipline labor in such a way that the economy developed smoothly. In the coming decades, as a sustained postwar economic boom transformed Mexico from an agrarian society into a more urbanized industrial nation, the conservative patriotism and anticommunism heard in 1930s Monterrey became the "official" discourse of Mexico's ruling elites. Indeed, as the Cold War developed, the federal government itself acted to eliminate Communists from the leadership of key unions like the Miner-Metalworkers. But as in the time of President Cárdenas, the steelworkers continued to use his language of revolutionary nationalism to maintain unity in their ranks and defend their interests.

## Notes

The author wishes to thank Andrew Wood, Christopher Boyer, and the collection's editors for their insightful and encouraging comments on earlier versions of this chapter. A Fulbright–García Robles Dissertation Fellowship and a grant from the Institute of Latin American Studies at the University of Texas funded research in Mexico.

1. From "Corrido del Sindicato Minero," written by Jerónimo Leija, Edmundo Ramírez Gómez, and Benjamín Argumedo. The original in Spanish is as follows: "El Sindicato Minero / Es organismo de hermanos / En él unidos estamos / Noventa mil mexicanos / Noventa mil mexicanos / Huarache, zapato y botas / Que sin presumir de ufanos / Somos de los más patriotas." Lyrics provided to the author by Dionisio Palacios, Monterrey, Nuevo León, January 3, 1996.

2. Manuel Gamio, *Mexican Immigration to the United States: A Study of Human Migration and Adjustment* (Chicago: University of Chicago Press, 1930), 31.

3. Interviews with Salvador Castañeda, December 5, 1995, and Manuel Carranza, January 5, 1996.

4. Michael Snodgrass, "The Birth and Consequences of Industrial Paternalism in Monterrey, Mexico, 1890–1940," *International Labor and Working-Class History* 53 (1998): 115–36.

5. *El Porvenir* (Monterrey), September 16, 1922, January 28, 1924; interviews with Palacios and Dionisio López, December 12, 1995.

6. Federación Regional de Sociedades Obreras to President Obregón, January 7, 1923, Archivo General de la Nación (AGN), Ramo Presidentes, 407-M-13; Michael Snodgrass, *Deference and Defiance in Monterrey: Workers, Paternalism, and Revolution in Mexico, 1890–1950* (Cambridge: Cambridge University Press, 2003), 107–44.

7. *El Porvenir*, June 5, 1924; Manuel González Caballero, *La Maestranza de ayer, la Fundidora de hoy* (Monterrey: Fundidora Monterrey, 1979), 34–37.

8. Alex Saragoza, *The Monterrey Elite and the Mexican State, 1880–1940* (Austin: University of Texas Press, 1988), 144–46; Gerónimo Dávalos et al., *Cuarenta años son un buen tiempo* (Monterrey, 1930), 11; *Trabajo y Ahorro*, September 15, 1923, September 22, 1928, April 13, 1929.

9. Interviews with María Oviedo, May 23, 1996, and Estela Padilla, November 20, 1995.

10. *Colectividad* (Fundidora company magazine), November 17, 1926; González Caballero, *La Maestranza*, 6, 21; "Memorias de Acero: Fundidora, 1900–1986," *El Diario de Monterrey*, May 9, 1996.

11. Interviews with Manuel González Caballero, June 30, 1995, and Juan Manuel Elizondo (with Raul Rubio Cano), April 9, 1996; plant director Melitón Ulmer, May 23, 1923, to Department of Labor, in AGN, Dirección General del Gobierno 2.331.8 (16)/32-A/34.

12. Interviews with Palacios and Antonio Quiroga, March 17, 1996.

13. Barry Carr, *Marxism and Communism in Twentieth Century Mexico* (Lincoln: University of Nebraska Press, 1992), 10.

14. Snodgrass, *Deference and Defiance*, 178–90; *El Porvenir*, January 10–21, 1936.

15. Documentation of the Monterrey Glassworks conflict in Archivo General del Estado de Nuevo León: Junta Local de Conciliación y Arbitraje (AGENL:JCA), 58/1788, 60/1815.

16. *El Porvenir*, February 3–5, 1936; *Excélsior* (Mexico City), February 2–5, 1936.

17. *El Porvenir*, February 3–5, 1936; *Excélsior* (Mexico City), February 2–5, 1936; AGN, Presidentes—Cárdenas, 432.2/184.

18. Jean Meyer, *The Cristero Rebellion: The Mexican People between Church and State, 1926–1929* (Cambridge: Cambridge University Press, 1976).

19. Lombardo Toledano to Cárdenas, February 14, 1936, AGN, Presidentes—Cárdenas, 432.2/184; Local 67 to Cárdenas, March 12, 1936, AGN, Gobernación: 2.331. (16) 32–A/76; López interview.

20. *El Porvenir*, February 8–10, 1936; Saldaña, *Crónicas históricas*, 250.

21. Jonathan C. Brown, "Acting for Themselves: Workers and the Mexican Oil Nationalization," in *Workers' Control in Latin America, 1930–1979*, ed. Jonathan C. Brown (Chapel Hill: University of North Carolina Press, 1997), 45–71.

22. César Gutiérrez González, "29 de julio de 1936 en Monterrey: Un caso de lucha de clases," *Cuadernos de cultura obrera*, no. 6 (Monterrey, 1983): 37–38; *El Porvenir*, July 1, 30–31, 1936.

23. *El Porvenir*, June 11 and 22, 1937; AGENL:JCA 94/2932; Federación de Trabajadores de Nuevo León, *La burguesía regiomontana y su verdadero rostro* (Monterrey, 1937), 41.

24. *Trabajo y Ahorro*, November 11, 1935; Snodgrass, *Deference and Defiance*, 251–65.

25. Snodgrass, *Deference and Defiance*, 265–81.

26. Interviews with Villarreal, Quiroga, Castañeda, Elizondo, and Salvador Solís Daniel, November 14, 1995.

27. *La Pasionaria* (Local 67), March 1938; *El Porvenir*, December 6, 1936, January 6, 1937; *El Norte* (Monterrey), August 8, 1939; interview with Máximo de León Garza, March 17, 1996.

28. Castañeda, López, and Palacios interviews.

29. Local 67 to President Cárdenas, December 14, 1939, AGN, DAT 290/4.

# Final Reflections:
# What Was Mexico's Cultural Revolution?

Mexico's was the first social revolution of the twentieth century, but it was also in some respects the nineteenth century's parting shot, the revolution that capped a century of revolutions and gave durable form to Mexico's modern state. Indeed, one significant peculiarity of the armed phase of the Mexican Revolution (1910–20) is its timing: late enough in the nation's process of modernization to radically reconfigure the Mexican state, too early in the history of state formation to forge a totalitarian or a fascist regime. Mexico's era of revolutionary reconstruction (1920–40) bore all the marks of this peculiar combination: the giddy realization that a new state was being shaped and the concordant sense that a new citizen, even a "New Man," needed to be molded for the occasion, but also a political and cultural inconsistency and pragmatism that was the inevitable consequence of having a comparatively weak state.

If Mexico's cultural revolution had radical foundational elements, exemplified in its rabid secularism, its educational programs, and its peculiar brand of modern art for the people, it was also prone to using new communications media and productive technologies in radio, film, and print to revel in narratives and cultural forms that were in no sense revolutionary: the romantic *indianista* themes of postrevolutionary Mexican cinema prolonged Porfirian fashion in many respects, as did the patriotic music of the military band, and "revolutionary" hygiene and urbanism, to name only a few examples.

## An Ideologically Inconsistent Revolution

As a result of this apparent inconsistency, the very nature of Mexico's revolution has become the subject of contention, since revolutionary reconstruction, while quite radical in many respects, never had the clout to promote a truly universal program. Even during the armed phase of the revolution, the revolutionary leadership tended to forsake ideological consistency in favor of politically expedient alliances: the socially conservative Venustiano Carranza was forced to back away from his high regard for private property and to promote edicts of agrarian reform in 1915,[1] while, conversely, Pancho Villa, who was sympathetic to agrarian reform, did not develop a coherent program of land distribution because he relied on hacienda production to purchase armament, and because he needed to keep his fighting men on the field, far away from their homes, rather than in their fields and close to their communities.[2] Zapatismo, which was the revolution's only ideologically consistent movement, paid a hefty price for its purity: by distributing lands to soldiers and destroying the productive capacity of haciendas, Zapata seriously impaired his ability to marshal troops beyond the confines of his native Morelos.[3] In short, any leader with a truly national vocation needed to make real ideological compromises.

Ideological inconsistency and political pragmatism were fostered not only by the need to forge alliances between heterogeneous, and sometimes opposed, social movements and interest groups but also by the fact that Mexico's northern border remained open and permeable throughout the revolutionary process. In this the Mexican Revolution differs from its French, Russian, Chinese, and Cuban counterparts, for whereas revolutionary governments in those countries were either surrounded by political adversaries or, at least, cut off from their traditional foreign trading partners, the Mexican export economy remained healthy throughout the revolutionary process. Despite the violence and destruction that the revolution wrought on the country as a whole, Mexico's overall economic performance in the export sector was not severely affected.[4] Revolutionaries such as Villa and Carranza needed to continue to export cattle, oil, and other goods to finance their armies. They also purchased their armaments across the border. Continued reliance on good relations with the United States was also a factor that prevented a coherent radical program from materializing in Mexico.

As a result of this combination of factors, revolutionary reforms tended to be applied on an ad hoc basis, rather than universally. The "terror" of anticlerical "defanaticization campaigns" was regionally confined, and revolutionary regimes were inconsistent in its application. Agrarian reform was deployed strategically, rather than universally, certainly until 1935, and even to some extent during Lázaro Cárdenas's presidency.[5] Socialist education became the object of negotiation and compromise. The nationalization of the oil industry never became a platform for a widespread socialist economy.

It would, however, be a mistake to reduce inconsistencies in policymaking to some sort of Porfirian inertia, or to a lack of intellectuals who might provide consistent ideological platforms. Inconsistency was an effect of social heterogeneity, a weak state, and dependency on the United States. Rather than a sign of intellectual deficiency, ideological inconsistency was an art that nationally successful politicians needed to cultivate. The pragmatism of a Villa, a Carranza, an Obregón, a Calles, or a Cárdenas can too hastily be chalked up to corruption, indifference, or ignorance, but it is more properly conceptualized as a necessary faculty for political survival, given the field in which these men operated. On the other hand, continuities with the Porfiriato were often consciously chosen rather than involuntarily adopted. The Mexican Revolution had thoroughly destroyed or disabled key sectors of the Porfirian state, and it gave armed expression to various social and political interests that would then vie for representation and expression in the construction of a new state. As a result, the revolution quickly became a highly contested set of state-building projects.

### Revisionism, Neotraditionalism, and the Cultural History of the Revolution

The interpretation of the nature of Mexican revolutionary reform has too often been held hostage to a debate on the causes and nature of the Mexican Revolution. In particular, contemporary interpretations in the United States and Britain have by and large accepted Alan Knight's proposed dichotomy between so-called traditional (or neotraditional) and revisionist interpretations as an adequate framework for describing the state of the art.[6]

According to Knight, the traditional interpretation of the revolution was initially put forward by the triumphant revolutionaries themselves: "The first generation of Revolutionary victors, penning their memoirs and apologias, gave substance to the idea of a nationalist, popular and agrarian revolution, the product of the legitimate egalitarian strivings of a people, especially a peasantry, oppressed by Mexican and foreign exploiters." Opposed to this view, counterrevolutionaries and embittered revolutionaries on the "outs" portrayed the revolution as the contrived and disastrous result of conniving bandits and revolutionary elites.

These two trends then filtered into academic positions, or so the story goes. The first, or pro-revolutionary trend, found its voice in the first generations of interpreters of the Mexican Revolution and dominated academic accounts into the 1970s. This initial generation of interpreters included both Mexican and foreign intellectuals. Like the successful intellectual movement in Mexican revolutionary *indigenismo*, the consolidation of the traditional or orthodox interpretation of the Mexican Revolution as a popular and agrarian uprising was coined simultaneously for internal consumption and to shape a new image abroad. The U.S. labor organizer and Columbia University professor Frank Tannenbaum, for example, penned one of the most influential early accounts of Mexico's revolution and personally brokered the relationship between the Calles government and the U.S. State Department in the 1920s.[7]

The presentation of the Mexican Revolution as a movement for social justice helped cleanse Mexico's international image: rather than a revolt of ignorant and bloodthirsty bandits and *caudillos*, the revolution was inscribed in the epic of national liberation as the culmination of a process that began with independence.

The second strand of historical interpretation, which Alan Knight has called "revisionism," only just became prominent and respectable in academic settings in the 1970s. This trend champions the idea that 1910–20 was principally a political, rather than a social, revolution, and that "elites," rather than "masses," played the dominant role. Although Knight, who is a British historian, claims that the revisionist label is neutral rather than pejorative, he also argues that revisionism has its intellectual roots in the writings of counterrevolutionaries, and that revisionist positions have an elective affinity to neoliberalism, the rehabilitation of Porfirio Díaz, and even the rehabilitation of the arch-villain and assassin Victoriano Huerta. Given these associations, it is no great surprise that Mexican historians have failed to self-identify as revisionists, despite Knight's coaxing insistence on the honorability and neutrality of the label. Still, this cosmology of revolutionary historiography—traditionalism versus revisionism, popular-agrarian revolution versus political revolt—dominates contemporary Anglo-American views of the field.

It is therefore pertinent to conclude this volume with some thoughts about how current work on social and cultural change in the 1920s and 1930s fits into, or subverts, the traditionalist/revisionist binary. Does this dichotomy inform the project of the authors of this volume? Do the chapters of this book uphold one of these positions over the other?

There are two very different sorts of issues underlying the view that would reduce interpretations of the Mexican Revolution to a field divided neatly into traditionalists (and neotraditionalists) and revisionists. The first is the question of whether the Mexican Revolution was a revolution or merely a change in the political guard, and the second concerns the hierarchy of determining factors within the revolution (whether the revolution was primarily a social, a political, or a cultural revolution, for instance, and what the determinations between these analytic levels might be).

The texts in this book all coincide in the notion that 1910–40 was a revolution rather than a rebellion, even if they may differ on the historical role of elites and masses: in its armed phase (1910–20), two of the central pillars of the Porfirian state were either destroyed or permanently debilitated (the army, and the landowning class of hacendados); the era of reconstruction (1920–40) was in fact a period in which the state was refounded (a fact that does not imply that all older forms and institutions were set aside); finally, the adoption, adaptation, and production of transnationally circulating ideological currents (such as modernism in aesthetics, or communism and fascism in politics) were all forged and reforged in the furnace of a revolutionary society, a fact that is obvious enough in the cultural vibrancy and originality of Mexico's intelligentsia in that period.

The second question, regarding the relationship between class conflict, political conflict, and cultural change, is more problematic. According to Knight, those who follow the traditional position subscribe to the notion that the Mexican Revolution was a social revolution first, and a political and cultural revolution only secondarily or even not at all. Conversely, those who would analyze the Mexican Revolution primarily as a political revolution (i.e., "revisionists") must deny any primacy to its social component. As a result, they naturally tend to pine for prerevolutionary or counterrevolutionary regimes (Díaz or Huerta), since "the Revolution" (or the "Great Rebellion") would in the last instance have few positive achievements and a great many crimes: the substitution of an individual dictator with a party dictatorship could hardly have been worth a million lives. Finally, according to the same account, those who would emphasize Mexico's cultural revolution are, at best, superficial analysts, since cultural change was an effect rather than a cause of revolutionary transformation.

Given the prominent attention that the authors of this volume have lavished on the cultural dimensions of the revolutionary process, this conclusion, if true, would be damning indeed. And yet the charges must be faced before they can be eschewed, and the handiest way to do so is to review Knight's position on the matter, since he has been the most vocal champion of neotraditionalism and the architect of the effort to reduce the historiography of the Mexican Revolution to two camps (traditionalists and revisionists).

For Alan Knight, culture is either superstructural or entirely all-encompassing, depending on the definition of the term. Rather than being a *level of analysis* that attends to semiosis (that is, to processes of signification and interpretation), culture is either a specific set of beliefs or a human faculty that is so ubiquitous that it cannot be used to explain anything. Thus, in a recent review, Knight argues that the culture concept is so general that it is conceptually useless: "Virtually all human activities (barring involuntary physical activities such as reflexes and twitches) fall into the cultural domain. . . . Thucydides and Herodotus therefore wrote cultural history. . . . Stephen Haber writes very good (somewhat quantitative) cultural history. It happens to be classified as economic history, but then economics are as much a part of culture . . . as anything else. . . . All history is cultural history, hence *cultural history* (old or new) cannot denote a particular subcategory."[8] It is clear from this excerpt that this tongue-in-cheek critique takes culture to be a discrete domain ("economics are a part of culture") rather than a level of analysis. The result is a reductio ad absurdum: authors such as Stephen Haber, who pay little attention to the *terms* in which economic activity unfolds through time, are still held up by Knight as good cultural historians because "economics are a part of culture." One might just as easily claim that the anthropologist Claude Lévi-Strauss is an excellent economist because culture is a part of economics.

Instead of opting for such a useless and overly general conception, the notion of culture that Knight himself uses is always deployed with qualifiers (for instance, "popular culture" or "political cultures") and seems to refer to discrete sets of traditions and beliefs. In their turn, these apparently manageable subsets of "culture" are then analyzed either as the reflection of social process or as irrelevant to it. Culture, in this account, is best represented as "baggage" that is riding on the locomotive of history. Take, for example, Knight's account of the relationship between popular culture and economic modernization during revolutionary reconstruction in Mexico:

> Thus, *traditional cultural baggage* was often the last item to be discarded along
> the path of "modernization." Often, it was never discarded at all: for example, in
> Mexico as in France, it seems, urbanization and industrialization did not neatly
> result in secularization. Such an argument suggests that old ideas survived lustily
> through—and despite—periods of rapid social change, such as 1910–1940. It also
> suggests that the motor of social change was to be found in the material rather
> than the ideological realm. The motor's machinery was replaced, overhauled, re-
> designed; but the *ghost in the machine* lingered. Much of Mexico changed during,

after, and often because of the Revolution, and this change was sometimes brusque and far-reaching (that is, revolutionary). But ideas and customs changed (if they changed at all) *at a more glacial pace*.[9]

This quotation, which is in many respects characteristic of social-historical approaches to culture, presents a telling mix of metaphors. Thus culture goes from being baggage, which might easily be cast off, to a spectral and intangible ghost in the machine, to a slow-moving, glacier-like thing with its own inertia. But culture cannot be at once an inert thing that is willingly cast off or carried along, and an intangible spirit that is perceived to drive a—material and also impersonal—"machine," and an object that moves according to its own inertia. The muddle stems from an implicit adscription to a base/superstructure model of society (in which culture is superstructural), as well as to a reification of "culture" as a thing (a "dependent variable") and to a false dichotomy between the "material" and the "ideal" that would relegate semiotic process to the level of the "ideal" or the "immaterial."[10]

It is curious, and to some extent fortuitous, that these misconceptions regarding culture, cultural analysis, and cultural history should have been incorporated in the debate concerning the nature of Mexico's revolution. After all, those who believe that Mexico did undergo a revolution (rather than a rebellion) need not subscribe to the notion that cultural and political transformations were epiphenomenal. Indeed, revolutionary violence itself can only be properly identified as such through cultural analysis: violence is both material destruction and symbolic transgression, and as such it is simultaneously instrumental and expressive in function. Therefore the nature of the revolution must in part be assessed by studying what violence *communicated*.

Recognizing these issues, the essays in this book take a third route, which cannot be folded neatly into the traditionalist/revisionist dichotomy. Like "traditionalists," they view 1910–40 as a revolution rather than as a rebellion. Like "revisionists," most authors place state building at the core of the revolutionary process. Most importantly, given this book's concern with historical agency, cultural analysis is neither trivialized nor secondary to the task of comprehending the nature of Mexico's revolution. It is fundamental. Conditions and relations of production are keys to the stories told in this book, but these conditions are shaped, understood, and contested in processes of signification, interpretation, and representation. In other words, culture is neither baggage, nor specter, nor glacier, and in no sense is it a "superstructure" of an ontologically prior "base." It is the very terms in which social action unfolds.

## Utopia and the Character of Revolutionary "Reconstruction"

Christopher Columbus thought he had sighted Eden off the coast of Vene-
zuela, and Mexican nationalists of the 1920s believed they had caught a glimpse
of Utopia in the remnants of the pre-Columbian world as they were refracted
in Mexican popular art. It was in the 1920s that both Aztec sculpture and
folk crafts were elevated to the status of "art." It was then that José Clemente
Orozco, Diego Rivera, Jean Charlot, and other Mexican artists first made
solemn pilgrimages to Mexico's National Museum to view pre-Columbian
sculpture. Up until that time, these figures had been attractive to erudite scholars and curious passersby, but not to Mexico's artists. As Diego Rivera put it:

> Al Museo Nacional solo van con el alma llena de devoción, y viva la sensibilidad,
> las gentes de calzón blanco. Los conocedores entran allí para estudiar y solazarse.
> Las clases medias y acomodadas para reírse de los ídolos.[11]

Similarly, as Rick López shows in his chapter in this volume, Mexican craft
production was elevated to the status of "popular art" by artists such as Dr. Atl
and Alfredo Best Maugard, often to the bewilderment of government officials,
who were not certain about how to identify popular arts or where to draw the
line between "artistic" and other forms of craft production. However, the dis-
cerning eye of the modernist artist was able to "capture" the indigenous spirit
and to offer it up as a kind of antithesis of bourgeois and colonial values; the
spirit of the people was like well-doused firewood, ready to kindle an Ameri-
canist revival, a Mexican utopia.

The projection of a glorified pre-Columbian world onto contemporary
popular culture generated a true aesthetic revolution in Mexico. This is true not
only at the level of appreciation (i.e., in the elevation of pre-Hispanic sculpture
and popular crafts to the status of universal art) but also in artistic production itself. The chapters on modern art in this book (Rochfort; Lowe, Zavala,
and Oles) and Velázquez and Vaughan's chapter on music and *mestizaje* suggest that there was a real awakening in the period, which extended beyond
its most explicitly ideological formulations in mural art and into a new, very
national, form of femininity and perhaps also into an incipient national form
of feminism. The identity of both women and Indians with the land, and the
carnivalesque inversions that characterized the revolutionary process, with its
*adelitas* and its *coronelas*, provided women of the twenties and thirties with
space for sexual redefinition, as is evident in several strands of Mexican artistic
production of the period. If "woman" stood for authenticity and for the land in

Diego Rivera's Chapingo murals, she subtly became the *subject* of sexual desire in María Izquierdo's canvases. If femininity was conventionally figured with tropes of fertility and reproduction, Frida Kahlo's earth mother wore a death mask. Alongside these expressions of female subjectivity in the arts, perhaps, the radio allowed housewives and working women to express desire through taste, in the safety and confinement of their homes. Thus a feminine public that could only rarely congregate in public spaces was shaped through radio.

The rise of mass culture, particularly through radio, but also in film and through incremental improvements in communication, through road construction, telegraph, and telephone, provided a growing and increasingly diversified market for the new mestizo aesthetics. As a result, the master narrative of revolutionary utopia, as it was first represented in the murals of Diego Rivera, quickly permeated commercial artistic genres and was playfully combined in seductive fashions and forms. This lighter form of nationalism tended to place utopian ideals at the personal level; mestizaje was realized in love and sex, in paternal pride and filial duties. Indeed, these lighter forms of nationalism for popular consumption made the fortunes of some of the emerging social types of the time: radio moguls and film producers, crooners and movie stars.

In the more political, and of course more solemn and self-important, cultural register, the movement to grasp and harness the purity of Mexican communitarianism, of Mexican solidarity and collective expression, was often thought of as a "second conquest." If the first conquest of Mexico had debased and defiled "the Indian," the second conquest (that is, the triumph over backwardness and ignorance by a state that was born of revolutionary violence) would extend the benefits of progress to Indians while taking their spirit to animate the collective project. Thus the chapter by Adrian Bantjes shows that revolutionary Jacobinism might have drawn its ideology from Bakunin, Lenin, or Robespierre, but its narrative about itself and its own mission relied strongly on specifically Mexican imagery.

Ironically, it would now be the revolution that would play "true faith" to Catholicism's "idolatry." If the devil had once misled Mayas and Aztecs with that mockery of truth that was idolatry, the church now misled the people with the falsehood of religion. If Mexico's state had originally been founded on religion and conquest, its new state would be erected on revolution and science.

In this matter, Tabasco's Tomás Garrido Canabal was explicit: "As long as man worships deities and believes in . . . an afterlife, he will remain mentally shackled and the enemy of his own liberation."[12] Revolutionary "defanaticization campaigns" in Yucatán, Veracruz, Tabasco, Michoacán, and Sonora cast the teacher in the role of priest, the law in the role of god, science in the role of religion, and work in the role of the religious cult, while Catholicism stood in the role of idolatry and superstition. In an uncanny replay of the Spanish conquest, the new state sought to supplant the old. Numerous church buildings, writes Adrian Bantjes in this volume, "were torched, dynamited, or demolished, sometimes by schoolchildren wielding pickaxes. Some states banned religious nomenclature for towns and streets. The most controversial acts of desecration involved the destruction of religious symbols, especially saints' images, which quemasantos incinerated or smashed, often during obligatory PNR rallies or school festivals. Many states outlawed public religious ritual, such as processions, pilgrimages, fiestas, and bell ringing. Mass became a clandestine activity celebrated in private homes."[13]

There was in this exercise of sympathetic magic a will both to re-create and to *reverse* the social order. The colonial state had enslaved the Indians, tearing them from a state of nature that was closer to scientific reason (and, for the communists of the 1920s and 1930s, closer too to scientific socialism), and led them astray with their false religion. Now was the time to burn the false idols of the colonial oppressors and to reinstate a rational state. The colonial state had been founded on the idea that Mexicans owed a spiritual debt to their colonizers, who were therefore owed tribute and privilege. This spiritual debt was based on trickery, on false religion. Now was the time to expropriate the heirs of these foreigners, and their new foreign allies. But one perceives in the pop culture that is described in the chapters by Velázquez and Vaughan, Hayes, and Hershfield a jumbling of these heroic ideals with the *jouissance* of the first waves of urban consumerism and leisure.


Memory

The question of memory and its connection to the era of revolutionary reconstruction can be conceptualized on two levels: the first is the question of historicity, that is, of the connection between revolutionary experience and the expectations of various social sectors in the 1920s and 1930s; and the second, of giving material form to the state's story of itself. This second aspect is treated in some depth in this book, and it reveals a fair amount of continuity with practices that were forged in the prerevolutionary period: the Mexican state renaming streets, monumentalizing its own version of national history, including the history of "the Revolution" itself, the appropriation of urban space as well as space and time in the media to guarantee the ability to give shape and content to what might be called "official memory."

In addition to using strategies that had had their origins under Porfirio Díaz (centennial celebrations, hero worship through death and birthdays, declaration of national holidays, inscription of holidays and heroes in the urban landscape), governments had a new way of building material sites of memory. The revolution's constitutional right to nationalize and expropriate lands, mines, and oil fields (a mechanism that was put into action through agrarian reform and the nationalization of oil but was also in evidence in the public use of church buildings, and in the redecoration of old government buildings with revolutionary murals) provided the revolutionary state with a much more powerful and convincing instrument for memorializing official history than any of its predecessors had ever had.

The connection between the active process of inscribing the landscape with a revolutionary interpretation of national history and collective experience and expectations is still a subject that we know relatively little about. How did the experience of internecine violence, fear, migration, and hunger contribute to shaping popular expectations in the 1920s and 1930s? What was the connection between these expectations and the official narratives that were taking material form during the same period? These are topics for future research. However, the chapters by Snodgrass, Fernández, and Meyer suggest that there may have been a significant disjuncture between popular experience and expectations and the material construction of sites of memory by revolutionary governments. In the case of Monterrey's workers, we observe a split between unions that embraced Cárdenas's leftward-leaning policies, and an alternative nationalism, sponsored by local patrons, that cast these policies as foreign to Mexican tradition. For their part, Meyer and Fernández show that the tensions between revolutionary secularism and popular Catholicism had real effects in popular identification with national history as told by revolutionary governments.

It is precisely this level of contention over memory or, to be more precise, the contention over the connection between stories about the past, the interpretation of the present, and expectations for the future that characterizes the 1920–40 era. This is the battleground of the cultural revolution itself. At the same time, the authors of this volume show that the parties of these conflicts often mimicked each other and ended up having similar effects on the social order. So, for instance, Snodgrass suggests that both the Cardenista and the anti-Cardenista unions of Monterrey had similar policies and effects on disciplining the workforce. Similarly, the "social Catholicism" that emerged in

the 1890s after *Rerum Novarum* and was refurbished in the postrevolutionary period both responded to and imitated social demands that came from
anarcho-syndicalists. We have already seen how the secularist and revolutionary state imitated the church's missionaries, with teachers being compared to
priests, laws to the gospel, schools to churches, and a puritanical work ethic
to the cult of the faithful.

These cases allow us to conclude with a tentative hypothesis: the violence
and depth of the struggle over historical memory was met with mimesis between the principal contenders; true difference in historical memory is to be
found on the margins of the core conflicts of the period and was more readily
expressed in consumer culture than on the ideological field. In their vehe-
mence against the church, Mexican Jacobins cast scientific reason as religion,
teachers as missionaries, and schools as churches. Catholic entrepreneurs took
up the trimmings of the emerging welfare state. Revolutionary bands were
like specters of professional armies. However, a kind of popular indifference
to these formal organizations, to the stories that emanated from state organs
of cultural production, was always in the air: indifference that was betrayed
both in the omnivorous tastes of new working-class consumers and in the persistence of popular Catholicism beyond the reach of both the state and the
church. These manifold forms of popular indifference were identified as the
horizon of reform, the space for state action, the very justification of the de-
velopmental state that would soon emerge.

## National Identity

A final comment on national identity. One of the key goals of Porfirio Díaz's
regime was to make Mexico internationally presentable. This ardent desire was
economically, politically, and culturally motivated. On the economic plane,
the Díaz government knew that foreign investment was necessary for Mexico
to modernize. It also knew, as John Hart has shown, that the regime's own
stability depended in good measure on good relations with foreign, and especially with U.S., investors.[14] On the other hand, Díaz also courted capital from
other foreign powers as a lever against the United States. Thus foreign prestige
was also politically relevant. Finally, on the cultural plane, important segments
of Mexico's ruling and middle classes wished to break out of the cultural confinement and isolation that went along with political turmoil and international
isolation.

In the first instance, the Mexican Revolution was a public-relations disaster. It proved that the Díaz miracle was a house of cards. Foreign commentators tended to frame the revolution as yet another bout of Mexico's ancient maladies: violence, intractable internal divisions, colorful bandits, a miserable people. However, the medium-term implications of the revolution for Mexico's international image and for national identity were in the end much sunnier. In part, this was due to the revolution's simultaneity with World War I, a war that was important both because Mexican allegiance was a bone of contention between powers and because the revolution's bloody side was to a degree overshadowed by the savagery of the Great War. In part, national prestige surged along with Mexico's great social movements, and its expressions of political independence, culminating with land reform, the oil expropriation, and political support for the Spanish Republic, all under president Lázaro Cárdenas. Finally, national prestige was strengthened by Mexico's vibrant postrevolutionary cultural milieu. All of this transpired in a context that was marked by multiple and sometimes multitudinous social movements, and by the excitement of an incipient mass society.

There is a remarkable sense of thrill and discovery surrounding Mexican national identity as it was formulated in the 1920s and 1930s. Mexican, U.S., Latin American, and European artists and intellectuals successfully wrote the savagery of revolutionary violence into a story of national redemption and managed, in the process, to shape Mexico's own brand of modernist aesthetics. Mexican modernism drew its vitality from three sources: pre-Columbian art, which became Mexico's classical art, its contribution to universal culture; popular art, which represented Mexico's revolutionary spirit; and international modernism, with its taste for modern materials, functional design, and its criticism of traditional bourgeois rationality and taste. The results were quite astonishing: Mexico's new bid on cultural modernity exuded energy and originality like never before.

At the same time, mass culture was emerging, and commercial mass culture was not always easy to romanticize or to assimilate to the national saga. The engraver José Guadalupe Posada, who illustrated sensational news stories and crime pages in the penny press until his death in 1913, might be held up by respected artists as a Mexican Goya, but it was tougher to incorporate the public's omnivorous appetite for fashion and novelty into a story of revolutionary redemption. In short, the modernist synthesis of Mexico's muralist painters, and subsequent developments in Mexican literature (culminating in the writings of Juan Rulfo and in Octavio Paz's *Labyrinth of Solitude*), was quickly competing in the internal market with wave upon wave of fashion and influence.

Moreover, revolutionary vanguards also confronted older forms of elite and popular nationalisms, especially in the form of politicized Catholic nationalisms.

The very intensity of these contests is what capped Mexican national identity's remarkable success: in this era of revolutionary change, only those who were entirely on the margins of the political process could afford to set the flag aside.

## Notes

1. Heather Fowler Salamini, *Agrarian Radicalism in Veracruz, 1920–1938* (Lincoln: University of Nebraska Press, 1978).

2. Friedrich Katz, *The Life and Times of Pancho Villa* (Stanford: Stanford University Press, 1998).

3. John Womack, *Zapata and the Mexican Revolution* (New York: Knopf, 1969).

4. John Womack, "The Mexican Economy during the Revolution, 1910–1920: Historiography and Analysis," *Marxist Perspectives* (1978): 80–123; Alan Knight, "Export-Led Growth in Mexico, c. 1900–1930," in *An Economic History of Twentieth Century Latin America*, vol. 1, ed. Enrique Cárdenas et al. (New York: Palgrave Publishers, 2001), 119–51.

5. For specific case studies, see Adrian Bantjes, *As If Jesus Walked on Earth: Cardenismo, Sonora, and the Mexican Revolution* (Wilmington, Del.: Scholarly Resources, 1998); and John Gledhill, *Casi Nada: A Study of Agrarian Reform in the Homeland of Cardenismo* (Albany: SUNY–Albany Press, 1991). For an overview of the Cardenista state as a relatively weak apparatus, see Alan Knight, "Cardenismo: Juggernaut or Jalopy?" *Journal of Latin American Studies* 26, no. 1 (1994): 73–107.

6. The clearest formulation of this cosmology is Alan Knight's "Revisionism and Revolution: Mexico Compared to England and France," *Past and Present* 134 (1992): 159–99.

7. Charles Hale, "Frank Tannenbaum and the Mexican Revolution," *Hispanic American Historical Review* 75, no. 2 (1995): 238.

8. Alan Knight, "Subalterns, Signifiers and Statistics: Perspectives on Mexican Historiography," *Latin American Research Review* 37, no. 2 (2002): 139.

9. Alan Knight, "Popular Culture and the Revolutionary State in Mexico, 1910–1940," *Hispanic American Historical Review* 4, no. 3 (1994): 399 (italics mine).

10. In short, Knight's critique of cultural and political interpretations of the Mexican Revolution is colored by philosophical premises that have been thoroughly criticized and rejected, not least within British Marxism itself. See Raymond Williams, *Marxism and Literature* (Oxford: Oxford University Press, 1977).

11. "Only the pajama-clad peasants go to the National Museum full of devotion

and 'Viva their sensibility!' Intellectuals go to study and amuse themselves; the middle classes and wealthy to laugh at the idols." "La pintura y otras cosas que no lo son," in *Diego Rivera: Textos de arte*, ed. Xavier Moyssén (1923; Mexico City: UNAM, 1986), 50.

12. Quoted by Adrian Bantjes, "Saints, Sinners, and State Formation" (pp. 139–40 in this volume), from Gaveta 35, Tomás Garrido Canabal, inv. 2312, exp. 140, legs. 517, 717, Archivo Plutarco Elías Calles (APEC).

13. See Bantjes, "Saints, Sinners, and State Formation," in this volume, p. 145.

14. John Hart, *Empire and Revolution: The Americans in Mexico since the Civil War* (Berkeley: University of California Press, 2002).

# Contributors

ADRIAN A. BANTJES is an associate professor of Latin American history at the University of Wyoming. He is the author of *As If Jesus Walked on Earth: Cardenismo, Sonora, and the Mexican Revolution* (Scholarly Resources, 1998) and of a series of articles on politics, culture, and religion during the Mexican Revolution. He is currently completing a book on revolutionary defanaticization and popular religion.

KATHERINE E. BLISS is a visiting scholar at the Center for Latin American Studies at Georgetown University, where she is also an adjunct associate professor. She is the author of *Compromised Positions: Prostitution, Public Health, and Gender Politics in Revolutionary Mexico City* (Pennsylvania State University Press, 2001), and coeditor with William E. French of a forthcoming volume entitled *Gender, Sexuality, and Power in Modern Latin American History*. She has written articles and book chapters on gender, health, and development.

MARÍA TERESA FERNÁNDEZ ACEVES is a research professor at the Centro de Investigaciones y Estudios Superiores en Antropología Social–Occidente, Mexico. Her most recent publications include " 'Once We Were Corn Grinders': Women and Labor in the Tortilla Industry of Guadalajara, 1920–1940," *International Labor and Working Class History*, 63 (2003): 81–101; and "La lucha por el sufragio femenino en Jalisco, 1910–1958," *La Ventana* 19 (March 2004). Her current research interests include Mexican women's and gender history and labor history.

JOY ELIZABETH HAYES is an associate professor of communication studies at the University of Iowa. Her research examines the role of radio broadcasting in identity formation in the United States and Mexico, focusing on the period between 1920 and 1950. She is the author of *Radio Nation: Communication, Popular Culture, and Nationalism in Mexico* (University of Arizona Press, 2000), and some of her recent work examines the history of community radio in Mexico and the construction of whiteness in U.S. radio and television programs.

JOANNE HERSHFIELD is an associate professor at the University of North Carolina, Chapel Hill, where she teaches media studies. She has authored numerous essays and book chapters on Mexican cinema as well as two books: *Mexican Cinema/Mexican Woman, 1940–1950* (University of Arizona Press, 1996) and *The Invention of Dolores del Río* (University of Minnesota Press, 2000). She also coedited (with David R. Maciel) *Mexico's Cinema* (Scholarly Resources, 1999). Currently she is working on a book-length study of women and visual culture during the postrevolutionary period.

STEPHEN E. LEWIS is an associate professor of history at California State University, Chico. His book *The Ambivalent Revolution: Forging State and Nation in Chiapas, 1910–1945* (University of New Mexico Press, 2005) examines the political, social, and institutional history of revolutionary Chiapas through the lens of the rural schoolhouse. At present he is researching the history of alcohol and *indigenismo* in modern Chiapas.

CLAUDIO LOMNITZ is Distinguished University Professor of Anthropology and Historical Studies at the New School University and is editor of the journal *Public Culture*. He is the author of a number of books, including *Exits from the Labyrinth: Culture and Ideology in Mexican National Space* (University of California Press, 1992), *Deep Mexico, Silent Mexico: An Anthropology of Nationalism* (University of Minnesota Press, 2001), and *Death and the Idea of Mexico* (Zone Books, 2005). Lomnitz's contributions to debates in contemporary cultural studies reach beyond the field of Latin American studies.

RICK A. LÓPEZ completed his Ph.D. at Yale in 2001. His research on Mexican national cultural integration won the Best Dissertation Award from the New England Council of Latin American Studies and the James A. Robertson Best Article Prize from the Conference of Latin American Studies. He has coedited a volume on violence and political marginalization in southern Mexico and is now working on a book manuscript entitled "Forging a Mexican Aesthetic and Integrating the Nation, 1921–1972."

SARAH M. LOWE is an art historian, curator, and writer who has written a number of books on Mexican art, including *The Diary of Frida Kahlo* (Abrams,

1995), *Frida Kahlo* (Universe, 1991), and *Tina Modotti: Photographs* (Abrams, 1995), the exhibition catalog for the first definitive retrospective of Modotti's photographs, which Dr. Lowe also curated. Her most recent publications include the exhibition catalog *Tina Modotti and Edward Weston: The Mexico Years* (Merrell, 2004) and the major essay for *Edward Weston: Life Work* (Lodima Press, 2004). Dr. Lowe lives and works in Brooklyn, New York, and Stanford, Kentucky.

JEAN MEYER, a researcher and historian at the Centro de Investigación y Docencia Económicas (CIDE) in Mexico City, has written more than thirty books on a wide range of topics in Mexican and European history. His classic three-volume study *La cristiada* is now in its thirteenth edition. His recent works include *Historia de los cristianos en América Latina* (Editorial Jus, 1999), *Samuel Ruiz en San Cristóbal, 1960–2000* (Tus-Quets, 2000), and *El sinarquismo, el cardenismo y la Iglesia, 1937–1947* (Tus-Quets, 2003). He is also a frequent contributor to several Mexican publications, including *Letras Libres*, *Proceso*, and *La Jornada*.

JAMES OLES teaches Latin American art at Wellesley College each spring and resides in Mexico City, where he works as an independent curator and art critic for the remainder of the year. He is the author of *South of the Border: Mexico in the American Imagination* (Smithsonian Books, 1993), *Helen Levitt: Mexico City* (W. W. Norton, 1997), and essays on the work of José Clemente Orozco, David Alfaro Siqueiros, and Lola Álvarez Bravo, among others.

PATRICE ELIZABETH OLSEN is an assistant professor of history at Illinois State University. Her manuscript "Artifacts of Revolution: Architecture, Society, and Politics in Mexico City, 1920–1940" received the Lewis Hanke and the Michael C. Meyer awards and will be published by Rowman and Littlefield. Her current research project "The Ferris Wheel on San Juan Hill: Remembrance and Adaptation in Contemporary Cuba" is a historical monograph and visual essay on national identity, collective memory, and revolution.

DESMOND ROCHFORT is University Professor and head of the School of Fine Arts at the University of Canterbury in New Zealand. As a mural painter, he became one of Britain's leading public muralists during the 1970s and 1980s. In 1986 he received his Ph.D. from the Royal College of Art in London for his research on Mexican muralist David Alfaro Siqueiros. He is the author of *The*

*Murals of Diego Rivera* (London, 1987) and *Mexican Muralists: Orozco, Rivera, Siqueiros* (London, 1993).

MICHAEL SNODGRASS is an associate professor of history at Indiana University–Purdue University Indianapolis. He most recently published the book on which his chapter in this volume is based, *Deference and Defiance in Monterrey: Workers, Paternalism, and Revolution in Mexico, 1890–1950* (Cambridge, 2003). His essays have also examined Cuban travel literature and the media's role in Mexico's transition to democracy. His current research projects explore neoliberalism's impact on Mexican steelworkers and the effects of emigration on Mexico's post–World War II history.

MARY KAY VAUGHAN is a professor of history at the University of Maryland. She is the author of *The State, Education, and Social Class in Mexico, 1880–1928* (Northern Illinois University Press, 1982). Her *Cultural Politics in Revolution: Teachers, Peasants, and Schools in Mexico, 1930–1940* (University of Arizona Press, 1997), received the Herbert Eugene Bolton Prize in Latin American history and the Bryce Wood Award from the Latin American Studies Association. She has edited collections and written articles on Mexican historiography, women and gender in Mexico, and the history of Mexican education.

MARCO VELÁZQUEZ is a professor of history at the Benemérita Universidad Autónoma de Puebla. As coordinator in the Ministry of Culture in Puebla, he revived traditional village bands and created new ones for adolescents. He also created the Orquesta Sinfónica de Puebla. He has published on the historiography of the Mexican Revolution.

WENDY WATERS received her Ph.D. in Latin American and comparative world history from the University of Arizona (1999). Today she is the research director at Avison Young Commercial Real Estate in Vancouver, Canada. Her current research interests relate to contemporary urban economic development, including the impact of hosting the Olympic Games; how information technology has transformed office work; and the effect of China's rapid economic growth on Vancouver's property markets. She has published reports on these and other topics through Avison Young.

ADRIANA ZAVALA is an assistant professor of art history at Tufts University, where she teaches modern Latin American art. Her publications include an essay entitled "The India Bonita Beauty Contest: Gender, Modernity and Tradition in Mexico City, 1921," in *Seeing and Beyond: Essays in Eighteenth- to Twenty-First Century Art in Honor of Kermit S. Champa*, ed. Deborah Johnson and David Ogawa (Peter Lang Publishers, 2005). She is preparing a book manuscript on images of women, nationalism, and modernism in Mexico City between 1900 and 1950.

# Index

LIBRARY OF CONGRESS CATALOGING-IN-PUBLICATION DATA

The eagle and the virgin : nation and cultural revolution in Mexico,
1920–1940 / edited by Mary Kay Vaughan and Stephen E. Lewis.
p. cm.
Includes bibliographical references and index.
ISBN 0-8223-3657-X (cloth : alk. paper)
ISBN 0-8223-3668-5 (pbk. : alk. paper)
1. Mexico—Civilization—20th century. 2. Mexico—History—1910–1946.
3. Arts—Mexico—History—20th century. 4. Art and state—Mexico—
History—20th century. 5. Nationalism—Mexico—History—20th century.
6. Identity (Psychology)—Mexico. 7. Ethnicity—Mexico. I. Vaughan,
Mary Kay, 1942– II. Lewis, Stephen E., 1967–
F1234.E15 2005
305.800972—dc22      2005028220